GROWTH CENTERS IN REGIONAL ECONOMIC DEVELOPMENT

GROWTH CENTERS IN REGIONAL ECONOMIC DEVELOPMENT

Edited by
Niles M. Hansen

The Free Press   New York
Collier-Macmillan Limited   London

The Free Press
A Division of The Macmillan Company
866 Third Avenue, New York, New York 10022

Collier-Macmillan Canada Ltd., Toronto, Ontario

Library of Congress Catalog Card Number: 73–151165

printing number

1 2 3 4 5 6 7 8 9 10

CONTENTS

PREFACE

Although there has been considerable interest in the past decade and a half in the role of growth centers in regional economic development, regional development legislation in the United States did not incorporate the growth center concept until the middle of the 1960s, and even then the commitment was vague and hesitant. Because past experience had shown that sprinkling regional development funds over wide areas was not very productive, the Appalachian Regional Development Act of 1965 and the Public Works and Economic Development Act of 1965 both called for the designation of centers with significant potential for growth so that resources could be used rapidly and effectively to create more employment and higher income for the residents of the centers and for the populations of their hinterlands. Nevertheless, there has been a pronounced tendency to neglect the growth center notion in favor of efforts to force-feed economic growth in lagging areas. Too often the "growth centers" that are the object of public policy have been merely the best locations available in an area of general economic lag, rather than urban areas characterized by rapid growth or genuine growth potential. This is why so-called growth center policy is frequently not only inefficient but also ineffective.

Whatever the practical and conceptual difficulties, it would appear that the growth center concept will be a major feature of new regional legislation. For example, in the summer of 1970 the White House's National Goals Research Staff suggested a growth center strategy that "would promote economic activity (notably, job opportunities) at the population center on the theory that it would spread to the rural periphery. In this way, the sparsely populated rural areas could be tied to the growth centers in a mutually beneficial relationship. At the same time, these centers would provide promising opportunities for more balanced growth and distribution of the Nation's population." In a related vein the Staff proposed that a " 'viable option' to deter growth in already congested megalopoli is a policy of encouraging growth in alternate growth centers away from the large urban masses, coupled with a complementary effort of the use of new towns."

Appealing though this approach may seem, it still poses a number of difficulties, especially with respect to its assumptions concerning beneficial spread effects from growth centers, and the balanced growth and "new town" concepts. As several of the papers in this volume point out, growth centers may drain their hinterlands (*polarization* and *backwash effects* are the terms generally used to describe this phenomenon) rather than induce prosperity in them. References to balanced growth are not amenable to concrete policy applications because of vagueness concerning what the term really means. Does it mean that equality of per capita income, public investment, or economic activity (however defined) should be the goal of development? Should the growth of large lagging regions be promoted solely by moving resources to them and stimulating the development of their existing resources? What effects will the location of various types of activities in a given region have on other regions as a result of induced activities (on both the supply and demand sides) of an interregional nature? What conflicts are likely to arise between maximizing regional and national welfare, and how should those conflicts be resolved?

Finally, as William Alonso has urged, a distinction must be made between growth centers and new towns, because the concepts are often associated or made identical. New town proposals are usually based on completely new places whereas growth center strategies are usually based on existing centers. New town advocates tend to stress self-contained labor markets whereas the growth center approach has emphasized the provision of jobs for people in the center's hinterland. In addition, new towns are proposed as means for channeling population growth away from large cities. Although growth centers may also perform this function, their primary role has been to provide economic opportunities for persons in lagging regions. Existing examples of new towns—most notably Columbia and Reston, both near Washington, D.C.—may prove successful as experiments in town planning, but they have little relevance to people in the income categories of migrants from distressed areas.

It should be pointed out, however, that the United States is a relative newcomer among industrialized nations that are attempting to guide regional resource allocation through public policy measures. Most countries in Western Europe, for example, have tried to attract economic activity to relatively poor, rural areas or to depressed industrial regions dependent on stagnating or declining industries. Many have also tried to check the growth of large, congested agglomerations by means of tax and credit devices, building permits, and similar measures. British policies with respect to southeast England and French policies with respect to the Paris region are cases in point. The growth of some large urban areas would perhaps have been greater if there had not been countervailing policy measures, but it is difficult to identify any case where hothouse efforts to promote the development of large lagging regions have met with more than very limited success. Although American and foreign evidence does indicate greater equality in the broad geographical distribution of manufacturing, this does not imply that small towns or lagging regions are becoming relatively more attractive. Today, growth in national employment is accounted for primarily by expanding tertiary activities that have been located for the most part in metropolitan areas. Those industries that have tended to leave metropolitan areas have been characterized by relative stagnation or decline; they frequently seek cheap labor in areas with surplus agricultural populations. Rapidly expanding sectors, on the other hand, have favored already concentrated regions because of their numerous external economies of agglomeration, especially tertiary services in the widest sense, including amenities as well as business services. (Originally the term *external economies* was used to describe cost reductions experienced by individual firms in a growing industry; the relevant economies, such as service activities and specialized education and training, were external to the firm but internal to the *industry*. External economies of agglomeration are also external to the firm, but they are internal to the *region* where the cost-reducing services and facilities have already been established.)

Although the polarization of population and economic activity in growth centers is increasingly bound up with the interplay of external economies, it is curious that contemporary growth center literature was initiated along different lines. The theory of *pôles de croissance* was first propounded by François Perroux in his well-known 1955 article, "*Note sur la notion de pôle de croissance.*" In contrast to balanced and steady growth theories, Perroux maintained that analysis of sustained growth of total production should concentrate on the process by which various activities appear, grow in importance, and in some cases disappear; and he emphasized that growth rates vary considerably from sector to sector. Like Schumpeter, he stressed the importance of entrepreneurial innovation in the growth process, which takes the form of a succession of dynamic sectors, or poles, through time. The pole concept was given a particularly regional flavor by emphasizing that growth is concentrated in various spatial loci as well as in certain leading industrial branches. Another key element in Perroux's dynamic interpretation of economic activity was the concept of dominance. For Perroux, dominance consists of an irreversible or only partially reversible influence exercised by one economic unit on another because of its dimension, its negotiating strength, the nature of its activity, or because it belongs to a zone of dominant activity. Moreover, Perroux held that as soon as any inequality appears among firms, the breach is opened by which the cumulative effect of domination insinuates itself. Given these theories, it followed that the dominant, or propulsive, firm would generally be large and oligopolistic and would exert a considerable influence on the activities of suppliers and clients. In addition, dominant and propulsive industries make the cities where they are located the development poles of their regions

In his contribution to this volume, J. R. Lasuén argues against Perroux's contention that cities grow and decay in such a manner as to create an unstable urban structure. However, Lasuén's data showing increasing stability in urban structure over time do not show that geographic polarization is not important in Western countries. Lasuén has pointed out a promising direction for future research on problems of regional development by linking growth center theory to the study of industrial organization, but nevertheless it is true that the changing structure of economic activity has reinforced rather than reduced spatial polarization. Indeed, the stability of the urban hierarchy is perhaps the best evidence of this phenomenon, for although the location of economic activity is more and more free with respect to large regions, it is less and less so with respect to size of community.

The earlier emphasis on big industrial undertakings by the French school of regional analysis (an emphasis still reflected in some of the pages of this volume) tended to shift the study of polarization away from what is perhaps its most operationally meaningful context—the increasing importance of external economies as the origin of spatial polarization. The advantages of larger urban areas cannot be explained simply in terms of the traditional economic base approach or in terms of classical location theory. The export base approach never really came to grips with the process by which an area builds up its overhead capital and acquires new export bases. Similarly, classical location theory, including central place theory, relied mainly on static analysis of the tranport costs required to overcome distance frictions under general equilibrium conditions. In contrast, the growth center approach attempts to explain the development process by concentrating on changes in the parameters of given systems. Thus, its concern with the complex interdependencies and dynamics of spatial resource allocation is perhaps more akin to the writings of, say, Wilbur Thompson than to much of the regional science literature derived from traditional location theory.

The papers presented in this volume bring together the thoughts of leading scholars, from various disciplines and countries, who are working at the frontiers of knowledge with respect to growth centers and related aspects of regional development. Collectively they represent a unique effort to present the state of the art and to indicate the likely paths growth center research may follow in the future.

The paper by Lloyd Rodwin sets forth the broad issues to which urban growth strategies, including growth center strategies, must address themselves. On the basis of considerable international experience, Rodwin argues that "no other aspect of our culture will receive more searching examination in the next generation" than the effort to achieve a national urban and regional growth strategy. He points out that present policies are primarily concerned with curbing metropolitan growth in one or more areas and with promoting growth in alternative locations, but he predicts that this emphasis will be modified in four ways. These new directions will involve policies for (1) dealing with massive linear megalopolitan clusters, (2) building up the resources and capabilities of local governments, (3) insuring that groups that should benefit from growth will do so, and (4) dealing with the changing functions performed by cities.

The articles by J. R. Lasuén, Morgan Thomas, and Tormod Hermansen are complementary critical reviews of the development and status of growth center theory. They represent excellent introductions to basic growth center concepts, pointing out theoretical and empirical problems as well as areas with promising potential for future research. They are particularly rich in suggestions on possible relationships between growth center theory and technological innovation, diffusion processes, and corporate and industrial organization.

Although the growth center notion has been widely utilized throughout the world, attempts to formulate a systematic and comprehensive theory of polarized development have been remarkably lacking. For several years John Friedmann has been developing such a theory. His paper, "A General Theory of Polarized Development," is the culmination of the thought-provoking core-periphery analysis first set forth in his book, *Regional Economic Policy: A Case Study of Venezuela*. Friedmann's formulation "assigns a decisive influence to the institutional and organizational framework of society and, specifically, to the patterns of authority and dependency that result from the unusual capacity of certain areas to serve as cradles of innovation." In developing his theory, Friedmann traces the complex interplay of innovation, the nature of social systems, authority-dependency relations, core-periphery interactions, city size, and the nested hierarchy of spatial systems.

Growth centers may benefit the residents of their surrounding hinterlands either by the opportunities they offer to persons attracted to the centers (as migrants or commuters) or through beneficial effects that spread from the centers to the hinterlands. Brian Berry's paper, "Hierarchical Diffusion: The Basis of Filtering and Spread," concentrates on the latter role of a growth center. Berry maintains that "the role played by growth centers in regional development is a particular case of the general process of innovation diffusion," and that "growth centers' development role involves the simultaneous filtering of innovations that bring growth down the urban hierarchy and the spreading of the benefits occurring from the resulting growth both nationally from the core to hinterland regions, and within these regions from their metropolitan centers outwards to the intermetropolitan periphery." Berry's theoretical discussion of hierarchical diffusion is given empirical verification by evidence on the diffusion of television stations and market penetration by the television industry in the United States from 1940 to 1968. Berry concludes that growth centers can be used to induce growth in lagging regions to the extent that (1) threshold limitations are reduced (innovations will not penetrate below a threshold size of town), (2) the diffusion process is hastened, and (3) accessibility to growth centers is increased.

The use of growth centers to induce growth in lagging regions is also the subject of Jean Paelinck's paper. Specifically, he deals with the need for guidelines about how to set up and stimulate an optimal cluster of industries in a growth center. He develops a model of an industry complex, taking account of industrial interrelations, externalities, and profitability conditions. A simple objective function is specified that, together with profitability and level constraints, permits selection of a minimal investment complex, given a group of feasible industries for a development region.

Although French growth pole theory has influenced regional policy in Canada, Benjamin Higgins points out that only the province of Quebec has seriously implemented a growth center strategy. Higgins contrasts large, fast-growing *pôles de croissance*, such as Montreal, which tend to drain their hinterlands, with those that raise income and employment in the hinterlands as well as in their own metropolitan areas. Quebec's growth center strategy will rely on three or four growth centers to the east of Montreal, selected and encouraged so as to pull development eastward toward Quebec City and beyond, with the aim of generating higher employment and income in the lagging areas of the province.

The remaining papers deal with the experience of the United States. William Alonso and Elliott Medrich, in their analysis of "Spontaneous Growth Centers in Twentieth Century American Urbanization," find that whereas migration from nonmetropolitan areas and from abroad was more evenly distributed among SMSA's in earlier decades, pronounced differences in growth rates in recent decades have been the result of intermetropolitan migration. They also show that SMSA's (Standard Metropolitan Statistical Areas) in the 50,000 to 250,000 range—which have been among the principal objects of federal policies to induce growth centers—have a declining share of all metropolitan population. These smaller areas have greater variability of growth rates than larger areas, and larger areas also have an increasing probability of being fast-growing. Although smaller growth centers may have considerable local regional importance, the authors conclude that they will not significantly affect national urbanization trends. With respect to lagging areas that are the object of growth center policy, they conclude that spontaneous growth centers are few and that growth might be neither possible nor desirable in terms of alternative opportunities. Rather, they suggest that particular programs and policies be geared to the development of the national system of urban areas in accordance with national objectives.

My evaluation of "Growth Center Policy in the United States" similarly maintains that lagging regions generally are not the appropriate places in which to implement growth center strategies. A growth center strategy is proposed based on intermediate-sized cities but linked to human resource investments in lagging areas. A general need to integrate manpower and regional development policies is indicated.

In the concluding paper, Gene Laber discusses the reasons why, at the county level, policies designed to reduce unemployment by inducing faster rates of employment growth may not be successful. During the 1950–1960 decade, about 36 per cent of all counties that experienced employment growth at or above the national average also experienced increases of 1 per cent or more in their unemployment rate. Laber concludes that change in unemployment in growth centers is a poor indicator of welfare increases because increased unemployment may be a result of higher labor force participation rates or immigration of persons who may be absorbed into the labor force only after a time lag.

Despite the contributions that the papers in this volume make to growth center theory and policy, it must be admitted that we still do not have specific criteria for identifying relevant urban centers, determining how big they should be, or deciding what kinds of investments should be placed in them. Perhaps this reflects a fundamental need to be more specific about the nature of spatial resource allocation problems to which growth centers should be related. A number of potentially promising lines of investigation are indicated, but several others may be mentioned here.

First, we need much more knowledge concerning the trade-offs between regional development and worker relocation programs. Many problems of regional development might be dealt with more rationally if they were treated more as problems of human resource development and labor mobility. There is a pressing need to integrate the research of place-oriented regional studies on the one hand and people-oriented studies concerned with manpower programs in the broadest sense on the other.

Theory of the dynamics of urbanization rests heavily on the notion of external economies of agglomeration, yet little progress has been made in dealing with them in quantitative terms. A similar situation exists with respect to the external diseconomies accompanying the expansion of congested cities. It may be noted here that a city may become too big even if marginal external diseconomies have not yet reached the level of the concomitant marginal external economies. The real question is whether the relationship between these variables is such that the net marginal social product would be greater in an alternative location.

Finally, regional research needs the help of students of human attitudes and preferences. When we speak of making spatial resource allocation more rational, we imply that we are—in some sense— trying to increase the aggregate level of welfare. However, this in turn implies that we know something about how satisfactions are related to location. Although economists have spent a great deal of time studying time preferences, they have given almost no attention to the preferences that policy makers presumably are trying to satisfy through regional policies.

In conclusion, I would like to express my gratitude to the Economic Development Administration, U.S. Department of Commerce, for its support of the Conference on the Role of Growth Centers in Regional Development held in Austin, Texas, in November, 1969, and sponsored by the Center for Economic Development of the University of Texas. The present volume is an outgrowth of that conference. Despite the invaluable help of numerous EDA officials, I would like especially to thank Gerald Duskin and Samuel Rosenblatt. Of course, the views of the various authors do not necessarily reflect those of the agency.

I also wish to thank N. Dann Milne, Pamela Pate, and Jackie Wallace for their aid in preparing this book. Mrs. Wallace deserves special recognition for her help in organizing the Austin conference.

Although the collective effort represented here is intended to give the reader a thorough exposure to issues being debated at the frontiers of growth center theory and policy, its greatest contribution would be to stimulate research on the problems that remain, particularly in formulating better criteria for regional policy. Growth center analysis implicitly or explicitly involves deliberate policies; otherwise, one is left with mere descriptions of the spatial distribution and growth of population and economic activity.

URBAN GROWTH STRATEGIES RECONSIDERED*

LLOYD RODWIN
M.I.T.

A number of diligent scholars have reproved their colleagues for misunderstanding Perroux's ideas, for shifting the emphasis of his notion of growth poles from sectors to areas, from *growth poles*, so to speak, to *growth centers*. The scholars were right, to be sure, but it is a trivial point. And in reverse, the colleagues might retort that Perroux was ambiguous as well as suggestive, and that, in any case, he had slighted the geographic implications of the growth pole concept. Fortunately, significant ideas are not inert. They suggest new ways of interpreting experience and solving problems; and so they undergo useful, and sometimes not so useful, extensions and misinterpretations in the course of their careers.

To make my position clear on this score, let me say that I find it intriguing, rather than scandalous, and helpful, rather than harmful, that growth poles have become synonymous in some quarters with growth centers and have then been linked to the concept of new towns, thereby making British and French economists perceive how an idea of physical planning could serve a significant regional growth function, a possibility they did not grasp at all in the past. And I find it equally intriguing and useful that the same notion has sparked a new *aperçu* for the city planners, making them aware of an inter-regional role for new towns as growth centers, a prospect that heretofore they hardly apprehended.

But we all know that economists and city planners are still learning the A, B, C's of their calling. For example, they still have to figure out how and where growth "genii" can be called into being when needed, or bottled up when they seem to be getting out of hand. And

---

* This paper is a slightly amended version of Chapter 8 of *Nations and Cities: A Comparison of Strategies* by Lloyd Rodwin. Reprinted by permission of Houghton Mifflin Company.

All notes appear at the end of their respective selections.

1

they need to learn about these matters in order to guide the urban growth strategies that nations are already deploying, wittingly or otherwise, regardless of the inadequacies of our state of knowledge and of our capacity to act. Since the bulk of the papers in this volume focus on growth centers, I should like to redress the balance somewhat by venturing a few tentative views concerning the nature of urban growth strategies of nations. These views, I should add, are based on a book I have recently completed that evaluates the experience with urban growth strategies of five countries—the United States, Britain, France, Turkey, Venezuela.[1] I propose to sum up four aspects of my evaluation of the experiences of these countries: (1) the conditions that generate these strategies; (2) the effects of similarities and differences in the environments of the five countries; (3) typical concepts and goals; and (4) the future directions they may be expected to take.

Germinating Conditions

Two conditions generate urban growth strategies: (1) growth problems must be recognized as critical and (2) they must also appear capable of solution. Otherwise, it would be hard to persuade the central government to redefine its aims and to reorganize its tools and organizations. Governments, like people, shy away from abstract issues and certainly do not bestir themselves very much unless an issue threatens to be persistent, prominent, and likely to cause trouble if ignored. Once an issue acquires these characteristics, however, it becomes part of the agenda of government and takes the status of what Hirschman has called a "privileged" problem. Urban growth strategies are especially interesting because they are in a transitional stage. They are on the verge of becoming privileged problems.

None of the central governments examined began to think in terms of such strategies until a wide range of specific and obdurate problems of cities, within cities, and between cities had become highly visible. At first they dealt with components of the problems, such as housing, industrial location, transportation, recreation, and education. Only later did they grapple with the more basic problems of suburban growth and of the relationships between metropolitan regions and central cities. At approximately the same time, the problems of poverty and of lagging regions came to be treated as specific components of the larger, more complex problem of managing the economy. The efforts to deal with the growth of cities and with the lagging regions proceeded independently at first, but they eventually converged. This convergence was accelerated once the essential interdependence of these programs began to be more fully appreciated. This, in turn, resulted in a quest for the elimination of inconsistencies, for more coherence, and for more effective means of execution.

Extreme phases of the economic cycle, particularly prosperity, also reinforced efforts to help lagging regions. This had not been true in the past when the economic crises as a rule diverted attention from the problem. More recently, however, they have not only spurred (or curtailed) building and development programs, but they have also highlighted regional discrepancies and problems of programming infrastructure investments equitably and inefficiently. A modicum of political stability, a moderately effective civil service, and some control or influence over capital allocations as well as tax policy sufficed to make the efforts appear practicable. All that was necessary to spark action was the conviction of key decision makers that they could do something to correct a serious imbalance and produce more efficient or more socially desirable patterns of development. This sense of need and opportunity impelled Great Britain to ring London with new towns, spurred France to counter Paris with equilibrium metropolises, prompted the United States to confront the suburbs with urban renewal, led Venezuela to exploit its oil economy to foster the regional development of Guayana, and induced Turkey to try to offset the growth of the Marmara by encouraging urban development in other regions.

Because this blend of circumstances is tantamount to a complex set of preconditions, the strategies evolved very gradually. This is not true for cases where there may be an extraordinary response to a special opportunity or need, such as in the relocation of a capital or in the decision to make massive investments to exploit the resources of a particular region. These efforts, because they are massive, constitute national policies even if they are only implicit, but they do not necessarily lead to systematic, formal policies and programs for the development of other cities and regions. In Turkey, under Mustafa Kemal and İnönü, they did not. The establishment of the new capital and the stress on urban development were important experiences and served as a reminder that new growth centers could be established, but the problem still had to be tackled afresh a generation later. On the other hand, in Britain, France, the United States, and Venezuela (and in Turkey, after the revolution of 1959), the adoption of national policies led to the creation of intellectual beachheads, of administrative mechanisms and staff that could spread the essential ideas to strategic points inside and outside the government. Over time, the increasing awareness of the commitments, the greater visibility of the policies and programs, and the egalitarian pressures on governments led to the extension of these policies and programs. In all five countries, it took at least a generation before goals and policies were even roughly articulated; and it will take many years, perhaps another decade or a generation, before these ideas are translated into effective, systematic strategies.

Nonetheless, we can expect more rapid introduction of such programs to guide urban growth in the future, for most of the essential components are now known. Whether one is concerned with policies, organizations, or instruments, there are now a number of operating models. They offer a starting point for thinking about a wide range of urban growth problems and of ways of dealing with them:

1. The choice of goals and development alternatives.
2. The administrative machinery.
3. The incentive, control, and review mechanisms.
4. The inescapable constraints.
5. The appropriate relationships between development and planning agencies at different levels of government.

The existence of such models accelerates similar efforts elsewhere. This is evident by the speed with which underlying ideas are spreading. The notion of new towns, basically British in origin, is now in vogue almost everywhere, and so are the ideas of urban renewal, an innovation of the United States, and of growth poles, a French doctrine, although none of these ideas was bruited about before the end of World War II.

The popularity of these ideas, however, is not at all a measure of their success. Actually, the difficulties encountered suggest that the problems of managing growth are formidable and are likely to evade easy solution. Britain has wrestled with some of them for more than a generation and is only now perhaps on the verge of achieving its objectives. The French started earlier but still have a long way to go—probably further than the British—even though their formal administrative machinery appears more highly developed, and their strategy of promoting equilibrium metropolises more explicit. Venezuela and Turkey are even further behind France.

One could roughly rate these and other countries on the relative sophistication of their efforts on a number of counts:

1. The adequacy of machinery to define development goals, not only aggregatively but by sectors and regions.
2. The means that exist to coordinate development programs by sectors and by regions.
3. The explicitness of the basic urban and regional development strategies.
4. The quality of staff and training programs.
5. The effectiveness of programs enlisting contributions from the private sector.
6. The linkages that exist among social, economic, and physical elements.
7. The capacity of local and regional organizations to handle their responsibilities.
8. The provisions for evaluation and improvement of performance as the program continues.

What is especially noteworthy is that, although such an examination would point up serious shortcomings in each of these countries, it would also disclose that the concern in each country was with how to refine policies and to improve mechanisms, not with how to get rid of them.

In short, gaps in the understanding of theoretical and pragmatic relationships have not precluded the adoption of such strategies. On the contrary, when the need to act was agreed upon, then the disposition was either to experiment and to learn or, as Hirschman suggests, to follow "The Principle of the Hiding Hand"—that is, to underestimate the difficulties or to overestimate the benefits.[2] In all the cases studied, recourse to action on a significant scale sooner or later began to spur the necessary theoretical and applied research to sustain and extend these efforts. Moreover, because of the rapid spread of knowledge and experience, future experiments with development policies and programs will acquire more of an adaptive character than an innovative one. This likelihood should further reduce the period between the initiation of such programs and the development of more explicit, systematic policies and provisions for their implementation.

The Environment
for Urban Growth Strategies

Britain, France, Turkey, the United States, and Venezuela differ in size, climate, resources, and location. They range from small to large, tropical to temperate, meager to well-endowed, and peripheral to central in their location. The five countries also differ in their institutions. Politically, they range from relatively centralized (France and Turkey) to relatively decentralized (United States). Socially, their cultures vary from relatively egalitarian (United States) to relatively hierarchical (Great Britain). All have varying elements of homogeneity and heterogeneity, depending on the criteria used for measurement. None of these differences has precluded the adoption of urban growth strategies, although they have influenced the effectiveness with which such strategies were carried out.

The economies of these countries also differ widely. Some are poor, others rich; some are narrowly diversified, others widely diversified. Turkey and Venezuela are in the take-off stages of industrialization; the others are highly industrialized and service-oriented. France, Britain, and Turkey face serious and immediate economic strains; the others do not. France had slow population and industrial development for more than a century; the others experienced the reverse. Both the more and the less economically developed countries are trying to spur national economic growth through the encouragement of growing regions. However, the advanced countries are also trying to arrest the decline of some regions, a decline stemming from changes in the location of industries, whereas the poorer countries are trying to induce development in primitive hinterlands. The lagging regions are prominent issues, particularly in the poorer countries, because of their magnitude and because a few of these regions may have very significant growth potentials.

These economic differences can affect urban and regional development strategies in fairly obvious ways. The most important involve the opportunities and constraints inherent in having relatively limited or relatively ample resources or in having a vigorous private sector and mature economic institutions or the reverse.[3] Another involves the differing psychological, as well as economic, significance of opening a hinterland rather than arresting its decline. What is intriguing, however, is that even though these differences have affected opportunities for development, they have not otherwise changed the main outlines of the urban and regional strategies adopted or the more general definitions of the problems on which they are based. Each of these countries believes it suffers from overconcentration in congested cities in some areas, underconcentration in others, and from undesirable and unnecessarily large regional differences in levels of social and economic development. All believe that they need to change the way the metropolis grows and to promote urban growth centers in the less prosperous regions.

Institutional differences can be significant factors also. An urban growth strategy involves controls, incentives, and pressures to influence the scale and pattern of development of metropolitan regions. It requires priorities for regional development and measures to implement them. It means favoring a West or a North against an East or a South. Even if the measures do not go counter to dominant trends or powerful interests, they presuppose choices among alternatives that will shift costs and benefits for cities and regions and arouse stormy conflicts. Such policies ought to be easier to work out in countries with centralized governments, hierarchical social systems, and homogeneous cultures. In point of fact, they are—but subject to a number of important reservations. In a country with a weak local system of government, opposition to the central government policy is crippled; but it is also harder to carry out the policy effectively in the field without able local or regional organs of government. The urban and regional aspects of growth strategy in Turkey and Venezuela betrayed serious weaknesses because of failings at this level. On the other hand, a weak national system of government is unable to develop a strong central policy for regional development, except through powerful incentives, relatively effective local, state, or provincial governments, or a vigorous system of private enterprise. The existence of any or all of these conditions is exceptional, but they did prevail in the United States in the nineteenth century and were responsible, in part, for its phenomenal western development.

A hierarchical social and political system—where the governing class is accustomed to govern, where other classes are accustomed to acquiesce, and where private interests have relatively less power—can more readily evolve urban and regional growth policies at the national level than systems under the sway of the market, local political jurisdictions, or egalitarian political processes. This is one reason why urban growth policies burgeoned earlier in France and Britain than in the United States. But a hierarchical system—whether social or administrative, or both—has serious weaknesses in execution. It generally suffers from "apoplexy at the center and anemia at the edges," problems that both France and Britain as well as Turkey and Venezuela are struggling to solve. On the other hand, if problems become serious enough (or simply appear to be serious enough), national strategies will emerge even in market-oriented environments. For example, the current furor over the problems of the central city in the United States, and, to a lesser extent, over the problem of energizing less prosperous areas, is prompting the government to follow roughly the same course taken in the more hierarchical and centralized environments—albeit with significant adaptations—to take account of racial issues and differences in planning institutions.

All told, the adoption of variants of the same strategies in a wide range of different environments underscores the common problems and trends and conventional ways of thinking about these matters. Even more significant, perhaps, is the fact that in all these countries, the common denominator is the conviction that the guidance of urban growth strategy cannot—or, rather, must not—remain only at the local level.

Concepts and Goals

The urban growth strategies of nations are hardly mature, but one can already speak of a "traditional" approach to urban growth issues and of problems characteristic of this approach. It has become increasingly customary for development specialists to consider the role different cities and regions might or ought to play in the development of a country and hence, in the programming of infrastructure and in the shaping of industrial and other development policies. In Britain, France, and Venezuela this definition of roles has led to quite different decisions about development priorities, and such differing results comfort planners who want urban and regional considerations taken more explicitly into account.

Nonetheless, there are difficulties imbedded in these ideas that need to be faced. Most planners, for example, are disposed to believe that development efforts will eventually founder if basic concepts are hazy and if development aims are obscure. Based on these assumptions, the future prospects of urban growth strategies are unattractive. This is because these strategies rest on two fuzzy assumptions—the disadvantages of big cities and the feasibility of promoting growth centers—that to date no one has been able to define operationally. We do not really know when a city is too big or too congested, rather than merely poorly organized. And we have, as yet, learned little more than the rudiments of how to convert an urban center into a growth center and how to radiate the effects of such growth centers over the surrounding hinterlands. But this is not the first time (and probably not the last) that decision makers have had to manipulate forces they do not fully understand.

The situation may appear to be all the more discouraging because development aims are defined obscurely in all the countries studied and not only in the United States, whose aims have scarcely been formulated at all. The British goals, for example, of encouraging growth centers and reducing unemployment in the lagging region, are still so vague that they hardly provide an adequate basis for evaluating progress or even for gauging how many of the changes in the character of urban development can be attributed to the measures undertaken. The French goals appear to be more explicit. The notion of equilibrium metropolises identifies the metropolitan regions where growth is to be encouraged and defines the strategy to build up large cities to compete with Paris. But conflicting national aims, not to mention pressures from other cities and regions, drain away much of the substance of this policy, so that in France, too, it is difficult to say what level of performance would represent satisfactory progress in carrying out its strategy within a reasonable period. The objectives in Turkey are far vaguer still. There are no explicit commitments, only general intentions of encouraging growth centers and correcting imbalance between growing and lagging regions. Plans are prepared that are supposed to be backed up by the Turkish government and private investments in the designated regions, but, more often than not, this fails to occur.

The sole exception, perhaps, is the experience of Venezuela. Plans for Guayana were incorporated into the national plan, and specific, staged targets for regional investment, production, and exports were linked to plans for national development. However, this was true only for the Guayana region. Indeed, the success of Venezuela's policy was possible only by focusing on one region whose development had national significance and by systematically exploiting the unique resource endowment of the region with relatively ample capital resources. Even under these highly favorable circumstances, the projected targets aggregated many important elements and were meaningful and well implemented only in comparison with the way regional plans were prepared elsewhere.

The experiences of these nations indicate the ambiguity and the range of variation that might be expected in the definition of aims in the early years of such a planning venture and perhaps for many years thereafter. They suggest that it may be impossible—at least at the outset—for a government to formulate adequate or precise national goals for urban and regional development. What appears to be a far more feasible approach is the preparation of some general guidelines that can later be successively redefined. It may also be possible to work out somewhat more adequate and more detailed development goals and programs in one or two regions. These can then be tried and evaluated and serve as a training ground and as a guide for efforts elsewhere.

Of course, it is more customary and attractive to argue that clear goals should be set from the start, but this does not appear to be an option. It is very hard in the early stages to devise solutions to complex problems or to obtain backing for new ways of dealing with them. However odd it may seem, it is easier and often more realistic to fix precise goals in the middle or toward the end of a program. Effective goals presuppose awareness of what is feasible and desirable. They are in effect the fruition of much thought and experience and substantial consensus. This implies a learning process, often stretching over a decade or two. During this period, however, vague formulations and limited efforts, for all of their inadequacies, serve a useful purpose. They indicate general directions and invite the necessary initial critiques and refinements of goals and methods. In the course of these efforts, the bureaucracy and the public are given time to familiarize themselves with the issues and time to devise ways and means of dealing with unsuspected difficulties, or of avoiding further entanglements.

Despite the relatively obscure objectives indicated in the case studies, the kinds of measures deployed in these different environments have been fairly limited. The principal ones involve changing the rate of growth of a major city and encouraging development in growth zones within metropolitan regions and in other areas. The traditional instruments for these purposes range from controls to a variety of incentive schemes for public and private investment programs. Of course, it makes a difference how these measures are applied: whether there are many loopholes in the controls, whether the incentives are significant enough to induce the desired outcomes, whether all or only some of these instruments are deployed, whether the diverse efforts are made by one organization or by several, whether the policies are reinforced by other policies and programs of the national government. The pattern to date—in Britain, France, and the United States and to a lesser extent in Turkey and Venezuela —is for simple, limited measures to be initiated at the outset, out of prudence and ease of innovation and possibly also out of lack of conviction or clarity either about the goals or the efficacy of the means.

This prudence is understandable. With a relatively new policy where it is difficult to foretell the problems that may be encountered or the consequences of policy choices, the best the decision maker can do in the beginning is to develop simple analytical and administrative machinery that may be made more efficient with time and to avoid major and relatively inflexible commitments until there is more of a consensus or until the decision maker is more certain about what is likely to happen. Later, as goals become clearer and if they still seem worth pursuing, he can either improve the tools (tighten or extend the controls, enlarge the premiums, change the definition of areas, perfect the coordinative mechanisms) or devise new tools to make the efforts more successful. He may also decide that the aims are wrong or, more probably, that they could be realized more efficiently by still other means. In that case, he might then relax controls and place more reliance on other tools, such as the price system, but such a reversal of official attitudes seems unlikely in any of the five countries studied.

This orientation today toward more controls and larger subsidies is all the more striking since, as we have observed, the experience with controls and incentives has been until recently somewhat disappointing. Controls and incentives have generally proved to be inadequate as a means of reversing a powerful force such as the expansion of a capital or a dominant metropolis. The opportunities for evasion are legion, and the strain of enforcement on the administrative apparatus is severe. In Britain and France, after a generation of effort, the controls and incentives are working better—but still not adequately. The principal justification for controls and incentives today is not that they prevent congestion or successfully induce new

growth. It is, rather, that in a territory containing several development possibilities, a well-designed system of controls and incentives
will prompt many firms and ministries to take advantage of these
other possibilities.

A national system of incentives and controls to reinforce an urban
growth strategy can be evolved in many ways. One possibility is to
start at the top, create an intelligence unit close to the chief executive,
and then develop a national strategy for area development. This is
doubtless the most appealing approach from one point of view, for
it is certainly possible now, in principle, for a small group of specialists to devise a fairly comprehensive strategy: to spell out goals, write
legislation, formulate policies, fashion administrative mechanisms,
and devise means to carry them into effect. Doubtless this can be
done all the more quickly and elegantly if there is a national planning
organization, but unless there is a large backlog of experience on
these matters, not to mention adequate staff and resources, such
efforts are apt to bog down. The ideas will not be fully understood
and therefore will not gain necessary backing in different quarters,
especially in the local regions. The programs in Britain, the United
States, Venezuela, and even France did not evolve in this way; and
the brief experience of Turkey with planning from the top down
suggests that when such an approach is followed, it will not be
effective. However simple and direct the centralized style may appear,
the lack of an adequate analytical, administrative, and political base
outside the political center often turns out to be a crucial weakness.
It would take a rare group of administrators, indeed, to overcome it.

An alternative approach is illustrated by the experience of Venezuela or by the later stages of the regional planning program in
Turkey. In these two cases, the emphasis was on promoting one or
more metropolitan regions; at the same time, or at some reasonable
period thereafter, these programs were linked into national development plans and policies. This approach built up the necessary experience and trained staff and gradually familiarized key elements of the
public and the government with the program and the issues. A basic
assumption here is that the essential ideas of the program have merit
and will win further support, that they will survive despite inconsistencies and conflicts between regions, and that over time they will
generate pressures for complementary programs.[4]

Despite the clarity of a nation's goals, political pressures can com-
plicate and dilute the effectiveness of development policies. The issue

of dispersal or concentration is an illustration of this. In the past, and even today, the pressure to satisfy political requirements has hobbled programs in Britain, France, and the United States (not to mention Italy and other countries in Western Europe). Dispersal was more effectively resisted in Venezuela, owing to a political leadership that created an extraordinary national consensus about an exceptional region; and it was also successfully resisted in Turkey under the leaderships of Kemal and Inönü but not thereafter. In general, however, the free market tends to favor concentration, whereas making the issues explicit often tends to consolidate political pressures and to favor dispersal. Thus, the great task of urban statesmanship is to develop the necessary political imagery to steer a middle course for a reasonable period in the future. This, however, is extremely difficult. To date, the issue of dispersal or concentration has proved so inflammatory, and the way it is resolved is so critical to the success of any policy of development, that governments have often found it necessary to talk one way and to act another. And although it is easier politically to advocate dispersal and then allocate resources otherwise (or allow such allocations to occur), the experience of France suggests that on occasion this process may be reversed. There, lip service has been paid to the ideology of concentration, but as yet this has imposed very few constraints on a far more permissive allocation policy.

The Next Phase
of Urban Growth Strategies

Urban growth strategies now address themselves to the curbing of metropolitan growth in one or more areas and to the promotion of growing points elsewhere. In the future, however, we can expect this emphasis to be modified in four ways.

The first change in emphasis will involve the responses of nations to the emergence of sprawling metropolitan areas along major transportation corridors forming massive linear megalopolitan clusters. Such patterns are already being formed along the Caracas-Valencia-Maracay axis in Venezuela and along the Istanbul-Izmit-Ankara sector in Turkey. They are visible in France along the east-west and north-south regional axes extending outward from Paris; and they are even more in evidence in Great Britain in the linear belt extending from London to Birmingham, Liverpool, Manchester, and Glasgow. Their most publicized expressions, of course, are the spreading metropolitan growth complexes along the eastern and western coastal areas of the United States and along the Great Lakes. Even new towns, which have been increasingly favored as instruments for linking decentralization and economic growth strategies, are no longer thought of as self-contained communities but rather as growing points generally connected on some linear pattern to larger urban complexes "along a band of communications, [or like] . . . beads on a string."[5]

The markets created by these vast concentrations of population and economic activity and the relative flexibility, compactness, and ease of extension of such patterns of development make it likely that the linear megalopolis form of growth will continue. Only inter-metropolitan and national policies can cope with the common problems facing such areas. The most important of these problems will concern transportation, water and sewage facilities, the handling of open space and recreational policies, and such special questions as air pollution and relationships with depressed areas, in addition to the general guidance of growth and development.

A second area of future concern will involve building up the resources and capabilities of local governments. At present, almost everywhere, local revenues are hopelessly inadequate, pay and staff poor, and local services in education, transportation, housing, recreation, social service, and basic information are in need of massive improvements. There are several reasons why these problems of local capability have not played a major role so far in national policy in relation to urban growth strategies. In the poorer nations, central governments have been in no position to transform local government services; nor have these problems been as pressing in the short run as the monetary exchange, general development, or minority problems that have faced the central governments. Moreover, in most of these countries, there exists no tradition of strong local government. There are often powerful landed or regional interests—vestiges of feudalism—that the central governments are trying to combat. These conditions, coupled with meager resources and inadequately trained professional staff, have made it unlikely for central governments to have either the capacity or the desire to strengthen local or regional independence. Overloaded central staffs and the need to stir local initiative will eventually spur efforts to solve these problems through some form of decentralization.

In the more developed countries, such as the United States, France, and England, the local governments had or have acquired greater responsibilities for territorial planning and development. Even these powers have proved inadequate. The mounting obligations accompanying increases in population, in welfare services, and in development responsibilities have compelled persistent efforts on the part of national governments to strengthen local capabilities. During the past generation, these efforts took the form of matched grants from the central government for specific services or of encouraging local public development corporations to build and manage housing, transportation, and other services. The current trend is toward enlarging local government boundaries, as in France and Great Britain, and toward providing unrestricted block grants to local communities, as in the United States.

One effect of these measures will be the weakening of the power of the central government to guide developmental strategy within the region. If communities do not require financial assistance, they will not be especially receptive to unpopular national policies. However, block grants and changes in boundaries will not alter the need for national efforts to induce desired changes in interregional or intraregional patterns of development. Therefore, national incentives are likely to be increased in order to aid lagging regions, to underwrite urban renewal, to siphon off population growth and industries from congested areas, and to support other programs favored by the central authorities.

Still a third question that will be of growing concern in the future is how to ensure that the groups who should benefit from growth will actually do so. Providing assistance from the well-to-do regions to the poorer regions by means of the central government often ends up with the giver as the principal beneficiary. It has therefore been urged that regions, and in particular the people of these regions, be given a greater voice in the administrative and political process. Mainly dissident minorities have expressed these views to date, but the ideas reflect the mood of the age and are neatly attuned to prevailing circumstances. It is hardly surprising that they are spreading and bid fair to become the conventional wisdom of the future.

One can see these tendencies in a number of different political and social contexts. For example, in the Guayana region of Venezuela, the dissidents stressed the importance of having the Guayana Development Corporation consult the views and needs of the local population—the merchants and political leaders and even the humbler elements of society. They wanted a greater emphasis placed on achieving high employment than on attaining a high rate of growth. They favored low density, more self-help, and owner-occupied housing in places where migrants could find jobs and learn more easily about new opportunities. They objected to the criteria used for housing selection and welfare, which some of the local populace considered to be inappropriate for many of the families the programs were intended to serve. A growing awareness of the discrepancy between the needs of the population and the policies of the administrators soon led some of the local leaders to explore ways of effecting change by pressures and other processes and even by violence.[6] Finally, the Guayana Development Corporation was forced to reverse its position on some matters such as the distribution of public land to the local community, in response to the pressures of the local leaders.

Other national programs have also been modified by local demands. In Turkey, despite the disdain for local views and a highly centralized administrative tradition, local and regional pressures have forced more attention to be paid to development in the East, though "participation" is still a long way off. In Britain, on the other hand, the claims for regional autonomy in Scotland and Wales have been asserted with increasing intensity. In France, even more than in Britain, the emphasis has changed from simply helping the lagging regions to providing more opportunity for their participation in the decision-making process. These views, expressed often enough before the revolutionary outbreaks in May and June, 1968, were clearly a reaction to the paternalistic and heavy-handed tutelage of the French administrative process. For a long time they were dismissed as con-trived political pressures encouraged by an intractable opposition; but after the events of May and June and even after the subsequent elections that gutted the opposition, the government radically reversed its position and supported the creation of regional assemblies as well as a gradual movement toward eventual fiscal autonomy. Moreover, the government favored these measures on the grounds that the people in the regions would thereby be more apt to pursue vigorous measures in their own behalf.[7]

As for the United States, although its long-established pattern of decentralized state authorities has been dwindling in importance, new pressures for more local control have arisen from certain militant leaders of the poor and the black. Only such power, it has been contended, will allow vigorous efforts at self-improvement, and only the possession of such power will transform the black population's image of itself and of its status. These views have come to the fore at approximately the same time that several experiments have been undertaken to encourage "maximum feasible participation" by low-income families in a variety of economic development, educational, and housing assistance programs designed to help them to improve their conditions. The ambiguity of the language and the inadequacies of certain programs have led some persons to dismiss such efforts as impractical and misguided, but it is far from certain that the programs have failed or that their limitations have been due to inherent weaknesses rather than to inexperience and limited resources.[8]

In any case, the evidence seems to suggest that in the future urban growth strategies will not be simply efforts of the central governments to aid lagging regions through incentives and controls. These strategies will be characterized by pressures and demands on the part of the populations of these lagging areas and their supporters for a greater share in the planning and administration of policies. Indeed, if these views prevail, the big question will be how to ensure that the programs undertaken will prove responsive to those groups they were designed to benefit.

The fourth set of issues will stem from the changed role of cities in the future. In the past, the basic functions of cities were economic. They still are. Cities provide a favorable location for all kinds of economic activities. And big cities, up to a scale we cannot yet identify with precision, tend to be the most favorable locations because of their markets, their wide range of public and private services, and the various opportunities and stimuli that accompany their growth and diversification. These, on balance add up to the advantages and "external" economies that families and firms find in the cities.

Cities also affect the way we live and enjoy ourselves and our capacity to change and grow. These functions are latent: they involve roles not usually associated with the city's *raison d'être*. But they are becoming more important. People today are increasingly present-

and pleasure-oriented. Preferred styles of living and sheer enjoyment rank far higher than they used to in the locational decisions of families and of firms, largely because they can now afford these preferences.

The educational function of cities is also receiving more recognition. In countries in transition from rural, traditional societies, the city concentrates and transmits a new tempo and new values. This effect is all the more significant in the poorer countries because schools reach only a limited portion of the population for a relatively short period. Even in the more developed countries, the city plays the role of educational center for in-migrants from rural areas.

Not the least important role of the city of the future, however, will be to help to direct the evolution of its own economy and culture. To be sure, a city's capacity to assist in its own transformation will be subject to serious constraints. Nonetheless, this role will become more crucial as our wealth increases, as we improve our tools and intelligence mechanisms, and as we more avidly explore feasible "alternative futures."

Given these prospects of the changing roles of the city, what are the implications for urban growth strategies? In general, we can expect still more emphasis on programs for renewal and for the control of the size or relative growth rates of the very largest cities because of the anticipated amenity and educational effects. There will also be renewed interest in optimum-sized cities. The quest will not prove any more amenable to analysis in the future; and as a by-product of this, attention may well shift to the problems of establishing critical *minimum* sizes for cities, especially in lagging regions, to sustain growth and to help cities to become more interesting. In addition, we can count on efforts not only to spread the influence of the city to the hinterland but also to expand the vistas of the city's own population, to get them to experience the whole city and the surrounding region. For, as John Dyckman has noted,

the West Side Puerto Rican or the Harlem Negro knows that he does not have access to the full meaning of the city of New York. Both the physical space apprehended by the individual and the Lewinian "life space" would have to be expanded. We make much of the city as a center of communication, but the information in the messages is received by a few while to the many the communication content is chiefly noise.[9]

Finally, there is sure to be much more exploration of the future for the purpose of guiding present national urban growth strategies.

We live in an age, many people believe, in which we can successfully accomplish most of what we seek to accomplish if we can only agree on what it is that we want. This faith, especially in the United States, is in large measure an outgrowth of the successes we have achieved in the realm of science and in the growth of our economy. Daniel Bell has even argued that

perhaps the most important social change of our time is the emergence of a process of direct and deliberate contrivance of change itself. Men now seek to anticipate change, measure the course of its direction and its impact, control it, and even shape it for predetermined ends.[10]

It is not at all certain that the response to this challenge will fortify the faith. The success of a national urban and regional growth strategy involves achieving consensus on values and resource allocation and resolving social conflicts that do not easily lend themselves to technical solutions. Nonetheless, the effort will surely be made; indeed no other aspect of our culture will receive more searching examination in the next generation.

Notes

1. See L. Rodwin, *Nations and Cities, A Comparison of Urban Growth Strategies* (Boston: Houghton Mifflin Company, 1970).

2. A. O. Hirschman, *Development Projects Observed* (Washington, D.C.: Brookings Institution, 1967), Chap. 1.

3. Examples are varied credit mechanisms and business and consumer services.

4. "Good" ideas do not always win further support: witness the limited success of the TVA in the United States. Also there is no guarantee, of course, that the eruption of conflicts and pressures will, in fact, prove benign.

5. J. James, "The Future of Urban Forms," in *The Papers and Proceedings of the International Symposium on Regional Development* (Hakone, Japan, April, 1967), p. 211. See also in the same collection K. Tange, "The Japanese Archipelago of the Future," pp. 79–92.

6. L. R. Peattie, *The View From the Barrio* (Ann Arbor: University of Michigan Press, 1968), Chaps. 6, 7.

7. L'équipe de la revue "2000," *Essai sur la Participation, Autonomie, et Solidarités*, Numero 9, "Special," Paris, June 1968. See also remarks of the Prime Minister M. Couve de Murville and General de Gaulle, cited respectively in *Le Monde*, December 15–16, 1968, and February 4, 1969.

8. See D. P. Moynihan, *Maximum Feasible Misunderstanding* (New York: The Free Press, 1969); P. Marris and M. Rein, *Dilemmas of Social Reform, Poverty and Community Action in the United States* (New York: Atherton Press, 1967); and J. A. Califano, Jr., "Moynihan: The Lasting Value is Dubious," *The Washington Post*, February 6, 1969.

9. J. W. Dyckman, "The Changing Uses of the City," in *The Future Metropolis*, ed. L. Rodwin (New York: George Braziller, Inc., 1961), pp. 161–62.

10. D. Bell, "Notes on the Post-Industrial System," *The Public Interest*, 2 (Winter 1967), 25.

ON GROWTH POLES

J. R. LASUÉN
Universidad Autonoma de Madrid

ABSTRACT   Perroux argued that economic space as an abstract field of forces leads to the notion of a vector of economic forces, and hence to the concept of growth poles.

His further view that economic development necessarily requires spatial polarization is an inaccurate and damaging limitation of this concept. Whilst the early stages of economic development must generate growth points due to a lack of entrepreneurship outside these centers, development in advanced countries is becoming less polarized. This is caused by the increasingly diversified structure of business which results in an extensive spatial spread of innovations and economic development. It follows that developing countries can accelerate their growth by creating diversified corporate structures which diminish the exigencies of a polarized strategy.

Introduction

The concept of *pôle de croissance* (growth pole),[1] along with related concepts such as growth centers, development poles, core regions, and regional centers, has become an idea in good currency.[2] It is referred to widely in the social sciences, on both sides of the Atlantic,[3] and enjoys the privilege of all mythic catchwords: on the one hand, it sounds like a useful concept for social policy; on the other, being loosely defined, it is not easily subject to meaningful tests. When the concept is used in planning, the failures of the policies centered upon it are normally attributed to the ways and means by which it has been implemented, never to the adequacy of the concept itself. As an

Reprinted from *Urban Studies*, Volume 6, Number 2, June 1969. Published by Oliver & Boyd Ltd., Edinburgh. Printed in Great Britain by Robert Cunningham & Sons, Ltd., Alva. Reprinted with permission of publisher and author.

idea in good currency, it can suffer the lot of most of them: they pass away, undestroyed, but tarnished by their inefficiency.

This paper's aim is to reduce the elusiveness of the growth pole concept. As a consequence, it may be taken as a critical note on some of the theoretical constructs of the French school of space economics[4] which has developed the concept. However, it is consistent with the original insights of the school's founding father, François Perroux. The reason is that Perroux has been a fecund source of ideas and insights, often unrelated, sometimes inconsistent and, rarely, developed further by him or his disciples. In the case of growth poles, I derive my arguments from some of the ideas of his first major paper.[5] The majority of his followers have based theirs on his second major paper,[6] which already diverges significantly from the former.

It is my conclusion that though the growth pole, and the notion of space on which it is built, are fruitful theoretical constructs, they do not necessarily lead to the traditional growth poles policy. Deeper analysis of those concepts is likely to lead to a new set of policies that will often compete advantageously with the crude version of spatial planning, now in vogue, in overcoming the frictions of geographical space to which the growth pole concept calls attention.

PERROUXIAN SPACE

Perroux is the latest important name in a long list of European economists concerned with space. It is a French name in an array of German and Scandinavian names. No doubt, he developed his interest in space economics from his exposure to the German literature,[7] for as Colin Clark[8] has pointed out, space economics has been a German speciality.

But Perroux added a significant Gallic contribution to the current. Von Thünen, Weber, Lösch, Predöhl, Palander, and so on[9] had been mostly concerned with explaining how economic activities organize themselves over geographic space. Perroux reacted against this approach. Viewed in this way, he felt that geography had been cast as a passive rigid container that conditions the dynamic evolution of the economic forces, and that this was only a partial, limiting, and dangerous perspective. In his view, geography does not rigidly limit the economic forces.

He has argued in fact, that the static, rigid, three-dimensional conception of space has led to unnecessary pathological evaluations and

psychopathic national policies in Europe.[10] To avoid these consequences he proposed[11] that this three-dimensional concept of space
should be replaced in economics by a type of abstract, topological
space. In that vein, space is the set of different relations that define
an object. Since there can be many systems of relations defining an
object, for any one object there are many different topological spaces.
For every object there are many different sets of relations, many
different space-sets.

This stated, he proceeded to put forward a threefold typology[12] of
topological economic spaces: (1) space as the planning area of the
decision units; (2) space as the field of forces acting upon the decision
units; (3) space as the field of homogeneous objects. The Euclidian
dimensions of any of those topological spaces will vary depending on
the decision under consideration.

I think Perroux was correct in his basic argument that a topological
view of space permits easier integration of the plans of different
decision units because it favors attitudes toward compromises on
complementaries between parties; contrariwise, that an Euclidian
('container-contained') view of space, a rigid ethological view of
space, leads to withdrawal and aggression.[13]

The growth pole concept is the logical derivation of one such
Perrouxian type of abstract spaces. Economic space as a field of
forces leads to the notion of a pole, a vector of economic forces.

THE CONCEPT
OF *PÔLE DE CROISSANCE*

In 1955, in his first paper on growth poles,[14] Perroux began his
argument by describing Gustav Cassell's stationary circuit[15] and
J. A. Schumpeter's use of it as a classification device to select out
the fluctuations and development changes occurring in real economic
life.[16] Then, following Schumpeter's main line,[17] Perroux succinctly
stated the essence of the structural or developmental change that
takes an economy away from the stationary circuit. To him, the basic
cause is "Schumpeterian innovations." They result in more desirable
products that replace previous ones. Development, in other words,
means to Perroux the birth of new and death of old industries; it
means the continuous differentiation of the rates of growth of the
new and old products and respective industries away from the equal
growth rates of the stationary circuit model. Development proceeds

by the direct and indirect effects of innovations. Highly income-elastic new products replace the low income-elastic old ones and call for smaller scale innovations in the products related to them. The adjustments in the products linked to the new ones, both through their forward and backward linkages, are caused both by the expectations produced by the new product and by their realized impacts, through prices and income channels. These impacts result in cumulative deviations from stationary equilibria (sectoral and geographical). Newer industries (and the cities where they are located) in which the developmental innovations take place grow at a faster pace than older industries and cities. Around the new industries and their locations, sectorally and geographically, the activities linked to the leading ones also grow faster than their counterparts elsewhere. Development therefore implies cumulative sectoral and spatial differentiation in impact; it implies sectoral and spatial clustering of activities around the leading activities and their faster growth than the rest.

In brief, the net contribution of Perroux to the basic Schumpeterian argument was that he took Schumpeter's tool-box of concepts and hypotheses from its original sectoral-temporal setting and applied it to a sectoral-temporal-geographical universe. He was able to do it, thanks to his concept of topological space. He viewed the changes in the system of industries as transformations in sectoral space and asked which form they would take in geographical space. The geographical pole is the geographical image of the newly innovated industry and its linked activities.[18]

In Perroux's framework, the basic definitions and hypotheses ought to answer: (1) what are the characteristics of a leading industry (*industrie motrice*)? (2) what are those of the industrial complex? (3) what are the sectoral and spatial interrelations between the leading industry and the industrial complex? (4) what are the interrelations between the growth of the polarized industrial clusters and that of the nation? He did not answer these questions properly. His definition of leading industry is imprecise[19]; that of the industrial complex is incomplete.[20] His explanation of the interrelations between the leading industry and the complex is partial[21]; that of the relations between the growth of the pole and that of the nation is at least partly erroneous.[22]

Perroux's inability to derive a clear analytical apparatus to describe the growth pole dynamics can be clearly attributed to his desire (and that of his followers) to make immediate use of the growth pole concept in planning. This led him to attempt to formulate the basic definitions and hypotheses using available quantitative methodological instruments. Eventually, the purpose has become self-defeating.[23] Worse still, as not all these methodological instruments are consistent with the growth pole concept, the concept itself has become a source of confusion in regional economics.[24] It is unfortunate that the usefulness of the growth pole concept is still to be realized. Its potential is high. The concept, better than any other, brings forward as relevant analytical questions whether national development implies polarizations over the different topological spaces, and which, if any, are the interrelations between these spaces. In consequence it extends the potential policy use of economics. Before Perroux introduced the notion of topological space, it was difficult to conceptualize that a phenomenon that was observed in sectoral space could be subject to a policy of geographical dimensions, and vice versa. His notion clearly implies that when a goal, represented in a topological space, cannot be attained by means of policies pertaining to that space, it can still be pursued by other policies in other topological spaces. These policies are addressed at the original goal but traced in the latter topological spaces.[25] The French school of space economics, which has striven to develop the growth pole concept, has failed to exploit its potential due to the special bias that has characterized its research.[26]

GROWTH POLES RESEARCH

The French and Belgian authors of the Perroux school have, in the last years, produced a considerable amount of research along the lines indicated by Perroux in his major second paper. The works can be classed in two major groups: (1) descriptive and (2) planning oriented. The works of Perroux on the Ruhr,[27] Bauchet on Lorraine,[28] and Derwa on Liège[29] belong to the first; those of Boudeveille on Minas Gerais,[30] Davin on Liège,[31] Rosenfeld on Turin,[32] and Paelink on Venezuela,[33] to the second.[34]

The distinguishing trait of all those works is a very restricted way of formalizing and measuring the concept of leading or dominant industries and that of a changing polarized system of industries. Reviewing the field, N. M. Hansen[35] has developed the same points, namely that their exclusive use of input-output analysis has: (1) reduced the usefulness of the growth pole concept and (2) unduly restricted the concept of leading or dominant sector to large industries with large matrix multiplier effects.

Some additional points are worth making concerning the causes and the results of the French school research bias. First, although Perroux deserves credit for the richness of the growth pole concept and for the notion of topological economic space on which it is based, he is responsible for the school's path.[36] Second, the research limitations of the French school of space economics cannot be attributed wholly to the limitations of the input-output analysis, their basic method. In a large part, it is the result of a lack of sophistication in the use of the analysis. The French school's use of input-output analysis has not evolved much over the state of the art in the 1950s.[37] Their planning objectives are not more novel: to identify and set up the activities with the highest supermultiplier effect (in their terms, *internal blocking*) and to identify and install the mechanisms to reduce the net outflow of the generated increments in regional income (*external blocking*).[38] The input-output techniques they have used to obtain those objectives are also old and unreliable.[39]

Yet, the highest cost that the French school has paid, by restricting its analysis to the interindustry technique,[40] is that it has drained the growth pole concept of its original temporal[41] and dynamic meaning and recharged it with a static[42] and/or comparative static content. The heavy use of the input-output technique has shifted the school's attention away from Perroux's original translation of Schumpeterian development. They have failed to develop the point that the activity creating a growth pole was essentially a sectoral and a geographical disturbance not because of its larger than average size, nor because of its higher multiplier, but because it was an *innovation*. The other characteristics of the leading activity explained exclusively the amount and direction of the spread effects of the innovation. In consequence, they have not been able to profit from Perroux's notion of topological space in the understanding of today's development process. Further, they have not been concerned with testing, reformulating and completing Perroux's hypotheses on growth pole dynamics in the context of recent economic development. That is what I undertake to do in the following sections.

Is economic development polarized? To focus the argument, the relevant questions are: is development today as polarized as it was before? Do innovations today lead to polarizations as much as they did in the past? Or better, is development today necessarily polarized in all topological spaces? If not, in which topological spaces is it polarized and under what conditions? What policies can be used to depolarize it?

Clearly, the French school takes it for granted that development is polarized in every topological space and that the only kind of intervening policy to correct geographical polarizations is some sort of industrial complex planning. Contrary to this, I believe: (1) there is enough available evidence to assert that, within nations at least, development is becoming decreasingly polarized over geographical space[43]; (2) there can be new policies complementary to or substitutable for physical and sectoral planning to correct economic disturbances over geographic space; (3) the original framework of Perroux, remodeled, may be of as great help in explaining present-day trends and in suggesting policies as it was in the past in detecting the geographical polarization of development.

Consider the first point. Over the historical record, the process of innovation is accelerating greatly, in any one line and in all lines. It has been estimated that while the lapse between successive waves of innovations took around thirty years before World War II, it was reduced to fifteen in the post-war and is approaching seven nowadays.[44] According to the original Perroux hypothesis, the acceleration of the process of innovation would mean a *pari passu* acceleration in the rise and decay of the corresponding industries and cities. As a consequence, one would expect the urban structure to have become very unstable, with the cities experiencing sudden, jerky, explosive bursts of growth and decay.

So far as I have been able to measure the process of urban growth, the contrary seems to have been the case. The data on the growth of the Spanish towns, in the last century, shows that the changes in city ranks by size have been much more pronounced in the past than in the present, reflecting a growing homogeneity in the process of growth of the system of cities. That can be clearly observed in Table 1.[45]

The same can be observed in Table 2, which records the results of a more formal test.[46] This test used Spearman rank correlation coefficients to compare the distributions by decreasing population size at every census year, of Spain's forty-nine provincial cities and of her 157 cities larger than 10,000 inhabitants in 1860, with their respective distribution in 1860.

TABLE 1

Major Shifts in Ordering of Spain's Provincial Capitals
(1867–1960)[a]

		Upward Shift in Rank YEARS OF MAIN SHIFT AND NUMBER OF RANKS OF SHIFT (IN BRACKETS; OVER 49 TOTAL)	
Cities	Final rank	Middle point shift	Total shift
Bilbao	7	1877 (9)	1900 (19)
San Sebastian	14	1900 (13)	1910 (17)
Santa Cruz	15	1877 (7)	1930 (19)
Huelva	26	1877 (9)	1930 (21)
Leon	28	1910 (8)	1950 (16)
Pontevedra	35	1877 (19)	1877 (19)

		Downward Shifts in Rank YEARS OF MAIN SHIFTS AND NUMBER OF RANKS OF SHIFT (IN BRACKETS; OVER 49 TOTAL)	
Cities	Final rank	Middle point shift	Total shift
Cadiz	19	1910 (5)	1930 (12)
Jaen	29	1877 (5)	1910 (10)
Lugo	34	1877 (9)	1877 (12)
Tarragona	38	1910 (8)	1960 (12)
Toledo	40	1910 (7)	1960 (12)
Gerona	12	1900 (8)	1960 (12)

[a] The table should be read as follows from the example of Bilbao. In 1867, Bilbao was the 28th largest provincial capital of Spain (out of 49). In 1960 it was the 7th. It had already attained that rank in 1900. The total shift of 19 ranks upwards was achieved in two sub-periods of roughly equal gain in ranks. From 1867 to 1877, Bilbao gained 9 (out of 19) ranks. From 1877 to 1900, the other 10.

I have picked Bilbao as the example, because it is the largest and best known city in the Table. Bilbao's rapid growth was based on its iron, steel and metal works base. Today it has Spain's highest disposable income per capita. It has diversified its base to engineering products, shipyards, chemicals, financing, etc. Its growth was anomalous. Its export staple was iron ore (to the U.K.), an unlikely base to industrialize upon. Bilbao developed its iron works and steel mills, because the iron ore ships had no return freight from the U.K. Rather than coming back with empty holds, the shippers loaded the boats with British coal at cheap rates. This made Bilbao a feasible site for an iron-steel complex.

Table 2 shows that the fall-off in the values of the coefficients decreased relatively as they approach the present, contrary to what would be expected if the acceleration of development meant higher instability in the urban structure.

Most data on other European nations also show an increasing

TABLE 2

Spearman Rank Correlation Coefficients among the
Different Rank-size City Distributions in Spain,
at the Different Census Years (1867–1960)
and that of 1860

Censuses	Provincial capitals (49)	Cities larger than 10,000 inhabitants in 1860 (157)
1860	—	—
1877	0.962	0.922
1887	0.941	0.866
1900	0.922	0.845
1910	0.896	0.792
1920	0.895	0.771
1930	0.864	0.727
1940	0.863	0.700
1950	0.846	0.673
1960	0.838	0.641

stability in the urban structure over time. The process is even clearer
in the United States, where the dramatic shifts in the urban
structure of cities like Chicago and Los Angeles in the nineteenth
and early twentieth centuries have disappeared, and where the urban
hierarchy now shows a remarkable relative stability, in spite of the
shifts of cities like Phoenix, Houston, and Miami.[47]

However, where one would expect the historical decline in geographical polarization effects to be less likely is in the newly developing countries, especially in those that have had a rapid growth, such
as Venezuela. This is precisely what Table 3 shows.[48]

In the table all coefficients are significant at the 1 per cent level and
show a relative decrease in the falling off of their values.

From available evidence, it is safe to conclude, then, that there is
no proof that the maturation of the development process significantly

TABLE 3

Spearman Rank Correlation Matrix among the
Venezuelan Cities: Rank-Size Distributions in Every
Census Year (122 Cities Larger Than 5,000 Inhabitants
in 1960)

	1881	1891	1936	1941	1950	1961
1881	1					
1891	0.744	1				
1936	0.740	0.738	1			
1941	0.756	0.722	0.924	1		
1950	0.685	0.652	0.738	0.850	1	
1961	0.717	0.649	0.606	0.688	0.829	1

increases the magnitude of the alterations in the relative ordering of the urban structure; on the contrary, available evidence suggests the opposite. Nowadays, the polarizations over topological sectoral space seem to distribute themselves over the urban structure so as to permit a stable pattern of growth of the system of cities.[49] The relative rise and decline of cities as a consequence of the localization of the successive transformations in the system of industries is becoming a minor issue, at the national level, in most countries.

What can account for it? Granted, as the evidence seems to support, that there were more geographical polarizations in the past than in the present, and that they are larger today the more underdeveloped the country is, what are the explanations for it? In the next section we present some hypothetical answers to these questions. Later, in the following section, we derive new criteria for regional development policy.

ECONOMIC DEVELOPMENT IN ORGANIZATIONAL SPACE

To start, let us view the economics of development of a country as the process by which its firms adopt successive sets of innovations, the time lapses between which become shorter,[50] and the scale of operations in any one line, larger.[51] From that perspective, the relevant development subprocesses are those relative: (1) to the generation of new innovations, (2) to the diffusion of knowledge of new innovations and (3) to the spread of adoptions. Then, the critical development factors are those determining the three subprocesses.

Once stated for reasons of logical presentation we can forget about the first subprocess. Most innovations today are developed in a small number of regions of an even smaller number of countries. For most countries and most regions, what matters is how the new innovations are diffused to their firms and how they adapt to the new knowledge.

The diffusion subprocess suggests an appealing hypothesis to explain the weaker geographical polarizations of the present. In fact, most people are inclined to think, off-hand, that the revolution in communications has favored not only a faster but a larger, more homogeneous, access of the population to any information.

For *general-purpose* information there seems to be evidence supporting the hypothesis. However, from this it is not safe to conclude that the diffusion of knowledge of innovations over geographical space was in the past more restricted than in the present. Diffusions in the past were no doubt slower but were at least as extensive. The hypothesis is wrong because it assumes equal characteristics to the diffusions of *general* and *specific* information. This neglects a critical fact, that is the existence, nature, and critical importance, of privileged or selective channels of communication for the diffusion of *specific-purpose* information. The farmer will listen more attentively, and will be more inclined to act upon, a new piece of farming information from another farmer than from most other news sources, media and agents; and the businessman, the professional, the academic, the politician, and so on, act in similar fashion.

Specific information is diffused through the same physical communication networks as general information but does not reach people the same way.[52] Before it can reach an audience it has to pass through an additional set of selective filters resulting from the specializations of individuals and organizations. In consequence, it can reach only those who are professionally interested. The revolution of communications essentially has only affected those who operate in several different lines of activity and whose business is to switch their focus from one activity to another, according to the evaluation of different specific information signals. That is due to the fact that most information flows, previously managed separately from every channel, are now diffused in such a way that they can be collected and synthesized fast. But for most of the people who, behaviorally (in their economic activity), are tuned only to certain specific signals, the communications revolution has not meant more than faster access to the new specific information and more exposure to the *general* information.

Looking at those who are the adaptors of innovations in any one line and in countries that do not create the innovations,[53] one always finds that they are either the manufacturers of previous products serving a similar need (the producers of bicycles in the case of new motorbike productions, for example), the middlemen who previously imported the product (in the case of import-substitution), the service-repair people of the same products, or any combination of them. Looking back in history,[54] looking back to archaeology,[55] if we want, we shall always find the same pattern. Whether faster or slower, there has always been a diffusion of specific knowledge directed particularly at people in the trade and fairly constant in its geographical extension, as Hägerstrand has indicated.[56] As the reader will realize, the cross-section and time-series evidence is extremely important because it extends the significance of the difference between general and specific information. What the evidence suggests is that the sensitivity to specific information depends on the intensity of the market-linkages of the audience to the specific information. Since the geographical pattern of adoptions of new innovations has been remarkably stable in the history of countries, it further suggests that the geographical distribution of evolving trades has been normally very stable. In consequence, within the physical communication networks there are subchannels of specific information determined by organizational factors whose stability over time and geographical space is considerable.

In resumé, the subprocess of geographical diffusion of knowledge on innovations can explain only the faster or slower rhythm of the geographical polarizations. It cannot explain why, in the past, the urban structure was much more unstable than it is today, why the temporal development sequence was more polarized over geographical space.

Necessarily, then, the explanation for the changes experienced in the process of geographical polarization must lie in the changes that have occurred in the subprocess of the spread of adoptions.

To clarify how the subprocess of adoptions has changed over time and how that change has affected the use of geographical space, it is convenient to distinguish clearly between the establishment or the plant, the firm, and the industry or product. The adopter of innovations has always been the firm, but the consequences of the adoptions for the nation have been and can be very different if the firm is of the one-product/one-plant type, if it is of the multiproduct/multiplant/multicity type, or if it belongs to any intermediate type.[57]

This agreed, it can be briefly and roughly stated that the transportation revolution together with the increasing scale of the successive sets of innovations, and the reorganization of the business firm (from the first to the last types referred to above) have been the outstanding factors determining the changing patterns of localization of innovations over time. The transportation changes and the increasing scale of the innovations have mostly worked in the same direction. The correcting force to the trend they have set forth has been the change in the mode of internal organization of the leading business firms and the resulting change in the pattern of interrelations between all the firms within an economy.

In spite of the fact that at any time with more or less hindrance all the would-be adopters have had access to the knowledge on the new innovation, the increasing size of operations has progressively reduced the actual number of adopters. Successively faster and cheaper modes of transportation of inputs and outputs have also favored the reduction in the number of adopters and their location in central places. Both those factors have, therefore, produced the fast growth of some areas and the compensating relative decay of some others, which the growth pole theory described. Naturally, the reorganizational structuring of the different trades over geographical space that the process brought about changed accordingly the networks of specific information, reinforcing the trend toward more intense geographical polarizations over time.

At first, the process of internal reorganization followed by the leading firms reinforced the previous trend. From the one-product/ one-plant mould, some firms evolved to adopt the multiproduct/ one-plant scheme, due to the advantages resulting from the production engineering revolution. The firms of vertically integrated plants were the result of the process. It reached maturity in the late 1800s and early 1900s, in the United States and Canada, where the first moves toward the multiproduct/multiplant/multicity firm were realized in the form of the holding corporation, a form that later became adopted as the typical industrial corporate structure. In Europe, due to institutional, cultural and sociological factors, and to the smaller national markets, the vertical complex reigned sovereign until World War II; the Ruhr combines, which influenced Perroux's thought, are the best examples.

Of late, the production engineering revolution has initiated an entirely new type of management and drastically changed the organizational structure of the leading corporations. The leading firm today is a loose organization that aims, not so much to make a better and cheaper product in one main line, but to be able to deliver to the market the most profitable mix among the changing flow of products and/or services the market wants. The idea of adaptiveness to innovations prevails over that of the breakthrough via one innovation. The latter is not safe any longer, not only because many other competitors have the ability to repeat the breakthrough, but because the result will fast become obsolete in any event. To the corporation, what matters is to be able to move in and out of any one line, at any point, and to mix the lines in the most profitable manner at any time. Consequently, firms seek to avoid slavish attachment to any particular line. If possible, they would subcontract out most of their activities and would seek to retain exclusive management over the assembly of all the pieces. They would give away the research, procurement, production, selling, servicing, and so on, and keep the designing, planning, marketing and financing functions. Moving in that direction the leading firms cut across all sorts of topological spaces. They operate plants all over the world, market thousands of products, produce many, assemble others, subcontract all sorts of functions, have footholds in agriculture, industry, services, and so on. In brief, to realize the change in corporate structure that has occurred in the last thirty years, just compare the tremendous rigidity of Krupp with the stupendous flexibility of Litton!

Besides, the change in the form of organization of the leading firms has had a no less dramatic repercussion in the pattern of inter-relations among firms across the business community. The linkages between large and small firms within an industry and between firms of all sizes in different industries have been enormously strengthened. These linkages take many forms. Firms are linked by subcontracting, custom manufacturing, licensing, know-how, marketing, management, and contracts. As a result, the channels of diffusion of specific information have been considerably enlarged and strengthened among firms. They have multiplied the previous sensitivity levels of firms to all innovations, making them receptive to more, because they have multiplied the intensity of the market-linkages between firms. The new linkages have also increased the potential spread of adoptions, because the large firms are now helping the small to adopt.

Because of those organizational (inter- and intrafirm) changes, the mapping of the activities of the Krupp-type firms and industrial complexes of the past is necessarily bound to be more polarized over geographical space than those of the Litton type. The successive tracing of the activities of the two is likely to give a repeated geographical pattern in the first and a rapidly changing pattern in the second. Today Litton is doing deep submarine research in California, space research in Boston, tourist development in Greece, and so on. Tomorrow it may be doing housing in Bedford-Stuyvesant or rice-seeds research in the Philippines. Nobody dares to predict! But everybody feels safe in foretelling that Krupp will be basically in

Essen working on something related to steel. The same can be said of the host of smaller firms linked up to the leading ones.

That is the reason why, from now on, when Litton (not Krupp) is likely to be the prototype of the leading adopters, with market-linkages between firms further strengthened, the acceleration of development is likely to result in much less geographical polarization than in the past. This is because the inter- and intrafirm reorganization processes now favor faster adoption of successive innovation sets. Further, if the processes of change of the scale of innovations, of the physical networks of transport and communication and of the form of business reorganization are not altered, the process above is likely to be cumulative: the diffusion channels of specific information will become less and less selective, the spread of adoptions more extensive over sectoral and geographical space, and economic development faster and less polarized.

Criteria
for Regional Development Policy
in Developing Countries

The scheme just outlined is helpful in understanding some previously unexplained events in recent experience of regional development policy.

The considerable success of dispersing industry to peripheral regions of the United Kingdom has not been explained relative to the failure of the same policy in Italy in the 1950s. Had it been, it probably would have come out quite clearly that the British firms of the time, already well diversified and managed in a sophisticated fashion, could install their new factories practically anywhere, once the supporting infrastructure was provided. On the other hand, the still primitive Italian firms could not. Up to the 1960s, it was very well known that it was socially more expensive to bring the Sicilians and Calabrians to Milan, the Andalusians to Barcelona and the north-eastern Brazilians to São Paulo, than to move the new plants being built in the opposite direction. Yet it was unfeasible to do it, no matter how hard it was tried. Meanwhile, since the capacity expansion of the "north" was of the one-plant/one-product firm, or even of the multi-product/one-plant firm, the building of new capacity could not move away from the "norths." The acceleration of growth in the Mezzogiorno in the later decade, in today's northeast Brazil, and the great success of Spain's growth poles in the last four years is also easily understood from this perspective. Most of the new employment created has taken place in plants that are extensions, filials, subsidiaries, licensees, subcontractors, and so on of the expanded and transformed firms in the "norths."

That is essentially the process W. Thompson has described as the "filtering down" process.[58] The large firms, of the multiproduct/multiplant type, set up the new product plants where it is most convenient and relocate the older lines plants placing them in the "souths." What is happening today, directly or indirectly, induced by government subsidies, in the countries mentioned, happened naturally in the United States about twenty years ago. The firms in the eastern seaboard started to locate their older lines plants (the ones that required less qualified labor) in the southern states.

Sometimes, when the leading business firms in the less developed countries reach the organization structure that is becoming predominant in the United States leading firms, and the intrafirm market linkages are strengthened, the filtering down effect, already in practice in many countries, will be complemented by the unpolarizing behavior of the modern inter- and intrafirm structure. Not only old line plants, but the very new, will move out to the functional equivalents of Florida, Tennessee, Arizona, and Texas.

Can we accelerate the process?

In a way, Hirschman anticipated most of my argument. Development he said,[59] needs to be geographically polarized in its early stages, concentrated in "growing points," because of lack of entrepreneurship outside those centers. To spend resources in building up infrastructures in the underdeveloped regions, hoping to attract industrial investments, is a wasteful strategy. I differ from Hirschman only in that I believe that the reasons for his strategy are very dependent on the type of prevailing business organization.[60] If the industrializing countries with geographical polarization problems are to repeat the stages of business reorganizations that the advanced ones have gone through, then his advice is sound. Under the one-product/one-plant model, even under the multiproduct/multiplant/one-city model of the individual entrepreneur type, to move the new plants from the "norths" to the "souths," actually means to move the whole family and family-environment of the entrepreneur from, say,

Barcelona to Andalucia. Clearly, this is something that can be done only on a small scale. The logical alternative, which is to create enough entrepreneurs in the "souths," is even more unrealistic. However, the less developed countries are not constrained to leapfrog over only the technological stages of the past. They can also leapfrog over the stages of business reorganization: they can successfully copy the forms of successful business organization. If they do, the inexorability of polarized development decreases and the need for Hirschman's strategy also decreases.

Put in a different way, Hirschman believes with Perroux and the French school in the inexorability of polarized development. He disagrees with them in that he believes that the best way to reduce the negative effects of geographical polarizations is not to set up compensating poles. Rather, he maintains that it is better: (1) to foster the growth of the existing ones, in the hope that they will eventually trickle down, and (2) to increase the attractiveness of the underdeveloped areas to increase the possibility of the trickling down.

I find Hirschman's advice half right and half ambiguous. Right in his critique of the French school; ambiguous in his proposal. Bringing cheap labor in unlimited supplies to Tokyo, Buenos Aires, Barcelona, Milan, and the like does not favor a fast trickling down *per se*. For a long time, it adds up to a tremendous messy urban sprawl around the growing points because the firms, even when they are organizationally capable of moving south, do not find enough wage differentials between their existing locations and the "souths" to build their capacity expansions in the "souths." However, to hold down migration does not help much either, until the firms have undergone sufficient reorganization. The firms in the "norths" are most of the one-product/one-plant type and due to market and financing limitations cannot expand capacity by adding plants but only by adding sections within the one plant they usually have. As a consequence, wage differentials between regions are unimportant location factors. Firms can increase production in the "norths," but they cannot move their plants to the "souths."

On the whole, to avoid the problems of geographical polarization in the countries that are still likely to face such a contingency, it could well pay to have a two-pronged strategy. On the one hand, there should be an effort to foster the fastest possible transformation of the structure of the leading business firms and achieve corresponding changes in the relationships between all firms, from the old mold to the new one, as the Japanese have so successfully done. That would accelerate the maturation of Hirschman's growing points. On the other, there should be efforts to increase the relative attractiveness of location in the underdeveloped areas, Hirschman's complementary strategy.

Concerning the latter, I would most heartily subscribe to a very flexible policy that would be directed basically at fulfilling the specific requirements of the business firms (private or public) to locate in the "souths" in lieu of a rigid policy aiming at providing a fixed set of incentives (financial, physical) for all firms. This I maintain because the requirements of the firms will be different depending on their organizational levels. Capital, credit, personnel training, complementary services and industry infrastructure, and so on have different priorities to the firms, depending on which stage of technological and organizational development they are at. Policies to attract firms may as well profit from those differential priorities, to increase their effectiveness.

Concerning the policy of business reorganization, what is required is to create, as soon as possible, stronger interrelations between all plants across all topological spaces (geographical, sectoral, and so forth). That can be achieved, as hinted, by consolidating all plants into large multiplant/multiproduct/multicity firms and/or by fostering interfirm linkages.

To be efficient, a policy directed toward the object of reorganizing the business world needs to take into account the present form of the business structure in the developing countries. *Ceteris paribus*, it will pay dividends to start with the firms that have already reached a certain size and diversification. Also, the policy action needs to start in the business areas where, due to their market ties, the pay-off is going to be higher, and leave to a later period those firms, sectors, and so on where it is more difficult to achieve business integration.

Whatever the firm type, firms tend to feel strongly linked to their buyers and sellers. The degree of directness in market contacts, between firms, determines, *ceteris paribus*, the degree of sensitivity of a firm to the other firms' fortunes. After the revolution in the communication of general information, whatever the prevailing form of business organization, firms tend to feel more strongly linked in the direction of their final product market than in the direction of their primary inputs market. These two psychological factors point out that, in general, it seems easier to foster the integration of firms starting from the final markets and moving gradually toward the factor inputs, proceeding along the route of direct contacts.

In the underdeveloped countries, firms in wholesaling, retailing, banking and other service activities are relatively larger and more diversified than manufacturing firms. This situation, contrary to the pattern in the developed world, is easy to explain by the infant industry argument. Nonmanufacturing firms have faced little competition from abroad and even with low protection have been able to develop faster. Consequently, they also have had the opportunity to diversify.

Since these nonmanufacturing firms are also closer to the final market, underdeveloped countries could very effectively bank on them (on the two accounts mentioned) in their policies to integrate their business world.

Several words of caution are needed. First, whether to diversify the large firms or to produce business integration through specialized interfirm contracts is a matter that depends greatly on the supply of qualified business executives who are scientific, energetic, willing to adapt and social minded. The smaller their supply the less convenient the holding approach. Second, business integration, to be a social asset instead of a liability, has to be pursued in such a way as to achieve higher levels of price and product competition. It has also to attain a situation in which the integrated firms compete more for innovation adoption than before. It is not difficult to conceive how this can be made feasible. In caricature, the degree of competition in an economy with a hundred large firms, putting out ten thousand similar products each, is likely to be higher than that resulting from the interaction of ten thousand firms, with one hundred products each. In the latter case, in many sectors and in many regions, there will prevail monopolistic conditions. Third, the size of the country market should not condition the pattern of business organization excessively in most countries. However, to avoid the market size problem, whenever it exists, countries could better think of their continental integration through multinational firms than through the standard trade agreements.

Finally, to plan for single region development, most of the guidelines pertaining to the business reorganization policy in the context of regionalization of *national* development are relevant. The emphasis should be placed on promoting firms catering for the final market and fostering them to branch out into other activities and, through different type contracts, helping to set up other firms in market-related activities.

Criteria
for Regional Development Policies
in Developed Countries[61]

With respect to the developed world, where pockets of regional disparities also exist (in some cases, increasingly so), the general argument that has just been developed requires several qualifications.[62]

On the whole, I fully agree with Hansen[63] that in developed countries tertiary and quaternary industries—not manufacturing—are the growth industries. I also agree with him that they expand cumulatively, concentrated geographically in the countries' developed areas, whereas they are relatively absent in their backward regions. In consequence, to catch up with the advanced regions, the lagging areas need to obtain a larger share of tertiary and quaternary activities.

In other words, on the whole, better schools and better roads in Appalachia make a lot of sense. If they fail to help the Appalachians in Appalachia, they will certainly help them to get to better conditions outside of the region.

What distresses me in the tertiary growth pole idea is not the emphasis on the policies that have been tried in Europe in the last forty years and that have failed, because what did not make sense in underdeveloped pre- and postwar Europe may make sense in the United States today. Rather, what distresses me is the implication that a geographical polarization of urban infrastructure to attract services or service-oriented manufacturing industries is going to result in the development of lagging areas.

From my perspective, it seems clear that the image of the Route 129 and El Camino Real complexes is not less dangerous than the image of the Ruhr complex. It leads to the false notion that to have the industries and services connected with Harvard and M.I.T. and with Stanford and Berkeley, the thing to do is to create smaller but similar research and education magnets. Or that to have small Manhattans, the thing to do is to create small First City Banks, Madison Avenue publicity firms, and insurance companies. If that were the case, the hope of the world's future Appalachias would be rather gloomy because the duplication of those magnets is simply not feasible.

However, I think that there are more efficient alternative strategies. In effect, in the advanced world today most of the tertiary activities and some of the service-oriented manufacturing activities are carried out by firms in a less integrated and diversified manner (in an organizational perspective) than the more traditional manufacturing firms. This forces them to cluster over geographical space. Physical proximity is the substitute for stronger intra- and interfirm organizational linkages. The lesson that can be learned both from the failure of attempts to duplicate physical clusters of traditional manufacturing firms (in the absence of a diversified business organizational structure) and from the success attained in the presence of an integrated and diversified (inter- and intrafirm) business structure is that, in order to break up the centripetal forces of physical linkages between firms, it pays to weaken their pull by strengthening the organizational linkages between firms.

It all amounts to applying to tertiary and quaternary activities in developed countries the two-pronged strategy indicated in the previous section. On the one hand, in perfect agreement with Hansen, this would call for building up urban infrastructures favoring the location of those activities; on the other, it would call for promoting the inter- and intrafirm integration of those activities to permit the branching off of operations from the original location to desired new locations.

I agree with Hansen that for developed countries the factors attracting tertiary and quaternary activities are urban infrastructures and that they are the ones to be set up and built upon. With regard to the developing countries, I agree with Hirschman that the factors attracting secondary activities are directly productive investments and incentives to invest, both of which need to be made available in the zones to be developed. But I think the respective policies for advanced and developing countries need to be supplemented with another favoring the diversification and integration of tertiary and secondary activities. In other words, the two policies differ exclusively in the content of the incentives to be located in the areas to be developed and in the types of firm to which reorganizational efforts should be addressed.

Given the interrelations between tertiary and secondary activities (in production and organization) and given the fact that nonmanufacturing firms in the developing world are relatively larger, more diversified, and integrated than are manufacturing firms, I stated in the previous section that underdeveloped countries "could very effectively bank on them (nonmanufacturing firms) in their policies to integrate their business world." Conversely, in developed countries it might be appropriate to use the existing network of manufacturing activities to promote a similarly homogeneous spatial spread of tertiary and quaternary activities. This general strategy can also be applied to specific proposals made to attract manufacturing firms into markets where public policy has not been successful, as in the case of public housing in the United States.

Summary

My specific attempt has been to fill in the space created by Perroux's conceptual insights and Hirschman's hypotheses and policy strategies in the field of regional development. I have taken only one line, and there can be many. Obviously, I have developed the one I think most important and neglected. However, the major conclusion I would draw is that reading with Hirschman-type empirical common sense, within the universe of abstract functional spaces of Perroux, there are many findings to be made that the present rigid orientation of the growth pole school has neglected. My argument, in fact, amounts to saying that the polarizations in geographic space today tend to be smaller than in the past because the transformation that has occurred in the form of business firms dilutes the geographical polarizations that development still produces in other topological spaces. By implication, then, an efficient way to alter geographical polarizations is to act upon the organizational structure of the business firms. Clearly, my conclusion can be generalized as follows: policy decisions are normally viewed as if they are to be based only on the impact of the obvious variables in narrowly defined systems. Whenever policies so conceived fail, it is necessary to enlarge the framework of analysis to cover the effects and interrelations of the variables entering more complex systems and base policies upon their impacts. The concept of related topological spaces is a useful notion in this context. This approach which was, in fact, implicit in Perroux's framework is what

I have aimed to bring forward in the realm to which he originally
addressed himself.

Notes

1. The meaning of the terms *pole* and *polarization* are treacherous. In the present
paper I use the meaning of Perroux, who introduced the concept in economic literature.
His meaning is different from the conventional sense of the word in English. I discuss
the two meanings in detail in note 43, when it is necessary. The reader can either
consult that note or proceed until then on the notion that Perroux views *pole* as a
protuberance sticking up from a homogenous surface, rather than the sense of opposing
extreme. Consequently, for him there can be more than two poles at a time. For
polarization, Perroux understands the process as creating the enlargement of a pole.

2. The term has become very popular and has given way to several related concepts.
Among them: development pole is also French, but I have not been able to trace its
precise origin. In Spanish, the French concepts have undergone changes, *i.e.*, in
Spain's II Development Plan, a growth pole (*polo de crecimiento*) is a growing center
in a relatively backward region that requires an additional push; a development pole
(*polo de desarrollo*) is a stagnant center in a backward zone that requires a considerable
push. J. P. Friedmann, dissatisfied with the identification of pole with city, coined
core region. *Regional towns*, *market centers* are somewhat related concepts. They derive
basically from central place theory but sometimes are understood as special type poles.
Regional towns being some sort of *tertiary* poles, market centers the *tertiary and secondary* poles of agricultural areas, according to J. Johnson who advanced the terms.
Hirschman's well-known *growing points* responds to the same general notion, and so do
many others. All of them convey the idea, more or less policy oriented, that economic
growth and development take place in an agglomerated (sectoral and geographical)
manner.

3. Theoretical research and policy use of the concept have been more intense in
Europe, where it originated. They have, however, made inroads in America.
In Latin America, the journal *Cuadernos de la Sociedad Venezonala de Planificacion*,
under the leadership of Eduardo Neira, has been the carrier of most of the relevant
literature; policy acceptance of the concept has been widespread. In the U.S., J. P.
Friedmann (see, for example, Friedmann and Alonso, eds., *Regional Development and
Planning* (Cambridge, Mass.: M.I.T. Press, 1964) and N. M. Hansen (see his papers
later quoted in note 35)) among others, have made available to the professional audience
the European concepts. Hansen is trying to use the approach in the development of
Appalachia. J. P. Friedmann has made several attempts to give an analytical explana-
tion to the core region concept. I do not deal with his interesting contribution because
I restrict my concern to the area delineated by Perroux.

4. J. R. Boudeville, *L'espace et les pôles de croissance*, Paris 1968—Avant-propos,
p. 1—claims that most of theory and policy evolved has been the result of the French
school.

5. F. Perroux, "Note sur la notion de Pôle de Croissance," in *Economie Appliquée*,
January-June 1955.

6. F. Perroux, "La firme motrice dans la région et la région motrice" in *Théorie et
Politique de l'Expansion Régionale*, Brussels, 1961. It is a largely intuitive idea, of great
appeal and acceptance. Since it has not been defined, hardly sketched, it is useful for
both the followers of Hirschman and Myrdal: the idea, in fact, is almost as essential
to those who believe in the initial inexorability of the agglomeration factors, and in their
eventual transformation into depolarizing factors, as to those who maintain that, since
the change in the behavior of the factors is not sure (or too remote) and they are not
inexorable, polarizations have to be fought against. In other words, the idea fulfils the
role of providing an accepted intellectual battleground. Under its umbrella an inter-

change of contradictory hypothetical information takes place. It is in this sense that I have used the term *idea in good currency*, borrowing it from D. A. Schon's communication to the HUD Summer Study in Berkeley, 1968.

7. F. Perroux has been one of the few leading French economists familiar with the German sources. Specifically, before he helped to introduce Keynesian economics in France, he was critically important in diffusing Schumpeter's thought. See his "La pensée économique de Joseph Schumpeter," introduction to the French translation of *Theorie der Wirtschaftlichen Entwicklung*, Paris, 1935.

8. C. Clark: *Localizzazione industriale e popolazione*, Milan, 1964, p. 7.

9. For an overall evaluation of the contributions to space economics and of their applicability to regional planning, see E. von Böventer, "Spatial Organization Theory as a Basis for Regional Planning," in *Journal of the American Institute of Planners*, May 1964.

10. For example, he has stated that four of the main complexes of European nations could be traced back to the rigid conception of space. Namely, these are the complexes of: (1) petite nation (small nation); (2) Einkreisung (encirclement); (3) Volk ohne Raum (landless nation); (4) natural and historical borders; all policies derived therefrom are partly the result of a Euclidian perception of space. See his introduction in F. Perroux: "Economic space: Theory and Applications" in *Quarterly Journal of Economics*, February 1950.

11. Ibid., Introduction.

12. Ibid., Introduction.

13. Today, after the work of K. Lorenz (*On Aggression*, New York, 1966) and R. Ardrey (*The Territorial Imperative*, New York, 1966) among others, his argument can be phrased as follows: a "territorial" perception of space, dominated by instinctual mechanisms, has reigned over the conceptualisations of European politics and economics. This perception, in addition to other factors, has resulted in undesirable behavior. It has led to the construction of inefficient ecological social systems, with an inherent propensity to explode as soon as the magnitudes within the systems reached certain thresholds. This is an avoidable trend. Man can visualize space in a different way. He is able to perceive it abstractly, not conditioned by instinctual categories. Hypothetically, an abstract conceptualization of space facilitates the construction of continuously expanding ecological systems, more explosion-safe. In case the hypothesis holds, what matters is to develop adequate typologies, into which to collapse the indefinite number of abstract spaces, and once that is done, to use them for the purpose of building expanding ecological systems over the barriers of "territorial" environments.

14. F. Perroux, op. cit. (note 5).

15. Op. cit. (note 5), first paragraph: ". . . an economy in regular growth in which the proportions among the different flows do not change and in which the global output grows at the same rate as the population. . . ." Perroux quotes G. Cassels' *Theoretische Sozialökonomie*, 4th ed., Leipzig, 1927.

16. Op. cit. (note 5), second and third paragraphs. Perroux's evaluation is in total agreement with Schumpeter's declared intention. In his *History of Economic Analysis*, Oxford University Press (I am using his 1954 edition), pp. 965–96, he acknowledges Cassel, explains that Cassel himself derived the notion from Marx's "simple reproduction" scheme, and traces how the subsequent business cycle theorists (both Wicksellian and Keynesian) have used Cassel's device to sort out the business cycles' deviations and factors. He, himself, used it to select business cycles and development effects and causes.

17. Most probably because of reasons of brevity, Perroux takes up only Schumpeterian product innovations and, among them, those of high-income elasticity of demand. J. A. Schumpeter, needless to say, also considered all the other types of innovations. (I have added this footnote on the advice of J. Polach, Resources for the Future, Inc.)

18. In a different manner, Perroux attempted to describe the industrial complexes of the Old World (Ruhr), and the newly planned ones in Siberia and Africa (as he acknowledged in his footnote 6, op. cit.) with the help of "spatialized" Schumpeterian concepts and hypotheses; then, on the basis of its descriptive power, he attempted to make his argument operational, so that it would serve as a base for regional development and for the regionalization of national development.

19. In his two major papers (op. cit.) he changed his definitions. In "Note sur la notion de Pôle de croissance" he talks of industries, in "La firme motrice dans la région et la région motrice" of both firms and industries (assuming the absence of significant inter-firm competition effects within the industry). In the second paper the leading "motrice" industry, as opposed to the induced industry, has the equivalent meaning of "autonomous" versus "induced" investment. To him, basic industries (*industries clef*) are those that induce a "global expenditure in the economy larger than the increment in their own expenditure; in other words, special kinds of "autonomous" industries reaching above certain induction proportions; however, all his examples are of "basic-type" industries (primary transformers) implying therefore not only specific magnitudes, but qualities.

In the second paper he rejects the term *industrie clef* because, as he explains in footnote 18, most of the definitions applied to industries: *clef, motrice, dominant, leader*, etc. have validity only within the theoretical frame in which they are used. Since in the second paper he used an input-output frame, the older concepts from his first paper were no longer useful. In fact, in that footnote 18 Perroux clearly implies the reason for his confused terminology. Since in his original frame, essentially Schumpeterian (where the basic variable is innovations), he has introduced (over time) business cycle, income analysis, imperfect competition and interindustry economics explanations (where the basic variables are different), he has been unable to avoid having the general meaning of the concepts, in any one of these approaches, creep into the specific ones he gave to them. Many times the reader is led to believe that the leading industry is innovative, of a high accelerator and/or multiplier, an autonomous spender, price and/or output leader, of a high matrix technical multiplier, and so on.

The most recurring meanings in his argument are: the leading industry is a new, technically advanced industry of high income elasticity of demand; also, it seems, the leading industry to him is one with high "propulsive power," but he did not indicate whether the propulsive power was forward or backward. Since his *industrie clef* (key industry) was, supposedly, a basic industry of great backward propulsion, it may be taken that leading industries are highly propulsive industries (both forward and backward) and that the key industries are a special (the backward propulsive) type.

20. In section II, point 2, of his first paper Perroux gives as one of the functional reasons for the industrial complex the oligopolistic character (not necessarily of the same oligopoly) of its constituent industries. Another is the high degree of internal technical interrelations between the inputs and outputs of the related industries. However, he explains the geographical agglomeration of the industrial complex, basically, by Scitovsky's external economies, and traditional location factors.

21. In sections A, B, C, D of his second paper, Perroux analyzed the effects of the actions of the leading industry over the industrial complex. He talks formally in terms of the large leading firm (instead of the leading industry) but, since he is not introducing competition among firms within the industry, the argument is consistent. The leading firm or industry effects are analyzed via prices and income. The analysis is classical and is carried out under two different hypotheses: with or without further technological change by the leading firm. Ups and downs in prices and incomes, carried forward and backward via leading firm linkages, result from miscalculations of demand by the leading firm in the second case, from the nature of its new production function in the first case. The analysis is further detailed by distinguishing the classical differential effects the leading firm produces, depending on whether the industrial complex is located in a developed or underdeveloped region (see his section E, "La firm motrice").

He does not explain the effects of the complex on the leading firm or industry, neither when the firm is established nor before. Specifically, he does not attempt to explain if there are factors other than natural resources which may attract the firm, or whether a small complex can call for another firm which in turn may make the complex grow. In short he does not provide a dynamic interpretation of the complex-leading firm interaction in the face of changing innovations.

22. In section 3 of "Note sur la notion" Perroux implies that sometimes the polarization may be beneficial to national growth, sometimes prejudicial, depending on the changing fortunes of any one of them. In respect to the evolution of the poles he was very clearcut. He visualized the destiny of the complexes themselves as rigidly tied to that of their leading industries: "The pole, which was a source of prosperity and growth,

becomes a centre of stagnation." (Section 2, point 3, end of third paragraph, "Note sur la notion.")

His overall evaluation was: the geographical polarizations are long-run deviations. Their effects on the region (positive or negative, according to whether they are growing or stagnant polarizations) and the nation (positive or negative in an unclear manner, depending on how the different polarizations interact) need to be corrected basically by means of policies aiming at compensating their effects with opposite sign geographical polarizations. As I develop later, the growth pole and the stagnation pole need not be long-run phenomena. Nor does the growth pole necessarily become a stagnation pole. Besides, thanks to his concept of topological space, the best policies to deal with those geographical polarizations need not be of the physical, geographical type.

23. While Perroux deserves all the credit for the conceptual richness of his first major theoretical paper, he is also responsible for the analytical retreat in which he indulged in his second paper, when he attempted to make his framework operational for planning purposes. Instead of developing his own analytical concepts and hypotheses (see note 19) to fill in his framework, he tried most of the available ones elsewhere. Eventually, he came to rely basically on interindustry analysis, thereby limiting his concept to only one (the technological) of its several dimensions. His adherence to the input-output technique excluded all the institutional, micro and macro economic factors he had listed as important. In practice, as a result, his analysis, and that of the French school, has become a special version of the intra- and interregional input-output approach. In short, Perroux has paid the price of restricting the potential theoretical usefulness of his concept to that of input-output analysis. He has not gained anything in exchange because of the general failure of input-output policies.

24. It can be stated safely that many of Perroux's readers have been attracted by the clear potential of the growth pole concept and imagery and, unaware of the conceptual and analytical limitations of its formulation, led to considerable confusion. Thus, for example, to many of his readers, growth pole theory appears as some sort of dynamic location theory. Yet, it is clear Perroux could not go further than Schumpeter whose frame and major hypotheses he adapted, transferring them from sectoral space to geographical space. If Schumpeter could not explain in which sector and at what time the innovations were likely to take place, Perroux could not explain where they were going to locate and where, therefore, subsequent industrial complexes were to arise. Like Schumpeter, he could only explain the derived effects (magnitude, direction, etc.) of the innovations, over geographical space. Even in that more limited attempt he had to rely on agglomeration economics, for without them he could not explain why sectoral polarization gave way to geographical polarizations.

It has taken time to evaluate unequivocally the contribution of the growth pole theory. J. Paelinck has accepted that it does not replace location theory nor agglomeration economics (J. Paelinck: "Systématisation de la Théorie du Dévelopement Régional Polarisé", synthesis A, in *Cahiers de l'I.S.E.A.*, series L, number 15). He has further defined its relationship to the body of economic theory by stating (op. cit. above, synthesis B) that it is "a conditional theory of regional development", meaning that it established the conditions for successful regional development in a flexible and non-deterministic manner.

25. Because of the new perspectives the concept opens, existing knowledge can be usefully related to its frame. For example, the unbalanced and balanced strategies in economic development literature can be profitably referred to point (1) before. They are the opposing views on sectoral polarization, and its relation to national development. Hirschman's "growing points" (A. O. Hirschman, *The Strategy of Economic Development*, New Haven, 1958), a view of the relations between geographical polarization and national development, also can be related easily to its frame. Most of the specific relationships (such as migration and regional income differentials) between sectoral polarizations and geographical polarizations analyzed by Schultz, Myrdal, Okun, and others, also relate to point (1). Concerning the second point J. R. Boudeville ("Les notions d'espace et d'intégration," op. cit, note 4, p. 24) who has succinctly summarized the relevant concept of economic space as the projection onto geographical space of all abstract economic systems, has pointed out that such a concept enhances the possibility of planning the economic integration of geographical spaces.

26. In spite of the more positive claims of Boudeville and Paelinck, for which there seems to be some evidence, the usefulness of the concept is still to be realized.

27. F. Perroux: "Matériaux pour une analyse de la croissance économique," in *Cahiers de l'I.S.E.A.*, series D, number 9.

28. P. Bauchet: *Les tableaux économiques. Analyse de la région Lorraine*, Genin, Paris, 1955.

29. L. Derwa: "Analyse input-output de la region Liégeoise," in *Revue du Conseil économique Wallon*, Sept.-Nov. 1957.

30. J. R. Boudeville: "Les Pôles de Croissance Bresiliens: La siderurgie du Minas Gerais," in *Cahiers de l'I.S.E.A.*, series L, number 9.

31. L. E. Davin: *Dynamique économique de la région Liégeoise*, Liege, 1959.

32. R. Rosenfeld: "Structure et perspective économiques de la Province de Turin," in *Metra*, vol. III, number 4, 1964.

33. J. Paelinck: *Note sur la programmation régionale au Venezuela*, mimeograph.

34. For a more complete bibliography, see J. Paelinck's "Nota Bibliografica," in *Cuadernos de la Sociedad Venezolana de Planificacion*, August-September 1963.

35. Niles M. Hansen: "Development Pole Theory in a Regional Context" in *Kyklos*, vol. XX, 1967. See also his other publications on the same and related topics: "Regional Planning in a Mixed Economy," in *Southern Economic Journal*, Oct. 1965; "Unbalanced Growth and Regional Development," in *Western Economic Journal*, Fall 1965; "Some Neglected Factors in American Regional Development Policy: The Case of Appalachia," in *Land Economics*, Feb. 1966.

36. Which was mostly diffused among regional analysts in Europe thanks to the 1960 Conference of Bellaggio, sponsored by the O.E.C.D. W. Isard and J. Cumberland edited the proceedings: *Regional Economic Planning: Techniques of Analyses for Less Developed Areas*, Paris, 1961.

37. As expressed by J. R. Boudeville and J. Paelinck, their leading advocates. See, for example, Paelinck, op. cit., note 24.

38. As the reader will recognize, the "internal blocking" objective was W. Isard's target in the late 1950s when he developed industrial complex analysis. See, for example: W. Isard and E. W. Schooler: "Industrial Complex Analysis. Agglomeration Economies and Regional Development," in *Journal of Regional Science*, Spring 1959. Also, W. Isard and T. Vietorisz: *Industrial Complex Analysis and Regional Development*, N.Y., 1959. Their "external blocking" aim is the general regional policy conclusion which was drawn in the early 1960s from H. B. Chenery's evaluation of the Mezzogiorno. See H. B. Chenery: "Development Policies for Southern Italy," in *Quarterly Journal of Economics*, November 1962.

39. As acknowledged by all authors (for example, J. Paelinck, op. cit. (note 24), J. R. Boudeville: *Problems of Regional Economic Planning*, Edinburgh, 1966, chap. 5) the identification of the propulsive industry is carried out on the basis of the highest matrix multiplier criterion, applied to highly aggregated tables. See, for example, J. de Caevel, J. Degueldre, J. Paelinck: "Analisis Cuantitativo de ciertos Fenomenos del Desarrollo Regional Polarizado" (Spanish translation), in *Cuadernos de la Sociedad Venezolana de Planificacion*, August-September 1963. That was the procedure investigated in the early 1950s which resulted in Chenery's, Clark's, Watanabe's, Rasmussen's works, published around the middle of the decade.

The high aggregation of the tables they have used has permitted no evaluation of the size of the establishments (only of large industries) and of the locational tendencies of these establishments. Facing the same problem, and realizing how critical was the size and the locational tendency of the establishments in determining whether the income flows generated by the leading industry would result in a geographical complex (as A. O. Hirschman had indicated, op. cit. (note 25), p. 101, quoted by J. R. Boudeville, op. cit. (note 39), pp. 115–117), W. Isard addressed himself to filling out the input-output industry flows with engineering interactivity analysis and locational analysis (the industrial complex analysis). See W. Isard, op. cit. (note 38). See also the bibliography he quotes on p. 412 of his *Methods of Regional Analysis: and Introduction to Regional Sciences*, New York, 1961.

The French school, though aware of the problem (see J. R. Boudeville's quote before) and of W. Isard's solution (see the same chapter in J. R. Boudeville's op. cit.), has not done anything to correct the problem posed by the high aggregation of the tables.

40. It may be worth mentioning also that because of the restricted input-output tables used, they have not paid enough attention to other more recent findings of agglomeration economics. In fact, they have hardly explored the theoretical and policy repercussions of R. Vernon and W. Thompson and others in the context of industrial and urban complexes. R. Vernon, in his *The Changing Economic Function of the Central City*, New York, 1959, and other authors after him, have shown evidence that a dynamic geographic pole does not need to be a vertical industrial complex of the Ruhr type, nor of the "interactivity" type. They have shown that a nebulous universe of small, differentiated firms, or different industries, could coalesce into a large dynamic center by way of external linkages of psychological, social, cultural, institutional character. In this way they have opened new ways to explain and develop policy for geographical polarizations.

Finally, W. Thompson, in his *A Preface to Urban Economics*, Baltimore, 1965, and in related papers with Mattila, and other authors have shown the locational pull and geographical polarizing effect of human resources and of the activities raising the quality of those resources (research institutions, universities, etc.). The French school has not modified its techniques to account for them.

41. In this context, they have not even recognized the fundamental issues of the regionalization of national development: is the investment in the undeveloped regions less efficient in all planning horizons, or only in the short run? This is the question to which P. Rosenstein-Rodan addressed himself in his *Reflections on Regional Development*, Center for International Studies, M.I.T. C/6325, July 1963. If only in the short run, as Rosenstein-Rodan believes, what is the acceptable limit of the "transfer" of investment resources from the developed to the underdeveloped regions which can be accepted from a national growth point of view?

42. The dynamic content of the Schumpeterian-Perrouxian frame was lost the moment that the events were not dated and their results in one period were not made dependent on the adjustments in the previous one. This happened when the role of innovations was removed from their framework.

43. In my paper "Some Traits of the Process of Growth of the System of Nations: Stability, Polarization, Diffusion," which is to be published in French shortly in *Economie Politique*, I have used the term *polarized* in an almost opposite sense to the one I am using in this paper, in which I follow Perroux's meaning. What I have attempted to show in that paper is that, over the available historical record, there have not been significant changes in the relative ordering of countries by their income per capita. Rather, that the countries have grown, in a tight pack, keeping their relative positions: the rich have got relatively richer; the poor, poorer; but yesterday's rich and poor are still today the same countries. In other words, a considerable stability in the relative ordering has been accompanied by an increasing polarization of the extremes, *i.e.*, the absolute and relative distance between the rich and the poor is increasing. As will be familiar to the reader, that is the conventional meaning of polarization, in the social sciences, in English. As Webster puts it: ". . . division into two opposites . . . ; the concentration about opposing extremes of usually conflicting groups, or interests, formerly ranged in a continuum . . ." etc. But it is not the sense which was used by Perroux. The image that the term conveys, in its common English meaning, is that of a continuum being gradually stretched toward its opposite extremes; that of two opposing poles generating forces which gradually alter the ordering of the elements in the space between them, attracting them. In Perroux's meaning, the image is that of a succession of different fields of forces which generate a changing sequence of different vectors over functional and geographical space. Essentially, the semantic confusion derives from the fact that in English, French, and Spanish the term *pole* (pôle, polo), conveys the meanings of the two different roots from which it has evolved: the Latin terms *palus* (stake) and *polus* (axis). The two different original meanings and associated senses (vector and extremes, respectively) were maintained in separated words as long as the spelling of the two evolving words was distinct. They became mixed under *pole*, when the spelling of the words became indistinct. For example (see Webster), in Middle English, *palus* had changed into *pol* (from Old English, *pal*), while *polus* was *pool*. After that tedious clarification it will be easy to understand the argument which follows in the text. In essence, it is: a polarized development sequence of a system of geographical units (of nations, of regions, of cities, etc.), in the first

meaning (*polus*), is consistent with both a polarized and depolarized sequence, in the second (*palus*). However, a polarized sequence of stable internal order, in the first meaning, is only consistent with a depolarized sequence, in the second. My data on nations (1930–1960) show increasing polarization in the first meaning and the absence of polarization in the second. The data on cities that I present in this paper and which will be reported fully in my forthcoming *Urbanization and Development*, show both a growing polarization (in the first sense) and a growing depolarization (in the second). All this in geographical space. In other relevant economic spaces, development can still be polarized. What this means is that, at least within nations [because for nations, the data do not show a clear depolarization (2) trend], the conversion rules to pass from those spaces onto geographical space have changed.

44. See, for example, D. A. Schon: "Forecasting and Technological Forecasting," in *Toward the Year 2000*, Daedalus, 1968.

45. J. R. Lasuén: "Urbanization Hypotheses and Spain's Cities System Evolution," to be published in the *Journal of the Institute of Social Studies*, The Hague (Paper to the Workshop on Regional Development Planning, 1967).

46. J. R. Lasuén: "Immigration et Aménagement Urbain," to be published by the Congrès International des Economies Régionales (paper presented at the meeting, Madrid, 1967). Translated into Spanish in *Cuadernos de la Sociedad Venezolana de Planificacion*, September 1967.

47. See, for example, Eric Lampard, "The Evolving System of Cities in the United States: Urbanization and Economic Development," in Harvey Perloff and Lowdon Wingo (eds.), *Issues in Urban Economics* (Baltimore: Johns Hopkins Press, 1968).

48. J. R. Lasuén, *Urbanization and Development* (forthcoming), chap. 10.

49. This is obviously one manifestation of the general process of regional convergence of income levels and economic structure.

In presenting this paper to the 1968 meeting of the Southern Economic Association I did not find it necessary to make explicit that relationship. Dr. Alexander Ganz of the Joint Center for Urban Studies at M.I.T./Harvard University, the main discussant of the paper, advised me to do it. I am most grateful for his comments. This and note 60 are the result of his advice.

The general process of regional convergence is the result of the increased mobility of capital and labor. It gives way to a growing similarity in the factor proportions of the different production functions, of the different industries and plants, in the different regions, and of the different regions. The mechanics of the process have received quite a lot of attention. An authoritative evaluation of the research is presented in Harvey Perloff *et al.*, *Regions, Resources and Economic Growth*, Baltimore, 1960. We have carried one in Chapter 2 of our forthcoming book, op. cit. (note 48).

Naturally, the growing convergence in production functions tends to result in a growing convergence in the cities' growth records and in the growing stability of the urban hierarchy.

As the reader will recollect, the analyses of the general process of regional convergence have been carried out in terms of productivity and income differentials created by resource rigidities and related population and capital movements. Our argument aims to explain some of the factors which can accelerate or retard the capital and labor movements, other than the transport and communication factors considered by the analyses.

50. See note 44.

51. That the newer products and processes in any one line normally have meant larger scales of operation than the previous ones has been common knowledge. The hard figures have been provided by E. Mansfield, *Industrial Research and Technological Innovation*, New York, 1968. In his book he shows that though small and medium firms keep on inventing as much as·the large ones (and many times more), the new innovations are adopted faster and more extensively by the large firms than by the small ones because of the increasing scale of the successive innovations.

52. For a general discussion of the differences in time and over geographical space of the diffusion of specific and general information see A. Rapoport, "The Diffusion Problem in Mass Behavior," in *General Systems Yearbook*, 1956.

53. This is the case of most countries in the world. The corresponding typological analysis and examples will appear in Chapter 3 of my above-mentioned book (note 48).

54. W. H. McNeill, *The Rise of the West*, Chicago, 1963, has given central importance (in the explanation of the historical evolution of the different countries) to the effects of diffusion of innovations. The reader can find there evidence of the overall importance of the diffusion of innovations and examples of them.

55. An impressionistic view is offered by J. Michener in *The Source*.

56. T. Hägerstrand, "Quantitative Techniques for Analysis of the Spread of Information and Technology," in C. A. Anderson and M. J. Bowman (eds.), *Education and Economic Development*, Chicago, 1963.

57. In Chapter 4 of my forthcoming book, I have developed the following typology:

Stages of Firms' Reorganization

	Firm/ Products	Firm/ Plants	Firm/ Cities (location)	Firm/ Regions (market)	Firm/ Processes
1.	One product	One plant	One city	One region	One process
2.	,,	,,	,,	,,	Multiprocess (vertical)
3.	,,	,,	,,	Multiregion	,,
4.	,,	Multiplant	Multicity	,,	,,
5.	Multiproduct	,,	,,	,,	,,
6.	,,	,,	,,	,,	Multiprocess (vertical- horizontal)

58. W. Thompson, op. cit., note 40.

59. A. O. Hirschman, op. cit., note 25.

60. Again on the advice of A. Ganz (see note 49), we must make it explicit that we are not challenging the existence of strong interrelationships between the processes of urbanization and development. On the contrary, using Perroux's concepts, I view urbanization and development as the successive mappings, on geographical and sectoral spaces respectively, of the transformations of economic activities over time.

What I am simply stating is that the interrelation between the two (urbanization and development) manifestations of the process of economic transformation is not unique. By that I mean both (1) that the characteristics of the relationship are different at the different stages of the two (a commonly accepted view), and (2) that even at similar stages, the relationship may differ; that the "conversion rules" to project the mappings of the economic transformations from sectoral space onto geographical space may change and may be changed. They change due to many factors. Most of them may not be subject to policy. At least one is, and that is the pattern of organization of the business firms. By acting upon it, *ceteris paribus*, one can act upon the urbanization pattern and/or the development pattern.

61. This section was absent when the paper was first published. It was added for the Growth Center Colloquium held at the University of Texas at Austin in November 1969.

62. These qualifications are extracted from my paper "Urban Hierarchy Stability and Spatial Polarization: Rejoinder," to be published in *Urban Studies*. I wrote this paper in response to several points Professor Hansen had raised in his "A Note on Urban Hierarchy Stability and Spatial Polarization," to be published in the same journal.

63. Op. cit., note 62.

GROWTH POLE THEORY: AN EXAMINATION OF SOME OF ITS BASIC CONCEPTS

MORGAN D. THOMAS*

University of Washington

Introduction

Contemporary governments in many parts of the world have accepted the concept of the growth pole as a tool of economic and even social transformation at the regional scale.[1] However, it seems that these governments and other proponents of the growth pole notion have not entirely solved the problem of just how to use this concept as a tool of economic and social policies for promoting basic changes in the distribution of population and economic activities. Probably part of the solution to such a problem awaits the formulation of a clearly articulated and approved set of nonconflicting, long- and short-term regional development goals.

The effective use of the growth pole as a policy instrument is inhibited also by the fact that it is, as Hansen recently stated, "characterized as an ambiguous concept composed of loosely related, vague sub-concepts."[2] Growth pole theory "is badly in need of a thorough semantic reworking; the concepts and the language which characterize it need more precise definition and more consistent usage."[3]

At this time, one may briefly mention two additional deficiencies that adversely affect the utility of the growth pole notion as a policy instrument. One deficiency is related to our lack of knowledge con-

* I would like to express my gratitude to my friends W. B. Beyers, G. Krumme, C. W. Moore and G. P. F. Steed for their help and constructive criticisms during the writing of this paper. At various stages the Ford Foundation, the University of Washington and the Economic Development Administration made it possible for me to develop my current ideas concerning growth poles as they are related to the process of regional economic development.

cerning the processes of growth within poles over time. The second deficiency is connected with the paucity of information about the nature and significances of the spatial components of interindustry linkages that exist between various kinds of industries found within growth poles.

OBJECTIVES

In this article my general objective is to try to reduce the ambiguity of growth pole theory by evaluating a number of its basic concepts and relationships. Like Hansen, Lasuén, and others, I believe a reduction in the elusiveness of the growth pole concept is necessary if we are to improve its utility and efficiency as a policy instrument for achieving regional economic development.[4]

I begin with a few comments on contemporary regional economic growth and location theories, for the theory of growth poles is closely connected with the questions of how and where does, or how and where should economic growth take place in a region. I then attempt to provide an historical perspective for growth pole theory as articulated in the 1950s by discussing various concepts found in the writings of such scholars as Perroux, Chenery, and Hirschman.[5] A major portion of my discussion is devoted to a critical evaluation of such conceptual elements as the disequilibria of propulsive industries, internal and external economies, technological change and productivity growth, and innovations and their diffusion. These elements, among others, appear to provide crucial foundations for growth pole theory and in particular, they are intimately connected with the growth mechanism of poles. The concluding section contains a few brief suggestions concerning work we need to do on some growth and spatial aspects of the growth pole notion. In addition, I note a number of policy implications stemming from some of the points discussed.

SPATIAL CONCENTRATIONS

If we examine the explanatory frameworks for regional economic growth, we will realize that they are usually devoid of spatial dimension. Yet we know that no economic activity is located at a point with no spatial dimension! An interesting theoretical problem is then the determination of an optimum spatial dispersion of all economic

activities. Bos has described the analytical aspect of this problem as
follows:

> Production, consumption, capital goods, population, etc. are not
> spread evenly and in a continuous way over the globe, its continents,
> national economies and their regions. With the exception of activities such
> as agriculture, forestry and fishery, production and population are con-
> centrated in agglomerations or centres. These concentrations of economic
> activity are not all of the same size, nor do they have the same economic
> structure.[6]

Economic theory has contributed very little to the explanation of
these spatial distributions of economic activities.[7] This situation is
unfortunate because such explanations are needed if we are to solve
some important practical contemporary economic problems—for
example, the planning problem of determining the optimum, or most
desirable, dispersion of economic activity to achieve a particular rate
of economic growth for a selected region. We should, however, note
that the choice of a different objective function would tend to result
in or necessitate the creation of different industrial and spatial
structures of the region's economic activities.

LOCATION

The development stages and export base theories provide us with
explanatory frameworks in our search for answers when we ask "How
and why does regional economic growth take place?"[8] Such theories,
however, tell us very little about where in the region economic
growth should take place so as to achieve a given objective(s). There
is an obvious need to integrate location and economic growth
theories.

It is appropriate that we look to location theories to provide us
with guidance as to where various kinds of economic activities should
be located in the region. We have, of course, a number of theories
purporting to explain the location of economic activities.[9] We may
classify these into three groups. These are concerned with explaining
(1) agricultural activities, (2) manufacturing, and (3) service activities
(chiefly retail activities). It seems that we have made little progress
toward developing a general theory designed to explain the location
of all economic activities. The theories we have tend to be normative
in nature, as in the case of industrial (manufacturing) location theory,
and pictorial model "realities," in the case of agricultural and service

activity location theories. All are placed in a timeless setting—*i.e.*, in the static frameworks of general or partial equilibrium theories. I suggest that our present location theories provide very poor explanatory and predictive frameworks for regional economic growth policy formulation. Such theories, among other things, should consider explicitly the effects of *time* in the location equation. Perhaps what I am saying is that we need dynamic location theories.

Be that as it may, we can point to work done by some theorists to dynamize regional economic growth theory. A number of these scholars have also been concerned with certain aspects of the location question. I am, of course, referring in particular to the work of the French school of space economics founded on what Lasuén has referred to as "the original insights of the school's founding father, François Perroux."[10] We are increasingly aware of the contributions of many scholars, particularly those French economists who have in recent years articulated the nature and significances of relationships that exist between growth poles and regional economic growth.[11]

Certainly, the notion of the growth pole has been a fruitful theoretical construct, and it has had a remarkably wide acceptance in recent times as a planning instrument. I therefore think it appropriate and useful at this time to examine in some detail some of the basic concepts underlying growth pole theory. However, before I begin the next section, I would like to note that scholars such as Perroux and Friedmann have now developed the idea of the growth pole to include social, institutional, organizational, and political as well as economic elements.[12] Perhaps this expansion has contributed to what Lasuén calls the elusiveness of the growth pole concept. I prefer to restrict my comments here to an examination of the economic and geographical concepts associated with the more "traditional" notion of growth poles, formed for example in Perroux's early views on this subject and expressed in his classic 1955 paper.[13]

Historical Perspective

Many theorists see the beginnings of the contemporary notion of the growth pole in one of Perroux's three types of economic space— namely, economic space as a field of forces.[14] In a paper published in 1950, Perroux seemed to visualize that there are within this field

of forces certain poles or foci or centers from which centrifugal
forces emanate and to which centripetal forces are attracted.

PERROUX

In 1955 Perroux developed further some of his ideas connected with
growth poles in his now classic article entitled, "*Note sur la notion
de pôle de croissance*."[15] However, according to Blaug, a number of
concepts found in Perroux's recent writings on growth poles, such as
"leading firms," "leading industries," and "points of growth," are
synonymous with what used to be called "the dominant economic
unit"—an idea associated with the theory of economic domination.[16]
An articulation of this theory was made by Perroux in papers
published in 1948, 1949, and 1950.[17]

Perroux's conception of economic growth has been reflected in his
examinations of the significance of "points of growth poles."[18] Blaug
suggests that economic growth manifested in the increase of total
output is necessarily accompanied by structural changes in the
economy. For Perroux, the problem of growth theory is to explain
the nature of those structural changes.[19] Dominant economic units
appear to play a major role in Perroux's explanatory framework. The
roles of such units within a points-of-growth context are largely
manifested through the crucial twin concepts of (1) a propulsive firm
or industry (*firme* or *industrie motrice*), and (2) a key firm or industry
(*firme* or *industrie clef*).[20]

Perroux states that when a propulsive industry raises its output, it
induces expansions in the outputs of other industries. In cases where
the induced growth in outputs is much greater than the initial growth
of the propulsive industry's output, such a propulsive industry is
called a *key* industry.[21] It should be noted that Perroux does not
confine the notion of growth induced by a key firm or industry to a
highly localized geographical area. He indicates that such induced
growth may be traced throughout a national economy when considering the question of whether or not a propulsive industry is also
a key industry.

AMERICAN CONTRIBUTIONS

Comments will be made later on the growth mechanism and spatial
relationships connected with Perroux's notion of points of growth.

Now I propose to examine very briefly the development in the 1950s of concepts in the United States that appear to be strongly related to many of the ideas articulated in the same period by Perroux and many of his French disciples.

In some respects, Perroux's propulsive and key industries have a strong input-output flavor. Indeed, he defines some of the salient characteristics of these industries within an industrial complex context.[22] Since the mid-1950s, Perroux and especially some of his French colleagues have made considerable use of the input-output analytical framework.[23] During the same period in the United States, Isard, together with many of his students and colleagues, contributed greatly to the development of the industrial complex as an analytical and economic planning instrument.[24] However, although Isard made significant contributions in the 1960s to the development of the input-output technique for regional analysis, he is not generally associated with growth pole analysis. In the United States, Hirschman is very frequently recognized as being one of the first scholars to discuss growth poles in a similar fashion to Perroux. In fact, in his book *The Strategy of Economic Development*,[25] published in 1958, he notes the closeness of his viewpoint on development theory to views held by Perroux, Svennilson, and Fellner.[26]

INPUT-OUTPUT LINKAGES

A crucial component of Hirschman's theory of development is the recognition of interdependence linkages (input-output) between industries and an articulation of their significances as they relate to the process of induced economic growth.[27] In this connection, Hirschman's thinking appears to have been greatly influenced by a paper presented by Chenery and Watanabe to the Econometric Society in 1956.[28] In that paper the authors made comparisons of the structure of production for the United States, Italy, Norway, and Japan. Chenery and Watanabe used an input-output model to show the various interdependence linkages between industries in the four economies, and they were able to indicate a way in which individual sectors are related to each other. This they did by taking ratios of intermediate transactions to total production and total demand. In their study, these ratios are worked out for each sector. The ratio of purchased inputs to total production measures the direct effect of increasing production in sector j on other sectors (backward linkages), while the ratio of intermediate to total demand measures the extent to which demand in sector i is derived from use in other sectors of production (forward linkages). The next step undertaken was to establish a hierarchy of sectors leading from raw materials to finished products. One-way sequences like raw cotton–textiles–clothing fit quite nicely into such a scheme, but circular relations like coal mining–steel production–mining equipment–coal mining do not. The sectors for each country are arranged in the order that gives a minimum of circular relationships—*i.e.*, one tries to make the flow matrix as nearly triangular as possible. Chenery and Watanabe noted that in the United States table, for example, only 12.7 per cent of inter-industry transactions lay above the diagonal.[29] The sectors are then classified according to their ratio of purchased inputs to total demand.[30] One can of course invert the matrix and use Rasmussen's "power of dispersion," which gives direct and feedback effects.[31]

The tables showing backward and forward linkages became an important part of Hirschman's theory of unbalanced growth and of his strategy for economic development. Hirschman recognized the importance of technical complementarities that work through vertical linkages. Chenery and Watanabe's tables showed that the degree of complementarity is stronger between some particular groups of industries than others.[32] These industries, called *master* industries by Hirschman, tend to have high forward and backward linkage effects, and they seem to correspond to Perroux's propulsive industries. Perroux's *industrie clef* (key industry) and Hirschman's "master industry" appear to have much in common, although Hirschman's definition is perhaps less specific than the one given by Perroux and noted earlier here. Hirschman indicates that "the direct and indirect repercussions of an increase in final demand requirements for any one industry on the other sectors of the economy" may be obtained from the inverse matrix. Such a measure may then be used to rank industries, and seemingly high-ranking industries are identified as key industries. Intermediate and final manufacturing industries in particular would tend to qualify as key industries.[33] One might add that the concept of key industry appears to be related to the concept of lead industry and sector as used by economic historians.[34]

BEHAVIORAL ASPECTS

Both Perroux and Hirschman draw heavily on behavioristic elements and psychological forces to provide, in part at least, the motive force for growth in their poles or foci—which are really their propulsive or master industries. The same holds true for key or lead industries. Hirschman feels that the dynamic process of growth will be kept alive by the tensions of shortages and excess supplies and by the disequilibria in the strategic sectors that are capable of responding to these pace-setting pressures.[35] Perroux and Hirschman seem to rely on such tensions to provide favorable conditions for the continuing creation of profit-motivated entrepreneurs capable of perceiving exploitable opportunities. Such entrepreneurs are vital to the continuance of growth. Perroux seems to stress the existence of a growth mentality and competitive spirit among businesses.[36] Economic historians have long noted a particular climate created by a lead industry as it bursts along a certain part of its growth curve.

SPATIAL ASPECTS

Initially, so far as Perroux was concerned, the spatial dimension did not receive much consideration in his development of the concept of growth poles. He simply comments vaguely about the territorial agglomeration of growth.[37] Hirschman, however, recognizes the areal concentration of various combinations of master or propulsive industries and that where found they form core regions. Core regions are sometimes ambiguously referred to by other authors as growth areas, growth points, growth and development poles, and even growth centers. Hirschman, by differentiating economic growth characteristics found in different parts of a country, explicitly introduces a spatial dimension into his notion of growth poles. In fact, Hirschman notes that "international and interregional inequality of growth is an inevitable concomitant condition of growth itself."[38]

Boudeville, greatly influenced by Perroux's thinking, maintained in 1965 that the theory of economic space "is the application of a mathematical space on or in a geographic space."[39] A few years later he wrote, "The concept of a growth pole is associated with the notion of propulsive industry. . . . it would be preferable to describe poles as a geographic agglomeration of activities rather than as a complex system of sectors different from the national matrix. In short, growth poles will appear as towns possessing a complex of propulsive industries."[40]

Today, the majority of those thinking and writing about growth poles as well as those who use growth poles as policy instruments do seem to visualize growth poles as having a spatial setting. Of course, even among the majority, there is considerable disagreement concerning the nature of the spatial setting, the areal dimensions, and the structural characteristics of growth poles.

Growth Concepts

If the growth pole concept is to have utility as a policy instrument designed to facilitate regional economic growth, then we need to know why, how, and where a growth pole grows. A perusal of the literature leaves one with the impression that the processes of growth within the pole are not well articulated and that they are in considerable need of closer scrutiny and elaboration. With these needs in mind, then, I shall discuss two important interrelated aspects of the growth pole concept, namely (1) the growth mechanism and (2) the spatial components of growth poles. In this section, major emphasis will be placed on conceptual elements such as the disequilibria of propulsive industries, internal and external economies, technological change and productivity growth, innovation, and the diffusion of new techniques. These elements, among others, appear to provide crucial underpinnings for growth pole theory. Toward the end of this section a few brief comments will be made about a number of spatial relationships connected with growth poles.

GROWTH ASPECTS

Let us begin by examining some of Perroux's statements concerning the process of growth. In 1955 he indicated that the spiral of growth received its initial stimulus from the propulsive industry lowering its cost curve.[41] Then Perroux noted that when the industry has reached its optimum output, it may be able to lower its prices. Perroux suggested that the effect of lowering the price of the propulsive industry's output will be the induction of new increases in the output of the vertically integrated industries that initially benefit from a reduction in input costs and subsequently from possible increased demand for their lower-priced outputs. A knowledge of the price elasticities for the propulsive industry's output would provide it with useful guidance with respect to the kind of price changes it should introduce. Such information, of course, would be desirable to have for all those industries linked to the propulsive industry.[42] Perroux thus focuses attention on cost reduction as an important means of bringing about economic growth.

COST REDUCTION

Cost reduction notions appear to be very important and strategic in their influences on the theory of unbalanced economic growth. In contrast, consumer income expansion concepts are stressed in "balanced" growth theory.[43] Of course, in both theories cost reduction and income expansion are vital components of the mechanism of economic growth. I feel that growth pole theory could greatly benefit from a greater stress on income expansion elements. Because Perroux placed great emphasis on the role of cost reduction in starting and fueling the engine of growth,[44] it may be desirable and appropriate to examine briefly a number of subconcepts related to the idea of cost reduction. A convenient way of discussing these aspects would be to examine subconcepts related to (1) economies external to the single plant firm, multiplant firm, or industry and (2) economies internal to the single plant firm, multiplant firm, or industry. Each of these different levels of structural disaggregation of an industry necessitates somewhat different kinds of analyses.

EXTERNAL ECONOMIES

As noted earlier, Perroux made considerable use of the concept of external economies as a vehicle for spreading the possibilities of growth into many sectors following a lowering of the propulsive industry's cost curve.[45] When it lowers the price of its output, the propulsive industry provides lower-priced inputs to user industries. One must assume the right kinds of price elasticities are present, and thus external economies act as a type of growth multiplier. It seems appropriate that the concept of external economies be examined further because of its apparent importance as an explanatory variable in growth pole theory.

One must first distinguish between the Marshallian concept of external economies and that of economic growth theorists. The Marshallian concept uses the assumptions of competitive equilibrium and pertains to costs and benefits of production not adequately reflected in the price mechanism. In growth theory, the concept refers to the effect of one investment on the profitability of another.[46] Scitovsky has referred to this latter type of interdependence as "pecuniary external economies."[47] It is important to realize that the concept of pecuniary external economies as used by growth pole theorists acquires its significance from the assumptions of *dynamic disequilibrium*.[48] The theoretical underpinnings for this dynamic concept have been largely worked out in connection with the formulation of growth theory applicable to the industrialization of lesser developed countries, as for example by Rosenstein-Rodan in his famous article on Southeast Europe.[49] How appropriate, then, are these concepts for use in the propagation or continuing development of growth poles in stagnant and/or fast-growing regions in economically advanced countries?[50] Unfortunately, this question cannot be considered within the scope of this article; it is assumed, however, that the concept of external economies *has utility* in considering the problem of economic growth in economically advanced regions even though little can be said at present about the *degree* of utility provided by the concept.

At the conceptual level and within the framework of dynamic disequilibrium, the cost-reducing and induced growth effects of dynamic external economies are readily understood. Nevertheless, it is very difficult to find studies that attempt to measure these external economies. Chenery has, however, tried to measure the importance of one type of external economies, namely that associated with interdependence in production. He has used Latin American examples to illustrate how the concept provides useful guidelines for investment decisions.[51] Although Chenery appears to feel that this type of external economies has greater significance for less developed countries than for more advanced countries, one intuitively feels that the concept may have considerable utility in planning growth in the less developed regions of the more advanced countries. One should note, however, that "interdependence is also more important for products sold to producers and hence it occurs typically in sectors related to manufacturing."[52] Despite these limitations and biases, the idea of interdependence in production has considerable appeal. For example, governments wishing to use pecuniary external economies for the achievement of general welfare goals may find the following statement by Scitovsky to be of interest: ". . . when an investment gives rise to pecuniary external economies, its private profitability understates its social desirability."[53] The recognition and measurement of the interdependence concept as defined by Scitovsky provide us with a measure of the difference between social and private profitability of investment decisions.[54]

Clearly, one may utilize the concept of pecuniary external economies at macro and micro levels of analysis. Here I would like to pursue the idea a little further at the micro level, which entails the consideration of this type of external economies as it refers to particular industries and plants. Chenery has shown that the principal effects of interdependence in production can be classified as *effects on users* and *effects on suppliers*. He has also illustrated, using Latin American examples, the differences in profitability resulting from partial and from complete coordination of investment decisions. In the same study, Chenery demonstrates that the external effects are not only more important when economies of scale are introduced, but it makes possible some types of external effects that do not exist in cases where costs are constant.[55]

In contemporary discussions of growth pole theory, especially by geographers and by economists steeped in classical location theory, I sense a heavy emphasis on agglomeration effects stemming from

the physical propinquity of different types of production. In part they consist of the Marshallian type of external economies—creation of a pool of skilled labor, common services, etc., which can result from the expansion of one or several industries in one place. In part, they are due to a reduction in the physical quantities of certain inputs required—particularly transport and storage.[56]

We may observe that apparently the concept of external economies as usually associated with agglomeration does not have the same meaning as the dynamic external economies of growth theorists such as Rosenstein-Rodan, who have found the constraints of competitive equilibrium too restrictive.

In his classic 1955 article on growth poles, Perroux makes considerable use of Scitovsky's earlier paper, "Two Concepts of External Economies." One may note that Scitovsky illustrates the process of growth in two industries, A and B, by making use of the concept of pecuniary external economies. He states that ". . . equilibrium is reached only when successive doses of investment and expansion in the two industries have led to the simultaneous elimination of profits in both. It is only at this stage, where equilibrium has been established, that the conclusions of equilibrium theory become applicable."[57] However, as Chenery has pointed out, "If the system does not start from a position of competitive equilibrium, it cannot be assumed that the investment that takes place will, necessarily lead toward such an equilibrium."[58] I feel an appreciation of Chenery's point underlies the use by some growth theorists of the concept of external economies within a dynamic disequilibrium framework.

I do not propose to discuss the relationship of agglomeration economies to growth pole theory here, but it should be pointed out that Perroux's disciples have been more interested than he in agglomeration economies, and one must agree that the concept can be tied in quite neatly to the whole idea of geographical growth poles, I believe that, in general, agglomeration economies have been discussed in too static a location theory framework. We have not tried hard enough to take more explicit note of the effect of *time*. In his 1955 paper, Perroux stresses the dynamism of industries and the agglomeration of industries in parts of geographic space. He notes the birth and growth of propulsive and linked industries and the role of agglomeration economies. These are the features most strongly stressed in our literature. However, Perroux indicates that industries, even propulsive industries, die. We then find that the positive multiplier effect of some of the external economies during the growth phases changes to a negative multiplier effect when the propulsive industry declines. We are all familiar with examples of this phenomenon in cities and regions throughout the world. Perroux puts it this way:

> The changes in technology, the vicissitudes of politics, the orientations of currents of world traffic between major poles are favorable or unfavorable to the poles which are territorially agglomerated. Concentrations of men and fixed capital, the rigidity of the installations and the structures which have accompanied the development of the pole also make all their consequences felt when their decline commences; the pole was an area of prosperity and growth, it becomes a center of stagnation.[59]

INTERNAL ECONOMIES

Let me now say a few words about internal economies, for these must also be considered in an examination of the concept of cost reduction. We find that the idea of internal economies, like its complement, external economies, is a significant conceptual component in growth pole theory. External economies reflect certain economic relationships between industries whereas internal economies are usually thought of as a manifestation of certain relationships within plants and firms and industries.

As I mentioned earlier, Perroux, Hirschman, and others stressed the vital role of propulsive industries in growth pole theory. We find the propulsive industry is, by definition, expanding at a relatively fast rate, it has a high level of output, and it has strong linkages with other activities of the region.[60] We are familiar now with the argument that the propulsive industry accrues internal economies by increasing its output. Average unit costs are lowered, and concomitant reductions in price brought about through scale economies and innovations are transferred to linked industries as pecuniary external economies. Eventually, these price reductions will tend to increase the effectiveness of given levels of personal incomes.

Scale economies and innovations are obviously thought to be major sources of internal economies, and thus they contribute substantially to the foundations of growth pole theory. There is a need for a rigorous examination of the relationships that exist between scale economies, innovations, and internal economies at the single and multiplant firm and industry levels, though only a few comments can be made in this regard here.

SCALE ECONOMIES

It is interesting to observe that a dynamic growth pole theory makes such extensive use of a concept such as economies of scale, which has been derived from the well-known static "envelope" curve of long-run average costs.[61] This curve shows "the lowest possible cost of producing at any scale of output when all possible adaptation to that scale of output had taken place."[62] However, relative factor prices and technical knowledge are held constant.[63]

There is a suggestion in growth pole literature that expansions in output are invariably accompanied by economies. Yet Bain, Haldi, Walters, Bruni, and others have shown that we have relatively little information about scale economies in the great number of different industries found in economically advanced economies of the world.[64] Scale economies seem to vary from industry to industry, although we have limited information about this. Such a situation might well be expected because of the various combinations of forces that determine economies of scale from industry to industry.[65] Here one would need to take into account the varying influences of such forces as indivisibilities, the economies of increased dimensions, specialization, and massed resources, the use of more efficient methods of organizing production and the learning effect.[66]

So far as improving growth pole theory is concerned, there is much we need to know about scale economies. We need information on main potential sources of economies of scale in single-plant and multiplant firms. Are these sources different? What effects do multiproduct mixes have on scale economies?[67] Growth pole theory has stressed the importance of increasing scale of production and the apparent concomitant increase in efficiency. Such a relationship needs further scrutiny because we need to know if increasing scale at the firm level is accompanied by an increase in concentration and if such concentration adversely influences competition in the industry. It is, of course, very difficult to assess the impact of changes in the level of competition on the efficiency of an industry.

RESEARCH AND DEVELOPMENT

We find in growth pole literature the suggestion that the lead firms and industries that supposedly accrue substantial scale economies also greatly benefit from the economies resulting from process, product, and organizational innovations. However, we have little quantitative knowledge of the economies that accrue as a result of investments in research and development by the firm or industry.

Today, we often hear that bigness is required to carry out the research and development vital to rapid technological change, which in turn is necessary if we are to have and benefit from dynamic internal economies. The concept of the necessity for research and development would appear, therefore, to be closely connected with the basic foundations of growth pole theory. It is pertinent that we examine some aspects of this concept. I am mainly concerned with the product of research and development as it contributes to economies internal to the firm or industry. Innovations derived from research and development carried out by a firm other than the one considered, or by an industry other than the one considered, may be examined within an external economy context.

Contemporary research has focused on, among others, these three questions: (1) What determines the level of a firm's privately financed research and development expenditures? (Research and development are mainly financed by government in aircraft, instruments, and electrical equipment industries.) (2) Do the largest firms in various industries spend more on research and development, relative to their size, than firms one-fifth or one-tenth their size? (3) What is the relationship between a firm's research and development expenditures and various crude measures of inventive output?[68]

With the usual caveats with respect to the small amounts of data available, the measurement techniques used, and so on, Mansfield found that in the chemical, petroleum, drug, glass, and steel industries:

    1. The expected ratios of return from reasonably promising research and development projects are distributed according to the Pareto law.

    2. The distribution of expected rates of return from research and development projects, together with a firm's size, determines the firm's desired level of research and development expenditures.

    3. The firm's speed of response toward this desired level depends on the extent to which desired levels differ from last year's spending and the percent of its profits spent last year on research and development.[69]

Mansfield found in the five industries studied that "except for the chemical industry, there is no evidence that the largest firms in these industries spent more on research and development, relative to sales, than did somewhat smaller firms."[70] In an empirical study of twenty-one three-digit industries, Comanor also concluded that there were few instances where the larger firms contributed a disproportionate share of industry resources for research and development. Yet firm size is said to be a significant factor influencing the rate of research spending, and doubtless the "lumpy" and discontinuous process of research poses a different problem for small as compared to large firms. However, in industries where firms are generally large, the relatively larger firms tend to account for only a proportional share of industry research. On the other hand, in industries where firms are generally small, the smaller firms that undertake research are likely to allocate a larger share of their resources for these purposes.[71] Thus one might conclude that increasing the degree of concentration, in terms of output, accounted for by the largest firms would be unlikely to lead to increased research.

There is some evidence, however, that in certain market situations higher concentrations, for given levels of firm size, are associated with greater research. This tends to be the case in industries in which the prospects of achieving product differentiation are limited.[72]

Similar conditions also appear to prevail where product differentiation exists, for product differentiation has the effect of insulating
submarkets and erecting entry barriers.[73] With respect to the association of entry barriers and research and development investments,
Comanor tentatively concluded that "technical entry barriers to
some moderate degree are associated with the highest levels of
industrial research."[74]

Now I shall discuss briefly the third question I mentioned earlier,
one which focuses on the productivity of industrial research and
development. The question is of interest because of the crucial role
played by innovations in growth pole theory. Perroux, like Schumpeter, has argued persuasively that large economic units are responsible for most innovating activities.[75] Large size and a high ability
to innovate are characteristics of the propulsive firms and industries
so important in growth pole theory.

We are, therefore, interested in knowing whether or not research
and development productivity is greater in the largest firms than in
somewhat smaller ones. Does this productivity increase with the
amount spent on research and development? Empirical information
on the productivity of industrial research and development is very
limited. The conceptual and measurement problems connected with
this subject must surely account in large part for the paucity of
information. One of the few studies we have concerning the extent
to which very large firms do the innovating was carried out by
Mansfield. He examined three industries: iron and steel, petroleum
refining, and bituminous coal. Mansfield admits that the industries
chosen were not entirely representative. He also finds it very difficult
to define particular innovations and to identify the innovations
responsible for increased productivity, as will as to gauge the relative
importance of various innovations. Consequently, he recognizes the
"very rough" nature of his findings.[76] Mansfield draws three tentative conclusions from these empirical studies. First, "it seems that
there is a close relationship over the long run between the amount a
firm spends on research and development and the total number of
important inventions it produces." Second, in two out of the three
industries examined (petroleum and steel), the results did not indicate
any marked advantage of very large-scale research activities over
medium-sized and large ones. Third, the evidence available suggests
that the productivity of a research and development effort of given
scale is lower in the largest firms than in the medium-sized and large

ones.[77] There is reason to believe that these results will vary somewhat from one time period to another.

INNOVATIONS

I now propose to examine briefly the concept of innovation that I
have already mentioned several times when discussing the closely
related idea of research and development. There seems little doubt
that research and development throw considerable light on the
technical characteristics and cost of production of an invention. This
is vital information when considering the process of transformation
from invention to innovation. Despite the availability of research
and development and other kinds of information such as market
research, there is still uncertainty involved in the utilization of an
invention by a firm. Traditionally, economists have stressed that
when the invention is applied, it becomes an innovation and until
then, it has little or no economic significance.

I have already mentioned the importance of innovations in
Perroux's articulation of growth pole theory, especially in his writings
of the mid-1950s. It seems pertinent, then, that we focus our attention
on a few aspects of the role of innovation in industrial development
and economic growth.[78] We should realize, however, that according
to such scholars as Schmookler, Brownlee, Salter, and Maclaurin,
the role of innovation in economic growth is not clearly and fully
understood at present.[79]

One aspect of interest is tracing the effects of innovations on
productivity increases and investigating how and why these changes
in productivity levels are related to economic growth. We are interested in the effect of innovations on not only the size but also the
quality of outputs.[80] One can readily appreciate the tremendous
difficulties of measuring these attributes of output! For example,
there is the difficulty of differentiating between the streams of output
of "old investment goods" and "new investment goods." In recent
years, studies of embodied technological changes by Solow, Brown,
Salter, and others have focused considerable attention on these
measurement problems.[81] Salter and Brown in particular have also
underscored the significance of high rates of *gross* investment on the
growth rates of firms and industries.

Harrod has drawn attention to the fact that in recent years technological innovations have received growing attention from economic

growth theorists.[82] Of particular interest is the effect of such innovations on capital coefficients. The objective is to lower the coefficient and thus increase the productivity of capital. In this way, there is an associated saving in capital needed to reach given levels of output.

We so frequently associate the need for investment with innovations. Yet some managerial and/or organizational innovations are usually cited as examples of disembodied technological progress, and as such they alter the production function without requiring gross investment. This type of innovation brings about rises in the productivity of old and new investment goods.[83]

DIFFUSION

Another aspect of interest in connection with innovations is the rate and nature of their diffusion throughout firms, industries, and various kinds of regions or growth poles. I am using the term *growth pole* in the sense of a specific part of earth space that represents coincident economic and geographic poles, as Boudeville has recently defined it.[84] It has been suggested that within the firm the response to new technology and its diffusion will be influenced by (1) the relative size of the firm, (2) its growth rate, (3) its profit position, (4) its liquidity position, (5) the anticipated profitability of the new technology, and (6) the age of its management. Solo has suggested that if we regard the adoption of innovations as a cognitive-formation process this would help to explain Mansfield's finding that the firm or industry's *accumulated* research and development expenditures rather than "its ratio of R and D expenditure to sales, its rate of growth, or its concentration ratio exert an important influence on its rate of technological change." Accumulated research and development expenditures are thus conceived by Solo to be an open-ended process of group learning.[85]

We are interested in knowing as much as possible about additional factors that influence the diffusion and acceptance of an innovation. One might ask: Is the rate of adoption of the innovation a function of the areal extent of the growth pole and the nature and ease of communication within it? What influences would the degree of similarity or uniqueness of potential adopters have on the rate of adoption? Does the number of potential adopters play any part in this process? Do business conditions in general or in the industry or firm concerned influence the rate of adoption? Do the size of the investment requirements and the amounts and age of existing capital influence the diffusion and acceptance processes? Certainly there are other relevant factors to be considered. Even though there is a paucity of empirical evidence, we do know that there is great variability in the rate of adoption of different kinds of innovations when considered on intrafirm and interfirm or industry or growth pole bases. There are also space-time variations in patterns of adoptions of innovations. From the competitive point of view of the firm and the growth pole within which it is located, the rate and form of the adoption of the innovation in the same and in other growth poles will also be significant. Here one is focusing attention on the role of "imitation." In addition, it would be relevant to know whether or not the particular innovation is likely to be an isolated element or part of a stream of innovations. Intuitively one feels the latter is the more prevalent situation. It seems plausible to assume that the rate of adoption of an innovation or set of innovations will influence the rate and amount of growth in a firm, industry, and growth pole in a given period of time.

We would expect different innovations to have different effects on the rates of growth of different firms, industries, and growth poles. The length of the time period over which an innovation will tend to influence the annual growth rate of a firm will be influenced by the nature of the innovation and the firm concerned. Insofar as such numbers are meaningful, Mansfield has stated "the average effect of a successful innovation was to raise the firm's annual growth rate by four to thirteen percentage points, depending on the time interval and the industry."[86] Despite this apparent beneficial impact of innovations on the growth rate of firms, it still seems to take a very long time for major new techniques to spread through an industry. It frequently takes some twenty years for such techniques to be adopted by all major firms in an industry, and seldom is the process of adoption completed in less than ten years.[87] We also find that innovations are more likely to be introduced during periods when industries are operating at 75 per cent of capacity, regardless of whether the output trend was up or down.[88]

Before I conclude this section on innovations, I wish to mention two things. First, it may be helpful for us to think of innovations as contributing to the continued growth or establishment of growth poles in several ways—for example, (1) by improving the competitive position of industries in which they are adopted, (2) by making it possible throught the development of new products to establish new industries in the growth pole, and (3) by making it possible to establish industries that for economic reasons could not have been previously located in the pole. Number (1) is relevant with respect to the pole's existing industries through time, whereas (2) and (3) focus on the pole's need and quest for new industries if it is to endure.

Second, I will acknowledge the neoclassical analytic apparatus underlying my discussion of innovations. This involves only one viewpoint, and of course a greater understanding of the process of innovation adoption requires insights generated by many viewpoints. Arrow has recently commented on the desirability and relevance of the viewpoints of sociologists, such as Rogers and Coleman, who "are concerned with the nature of the channel connecting the adopters of an innovation with potential followers."[89] Solo believes that such an understanding of the process of innovation adoption requires the development of a conceptual framework "that can contain the generation, recapitulation, dissemination of information, the determinants of creativity, the process of learning by individuals and groups, the disintegration and re-creation of ideology and values, the receptivity or resistance to novelty, and the scope of the power and the nature of opportunity and the motivation to transform technology."[90] Obviously, the neoclassical economic framework would be inadequate for such an Herculean task! I believe Solo's suggestion points the way to much needed research. It also underscores our needs, so far unsatisfied, if we are to have knowledgeable influence over the process of innovation and change within growth poles.

Spatial and Growth Elements

I have clearly been concerned with the problem of improving existing explanatory frameworks for growth poles. If we are to develop growth pole policies, we will have to achieve much higher levels of understanding of the processes of economic growth in a growth pole context. In this concluding section I wish to continue to use a similar orientation for my discussion, although I will suggest possible policy implications more frequently than I did earlier. I also propose to comment very briefly on a number of additional spatial and growth elements in growth pole theory that appear to need further examination.

SPATIAL RELATIONSHIPS

The spatial ramifications of industrial change are very poorly developed in growth pole theory. We also have very little knowledge of the spatial dimensions of the interindustry linkages that are so important in a theory stressing the significance of induced economic growth. Information on these aspects are crucial to the development of a location theory that would explain the location of poles having different or similar industrial structures. There are important theoretical and practical reasons, then, for knowing the spatial structure of interindustry linkages that exist between growth poles as well as those that exist between establishments and firms within a pole. Such spatial structures are reflected in the cost schedules of plants and firms, affecting their viability and consequently influencing the growth prospects of the pole itself.

The notion of the growth pole should also throw some light on the nature and significance of the spatial relationships existing between a growth pole and its surrounding area. These are dynamic relationships, but how much do we know about their dynamism? We have, of course, some information about labor sheds and retail and wholesale links for a town or city's so-called "tributary" region.[91] Little do we know about the spatial characteristics of the input and output linkages of the town and city's industrial sectors or plants and offices, and so on.[92] How do size and industrial structure influence the spatial relationships of the pole with its surrounding area? Before answering such a question we need to know more about what we mean by the terms *size* and *surrounding area*.[93] These are significant concepts when we come to consider such issues as the spatial concentration and backwash or spread effects of growth poles.

We need to know a great deal more than we do now about the spatial dimensions of the centripetal and centrifugal forces connected with growth poles of various kinds. This knowledge is especially desirable if we intend to set up growth poles in a region to serve as demagnetizers for an existing pole or poles.

LOCATION ANALYSIS

Growth pole theory tells us very little about *where* in the region growth poles should be established. Nor does it provide, for that matter, a coherent explanation for various kinds of growth poles found in specific locations over the surface of the earth. There is an obvious need to integrate and improve location and growth theories. The unsuitability of classical location theory for the consideration of plant location within the framework of a long period of economic growth has been recognized.[94] The Economic Commission for Europe (ECE) recently noted that, with respect to the general consideration of criteria used in the location of industrial plants, two major interrelated observations emerge—"the first is the emergence and growing importance of macro-criteria, and the second is the basic change in the structure and mechanism of the decision-making process in the field of industrial location."[95] These observations are worthy of further investigation.

There is also a need to examine the possibilities of using industrial or economic activity location analysis as a tool for long-run growth pole policy formulation and implementation. It is clear that many problems inhibit the effective use of location analysis as a tool for such purposes. One set of such problems is connected with the spatial elasticity associated with the allocation of industrial investment. We need to identify and evaluate the significance of factors that influence such spatial elasticity. In this connection, is the rate of industrial growth an important factor? Different industries have different degrees of locational choices. For example, the establishment of new mines and steel plants tends to reflect spatially inelastic industrial growth, whereas new light metal fabrication plants tend to represent more spatially elastic industrial growth. However, *ceteris paribus*, does a high rate of growth generate more locational choices than a low rate? We also need to investigate the effect on such spatial elasticity of changing shares of footloose industries and new plants in total industrial investment. Another factor whose impact is worthy of study is represented by the identified tendencies of large plants to account for a growing share of total industrial investment and new units constructed.[96]

The conflict between sectoral and regional approaches to industrial location represents another set of problems that influences the utility of industrial location as a policy instrument. The ECE report states that, "In most cases the sectoral approach stresses the economic advantages of spatial concentration and the regional approach the advantages of spatial dispersion. . . . Generally, the sectoral approach is represented by private industry and the regional approach by various public authorities."[97] What are the conflicts, if any, that exist between the sectoral and growth pole approaches?

LOCATION THEORY

If we are to improve the efficiency of industrial location as an economic development policy tool, work must proceed on many problems in addition to those mentioned above. For example, how do we take explicit consideration of the effects of time in the location equation? It is also clear that we need to know a great deal more than we now do about location decision making at the single plant and multiplant firm levels as well as at various national and subnational governmental levels.[98] Not only do we need to know more about how location decisions are made, but we need to know why. What degree of correspondence exists between the location, production, and growth goals of single and multiplant firms in the same and in different industries? How similar are these objectives to those held by governmental authorities pursuing specified kinds of long-run economic development patterns at national and subnational levels? If they are not identical or harmoniously related, what happens? In addition, how do we deal with goals that represent a mixture of quantitative and qualitative elements?

QUALITY OF GROWTH

In the past our location theories have tended to evaluate the economic costs of inputs involved at various alternative locations. If industrial location analysis is to be used as a long-run economic development tool by government authorities, will we need theories to take explicit account of social, political, and other kinds of costs associated with various combinations of inputs used by plants in specified locations? Should we also be concerned with the noneconomic as well as the economic implications of different levels and kinds of output that follow industrial location decisions relating to specific locations such as growth poles? Increasingly today, one hears comments to the effect that we should be concerned with the *quality* of economic development.[99] Perhaps another way of saying some of these things is to call attention to the need for further study of the links between economic development and the more comprehensive concept of development at national and subnational levels. These, then, are some of the questions that are pertinent to ask. The answers we find will help us to understand better the growth processes and some of the spatial relationships of growth poles. Such insights should help us to increase the efficiency and utility of the growth pole concept as a policy instrument.

GROWTH ELEMENTS

I will now say a few words on a number of growth elements worthy of much greater scrutiny than is possible here. First, and without elaboration, we note that there is no clear distinction drawn between extensive and intensive components of economic growth in growth pole theory. Surely it would be useful to know to what extent the pole's growth represents a spatial transfer of growth from some other region or part or parts of a region to the pole.

Growth is a process that takes place over time. The crucial concept of interindustry linkages is derived from the static input-output matrix. To use the concept in a dynamic framework requires a great deal of knowledge about the stability over time of the technical coefficients as well as the stability of the composition of sectors in the pole. Relevant here would be information on aspects discussed earlier, such as technological change, factor substitutions, and changes in product mix of plants and firms over time. Initially, the concept of a propulsive industry was developed at a highly abstract or aggregated level. We need input-output linkage information at plant or firm level for growth poles. Perhaps we need to investigate in this connection the utility of activity and process analysis.[100] Clearly there is a need to construct a bridge between the concept of Schumpeterian sectoral growth found in Perroux's writings of the mid-1950s and the concept of induced growth based on interindustry linkages characterizing his work of the early 1960s.

INDUSTRY GROWTH PATTERNS

We should also attempt to integrate into the growth pole conceptual framework insights gleaned from the study of industry growth patterns. It is well known that the rates of growth of output and productivity are closely related to per capita income growth in a pole or region. The welfare implications of these connections suggest that we should be interested in knowing as much as we can about the pattern of industry growth in particular poles as well as in the region in general. In this connection, one can readily appreciate the value of knowing if individual industries have uniformities in their growth patterns. In the United States, the search for such uniformities reached a peak in work carried out by Kuznets and Burns over thirty-five years ago.[101] Interest in this kind of work has recently revived. Gaston's publication of *Growth Patterns in Industry* in 1961 and his use of the Gompertz curve exemplify this renewed interest.[102] They also illustrate the fact that Burns' significant work of the 1930s on industry growth patterns has had a tremendous effect on subsequent thinking on this subject. In particular, Burns's law has had enduring impact on scholars concerned with the study of industrial growth. This law was summarized by Burns in his statement, "An industry tends to grow at a declining rate, its rise being eventually followed by a decline."[103] Contemporary trenchant criticism of Burns's work by Bela Gold involved an extension of Burns's results over a subsequent twenty-five-year period and the review of Burns's expectations.[104] Gold's series show a variety of industry expansion paths and, in many instances, individual industries exhibit a number of distinct peaks. Yet, according to Burns, the estimated peak for each industry represents the year in which the logarithmic parabola fitted by him reached its maximum. These findings obviously conflict with the expectations based on Burns's law.[105]

If these findings of Gold are correct and general, then the search for uniformities needs the guidance of supporting theories of the economic processes involved in describing and explaining the pattern of industrial growth. This is very much the case when we come to the problem of forecasting the volatile patterns of growth for individual industries at regional (subnational) and especially growth pole levels. Recent work by Hirsch provides very interesting insights on this topic.[106]

One intuitively feels that an industry's ability to change its product mix and thus effect necessary structural changes are important elements in the articulation of patterns of growth. To what extent, then, are these product and structural changes compatible with changes in the sources, kinds, amounts, and qualities of inputs? We quickly realize that answers to these questions will focus on the roles of concepts discussed earlier, such as income elasticity of demand, innovations, and external economies. With respect to the pattern of industry growth, changes in outputs and markets for an industry's products condition the nature of the industry's expansion path.[107] Unfortunately, in attempting to identify the expansion paths of particular industries, it is found frequently that the paths are aggregated with those of related industries. Identification problems also result from changes that occur in industrial classification schemes during the time period considered.

There is an important relationship between the concepts of productivity and an industry expansion path. It is useful to think of the growth or expansion path as being usually a composite of movements by the firm or industry over parts of a number of possible expansion paths. In fact, it may be useful to think of a firm or industry moving along parts of a number of possible expansion paths. If the firm's or industry's output and productivity levels are to grow, the objective is to try to keep moving to higher and still higher expansion paths to avoid the inhibitive effects of diminishing marginal outputs.[108]

Concluding Comment

I have made no attempt to tie the notion of growth poles into a broader regional economic growth theory or to indicate its place in a much more generalized theory of polarized development. Like Paelinck, I have tended to treat growth pole theory as "a *conditional* theory" of regional economic growth. However, I do not feel that at present we have a clear indication of "the conditions under which accelerated regional development can occur."[109] I should say that the predictive and even explanatory qualities of contemporary growth pole theory leave much to be desired, even though the regional economic growth theories seem to be no better.

The concepts and subconcepts so frequently encountered in the literature on growth poles and examined in this paper are still ambiguous. The relationships between these concepts and subconcepts are also not clear. I have tried to give meaning within a growth pole framework to such terms as propulsive industries and firms, external and internal economies, research and development, diffusion, innovation, spatial components of industries, and expansion paths. Obviously, I chose to discuss concepts and aspects that seemed to me to be basic to the notion of the growth pole. I am aware of concepts and aspects equally important, if not more so, than the ones I have examined. However, if we are to reduce appreciably the elusiveness of the growth pole notion, it will require a tremendous amount of work on the part of a large number of researchers from many disciplines. I have tried to focus attention on the interrelatedness and dynamism of elements of the growth pole conceptual framework. I have also attempted to throw some light on the processes of economic growth within a growth pole context. Many pertinent questions have been left unanswered—perhaps some are unanswerable with our present level of knowledge. Be that as it may, it is hoped that in some small measure I have served to identify ways and means of achieving a greater understanding of the process of economic growth within growth poles. Certainly, such understanding is a prerequisite if we are to improve the efficiency of the growth pole theory as a policy instrument for achieving regional economic development.

Notes

1. K. Allen and T. Hermansen, *Regional Policy in EFTA: An Examination of the Growth Centre Idea* (Geneva, Switzerland: European Free Trade Association, 1968.) European Economic Community, *Study for the Promotion of an Industrial Development Pole in Southern Italy, Vol. 1* (Brussels, Belgium: 1966). T. Hermansen, *Growth Poles and Growth Centres in National and Regional Development—A Synthetical Approach* (Geneva, Switzerland: United Nations Research Institute for Social Development, 1969), UNRISD/69/C.26. Hermansen's study is excellent. P. Bernard, *Les pôles et centres de croissance en tant qu'instruments de développement régionale et de la modernisation* (Geneva, Switzerland: United Nations Research Institut for Social Development, 1969), UNRISD/69/C.32.

2. N. M. Hansen, "Development Pole Theory in a Regional Context," *Kyklos*, Fasc. 3, 1967, p. 723.

3. Ibid., pp. 723–24.

4. J. R. Lasuén, "On Growth Poles," *Urban Studies*, June 1969, pp. 137–61. Hansen, "Development Pole Theory." D. F. Darwent, "Growth Poles and Growth Centers in Regional Planning—A Review," *Environment and Planning*, 1969, pp. 5–31.

5. F. Perroux, "Note sur la notion de 'pôle de croissance'," *Economie appliquée*, janvier-juin, 1955, pp. 307–20. A. O. Hirschman, *Strategy of Economic Development* (New Haven, Conn.: Yale University Press, 1958). H. B. Chenery, "The Interdependence of Investment Decisions," in M. Abramovitz, et al., *The Allocation of Economic Resources* (Stanford, Cal.: Stanford University Press, 1959).

6. H. C. Bos, *Spatial Dispersion of Economic Activity* (Rotterdam, The Netherlands: Rotterdam University Press, 1965), p. 1.

7. Ibid., p. 9.

8. D. C. North, "Location Theory and Regional Economic Growth," *Journal of Political Economy*, June 1955, pp. 243–58. C. M. Tiebout, "Exports and Regional Economic Growth," *Journal of Political Economy*, April 1956, pp. 160–69. M. D. Thomas, "The Export Base and Development Stages Theories of Regional Economic Growth: An Appraisal," *Land Economics*, November 1964, pp. 421–32.

9. P. Hall, *Von Thünen's Isolated State* (Oxford, England: Pergamon Press, 1966). A. Weber, *Theory of the Location of Industries* (Chicago: University of Chicago Press, 1928). W. Christaller, *Central Places in Southern Germany*, trans. C. Baskin (Englewood Cliffs, N.J.: Prentice-Hall, Inc., 1966). A. Lösch, *The Economics of Location*, trans. William H. Woglom (New York: John Wiley and Sons, Inc., 1967). E. M. Hoover, *The Location of Economic Activity* (New York: McGraw-Hill Book Company, 1968). W. Isard, *Location and Space-Economy* (New York: The Technology Press, 1956). M. Greenhut, *Microeconomics and the Space Economy* (Chicago: Scott, Foresman Company, 1963).

10. Lasuén, "On Growth Poles", p. 137.

11. L. E. Davin, L. Degeer, J. Paelinck, *Dynamique économique de la région liégoise* (Liège, Belgium: Editions de l'A.S.B.L. "Le Grand Liège", 1959). L. E. Davin, *Economie régionale et croissance* (Paris, France: Editions Génin, 1964); J. R. Boudeville, *Problems of Regional Economic Planning* (Edinburgh, Scotland: Edinburgh University Press, 1966). J. Paelinck, "La theórie du développement régionale polarisé," *Cahiers de l'I.S.E.A.*, series L, no. 15, 1965.

12. Perroux, "Note sur la notion," pp. 319–20; J. Friedmann, "The Strategy of Deliberate Urbanization," *Journal of American Institute of Planners*, November 1968, pp. 364–73.

13. Lasuén, "On Growth Poles", p. 138 makes a similar decision.

14. F. Perroux, "Economic Space: Theory and Applications," *Quarterly Journal of Economics*, February 1950, pp. 90–97, in W. Alonso and J. Friedmann, eds., *Regional Planning and Development—A Reader* (Cambridge, Mass.: M.I.T. Press, 1964), pp. 21–34. The other types of economic space are (1) defined by a plan and (2) economic space as a homogeneous aggregate.

15. Perroux, "Note sur la notion."

16. M. Blaug, "A Case of the Emperor's Clothes: Perroux's Theories of Economic Domination," *Kyklos*, Fasc. 4, 1964, pp. 551–64.

17. See F. Perroux, "The Domination Effect and Modern Economic Theory," *Social Research*, June 1950, pp. 188–206.

18. Blaug, "A Case of the Emperor's Clothes," p. 556.

19. Ibid.

20. Davin, *Economie régionale*, p. 56.

21. Perroux, "Note sur la notion," p. 315.

22. Ibid.

23. F. Perroux, *L'économie de XXe siècle* (Paris, France: Presses Universitaires de France, 1961), pp. 192–241.

24. W. Isard and R. E. Kuenne, "The Impact of Steel Upon the Greater New York–Philadelphia Industrial Region," *Review of Economics and Statistics*, November 1953, pp. 289–301. See also W. Isard and J. H. Cumberland, eds., *Regional Economic Planning: Techniques of Analysis for Less Developed Areas* (Paris, France: Organization for Economic Cooperation and Development, 1961).

25. Hirschman, *Strategy of Economic Development*.

26. T. Svennilson, *Growth and Stagnation in the European Economy*. W. Fellner, "Long-Term Tendencies in Private Capital Formation," in *Long-Range Economic Projections* (Princeton, New Jersey: National Bureau of Economic Research, 1954).

27. Hirschman, *Strategy of Economic Development*, pp. 98–119.

28. This paper was later published—H. B. Chenery and T. Watanabe, "International Comparisons of the Structure of Production," *Econometrica*, October 1958, pp. 487–521.

29. Ibid., p. 497.

30. Ibid., pp. 507–20.

31. P. N. Rasmussen, *Studies in Inter-Sectoral Relations* (Copenhagen, Denmark: Einar Harcks Forlag, 1956). See also M. D. Thomas, "Programming, Industrial Interdependence and Economic Development," University of Washington *Business Review*, October 1960, pp. 48–57. C. Michalopoulos, "Inter-Industry Relations, External Economies, and Regional Development," paper presented at the Interregional Seminar on Industrial Location and Regional Development, Minsk, August, 1968, pp. 1–34, ID/WG.9/7. H. Aujac, "La hiérarchie des industries dans un tableau des échanges interindustriels," *Revue économique*, mars, 1960, pp. 164–238.

32. Chenery and Watanabe, "International Comparisons."

33. Hirschman, *Strategy of Economic Development*, p. 108.

34. J. Marczewski, "Some Aspects of the Economic Growth of France, 1660–1958," *Economic Development and Cultural Change*, April 1961, pp. 369–86. W. G. Hoffman, *The Growth of Industrial Economies* (Manchester, England: Manchester University Press, 1958).

35. H. Myint, *Economies of the Developing Countries* (London, England: Hutchinson of London, 1964), p. 123.

36. Perroux, "Note sur la notion," pp. 312–13.

37. Ibid., p. 318.

38. Hirschman, *Strategy of Economic Development*, pp. 183–84.

39. J. R. Boudeville, "Les notions d'espace et d'intégration," paper given at the International Congress for Town and Regional Planning, Basle, Switzerland, September 22–25, 1965, p. 2, cited by Hansen, "Development Pole Theory," p. 713.

40. Boudeville, *Problems of Regional Economic Planning*, p. 112.

41. Perroux, "Note sur la notion," p. 309.

42. Ibid., p. 315.

43. Chenery, "The Interdependence of Investment Decisions," p. 338.

44. Perroux, "Note sur la notion," p. 309.

45. Ibid., p. 315.

46. Chenery, "The Interdependence of Investment Decisions," p. 337.

47. T. Scitovsky, "Two Concepts of External Economies," in A. N. Agarwala and S. P. Singh, eds., *The Economics of Underdevelopment* (New York: Oxford University Press, 1963), p. 300.

48. Chenery, "The Interdependence of Investment Decisions," p. 337. Scitovsky, "Two Concepts of External Economies," pp. 303–08.

49. P. N. Rosenstein-Rodan, "Problems of Industrialization in Eastern and South-Eastern Europe," *Economic Journal*, June–September 1943, pp. 202–11.

50. Chenery, "The Interdependence of Investment Decisions," p. 339.

51. Ibid., pp. 336–71.

52. Ibid., pp. 339–40.

53. Scitovsky, "Two Concepts of External Economies," p. 304.

54. Chenery, "The Interdependence of Investment Decisions," p. 348.

55. Ibid., pp. 349–61.

56. Ibid., p. 362.

57. Scitovsky, "Two Concepts of External Economies," p. 304.

58. Chenery, 'The Interdependence of Investment Decisions," p. 338.

59. Perroux, "Note sur la notion," p. 318. Dr. G. Krumme has suggested that the multiplier at work here be described as a "post-mortem multiplier-effect" (positive or negative).

60. H. Siebert's interpretation of a statement by N. Hansen, "Development Pole Theory," p. 717 in *Regional Economic Growth: Theory and Policy* (Scranton, Pennsylvania: International Textbook Co., 1969), p. 191.

61. This concept was first discussed by J. Viner in *Zeitschrift für Nationalökonomie*, 1931, pp. 23–46.

62. C. Pratten and R. M. Dean in collaboration with A. Silberston, *The Economies of Large-Scale Production in British Industry* (Cambridge, England: University Press, 1965), p. 12.

63. For a good discussion on this general subject of cost curves see J. Johnston, *Statistical Cost Functions* (New York: McGraw-Hill Book Company, 1960).

64. J. S. Bain, *Barriers to New Competition* (Cambridge, Mass.: Harvard University Press, 1956); J. Haldi, *Economies of Scale in Economic Development* (Memorandum No. E-7, Stanford Project for Quantitative Research in Economic Development, Stanford University, 1960); A. A. Walters, 'A Note on Economies of Scale," *Review of Economics and Statistics*, November 1963, pp. 425–27; L. Bruni, "Internal Economies of Scale With a Given Technique," *Journal of Industrial Economics*, July 1964, pp. 175–90.

65. See E. A. G. Robinson, *The Structure of Competitive Industry* (Cambridge, England: Cambridge University Press, 1958).

66. Pratten and Dean, *Economies of Large Scale Production*, pp. 17–19.

80 *MORGAN D. THOMAS*

67. Ibid., p. 103.

68. E. Mansfield, *Industrial Research and Technological Innovation: An Econometric Analysis* (New York: W. W. Norton Company, Inc., 1968), pp. 21–22. See also R. R. Nelson, M. J. Peck, E. D. Kalachek, *Technology, Economic Growth and Public Policy* (Washington, D.C.: Brookings Institution, 1967), pp. 66–88.

69. Mansfield, *Industrial Research and Technological Innovation*, pp. 42–43.

70. Ibid., p. 43. These conclusions reached by Mansfield are certainly not definitive and are not representative of the full spectrum of manufacturing activities. However, they suggest that we do need to make similar and other tests to identify and measure the patterns of relationships between innovations and internal economies within various propulsive and "lead" industries so vital to the whole notion of growth poles.

71. W. S. Comanor, "Market Structure, Product Differentiation and Industrial Research," *Quarterly Journal of Economics*, November 1967, pp. 656–57.

72. Ibid., p. 657.

73. Ibid., p. 646.

74. Ibid., p. 657.

75. F. Perroux, *L'économie du XXᵉ siècle*, quoted from N. M. Hansen, "Development Pole Theory," p. 714.

76. Mansfield, *Industrial Research and Technological Innovation*, p. 108.

77. Ibid., p. 199. Mansfield has also suggested that where the largest firms account for a disproportionately large share of the innovations as, *e.g.*, in the chemicals industry, the following conditions appear to hold: (1) the innovation requires a large investment relative to the size of the potential users of the innovation, (2) the minimum size of firm to which the innovation would apply is large relative to the average size of firm in the industry, and (3) the average size of the largest four firms in the relevant industry is much greater than the average size of all firms that are potential users of the innovation. See E. Mansfield, *The Economics of Technical Change* (New York: W. W. Norton Company, Inc., 1968), p. 110.

78. Lasuén, "On Growth Poles," has a most perceptive discussion of this aspect.

79. See J. Schmookler and O. Brownlee, "Determinants of Inventive Activity," *American Economic Review, Papers and Proceedings*, May 1962, pp. 165–76; W. E. G. Salter, *Productivity and Technical Change* (Cambridge, England: Cambridge University Press, 1960); and W. R. Maclaurin, "The Sequence from Invention to Innovation and its Relation to Economic Growth," *Quarterly Journal of Economics*, February 1953, pp. 97–111.

80. M. D. Thomas, "Regional Economic Growth and Industrial Development," *Papers of the Regional Science Association*, Zurich Congress, 1962, p. 71.

81. See Salter, *Productivity and Technical Change*, p. 63; R. M. Solow, "Investment and Technical Progress," in K. J. Arrow, S. Karlin and P. Supes, eds., *Mathematical Methods in the Social Sciences*, 1959 (Stanford, Cal.: Stanford University Press, 1960), p. 91, and R. M. Solow, "Technical Progress, Capital Formation, and Economic Growth," *American Economic Review, Papers and Proceedings*, May 1962, pp. 76–86; M. Brown, *On the Theory and Measurement of Technological Change* (Cambridge, Mass.: M.I.T. Press, 1966), pp. 77–92.

82. R. Harrod, "Dynamic Theory and Planning," *Kyklos*, Fasc. 1, 1962, p. 73.

83. See Brown, *Theory and Measurement of Technological Change*, pp. 77–8.

84. Boudeville, *Problems of Regional Economic Planning*, p. 112.

85. See R. A. Solo's review of E. Mansfield, *Industrial Research and Technological Innovation* in *Journal of Economic Literature*, vol. 7, no. 3 (September 1969), p. 863. See also K. J. Arrow, "Classificatory Notes on the Production and Transmission of Technological Knowledge," *American Economic Review, Papers and Proceedings*, May, 1969, pp. 29–35.

86. Mansfield, *Industrial Research and Technological Innovation: An Econometric Analysis*, p. 204. See also T. Barna, *Investment and Growth Policies in British Industrial Firms* (Cambridge, England: Cambridge University Press, 1962).

87. See the excellent article by G. F. Ray, " The Diffusion of New Technology: A Study of Ten Processes in Nine Industries," *National Institute Economic Review*, no. 48, May 1969, pp. 40–83. Mansfield, *Industrial Research and Technological Innovation: An Econometric Analysis*, p. 204.

88. Ibid., p. 203.

89. Arrow, "Classificatory Notes," p. 33.

90. Solo, *op. cit.*, p. 862.

91. See a discussion of work done on these aspects by K. Fox and his colleagues at Iowa State University, Ames, in, *e.g.*, K. Fox, *The Role of Growth Centers in Regional Economic Development* (Ames, Iowa: Department of Economics, Iowa State University, 1966).

92. B. G. S. James has interesting insights concerning some of these aspects in "The Incompatibility of Industrial and Trading Cultures: A Critical Appraisal of the Growth-Point Concept," *Journal of Industrial Economics*, November 1964, pp. 90–94.

93. There is an interesting discussion of these terms by K. Allen in K. Allen and T. Hermansen, *Regional Policy in EFTA*, pp. 85–97.

94. M. D. Thomas, "Regional Economic Growth: Some Conceptual Aspects," *Land Economics*, February 1969, pp. 45–46.

95. Economic Commission for Europe Secretariat, *Criteria for Location of Industrial Plants, Changes and Problems* (New York: United Nations, 1967), pp. 12–14.

96. Ibid., pp. 17–25.

97. Ibid., p. 68.

98. A. Danielsson, "The Locational Decision from the View of the Individual Company," *Ekonomisk Tidskrift*, June 1964, pp. 47–87; W. F. Luttrell, *Factory Location and Industrial Movement: A Study of Recent Experience in Great Britain* (London, England: National Institute of Social and Economic Research, 1962); G. C. Cameron and G. L. Reid, *Scottish Economic Planning and the Attraction of Industry*, University of Glasgow Social and Economic Studies, Occasional Papers, No. 6 (Edinburgh, Scotland: Oliver and Boyd, 1966); G. C. Cameron and B. D. Clark, *Industrial Movement and the Regional Problem*, University of Glasgow, Social and Economic Studies, Occasional Papers, No. 5 (Edinburgh, Scotland: Oliver and Boyd, 1966); G. Krumme, "Towards a Geography of Enterprise," *Economic Geography*, January 1969, pp. 30–40. G. A. Churchill, *Plant Location Analysis: A Theoretical Formulation* (Indiana University, unpublished D.B.A. dissertation, 1966).

99. See in this connection J. H. Cumberland, "A Regional Interindustry Model for Analysis of Development Objectives," *Papers, The Regional Science Association*, 17 (1966). J. H. Cumberland, and F. van Beek, "Regional Economic Objectives and the Subsidization of Local Industry," *Land Economics*, 43, (1967), p. 3. W. Isard, *et al.*, "On the Linkage of Socio-economic and Ecologic Systems," *Papers of The Regional Science Association*, 21 (1968).

100. A. S. Manne and H. M. Markowitz, eds., *Studies in Process Analysis*, Cowles Foundation for Research in Economics, Yale University, Monograph 18 (New York: John Wiley and Sons, Inc., 1963). A. S. Manne, ed., *Investments for Capacity Expansion: Size, Location, and Time-Phasing* (Cambridge, Mass.: M.I.T. Press, 1967).

101. S. S. Kuznetz, *Secular Movements in Production and Prices* (New York: Houghton Mifflin Company, 1930). A. F. Burns, *Production Trends in the United States Since 1870* (New York, National Bureau of Economic Research, 1934).

102. J. F. Gaston, *Growth Patterns in Industry: A Reexamination* (New York: National Industrial Conference Board, 1961).

103. Burns, *Production Trends in the United States*, p. 173.

104. B. Gold, "Industry Growth Patterns: Theory and Empirical Results," *Journal of Industrial Economics*, November 1964, p. 53.

105. Thomas, "Regional Economic Growth: Some Conceptual Aspects," p. 50.

106. S. Hirsch, *Location of Industry and International Competitiveness* (Oxford: Oxford University Press, 1967).

107. T. Y. Shen, "Economies of Scale, Expansion Path, and Growth of Plants," *The Review of Economics and Statistics*, November 1965, pp. 420–28; and "Competition, Technology and Market Shares," *The Review of Economics and Statistics*, February 1968, pp. 96–102.

108. Thomas, "Regional Economic Growth: Some Conceptual Aspects," pp. 50–51.

109. Quoted by Hansen, "Development Pole Theory," p. 725.

A GENERAL THEORY
OF POLARIZED DEVELOPMENT

JOHN FRIEDMANN
University of California at Los Angeles
School of Architecture and Urban Planning

Introduction

In many parts of the world today, regional development planning, along with national planning, is considered to be an important aspect of guided change in societal systems. Regional planning is characterized by its focus on the attainment of objectives for territorially organized—or spatial—subsystems of national societies and, with growing frequency, also of multinational systems. Although the practice of regional planning in this sense is becoming increasingly common, it still needs to be put on an adequate theoretical foundation. And the most appropriate theory, it would seem, is one that would set forth and explain systematic interrelations between development and space—a theory, in other words, of the development process in its spatial dimension.[1]

Before presenting this subject, existing theories will be reviewed.[2] Despite their relative shortcomings, these theories complement each other in a number of ways and may each be relevant for specific kinds of planning analysis. In several important respects, however, none of them can be accepted as an adequate framework for regional development planning in its more general connotation.

Classical location theory is concerned with the optimum location of the firm.[3] More recently, it has been expanded to include industrial complex analysis which, in turn, has led to the theory of growth centers as formulated by François Perroux and others.[4] In a perspective of regional planning, however, classical location theory must be considered deficient because its concern is essentially with point locations rather than regional (or spatial) systems. The link between the location of economic activities (microtheory) and the development of a system of regions (macrotheory) is not yet clearly established.

Spatial organization theory has been specifically advanced as a basis for regional planning.[5] This theory focuses on the structural characteristics of a system of point locations. To the extent that it adopts a systems approach, spatial theory represents an advance over classical location theory. It remains unsatisfactory for our purposes, however, because it is formulated in terms of a general equilibrium model. The theory can explain the patterns of point locations at two separate periods of time; it contributes little to our understanding of the processes by which the historical transformation of spatial systems occurs.

In regional growth theory an attempt is made to overcome this difficulty and to treat specifically the dynamics of spatial systems. Separate theories have been evolved for individual regions[6] and for systems of regions.[7] In the case of the former, the theory presents some of the same difficulties that restrict the applicability of classical location theory to regional policy formation: its analysis falls short by concentrating exclusively on the case of single regions. In the more elaborate attempts to deal with the dynamics of a system of regions, the theory tends once more to revert to a general equilibrium formulation, where interregional flows of labor and capital are looked upon as the principal mechanisms for reestablishing a balance that might have been disturbed.[8] Although superior to all preceding theories as a foundation for regional development planning, it suffers the additional limitation—contrary to national growth theory—of being formulated entirely in economic terms. Albert Hirschman and Gunnar Myrdal have attempted to advance beyond these limitations, but their ideas have not been fully elaborated.[9]

Perhaps the most comprehensive theoretical text on regional growth published until now is that of Horst Siebert, who proceeds to formulate models for both an individual region and a system of regions.[10] Although an economist, Siebert deals imaginatively with significant topics, such as technical knowledge, diffusion of innovations, and communication, which brings his formulation close to the present one.

The avowed purpose of this chapter, then, is to formulate a theory of the development process in its spatial dimension. Society is spatially organized in the sense that human activities and social interactions are space-forming as well as space-contingent. It follows that as a society undergoes development, its spatial structure will be transformed, but the development process will also be influenced by the existing patterns of spatial relation and the dynamic tensions that result from them. Space is used here in the nonphysical sense of a field of forces (*e.g.*, energy levels, decision-making power, communications) that obeys its own laws of transformation.[11] In order to state a spatial theory of the development process, therefore, it is necessary to establish a linkage between the separate but correlative theories of social change and spatial organization.

There are two main contenders for a relevant theory of social change, Everett Hagen and Ralph Dahrendorf.[12] Hagen's theory is grounded in individual psychology and is consequently difficult to integrate with a theory of spatial organization. Dahrendorf works with a conflict model of social change in which the principal variable is the pattern of authority-dependency relationships that characterizes any organized social system. Because spatial systems are territorially organized systems of social relation, the Dahrendorf model was selected as a promising beginning for formulating a general theory of polarized development.[13]

The theory is stated in the five sections that follow. In the first section, "development" is distinguished from "growth" and is characterized as an innovative process leading to the structural transformation of social systems. Societies that fail to achieve such transformations either become arrested in their growth or start to degenerate as their internal order breaks down into increasingly unstable and random relations.

In the second section, six conditions favorable to innovation are discussed. These conditions, it is claimed, are generally present in large and rapidly growing urban systems or, more generally, at the points of highest potential interaction in a "communication field."

In the third section, innovation is linked to the concepts of power and authority in territorially organized social (spatial) systems. Innovations enhance the potential power of the innovating agents over a given environment, but the full possibilities for increased environmental control can be extracted from an innovation only if the powers inherent in it are accepted as socially legitimate. Socially legitimate power is called authority. The conflict that may result from the efforts of innovating agents to legitimate their power is seen as frequently involving a wider conflict over the legitimacy of some or all authority-dependency relations within a spatial system. It consequently bears directly on the social bases for integration of that system and on its ability to achieve development.

In the fourth section, the preceding argument is carried further by a discussion of authority-dependency relations in a spatial system. If innovations coincide in large measure with the points of highest interaction potential in a communications field, their origin will be found in a relatively small number of centers of change from which innovations tend to diffuse downward (and outward) to areas of lower potential interaction. Centers of innovative change are called core regions. With respect to any core region, a periphery may be defined by its relation of dependency to the core. This relationship is further analyzed in terms of the self-reinforcing effects of core region growth and the rising opposition of peripheral elites to being dominated by the core, a condition that, to a large extent, is based on the core's superior capacities for innovation. The ensuing conflict may lead, among other possible outcomes, to a sharing of core region authority with peripheral areas or the replacement of core region elites by others whose political strength lies essentially with peripheral populations.

In the fifth section, the core-periphery relation is generalized to an hierarchical order of spatial systems. A nested hierarchy of five spatial systems is posited, including the world, the multination region, the nation, the subnational region, and the province. Specific mechanisms of core region dominance are discussed, and the ability to challenge core region elites successfully is stated as a basic condition for the structural transformation of spatial systems. This can occur through the establishment of new core regions in the periphery and the gradual linkage of core regions, old as well as new, into more encompassing spatial systems. One result of this process will be the exponential growth of innovations and the consequent acceleration of developmental change in society.

The chapter concludes with a brief discussion concerning the relation of the general theory to existing theories of regional growth. The latter are shown to be special cases of the general theory of polarized development.

The Theory

DEVELOPMENT AS INNOVATION

1.1. (D)* Historical progress may be understood as the temporal succession of one sociocultural paradigm by another.[14] Simon Kuznets attributes this succession of paradigms to the appearance of what he calls epochal innovations.[15] He writes:

> The pattern of life during the epoch must be seen as the realization of the potentialities involved in the single complex identified as the epochal innovation. . . . To put it in technical terms, the epoch must be defined so that a single trend line can be effectively fitted to it.[16]

These innovations have the capacity of transforming social values in such a way that all presuccession history will tend to be rewritten from the vantage point of new perspectives. Epochal innovations are self-validating because initial opposition to them is changed into support, and a new world view, expressing the new norms, is born.[17]

According to Kuznets, the major innovation of our own epoch is the "extended application of science to problems of economic production."[18] This innovation—in reality a vast complex of interlocking institutional, technical, and cultural innovations—had long antecedents in the past.[19] It began as a series of isolated innovations that occurred at different moments in history and gradually became linked to each other, inducing a structural transformation of the traditional social system from which they had emerged. The transformation toward which contemporary—or modern—development is moving is a social system that has a high capacity continuously to generate and adapt to innovative change.[20]

1.2. (D) In accordance with this interpretation, development may be studied as a discontinuous, cumulative process that occurs as a series of elementary innovations that become organized into innovative clusters and finally into large-scale systems of innovation.[21] The innovations may be technical or institutional and, if the latter, may be usefully subsumed under the customary categories of social, economic, political, and cultural.

1.2.1. (D) With reference to societal systems, *growth* should be conceptually distinguished from *development*. The former refers to an expansion of the system in one or more dimensions without a change in its structure. Such growth normally follows the general form of an

* D stands for a statement of definition.

S-curve so that if system-wide growth is to continue, a transformation of the constraining structural relations becomes necessary.[22]

1.2.2. (D) *Development* refers to the unfolding of the creative possibilities inherent in society. But this can occur only if growth is allowed to pass through a series of successive structural transformations of the system.

1.2.3. (D) Societies that fail to achieve such transformations either become arrested in their growth or start to degenerate as their internal order breaks down into increasingly unstable and random relations.

1.3. Development always occurs through asynchronic processes in which leading, innovative forces arise from or are injected into an existing mold of traditional structures.

1.3.1. (D) No particular model of traditional society has to be assumed; traditional is simply that which, at any given moment, is established and with respect to which an innovation is defined.

1.3.2. The cumulative effect of successive innovations is to transform the established structure of society by attracting creative or innovative personalities into the enclaves of accelerated change;[23] by encouraging the formation of new values, attitudes, and behavior traits consistent with the innovation;[24] by fomenting a social environment favorable to innovative activity; and by bringing into existence yet further innovations.[25]

THE CONDITIONS OF INNOVATION

2.1. (D) Invention is the act of conceiving and presenting new structural combinations of preexisting cultural elements or ideas; it may also refer to the result of an inventive act; invention is an idea or artifact discovered.

2.2. (D) Innovation is the successful introduction of ideas or artifacts perceived as new into a given social system.[26]

2.2.1. (D) Innovations may be based on ideas or prototypes that are invented, borrowed, or imitated. What is already established in one place may, by borrowing or imitation, become an innovation in another. It is its perception as something new that is the decisive criterion for innovation.

2.2.2. Every innovation requires a measure of organization and adaptation to the conditions and functional requirements of the medium into which it is introduced or, alternatively, a change in certain aspects of the medium itself. Innovation and medium must be structurally compatible.[27]

2.2.3. Innovations require individuals or institutions that will organize the necessary resources and assume the risks of failure; every innovation requires an innovative agent.[28]

2.3. The likelihood that innovative activities will be generated at a given location and be ultimately successful depends on six basic conditions, including:

2.3.1. *First*, the number of problems resistant to solution by traditional means.[29] This may be said to represent the effective demand for innovation. The greater this demand, the higher will be the probability of innovation.

2.3.2. *Second*, the probability that two or more previously unconnected mental frames of reference have for mutual confrontation.[30] Such confrontations raise the likelihood that innovations will occur.

2.3.2.1. (D) This probability may be expressed in terms of a concept of information exchange or communication in open systems.

2.3.2.1.1. (D) For every territorially organized social system—henceforth to be called spatial system—a communication field may be defined in which the probability of information exchange may vary from o to 100, forming a spatial frequency distribution.[31]

2.3.2.1.2. Innovations are more likely than elsewhere to occur at those points in a given communication field where the probability of information exchange is relatively high (see 2.3.2.).

2.3.3. *Third*, the capacity of the existing social system to absorb proposed innovations without itself undergoing major structural changes.[32] The greater this capacity, the greater will be the probability of innovation.

2.3.3.1. Hierarchical, centrally controlled social systems (Type I) tend to have a relatively low capacity for continuously generating and absorbing innovations.[33]

2.3.3.2. Nonhierarchical, multicentric, horizontally integrated social systems (Type II) tend to have a high capacity for generating and absorbing innovations.[34]

2.3.3.2.1. Where power approximates an even distribution among multiple centers of decision, however, and agreement on objectives is lacking among them, Type II systems may also display a low capacity for innovation because multiple interests in a horizontally integrated social system are able to exercise effective veto power over the initiatives of any one of them.[35]

2.3.3.3. From the standpoint of innovative capacity, the optimum system of social organization appears to be a combination of Types I and II where leadership, central information, and certain conflict-resolving functions are hierarchically superimposed upon Type II systems.[36]

2.3.4. *Fourth*, the frequency of innovative personality traits in the population of a given society.[37] The greater the innovative propensity of a population, the higher is likely to be the frequency of innovation in that population.

2.3.4.1. Sociocultural systems will significantly differ in the proportion of innovative personalities they produce or attract from the outside.

2.3.4.2. The propensity to innovation may also result from the social position occupied by certain collectivities. Foreign immigrant groups or deviant subcultures often account for a substantial share of total innovative activity in a society.[38]

2.3.5. *Fifth*, the ability to marshal the human and material resources sufficient for effective innovation, from the initial introduction of a new idea to its ultimate adoption and diffusion through the social system.

2.3.6. *Sixth*, the social rewards offered for innovative activity. The higher these rewards, the more are innovations likely to occur.

2.4. Historically, conditions especially favorable to innovation are generally present in large and rapidly growing urban systems.[39] Ten conditions appear to favor innovative activity in the urban complex (see 1.3.2.).

2.4.1. The pressure of unprecedented problems resulting from rapid growth, high densities, and the presence of culturally heterogeneous population groups in large cities generates urgent demands for solution (see 2.3.1.).

2.4.2. The traditional frames of reference are incapable of solving many of the new problems arising from accelerated urbanization (see 2.3.1.).

2.4.3. The bankruptcy of traditional mental frames leads to an intense search for new and adequate solutions (see 2.3.1.).

2.4.4. A relatively heavy volume of information from outside the urban center transmits new knowledge together with new ways of looking at the world. Elements of "exotic" culture encounter in the city a pattern of established beliefs and practices from which they are set apart and with which they often come into conflict (see 2.3.2.1.2. and 2.3.4.2.).

2.4.5. The resulting clash of new and existing culture elements in an environment of high potential interaction leads to substantial exposure of certain population groups to different mental frames of reference (see 2.3.2.).

2.4.6. The large city or urban region tends to have a relatively loose, if complex, social structure as well as a relatively diffused structure of power. Both conditions will tend to encourage and facilitate experiment and innovation (see 2.3.3.).

2.4.7. The large city or urban region tends to attract creative personality types in a proportion greater than their frequency in the population as a whole (see 2.3.4.).

2.4.8. The large city or urban region provides exceptional opportunities for marshalling the necessary human and material resources for innovation (see 2.3.5.).

2.4.9. The large city or urban region reinforces creative responses to new situations by extending economic, social, and political rewards for innovative activity (see 2.3.6.).

2.4.10. A process of innovation sustained over long periods of time is likely to lead to the institutionalization of this process.

2.5. These ten conditions, however, are not equally satisfied in all large-scale and expanding urban systems. Holding size constant, urban systems may differ, for example, with respect to their rates of growth (and consequently the urgency of their demands), cultural heterogeneity, degree of openness to external information, and social organization conducive to innovation.[40] Theocratic cities, for instance, will tend to be less innovative than large commercial-industrial centers.

2.5.1. The historical correlation between large city size and rapid urbanization on the one hand and innovation on the other seems nevertheless to be well established, especially if it is borne in mind that innovation may result from borrowing and imitating no less than from invention.

INNOVATION, POWER, AND AUTHORITY IN SPATIAL SYSTEMS

3.1. (D) To have power is to exercise a measure of autonomy in decisions over a given environment and to have the ability to carry out these decisions.[41]

3.1.1. Successful innovation gives to both innovators and initial adopters a relative advantage over possible competitors in controlling a given environment. Successful innovation tends to increase the potential power of innovators.

3.2. The full possibilities for increased control over an environment can be extracted from an innovation only when the potential power inherent in it is institutionalized: in other words, when the full exercise of its power is accepted as socially legitimate.

3.2.1. (D) Socially legitimate power will be called authority.[42]

3.2.2. Innovators generally seek to translate a prospective gain in power into some form of (legitimate) authority.[43]

3.2.3. Where the innovation is socially compatible (see 2.2.2.), this process is relatively automatic. Society will reward the innovator with esteem and invest him with a measure of authority (see 2.3.6.).

3.3. Where the innovation is incompatible with the social medium, however, efforts to render legitimate a prospective gain in power will put innovators in conflict with the holders of established authority (see 1.3.).

3.3.1. Individuals or groups seeking to legitimize prospective gains in power frequently establish alliances among themselves in order to confront established authorities from a position of collective and, consequently, greater strength.

3.3.2. (D) Such alliances lead to the formation of counter-elites to established authority.

3.4. (D) The presence of groups exercising authority within a territorially organized social (spatial) system implies the existence of other groups dependent on them for vital decisions.[44]

3.4.1. Spatial systems are integrated through a given structure of authority-dependency relations that is maintained partly by a belief in the legitimacy of the relation itself and partly by coercion.[45]

3.5. The conflict between innovating counter-elites and already established authorities (see 3.3.) is often posed as a wider conflict over the legitimacy of some or all authority-dependency relations within a given spatial system.[46] It is consequently a conflict that may bear directly on the social bases for integration of that system (see 3.4.1.).

3.5.1. This conflict can have four possible outcomes:

3.5.1.1. *Suppression*: counter-elites are prevented from gaining access to positions of authority (their attempt to legitimize prospective gains in power is frustrated).

3.5.1.2. *Neutralization*: established authorities oscillate between acceptance and rejection of the proposed innovations, frequently adopting their external forms but managing them so as to neutralize their effects.[47] Counter-elites fail in gaining full access to authority.

3.5.1.3. *Cooptation*: counter-elites are drawn into the established structure of authority.[48] Their innovations may be adopted but in a highly restricted form. Counter-elites are pacified by being allowed to share to a limited extent in the exercise of established authority.

3.4.1.4. *Replacement*: counter-elites are successful in replacing the established authorities and substituting their own authority for them.

3.5.2. Conflict over authority may take either legitimate or illegitimate forms.

3.5.2.1. (D) Conflict is legitimate when it (1) occurs within a framework of rules established for regulating social conflict and/or (2) does not challenge the fundamental bases for social integration of the spatial system (see 3.2.3. and 3.4.1.).

3.5.2.2. (D) Conflict is illegitimate when it fails to meet either of these two criteria.

3.6. Where the outcome of conflict over authority is resolved in favor of the counter-elites (see 3.5.1.3. and 3.5.1.4.), the existing structure of authority-dependency relations and, consequently, the social bases for integration of the spatial system will be transformed (see 3.5.).

3.6.1. The magnitude of this transformation will depend on the extent of the claims made on authority.

3.6.1.1. Since authority in complex spatial systems tends to be fragmented, it may be possible for the system to absorb relatively minor and compatible innovations without a change in its fundamental structure; in this case, the effects of individual innovations are contained although their cumulative impact may be very large.

3.6.1.2. Substantial transformation occurs when authority-dependency relations important for the social integration of the system are successfully challenged. In this case it is possible to speak of the "development" of that system (see 1.2.1.).

3.6.2. If successive counter-elites are gradually absorbed into the established ruling stratum (see 3.5.1.3.), the transformation of the social bases for integration will tend to occur as a gradual, evolutionary process.

3.6.3. If the conflict is resolved with innovating groups replacing the established authorities (see 3.5.1.4.), the consequent changes in the social bases for integration will tend to be violent, rapid, and far-reaching.

3.6.4. Having once gained access to positions of authority, former counter-elites may either foreclose further innovative efforts or create a social environment capable of absorbing successive innovating groups into an adaptive system of authority-dependency relations (see 3.6.1.).

AUTHORITY-DEPENDENCY RELATIONS IN A SPATIAL SYSTEM

4.1. Development, viewed as occurring through a discontinuous but cumulative process of innovation (see 1.2. and 1.3.), will tend to have its origin in a relatively small number of *centers of change* located at the points of highest potential interaction within a communication field (see 2.3.2.1.2.); innovations will tend to spread downward and outward from these centers to areas where the probability of potential interaction is lower.[49]

4.1.1. (D) Major centers of innovative change will be called *core regions*; all other areas within a given spatial system will be defined as *peripheral*.[50] More precisely, core regions are territorially organized subsystems of society that have a high capacity for innovative change; peripheral regions are subsystems whose development path is determined chiefly by core region institutions with respect to which they stand in a relation of substantial dependency.

4.1.2. (D) Peripheral regions can be identified by their relations of dependency to a core area.

4.1.3. (D) Core and periphery together constitute a complete spatial system.

4.1.4. (D) A spatial system is integrated through a pattern of authority-dependency relationships that is focused on the dominant core regions (see 3.4. and 3.4.1.).

4.1.4.1. The domination of the periphery by its core is the result of earlier and critical innovations that were incorporated into the central authority structure of the system (see 3.5.1.3. and 3.5.1.4.).[51]

4.1.5. The conflict over the legitimacy of established authority-dependency relationships resulting from continuing core region growth may undermine the bases for social integration of the spatial system and give rise to prolonged conflict between core and peripheral elites.

4.1.5.1. This conflict will be especially severe where core region elites belong to a cultural tradition different from that of peripheral populations.

4.2. Four major propositions may be advanced concerning the relations of core regions to their peripheries:

4.2.1. First, core regions impose a condition of organized dependency on their peripheries.

4.2.1.1. This dependency relation results from a penetration of the periphery by institutions that are effectively controlled by core region authorities (see 5.2.1.).

4.2.1.1.1. In the perspective of the periphery, many of these institutions will be perceived as innovations (see 2.2.1. and 4.1.4.1.).

4.2.1.1.2. Peripheral elites will attempt to resist those innovations that they regard as threatening their own authority positions and as imposing a lasting dependency on external authorities (see 3.3.).

4.2.1.1.3. From the standpoint of the periphery, core region elites may be viewed as counter-elites intent on usurping peripheral authority positions (see 3.3.2.). However, where the structural conditions are roughly compatible, certain core region innovations may be integrated into the periphery with relatively little difficulty (see 2.2.2.).

4.2.1.1.4. Massive psychological, material, and coercive resources at the disposal of core region elites give them a significant advantage in their struggle to reduce peripheral areas to a status of dependency. Local elites may be suppressed, neutralized, coopted, or replaced (see 3.5.1.).

4.2.1.2. (D) Successful penetration of the periphery by core region institutions implies that decisions vitally affecting local populations will henceforward be made by relevant core region authorities.

4.2.2. The process by which core regions consolidate their dominance over the periphery tends to be self-reinforcing.[52] This may be ascribed to six major feedback effects of core region growth:

4.2.2.1. *Dominance effect*, or the steady weakening of the peripheral economy by a net transfer of natural, human and capital resources to the core.[53]

4.2.2.2. *Information effect*, or the increase in potential interaction within a given core region resulting from its own growth in population, production and income. Among other things, this effect will tend to induce a higher rate of innovation (see 2.4.4. and 2.4.5.).[54]

4.2.2.3. *Psychological effect*, or the creation of conditions favorable to continued innovation at the core, such as rendering the opportunities for innovation more visible, reducing the risks of innovation through imitation, and creating expectations for further innovation (see 2.4.5., 2.4.7. and 2.4.9.).[55]

4.2.2.4. *Modernization effect,* or the transformation of existing social values, behavior, and institutions in the direction of greater acceptance of and conformity with rapid cumulative change through innovation (see 1.3.2.).[56]

4.2.2.5. *Linkage effects,* or the tendency of innovations to breed other innovations by creating new service demands as well as new markets for the services the core region is itself able to supply to other areas. However, not all innovations will have the same capacity in this respect; the multiplier or linkage effects of certain innovations will be greater than for others.[57]

4.2.2.6. *Production effects,* or the creation of an attractive reward structure for innovative activity operating through the exploitation by innovators of their temporary monopoly position, the appearance of linked systems of innovations, and growing specialization. All of these will tend to increase economic returns, while increasing external economies to scale and urbanization economies (*e.g.,* greater efficiency in the use of social overhead facilities) will tend to reduce the costs of innovation (see 2.4.10).[58]

4.2.3. Introducing core region innovations into the periphery will augment the flow of information to the dependent region from the core (see 4.2.1.1.). This will tend to be an unanticipated side-effect of core region dominance.

4.2.3.1. Sustained contact with the core region will tend to arouse portions of the peripheral population, not only to possible new ways of life, but also to their own comparative disadvantage in gaining access to them. New desires and frustrations will encourage demands for greater regional autonomy in areas of vital decision and may lead to a prolonged conflict with the core (see 4.1.5.).[59]

4.2.3.2. Individuals and groups most directly exposed to information originating in core regions will gradually awaken to the periphery's and their own dependency (and powerlessness) and will be among the first to insist upon greater autonomy for the periphery. Alternatively, they will emigrate to the core to be drawn there into the established structures of authority.

4.2.3.3. To stem off the pressures for greater autonomy on part of the periphery and possibly to avoid violent conflict, core region elites may move to implement a policy of limited decentralization which, among other things, may project the build-up in the periphery of new, subsidiary core regions.[60]

4.2.4. If the outcome of this conflict should favor the interests of core region elites, the subsequent acceleration of spread effects to the peripheral region will lead to a substantial sharing of decision power between the old and newly implanted core areas (see 3.5.1.3.).[61]

4.2.4.1. Such sharing of authority is not likely to be fully equal, however. In many important respects, the spatial system will continue to be dominated by the older core regions; the relation will be asymmetrical.

4.2.4.2. But such an outcome is not inevitable. In the process of extending their institutions into the periphery, older core regions may at some point exhaust their capacities for further creative response and decline to a subordinate, peripheral position relative to the new cores they helped to bring into existence.

4.2.4.2.1. Specifically, former peripheral elites successful in their endeavors to rise to positions of core region authority may act to foreclose further innovative activity (see 3.6.4.), while the positive feedback effects of growth in the old core regions (see 4.2.2.) may be weakened as control over their former peripheries is lost.[62]

POLARIZED DEVELOPMENT IN A HIERARCHY OF SPATIAL SYSTEMS

5.1. (D) Core regions are located within a nested hierarchy of spatial systems (see 4.1.1.).

5.1.1. (D) Possible spatial systems are the world, the multination region, the nation, the subnational region, and the province.

5.1.1.1. (D) Whether or not a given area constitutes a spatial system depends on the pattern of its internal relations. Where a core can be shown to dominate some of the vital decisions of populations in areas external to itself, a spatial system will be said to exist.

5.1.2. A given spatial system may have more than one core region.

5.1.3. The territorial extent of a given core region will tend to vary with the physical size or scope of the relevant spatial system of which it forms a part. For a major world region, the appropriate core may be a vast and complex area such as the megalopolis of the northeastern part of the United States. At the level of provincial systems, the relevant core may be a single city region of moderate size.

5.1.4. Core regions generally perform a wide variety of functions for their dependent areas; some specialization may occur, however, especially in the cores of lower-order spatial systems.[63]

5.2. Five major propositions concerning the role of core regions in the development of spatial systems may be suggested:

5.2.1. Core regions organize the dependence of their respective peripheries through systems of supply, market, and administrative areas (see 4.2.1.).[64]

5.2.1.1. As centers of production and consumption, core regions organize their peripheries into sets of supply areas for furnishing the raw materials, food stuffs, and semiprocessed commodities needed by the core regions.

5.2.1.2. As supply centers, core regions organize their peripheries into sets of market areas (*e.g.*, through the establishment of regional sales and service offices or a "colonial" pattern of transport and communication services that generally serves the needs of the core region more than those of the periphery).

5.2.1.3. As centers of legitimate decision-making power, core regions organize their peripheries into sets of administrative areas for the purpose of securing central bureaucratic domination over them.[65]

5.2.2. For any spatial system, a loose hierarchy of core regions may be identified in accord with the functional importance of each core for specified characteristics of system performance. This hierarchy will tend to be asymmetrical, however, with some functions placing a core region at one hierarchical level while others may indicate a different position.[66]

5.2.2.1. For the same spatial system, any two core regions of approximately the same level in the hierarchy will tend to have a greater and more balanced volume of mutual interaction, modified by distance, than either will have with individual lower-order cores.

5.2.2.2. Within a given spatial system, the competition for the exploitation of specific innovations will be greatest among core regions of approximately the same hierarchical level.

5.2.2.3. A core region may, at the same time, belong to the hierarchies of two spatial systems. Thus, a second-order core region for a higher spatial system may also appear as a first-order core for a lower ranking system. The inverse of this situation is not possible.

5.2.3. Core regions systematically transmit impulses of innovation to the peripheries they dominate (see 4.2.1.1.).[67]

Three further propositions may help to clarify this process.

5.2.3.1. The rate of innovation tends to be greatest in core regions corresponding to high-level systems. Innovations tend to be propagated from high-order cores downward to lower-order cores of the same spatial system or laterally to similarly ranking core regions in parallel systems.[68]

5.2.3.2. The successful diffusion of innovations from given core regions will partly depend on the structural and behavioral characteristics of the receiving areas which must, in at least some respects, be consistent with those of the sending area;[69] on the ability of the innovative forces to overcome the resistance of local authorities likely to be encountered (see 4.2.1.1.2.); and on the general conditions prevailing in the receiving areas that may favor or not a sustained process of innovation (see 2.3.3.).[70]

5.2.3.3. Because of their greater and more effective control over both external and policy variables and because of the larger volume of resources at their command, higher-order core regions are more autonomous than lower-order cores with regard to their ability to make critical development decisions.[71]

5.2.3.3.1. Because of the asymmetrical nature of their relationship to higher-order cores and their partial dependency on them, all lower-order cores are also peripheral to a set of dominant core regions (see 4.1.2.). All propositions concerning core-periphery relations stated above apply also, therefore, to the hierarchical relations *among* core regions in Section 4.

5.2.4. Up to a certain point in time, the self-reinforcing character of core region growth (see 4.2.2.) will tend to have positive results for the development process of the relevant spatial system; eventually, however, it will become dysfunctional, unless the spread effects of core region development to the periphery can be accelerated and the periphery's dependence on the core region reduced (see 4.2.3.).[72] The approach of this critical turning point will be registered in the growing political and social tensions between core and periphery (see 4.1.5.) that are likely to drain core region strength and reduce its capacity for further development (see 1.2.3.).

5.2.5. The probability of innovation will increase over the surface of a given spatial system with increases in the probability of information exchange over that system.[73] This tendency—the result of a successful challenge of core region autonomy by their peripheries—will induce the physical spread of existing core regions, a weakening of their hierarchical order, the emergence of new core regions on the periphery, and the gradual incorporation of large parts of the periphery into one or more system cores.[74]

5.2.5.1. Enclaves of economic backwardness will appear in the areas lying between expanding core regions and/or in limited urban sectors of the cores themselves.[75]

5.2.5.2. The theoretical upper limit of core region spread is given by the extension of a single core region over the inhabited parts of the entire globe.

Relation of the General Theory to Current Theories of Regional Growth

As noted earlier, existing growth theory for regional economies is fundamentally a variant of classical location theory.[76] The economic growth of a single region is usually traced to some natural and consequently immobile resource for which an external demand exists. Investments to exploit this resource are attracted and lead to the further expansion of productive activity in the region through the stimulation of local demand and the creation of substantial external economies.[77] The region's growth relative to that of competitive subnational economies is in the long run made to depend on the extent of its participation in the rapidly expanding sectors of the total economy, but this participation can similarly be treated as a question in the economics of location. Finally, it is customary to emphasize that any welfare disequilibria that may result from the differential location behavior of economic activity will ultimately be restored to balance by compensatory flows of labor (and capital) from "surplus" to "deficit" regions.[78] That, in brief, is the substance of contemporary regional growth theory; the General Theory of Polarized Development discussed here goes considerably beyond it.

The General Theory treats economic growth as a function of changes in the structures that inevitably limit a system's capacity for expansion and, in the specific case of growth based on the application of science to problems of economic production, also the system's capacity for the continuous generation and absorption of innovations. This formulation assigns a decisive influence to the institutional and organizational framework of society and, specifically, to the patterns of authority and dependency that result from the unusual capacity of certain areas to serve as cradles of innovation. In this view, it is by no means indifferent what regions organize the new investments and make the relevant decisions on location, or what purposes are to be served by these activities. Dominant core and dominated periphery together constitute a relatively stable spatial system in which the latter is successfully "colonized" chiefly to sustain the continued growth of the former.

In the final analysis, however, the further growth of core regions is constrained by the tensions that tend to build up from the ever more visible discrepancies in the rates of expansion and modernization between core and periphery. The increasing flow of information from core to periphery, together with an aroused awareness of the conditions of their own dependency on the part of potentially modernizing elites in the periphery, produces conflict with core region authorities over the extent of permissible autonomy. This conflict, capable of seriously affecting the social bases of integration in a spatial system, may have four possible outcomes: first, the violent repression of peripheral elites by the core so that the existing spatial system is maintained even though its overall potential for growth may decline; second, the neutralization of peripheral elites, a process that may occasionally lead to a gradual, if inadequate, modification of the system's authority-dependency structure; third, the replacement of core region elites by peripheral elites followed by either the acceleration of system-wide growth (where the new elites are dedicated modernizers) or stagnation and even retrogression (where the new elites follow a traditional orientation); and fourth, the cooptation of peripheral elites by core region elites, leading to a more equitable sharing of powers that may be accompanied by a process of political and economic decentralization and the creation of new, or the expansion of already existing, core regions in the periphery. Under cooptation, the authority-dependency relations between cores and their peripheries are likely to diminish and may eventually disappear altogether except for relatively minor enclaves of economic backwardness located in interstitial areas or in limited urban sectors in the cores themselves. The actual working out of core-periphery relations, however, is made exceedingly complex by the hierarchical superposition of spatial systems ranging from subnational province to a (theoretical) world system.

In the context of the General Theory, contemporary regional growth theory may therefore be treated as a special case, applicable only to situations where the dualism of core and periphery is of relatively little consequence, such as the reasonably advanced and integrated spatial systems of the United States, West Germany, or Sweden. It is applicable neither to the industrializing countries nor to multinational regions where core-periphery dependency relations are still predominant influences. In their case, the transformation of authority-dependency patterns in spatial systems is a fundamental condition of development and, consequently, also of sustained economic growth.

Notes

1. Between theory and practice there is inevitable tension. Nevertheless, they mutually enrich and reinforce each other. See John Friedmann and Walter Stöhr, "The Uses of Regional Science: Policy Planning in Chile," in *Regional Science Association Papers* 18 (1967), (European Congress, Vienna, 1966): 207–22.

2. Horst Siebert has recently published an excellent survey of the literature: "Regionalwirtschaftslehre in den USA: Ein Überblick," *Jahrbuch für Sozialwissenshaft* 20 (1969): 51–83. For an earlier but still excellent review in English, see John R. Meyer, "Regional Economics: A Survey, *American Economic Review*, 53 (1963): 19–54.

3. An excellent summary statement of classical location theory is William Alonso, "Location Theory," in John Friedmann and William Alonso, eds., *Regional Development and Planning: A Reader* (Cambridge, Mass.: M.I.T. Press, 1964), pp. 78–106. For a more extended treatment, see Martin Beckmann, *Location Theory* (New York: Random House, Inc., 1968) and L. H. Klaassen, *Methods of Selecting Industries for Depressed Areas* (Paris: Organization for Economic Cooperation and Development, 1967).

4. On the subject of industrial complex analysis, see chapter 9 of Walter Isard, *Methods of Regional Analysis* (Cambridge, Mass.: The Technology Press of the Massachusetts Institute of Technology, 1960). This still serves as a useful introduction to the subject. On the concept of *pôle de croissance*, see François Perroux, *L'économie du XXe siècle* (Paris: Presses Universitaires de France, 1961), Part II. Other French literature on the subject is cited in *Cuadernos de la Sociedad Venezolana de Planificación* (1963): 74–77, and in Niles M. Hansen, "Development Pole Theory in a Regional Context," *Kyklos* 20 (1967): 709–26. An excellent recent contribution to growth pole theory is Heiko Körner, "Industrielle Entwicklungspole als Instrumente der Regionalpolitik in Entwicklungsländern," *Kyklos* 20 (1967): 684–708, which also contains comprehensive references. The entire body of literature is critically reviewed by David F. Darwent, *Growth Pole and Growth Center Concepts: A Review, Evaluation and Bibliography*, Working Paper No. 89, Center for Planning and Development Research, Institute of Urban and Regional Development, University of California at Berkeley, October 1968.

5. Edwin von Böventer, "Spatial Organization Theory as a Basis for Regional Planning," *Journal of the American Institute of Planners* 30 (1964): 90–99; and by the same author, "Toward a Unified Theory of Spatial Economic Structure," *Regional Science Association Papers* 10 (Zurich Congress, 1962): 163–88. Other major theoretical statements are: Walter Isard, *Location and Space Economy* (Cambridge, Mass.: The Technology Press of Massachusetts Institute of Technology, 1956); L. Lefeber, *Allocation in Space Production, Transport and Industrial Location* (Amsterdam, North Holland Publishing Co., 1968); H. C. Bos, *Spatial Dispersion of Economic Activity* (Rotterdam, The Netherlands: Rotterdam University Press, 1965); and Brian J. L. Berry, *Geography of Market Centers and Retail Distribution*. Foundations of Economic Geography Series. (Englewood Cliffs, N.J.: Prentice-Hall, Inc., 1967).

6. Harvey S. Perloff (with Vera W. Dodds), *How a Region Grows: Area Development in the U.S. Economy*. Supplementary Paper No. 17. (New York: Committee for Economic Development, 1963). See also Charles M. Tiebout, *The Community Economic Base Study*. Supplementary Paper No. 16. (New York: Committee for Economic Development, 1962).

7. Harvey S. Perloff, Edgar S. Dunn, Jr., Eric E. Lampard, and Richard F. Muth, *Regions, Resources and Economic Growth* (Baltimore, Md.: The Johns Hopkins Press,

1960); George H. Borts and Jerome L. Stein, *Economic Growth in a Free Market* (New York and London: Columbia University Press, 1964); John Friedmann, *Regional Economic Policy: A Case Study of Venezuela* (Cambridge, Mass.: M.I.T. Press, 1966); and L. B. M. Mennes, Jan Tinbergen, and J. George Waardenburg, *The Elements of Space in Development Planning* (Amsterdam and London: North Holland Publishing Co., 1969).

8. For a critique of equilibrium models in regional analysis, see John Friedmann, *Regional Economic Policy*, chap. 1.

9. Albert O. Hirschman, *The Strategy of Economic Development* (New Haven: Yale University Press, 1958), and Gunnar Myrdal, *Rich Lands and Poor* (New York: Harper and Brothers, 1957).

10. Horst Siebert, *Zur Theorie des regionalen Wirtschaftswachstums* (Tübingen: J. C. B. Mohr, 1967), translated as *Regional Economic Growth: Theory and Policy* (Scranton, Pa.: International Textbook Co., 1969).

11. General systems theory is relevant here. See, for example, James G. Miller, "Living Systems: Basic Concepts," *Behavioral Science* 10 (1965): 193–237; "Living Systems: Structure and Process," *Behavioral Science* 10 (1965): 337–79; and "Living Systems: Cross-Level Hypotheses," *Behavioral Science* 10 (1965): 380–411. On the concept of nonphysical space, see François Perroux, "Economic Space: Theory and Applications," in John Friedmann and William Alonso, eds., *Regional Development and Planning*, pp. 21–36.

12. Everett E. Hagen, *On the Theory of Social Change* (Homewood, Ill.: The Dorsey Press, 1962); Ralph Dahrendorf, *Class Conflict in Industrial Society* (Stanford, Cal.: Stanford University Press, 1959).

13. This is not the place for a full critique of Dahrendorf's model. Nevertheless, some important qualifications must be mentioned because they are relevant to what follows. According to Dahrendorf, authority-dependency relations are maintained only by restraint and coercion (pp. 158 ff.). Without denying the fundamental importance of coercion in system maintenance, it is necessary to point out that social values also play a significant role. This is implicit in the legitimacy accorded authority, and more specificially, the authority-dependency relation itself. Any conflict arising out of a given authority-dependency relation may therefore be either legitimate or illegitimate. It is illegitimate only when the legitimacy of the authority is itself put in question. Not all social conflicts, however, turn on this issue.

A second objection to Dahrendorf is his insistence that for any given social system there is only one authority when, in fact, authority is rarely, if ever, either unitary or absolute (pp. 296 ff.). Any complex organization is structured as a system of polyarchy in which there are many leaders whose authority is limited with regard to both function and the control of the leaders themselves, and is limited by those who are dependent on them. On this point, see the excellent discussion in Robert A. Dahl and Charles E. Lindblom, *Politics, Economics and Welfare* (New York: Harper and Brothers, 1953), Part IV.

14. This is the basic thesis of Thomas S. Kuhn's excellent study, *The Structure of Scientific Revolutions* (Chicago: The University of Chicago Press, 1962). A closely related idea is Joseph A. Schumpeter's concept of "creative destruction" explained in *Capitalism, Socialism and Democracy* (New York and London: Harper and Brothers, 1947), chap. 6.

15. Simon Kuznets, *Modern Economic Growth* (New Haven and London: Yale University Press, 1966), chap. 1.

16. Ibid., pp. 4.

17. Thomas S. Kuhn, *Structure of Scientific Revolutions*, chap. 10.

18. Ibid., pp. 9.

19. Charles C. Gillespie, *The Edge of Objectivity: An Essay in the History of Scientific Ideas* (Princeton, N.J.: Princeton University Press, 1960).

20. This view of the development process is elaborated in a brilliant essay by Manfred Halpern, "The Revolution of Modernization in National and International Society," in Carl J. Friedrich, ed., *Revolution*. Yearbook of the American Society for Political and Legal Philosophy, Vol. VIII (New York: Atherton Press, 1966). According to S. N. Eisenstadt, "the structural propensity to continuous change" is a crucial aspect of modernization. See "Breakdowns of Modernization," *Economic Development*

and Cultural Change 12 (1964): 347. For a more extended treatment, see Eisenstadt's *Modernization: Protest and Change* (Englewood Cliffs, N.J.: Prentice-Hall, Inc., 1966).

21. The view of development as innovation is fundamental to Hagen's analysis, *On the Theory of Social Change*. Less explicitly, innovation enters as a primary datum in Albert O. Hirschman's well-known study, *The Strategy of Economic Development*.

22. This extremely important principle is stated in K. E. Boulding, "Toward a General Theory of Growth," in Joseph J. Spengler and Otis Dudley Duncan, eds., *Population Theory and Policy* (New York: The Free Press, 1956), pp. 118–19. See also Chandler Morse, "Becoming versus Being Modern: An Essay on Institutional Change and Economic Development," in Chandler Morse *et al.*, *Modernization by Design: Social Change in the Twentieth Century* (Ithaca and London: Cornell University Press, 1969). The need for structural change lies, of course, also at the root of the developmental theories of Kuznets and Kuhn.

23. For detailed discussion of the concept of creative personality and its possible role in the process of social change, see Everett E. Hagen, *On the Theory of Social Change*, chap. 5–7.

24. A basic postulate of the theory of cognitive dissonance is that perceptions, attitudes, and ultimately values tend to become consistent with experienced reality and thus to maintain (or reestablish) the psychological equilibrium of a person. See Leon Festinger, *Theory of Cognitive Dissonance* (New York: Harper and Row, 1957).

25. For an extended discussion of this idea, see especially Hirschman, *Strategy of Economic Development*, chap. 4 and 6, and Gunnar Myrdal, *Rich Lands and Poor*, chap. 3.

26. The definitions of "invention" and "innovation" are generally consistent with the usage in Everett M. Rogers, *Diffusion of Innovations* (New York: The Free Press, 1962), pp. 195 and 13 respectively. Rogers, however, further distinguishes between innovation as a new idea and its successful introduction or adoption, a distinction not made here. Unfortunately, the empirical measurement of invention and innovative activity presents countless problems for which no adequate solution exists at the moment. For a penetrating discussion, see the papers in National Bureau of Economic Research, *The Rate and Direction of Inventive Activity: Economic and Social Factors*, Part I (Princeton, N.J.: Princeton University Press, 1962).

27. Rogers, *Diffusion of Innovations*, pp. 127–30.

28. In usage, the term innovative agent here is roughly analogous to Schumpeter's image of the "entrepreneur." See Joseph Schumpeter, *The Theory of Economic Development* (New York: Oxford University Press, 1961).

29. Kuhn, *Structure of Scientific Revolutions*, chap. 6–9. See also Rogers, *Diffusion of Innovations*, p. 125.

30. Arthur Koestler, *The Act of Creation* (New York: Macmillan, 1964). Koestler refers to this basic mechanism as "bi-sociation."

31. The concept of a "communication field" in relation to urbanization is discussed in John Friedmann, "An Information Model of Urbanization," *Urban Affairs Quarterly* 4 (1968): 235–44. See also the related treatment of the "mean information field" in Torsten Hägerstrand, *Innovation Diffusion as a Spatial Process* (Chicago: University of Chicago Press, 1967), chap. VII.

32. The relation between organizational structure and innovation is discussed in James G. March and Herbert A. Simon, *Organizations* (New York and London: John Wiley & Sons, Inc., 1958), chap. 7.

33. According to Young and Moreno, historical experience in the United States suggests the following conclusion: "Social rigidity and political rigidity have been shown to be related to attributes of stagnant economic structure; they are inversely correlated with innovation, risk-taking, technical proficiency, organizational complexity, and distributive economic development, over and above the expected value of these attributes based on the general level of industrialization of these areas." Ruth C. Young and José A. Moreno, "Economic Development and Social Rigidity: A Comparative Study of the Forty-Eight States," *Economic Development and Cultural Change* 13 (1965): 449. See also Michel Crozier, *The Bureaucratic Phenomenon* (Chicago: University of Chicago Press, 1964).

34. This hypothesis is derived from Warren Bennis, "Beyond Bureaucracy"

104   *JOHN FRIEDMANN*

Trans-action 2 (1965): 31–35. See also Paul R. Lawrence and Jay W. Lorsch, *Organization and Environment* (Boston: Harvard University, Graduate School of Business Administration, 1967).

35. This thesis is brilliantly demonstrated in Edward C. Banfield's study of interest group politics in Chicago, *Political Influence* (New York: The Free Press, 1961). Its theoretical statement is found in James Q. Wilson, "Innovation in Organization: Notes Toward a Theory," in James D. Thompson, ed., *Approaches to Organizational Design* (Pittsburgh: University of Pittsburgh Press, 1966).

36. This appears to be the main conclusion of Emmette Redford, "Centralized and Decentralized Political Impacts on a Developing Economy: Interpretation of American Experience," *Comparative Administration Group Occasional Papers*, February 1967.

37. The concept of innovative personality is discussed by Everett Hagen, *On the Theory of Social Change*, pp. 88–97.

38. This point is stressed, for example, by Seymour Martin Lipset, "Values, Education, and Entrepreneurship," in Lipset and Solari, eds., *Elites in Latin America* (New York: Oxford University Press, 1967), pp. 3–60. It is a basic point also in Hagen, *On the Theory of Social Change*, chap. 12, and in Rogers, *Diffusion of Innovations*, pp. 196–98.

39. Wilbur R. Thompson, "Locational Differences in Inventive Effort and their Determinants," in National Bureau of Economic Research, *Rate and Direction of Inventive Activity*, pp. 253–72. Many of the hypotheses in this section are also consistent with the empirical findings of Alan R. Pred, *The Spatial Dynamics of U.S. Urban-Industrial Growth 1800–1914* (Cambridge, Mass.: M.I.T. Press, 1966), chap. 3. See also John Friedmann, "The Role of Cities in National Development," *American Behavioral Scientist* 12 (1969): 13–21.

40. On the variety of urban structures relative to economic growth and development, see Bert F. Hoselitz, "Generative and Parasitic Cities," in *Sociological Aspects of Economic Growth* (New York: The Free Press, 1960), chap. 8. An especially interesting study, relevant in this context, is A. L. Epstein, "Urbanization and Social Change in Africa," *Current Anthropology* 8 (1967): 275–84.

41. In this definition, I follow Dahrendorf, *Class Conflict*, p. 166, who, in turn, bases his concept on Max Weber. For Weber, power is the "probability that one actor within a social relationship will be in position to carry out his own will despite resistance, regardless of the basis on which this probability rests." I have found it convenient, however, to alter the wording of this definition. See also Hans Gerth and C. Wright Mills, "Power and Authority: A Summary," in Lewis A. Coser and Bernard Rosenberg, *Sociological Theory: A Book of Readings* (New York: The Macmillan Company, 1957 and 1964), pp. 156–58.

42. Dahrendorf, *Class Conflict*, p. 166.

43. Dahrendorf states that ". . . all that is creativity, innovation and development . . . is due to no small extent, to the operation of conflicts. . . ." Dahrendorf, *Class Conflict*, p. 208.

44. "Authority relations exist whenever there are people whose actions are subject to legitimate and sanctioned prescriptions that originate outside them but within social structure." Dahrendorf, *Class Conflict*, p. 168. See also pp. 171 ff.

45. Dahrendorf, *Class Conflict*, pp. 162–63. How this integration is achieved specifically through systems of communication is explored in Philip E. Jacob and James V. Toscano, *The Integration of Political Communities* (Philadelphia and New York: J. B. Lippincott Co., 1964). See especially the contributions of Karl W. Deutsch.

46. Ibid., p. 184. See also Gino Germani, "Social Change and Intergroup Conflict," in I. L. Horowitz, *The New Sociology* (New York: Oxford University Press, 1964), chap. 23.

47. S. N. Eisenstadt, "The Development of Socio-Political Centers at the Second Stage of Modernization—A Comparative Analysis of Two Types," *International Journal of Comparative Sociology* 7 (1966): 119–37.

48. According to the inventor of the concept, "The process of absorbing new elements into the leadership or policy-determining strata of an organization as a means of averting threats to its existence or stability is called coöptation." Philip Selznick, *TVA and the Grass Roots* (Berkeley, Cal.: University of California Press, 1949), p. 259.

49. Kuznets, *Modern Economic Growth*, chap. 1 and 9. Of the six variables identified as having a decisive influence on the probability of interaction, the communication variable is here singled out as having probably greater importance than the remaining ones. The surface of the communication field will subsequently have to be modified to take account of the other variables, including differences in the demand for innovation, pattern of social organization, frequency of innovative personality traits, initial resource availabilities, and the pattern of social rewards for innovation, if it is to give a faithful expression of localized capacity for generating innovations. Though relative values may change topographical details of the communication field as a result of this operation, its general morphology will probably remain the same.

Concerning the mechanisms of innovative spread, see Lawrence A. Brown, *Diffusion Processes and Location* (Philadelphia: Regional Science Research Institute, 1968).

50. The concept of core region and periphery were first introduced to systematic regional analysis in John Friedmann, *Regional Development Policy*. See especially chap. 2. The present definitions, however, go considerably beyond the first conceptualization.

51. No separate explanation for the origins of core regions is here offered (but see note 50). They are posited to arise at points of relative initial advantage in terms of the structure of a given communication field. This initial structure may be assumed to be the result of randomly operating forces. For a very interesting but more deterministic study of the economic origin of core regions, see Eugene Smolensky and Donald Ratajczak, "The Conception of Cities," *Explorations in Entrepreneurial History*, second series, 2 (1965): 90–131.

52. The implication of a relatively stable system of cities and regions has been frequently noted. See, for instance, the discussion by Eric E. Lampard, "The Evolving System of Cities in the United States: Urbanization and Economic Development," in Harvey S. Perloff and Lowdon Wingo, Jr., eds., *Issues in Urban Economics* (Baltimore: The Johns Hopkins Press, 1968), pp. 126–30.

53. Horst Siebert, *Regional Economic Growth*, pp. 57–76. The phenomenon is widely noted and politically one of the most explosive in regional relations.

54. Ibid., pp. 70–74.

55. For a penetrating discussion of this effect, see Heiko Körner, "Industrielle Entwicklungspole als Instrumente der Regionalpolitik."

56. Ibid.

57. Ibid.

58. Tibor Scitovsky, "Two Concepts of External Economies," in *Papers on Welfare and Growth* (Stanford: Stanford University Press, 1964), chapt. 3.

59. The results for political development of a rising want/get ratio are most recently discussed by Daniel Lerner, "Conflict and Consensus in Guayana," in Frank Bonilla and José A. Silva Michelena, *Studying the Venezuela Polity* (Cambridge, Mass. and Caracas, Venezuela: Center for International Studies, Massachusetts Institute of Technology and Centro de Estudios de Desarrollo, Universidad Central de Venezuela, 1966), pp. 479–512.

60. See, for example, Robert C. Fried, "Administrative Pluralism and Italian Regional Planning," *Public Administration* (London), Winter 1968, pp. 375–91. See also Niles Hansen, *French Regional Planning* (Bloomington: Indiana University Press, 1968), and John Friedmann, *Venezuela: From Doctrine to Dialogue* (Syracuse, N.Y.: Syracuse University Press, 1964). A full-fledged study of the politics of regional development policy is still lacking, however.

61. Some empirical evidence for this hypothesis is found in the best documented study to date of core region development: Lloyd Rodwin and Associates, *Planning Urban Growth and Regional Development* (Cambridge, Mass.: M.I.T. Press, 1969), chapt. 24.

62. The former case may be illustrated with the example of post-liberation Rangoon, where authority was transferred to a non-innovative, religious elite; the latter case may be exemplified by post-World War I Vienna and post-World War II London, where the loss of empire led to a decline in innovative capacity.

63. Evidence on this point is presented in Otis Dudley Duncan et al., *Metropolis and Region* (Baltimore: Johns Hopkins Press, 1960), chapt. 11.

64. Studies of regional dependency relations are rare, partly, I suppose, because

"dependency" is a value-laden term and, according to the traditional academic view, social science should be neutral with respect to values. (See Alvin W. Goulder, "Anti-Minotaur: The Myth of a Value-Free Sociology," in I. L. Horowitz, *New Sociology*, chap. 13.) For contributions to the study of regional dependency, however, see Chandler Morse, "Potentials and Hazards of Direct International Investment in Raw Materials," in Marion Clawson, ed., *Natural Resources and International Development* (Baltimore: Johns Hopkins Press, 1964), pp. 397–414; Espartaco, "La 'crisis Latino-americana' y su marco externo," *Desarrollo Económico* (Buenos Aires) 6 (1966): 319–54; and Oswaldo Sunkel, "Política Nacional del Desarrollo y Dependencia Externa," *Estudios Internacionales* (Santiago) 1 (1967): 43–75.

65. James W. Fesler, *The Political Role of Field Administration: Papers in Comparative Public Administration* (Ann Arbor, Michigan: University of Michigan, 1962), and "Approaches to the Understanding of Decentralization," *Journal of Politics* 27 (1965): 536–66.

66. This hierarchy may be identified empirically by studying the organization of decision making in the political-administrative space of the system and by the spatial linkages of the different cores to their markets and supply areas. Much empirical work remains to be done in this field. For the concept of a loose, asymmetrical hierarchy of core regions, see Otis Dudley Duncan *et al.*, *Metropolis and Region* (Baltimore: Johns Hopkins Press, 1960), chap. 3 and 11.

67. For a fascinating discussion of this subject, suggesting a number of lines of inquiry, see Kuznets, *Modern Economic Growth*, chap. 9. Also Torsten Hägerstrand, "The Propagation of Innovation Waves," *Lund Studies in Geography*, Series B, Human Geography, 1952. See also, by the same author, "Aspects of the Spatial Structure of Social Communication and the Diffusion of Information," *Regional Science Association Papers*, 16 (1966) (European Congress, 1965): 27–42.

68. Poul Ove Pedersen, "Innovation Diffusion Within and Between National Urban Systems" (Copenhagen: Technical University of Denmark, Department of Road Construction, Traffic Engineering, and Town Planning, 1969). This relation holds especially where the distance decay function is relatively high, *i.e.*, during the early phases of industrialization. It may not hold for post-industrial systems like the United States.

69. For evidence, see Norman E. Whitten, "Power Structure and Socio-Cultural Change in Latin American Communities," *Social Forces* 43 (1965): 320–29, and John H. Kunkel, "Economic Autonomy and Social Change in Mexican Villages," *Economic Development and Cultural Change* 10 (1965).

70. John Friedmann, "The Future of Urbanization in Latin America" in *Studies in Comparative International Development* Vol. 5, No. 9 (1969–70), pp. 179–97.

71. See Kuznets, *Modern Economic Growth*, chap. 6, for evidence with respect to world patterns of international trade and their bearing on political relations.

72. This hypothesis is consistent with the empirical finding that "rising regional income disparities and increasing North-South dualism is typical of early development stages, while regional convergence and a disappearance of severe North-South problems is typical of the more mature stages of national growth and development." Jeffrey G. Williamson, "Regional Inequality and the Process of National Development," *Economic Development and Cultural Change* 13 (1965): 44.

73. On the close correlation and interaction between communications and urbanization indices and the use of these indices for predicting political change, see Phillips Cutright, "National Political Development: Measurement and Analysis," *American Sociological Review* 28 (1963): 253–64.

74. Poul Ove Pedersen and Walter Stöhr, "Economic Integration and the Spatial Development of South America," *American Behavioral Scientist* 12 (1969): 2–12.

75. John Friedmann and John Miller, "The Urban Field," *Journal of the American Institute of Planners* 31 (1965): 312–19.

76. The one notable exception to this generalization is Horst Siebert, *Regional Economic Growth*.

77. The process measured by the regional multiplier is normally assumed to be an automatic result of initial investment. That this is by no means so is demonstrated and made the basis of important modifications of regional growth theory by Robert E. Baldwin, "Patterns of Development in Newly Settled Regions," in John Friedmann

and William Alonso, *Regional Development and Planning* and John Friedmann, "The Future of Urbanization in Latin America."

78. See for instance, Charles M. Tiebout, *The Community Economic Base Study*; Harvey S. Perloff (with Vera Dodds), *How a Region Grows*, and Hugh O. Nourse, *Regional Economics* (New York: McGraw-Hill Book Company, 1968).

HIERARCHICAL DIFFUSION: THE BASIS OF DEVELOPMENTAL FILTERING AND SPREAD IN A SYSTEM OF GROWTH CENTERS

BRIAN J. L. BERRY
The University of Chicago

Introduction

"Growth," wrote Perroux in 1955, "does not appear universally at any one time but manifests itself at points or poles of growth . . . and diffuses through the economy in definite channels." Growth cannot, in this view, be separated from the diffusion of innovations, a process involving the "acceptance over time of some specific idea or practice by individuals, groups or other adopting units linked to specific channels of communication, to a social structure, and to a given system of values or culture."[1]

I shall try to expand here upon Perroux's original notion, arguing that the role played by growth centers in regional development is a particular case of the general process of innovation diffusion, and therefore that the sadly deficient "theory" of growth centers can be enriched by turning to the better developed general case.[2] In particular, I shall argue that the developmental role of growth centers involves the simultaneous *filtering* of the innovations that bring growth down the urban hierarchy and the *spreading* of the benefits accruing from the resulting growth, both nationally from core to hinterland regions and within these regions from their metropolitan centers outward to the intermetropolitan periphery. Regional inequities arise in this scheme because the income effect of a given innovation is a declining function of time and is also subject to a threshold limitation—a minimum size of region—beyond which diffusion will not proceed. As a consequence, the lowest levels of

108

welfare are found in areas peripheral to small urban centers in outlying hinterland regions.

A Model
of the Hierarchical Diffusion Process:
Derivation and Proofs

Previous attempts to model the hierarchical diffusion process have been made by Boon, Hudson, and Pedersen following earlier suggestions by Bowers, McVoy, Hägerstrand, Crain, Friedmann, and Thompson.[3] In this chapter I shall build upon these contributions, drawing together and extending the insights they provide by focusing on models that involve probability maximizing assumptions, and linking national spread and hierarchical diffusion of growth opportunities from one urban center to another to the spread effects within urban fields arising from the use households make of these opportunities. Thus, at the broader scale we are concerned with what Pedersen terms "entrepreneurial innovations," *i.e.*, those innovations that, when applied, have direct consequences for people other than the adoptor (which may be a person, a business, a city, or some other institutional unit), whereas the spread effects within urban fields involve "household innovations" whose immediate impact is on the adopting unit only (usually the person or the family).[4] Regional growth always involves both types of innovation in that it depends upon diffusion of the growth opportunity on the one hand and the utilization of the opportunity by potential beneficiaries on the other.

THE URBAN SYSTEM

The first step is to characterize the urban system in which the entrepreneurial innovations take place. As a first approximation, define an urban hierarchy $H(u,k,r',)$ where $P_{r'}$ is the population of a center of level r' in the hierarchy ($P_1 > P_2 > P_3 \ldots$). There are r'_{max} such levels, k is the ratio of the number of centers of population $P_{r'+1}$ to the number of centers of population $P_{r'}$, and u relates the population of a center $P_{r'}$, to that of its market area $M_{r'}$. At the lowest level

$$P_{r'_{max}} = u M_{r'_{max}} \qquad (1)$$

$$M_{r'_{max}} = P_{r'_{max}} + m. \qquad (2)$$

In equation (2) m is the rural population served by a center of lowest level; and therefore if the rural population density is known, the average spacing of these centers can be calculated quite readily. Call this spacing a. Then in the tessellation based on a triangular-hexagonal ($k = 2$), lattice, the next higher order of centers will be spaced $a\sqrt{3}$ apart, whereas in the rectangular-rhomboidal ($k = 3$) case the spacing will be $a\sqrt{4}$, and in the completely nested ($k = 7$) tessellation it will be $a\sqrt{7}$.

From equations (1) and (2)

$$P_{r'_{\max}} = \frac{u}{1-u}\, m. \tag{3}$$

The expression $\dfrac{u}{1-u}$ is, of course, the urban multiplier. It follows from the nesting relationship k in a regular central place hierarchy[5] that

$$M_{r'} = kM_{r'+1} + M_{r'+1} - P_{r'+1} + P_{r'}. \tag{4}$$

That is, the total population served by a center of level r' comprises the total population served by the k centers of next lower order it dominates, plus its own $r' + 1$ level area, plus the population it has because it lies at the r'th level of the hierarchy minus the population it would be if it were an $r' + 1$ level center, to avoid double counting.

Therefore, gathering the terms

$$M_{r'} = (k+1)M_{r'+1} - uM_{r'+1} + uM_{r'} \tag{5}$$

$$= \left(\frac{1+k-u}{1-u}\right)M_{r'+1} \tag{6}$$

$$= \left(\frac{1+k-u}{1-u}\right)^{r'_{\max}-r'} M_{r'} \tag{7}$$

so that

$$P_{r'} = \left(\frac{1+k-u}{1-u}\right)^{r'_{\max}-r'} P_{r'_{\max}} \tag{8}$$

A constant ratio $\left(\dfrac{1+k-u}{1-u}\right)$ is thus maintained between the sizes of centers at one level of the hierarchy and those of the next level size.

Now if such an urban hierarchy experiences geometric random stochastic population growth, the most probable distribution of cities by size is lognormal (*i.e.*, rank-size) possessing, therefore, the maximum entropy subject to the generating process.[6]

To demonstrate, let P_t be the population of a randomly selected city at time t. Then the city's relative growth G is

$$G_1 = (P_1 - P_0)/P_0 \qquad (9)$$

and

$$P_1 = (G_1 + 1)P_0. \qquad (10)$$

Letting G_1 be independent of P_0, to satisfy an assumption of geometric random stochastic growth, following $t = n$ time intervals the growth will be

$$\sum_{t=1}^{n} G = \sum_{t=1}^{n} \left[(P_t - P_{t-1})/P_{t-1} \right] \qquad (11)$$

which can be approximated in continuous form as

$$\int_{P^0}^{P_n} dp/P = lnP_n - lnP_0 \qquad (12)$$

i.e.,

$$\sum_{t=1}^{n} G_t = lnP_n - lnP_0 \qquad (13)$$

and

$$lnP_n = lnP_0 + G_1 + G_2 + \ldots + G_n \qquad (14)$$

$$P_n = P_0(1 + G_1)(1 + G_2) \ldots (1 + G_n). \qquad (15)$$

By the additive form of the central-limit theorem, $\log P_n$ is asymptotically normally distributed, and P_n is therefore asymptotically lognormally distributed. Generalizing to the set of cities, growth that is geometric random stochastic (*i.e.*, when a "law of proportionate effect"—Gibrat's law—holds and all cities have the same expected growth rate) leads to a lognormal size distribution.

The probability density function of cities according to size is then

$$f(x) = \frac{1}{\sqrt{2\pi}} \exp. \left[\tfrac{1}{2} x^2 \right] \qquad (16)$$

where x is a standard normal deviate $x_i = (\log P_i - \mu)/\sigma$ with μ and σ the mean and standard deviation of the $\log P_i$'s. The quantile relationship is $\log P_i = \mu + x_i \sigma$ which means that there is a linear relationship between the $\log P_i$'s and the x_i's.

Now the cumulative distribution function is

$$F(x) = \int_{-\infty}^{x} \frac{1}{\sqrt{2\pi}} \exp. \left[-\tfrac{1}{2}t^2\right] dt \tag{17}$$

which implies a linear relationship between the logarithm of $F(x)$ and the x_i's. Since both $\log P_i$ and $\log F(x)$ have a linear relationship to the x_i's, they in turn have a linear relationship to each other, so that we can write

$$P = a[F(x)]^b \tag{18}$$

which is a Pareto distribution with intercept a and exponent b.

But if we let r be the rank of a center in decreasing order of population $P_1 > P_2 > \ldots > P_r \ldots > P_n$ in an array of n centers, we observe that $1 - \left(\dfrac{r}{n}\right)$ is the complement of $F(x)$, so that rank will bear a linear inverse relationship to the $\log P_i$'s. Hence

$$P_r = K r^{-q} \tag{19}$$

which is the rank-size distribution.

In what follows we therefore use a rank-size distribution of cities as the most relevant model of the urban system against which to study the innovation diffusion processes because it is the most probable distribution. When innovations filter downward in the ranks of centers, we shall term the process *hierarchical filtering*. However, one requirement of using such a model should be noted: the diffusion process should be one that leads to equal expectations of population growth in all centers above some threshold. Hence, any regional inequities can arise only because the income effect imparted by a given innovation decreases in time whereas the growth of population proceeds steadily.

THE DIFFUSION PROCESS

Several possible reasons for hierarchical filtering can be posited[7], among them a "market-searching" process in which an expanding industry exploits market opportunities in a larger-to-smaller sequence,[8] a "trickle-down" process in which an activity faced with rising wage rates in larger cities moves to smaller cities in search of cheaper labor,[9] an "imitation" process in which entrepreneurs in smaller centers mimic the actions of those in larger cities,[10] or a simple probability mechanism in which the probability of adoption depends upon the chance that a potential entrepreneur residing in a given town will learn of the innovation, a probability which declines with size of town.[11]

Any or all of these reasons would result in a pure form of hierarchical diffusion in which α, the innovation potential, varies directly with city size:

$$\alpha = c + dP_r \qquad (20)$$

and therefore, from the rank-size expression

$$\alpha = c + d[Kr^{-q}]. \qquad (21)$$

Rescaling so that $\alpha' = \dfrac{\alpha - c}{\varepsilon}$ with $0 \leqslant \alpha' \leqslant 1$, we find that $\alpha' r^q = dK$ is a constant, so that the relationship of innovation potential, α', and rank in the urban hierarchy, r^q, is hyperbolic.[12]

An energetic model borrowed from particle physics enabled Boon to compute relative diffusion times in such a system, given that the innovation enters the urban system at the largest city at time $t_0 = 0$ and arrives at the smallest that satisfies threshold conditions at $t = Z$. The solution is that relative diffusion $\dfrac{t_i}{Z}$ is given by

$$\frac{t_i}{Z} = \frac{1}{N}\left[\frac{r_i^{-q}-1}{ln r_i - q}\right] \operatorname{arctanh}(1-\alpha_i')^{\frac{1}{2}} \qquad (22)$$

with

$$N = \left[\frac{r_{max}^{-q}-1}{ln r_{max}^{-q}}\right]\operatorname{arctanh}(1-\alpha_{min}')^{\frac{1}{2}}. \qquad (23)$$

This is a useful result, but it begs the question of exactly what the innovation potential α is, and it does not permit a national core-to-hinterland spread effect to take place simultaneously with hierarchical diffusion, in keeping with the observation that smaller centers located close to large centers that have already adopted an innovation are likely to innovate as early, or earlier, than larger but more peripheral centers.

The reason is, of course, that the urban hierarchy is not simply a functional hierarchy but also a spatial one. Any hierarchical diffusion process, therefore, must combine the effects of both hierarchical level and relative location.[13] To this end, Pedersen used an elementary

gravity construct, postulating that the information flow per unit time
between two urban centers i and j, I_{ij}, is

$$I_{ij} = K' \frac{P_i P_j}{s_{ij}^x} \qquad (24)$$

and s_{ij} is, of course, the distance between i and j.[14] Assuming that a
town that has adopted an innovation sends out a constant flow of
information to other towns, the information received in town j by
time t from the n towns that have adopted in this time span is

$$I_j^t = \sum_{t=1}^{n} K' \frac{P_i P_j}{s_{ij}^x} \qquad (25)$$

so that I_j^t measures the innovative pressures felt by town j. But there
is a "threshold" size of town P_{min}, beneath which an innovation will
not penetrate, and an amount of information, F, that a town must
receive before it will innovate; and because I_j^t can change only when
an additional town innovates and thereby increases the innovative
pressures on all centers that have not yet adopted, the diffusion
sequence starting with the largest place will be given by the succession
of additional terms that satisfy the inequality

$$\sum_{i=1}^{n} K' \frac{P_i P_j}{s_{ij}^x} \geqslant F \qquad (26)$$

which is computed after each adoption. Time t in I_j^t is therefore
simply order in the adoption sequence and needs further calibration
in the manner of equation (22).

The left-hand side of equation (26) converges on the product of
size of the city receiving the information flows, and population
potentials:

$$K' P_j \sum_{i=1}^{n} \left(\frac{P_i}{s_{ij}^x} \right) \geqslant F. \qquad (27)$$

In other words, the innovation potential of a center is a product of its
position in the urban hierarchy, and the force exerted on it by centers
that have already adopted the innovation (recall that in physics,
energy is $(GM_i M_j)/s_{ij}$ whereas force is $(GM_i M_j)/s_{ij}^2$). Therefore,
looking back at an entire diffusion sequence, adoption time should
be a function of the product of hierarchical position and population
potential.

To rephrase the conclusion, the innovation potential of a center is a function of its own rank in the urban hierarchy, and the force exterted on it by virtue of its location relative to the other centers in the hierarchy that have already adopted the innovation, for from equations (19) and (27) we can write

$$(K'K^2)r_j^{-q} \sum_{i=1}^{n} \left(\frac{r_i^{-q}}{s_{ij}^x} \right) \geqslant F. \qquad (28)$$

The limiting cases of equation (28) are those of pure hierarchical diffusion as the distance exponent x approaches zero, and a pure spread effect as x goes to infinity. Thus, as accessibility improves, one should expect the spread-type of diffusion wave to be replaced by a functional pattern of hierarchical filtering.

What justification is there for using a simple gravity model to estimate probable information flows between cities? Wilson provides an answer.[15] Define I_{ij} as before to be the information flow from i to j and let

$$I_{ij} = A_i O_i B_j D_j f(c_{ij}) \qquad (29)$$

where A_i and B_j are balancing factors calculated to let

$$\sum_j I_{ij} = O_i \qquad (30)$$

and

$$\sum_i I_{ij} = D_j \qquad (31)$$

so that

$$A_i = \sum_j \frac{1}{B_j D_j f(c_{ij})} \qquad (32)$$

$$B_j = \sum_i \frac{1}{A_i O_i f(c_{ij})} \qquad (33)$$

and $f(c_{ij})$ will, in general, be some distance-decay expression such as s_{ij}^{-x}, for example.

Rewrite

$$O_i - \sum_j I_{ij} = 0 \qquad (34)$$

$$D_j - \sum_i I_{ij} = 0 \qquad (35)$$

and also define

$$C - \sum_{ij} T_{ij} c_{ij} = 0 \qquad (36)$$

to indicate that there is some total expenditure of travel effort made.

The number of different ways messages can be assigned to information flows (disregarding rearrangements within information packages) is then

$$w(I_{ij}) = \frac{I!}{\pi_{ij}I_{ij}!} \tag{37}$$

and the total number of states possible is $W = \Sigma w(I_{ij})$. Now if Lagrangian multipliers are introduced to maximize equation (37) subject to equations (34) to (36), the solution for I_{ij} in terms of the other variables is

$$I_{ij} = A_i B_j O_i D_j e^{-\beta c}{}_{ij} \tag{38}$$

which is a gravity-type model that arises when information flows assume their most-probable state.[16] In equation (37) log w is, of course, the entropy, and it is this that the gravity model maximizes. An alternative statement involving $p_{ij} = I_{ij}/I$, maximizing $H = -\underset{ij}{\Sigma\Sigma}p_{ij} \log p_{ij}$ gives the same results.

Substituting populations of centers and appropriately modified balancing constants, the expression then can be rewritten

$$I_{ij} = K'P_i P_j e^{-\beta s_{ij}^x} \tag{39}$$

if s_{ij}^x is an estimate of overall distance impedance c_{ij}. Then, from equation (28), the expression for the most probable timing of innovations is

$$(K'K^2)r_j^{-q} \sum_{i-1}^{n} (r_i^{-q}e^{-\beta s_{ij}^x}) \geqslant K \tag{40}$$

or in terms of populations

$$K'P_j \sum_{i=1}^{n} P_i e^{-\beta s_{ij}^x} \geqslant K \tag{41}$$

which is still the product of size and a potential-like measure. The probability that the information leading to the adoption came specifically from i to j is

$$\rho_{ij} = \frac{P_j e^{-\beta s_{ij}^x}}{\sum\limits_{i=1}^{n} P_i e^{-\beta s_{ij}^x}} = \frac{r_j^{-q}e^{-\beta s_{ij}^x}}{\sum\limits_{i=1}^{n} r_i^{-q}e^{-\beta s_{ij}^x}} \tag{42}$$

which is essentially the expression one would obtain from an "intervening opportunities" model when opportunities are relatively uniformly distributed in space. Since a uniform distribution of opportunities is the case for each level of a regular urban hierarchy, further support is lent to the use of this type of model to study hierarchical diffusion.

Following Hudson, it would be possible to restate the above equations in the special case of the pure central-place hierarchy discussed earlier.[17] For example, where r' is level of centers in the hierarchy, the spacing of centers of a given level, s_r', can be written as

$$s_r' = a(k+1)\exp.[(r'_{max}-r')/2]. \tag{43}$$

Thus, in the hexagonal-triangular lattice, the spacing of centers of successive levels is the geometric series a, $a\sqrt{3}$, $a3$. . . . Since urban populations in such a hierarchy are similarly geometric [equation (8)] and proportional to area served, the gravity models resolve to simple binomial series, the probability that a message will first reach a town at time t is a binomially distributed random variable [from the gravity model $I_{ij}^2 = k'P_iP_j/s_{ij}$ Hudson derives the expression

$$\rho(t) = \frac{(r'_{max}-1)!}{t!(r'_{max}-1-t)!}\left(\left(1-\frac{1}{k+1}\right)^t(1/(k+1)^{r'-1-t}_{max}\right. \text{ with } t = 0,1,2\ldots,$$

$r'_{max}-1$],
and the cumulative proportion of towns receiving the innovation converges on an S-shaped distribution, consistent with empirical knowledge of the time distribution of adoptions. Such a time-path can be written

$$\rho(t) = 1/(1+e^{a-bt}) \tag{44}$$

where $\rho(t)$ is the proportion of potential adopters who have done so.[18] Clearly, such a logistic expression provides the way to relate the adoption sequence that can be obtained from successive application of equations (40) and (41) to relative and to real diffusion time.

HOUSEHOLD INNOVATION

The most probable time that an innovation becomes available to the households within an urban region, therefore, depends upon the functional location of the urban center within the hierarchy of towns and its geographic location or centrality within the force field of innovative potentials arising from general access to information provided by the early adopters. After the town has adopted, a logistic spatial-temporal trend may be postulated for the utilization of the innovation by households within its field of influence.[19] For example,

$$y(t,s) = 1/[1 + \exp.(a_0 + a_1 s + a_2 s^2 + b_0 t + b_1 st + b_2 s^2 t)] \quad (45)$$

where the a's and b's are parameters, t is time and s is the effective distance that a household resides from the urban center. "Effective distance" may, of course, be expressed in a variety of ways, but whatever the particular expression, a wavelike process of household innovation is therefore envisaged; and at any moment the spatial pattern of relative use of the innovation by people living within an urban region will be a negative exponential function of this effective distance from the urban center.[20] Again, it is relatively easy to demonstrate that the negative exponential is a maximally-probable state.[21]

Empirical Verification: Diffusion of Television Stations and Market Penetration by the Television Industry in the United States 1940–1968

The concepts outlined above are clearly borne out by the evidence on diffusion of television stations and progressively greater market penetration by the television industry in the United States in the years 1940–1968. This joint process of entrepreneurial and household innovation was characterized, quite clearly, by a combination of hierarchical diffusion and spread effects.

Three cities opened TV stations on the eve of the World War II (New York, Chicago, and Philadelphia), but there was a wartime cessation of activity. Another fifty-eight cities opened stations in the years 1947–1950, but again diffusion was ended for two years by an FCC-ordered freeze during the Korean war. In the two years following Korea, 144 cities opened stations for the first time. By 1958 complete national coverage had been obtained, and thereafter only ten more cities opened their first TV stations. Allowing for the two periods of war, the time-path of the entrepreneurial innovation was logistic (see Figure 1 where the solid line is an actual and the dotted line a perfect logistic). Moreover, the time-path was essentially hierarchical; the smaller the city, the later the opening of its TV station, as Figure 2 clearly reveals. Figure 2 displays other things too. For example, the greater density of points immediately following the

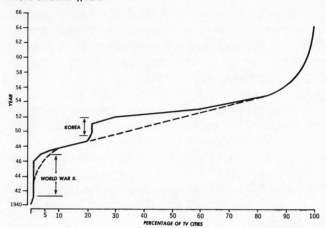

Figure 1.

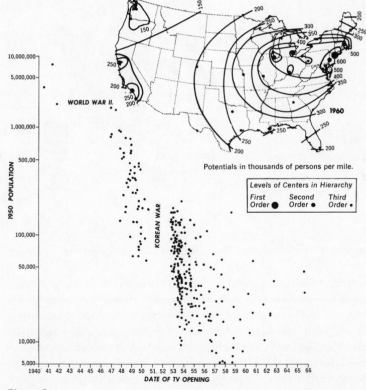

Figure 2.

Korean war unmistakably shows that the FCC-imposed wartime freeze simply postponed openings of TV stations that would normally have occurred between 1950 and 1952, and therefore that in the absence of the war the actual time-sequence of adoptions would have been closer to a perfect logistic trend.

Similarly, market penetration (measured by the percentage of households innovating) progressed in the manner predicted. Satisfactory national data on the spread of TV ownership are unavailable for the first seven years following World War II, although we do know that in 1946 only 6,500 television sets were produced, increasing to 178,000 in 1947, 867,000 in 1948, exceeding a million sets annually thereafter. We have to pick up the process in 1953, just as the Korean embargo was lifted, using the industry's estimates of "TV households."[22]

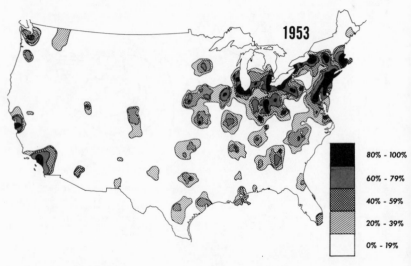

Figure 3. *Market Penetration: Percentage of Households Having Television Receivers.*

Figure 3 shows the pattern of market penetration in 1953. At that time all the nation's highest-order urban centers had opened TV stations. Market penetration declined with distance from these centers and was uniformly high in the zones of highest population potentials (see Figure 2, inset map). Large areas of the country remained unserved. Interestingly, all those larger American cities that have never opened their own television stations are located in these zones of fairly rapid complete initial market penetration of the yet-larger nearby metropoli—Fall River, Lawrence, Bridgeport, New London, Norwalk, Stamford, and so on between Boston and New York; Newark, Paterson, and Trenton in New Jersey; Canton in Ohio; Ann Arbor, Battle Creek, and Jackson in Michigan; Kenosha and Racine between Chicago and Milwaukee; Council Bluffs on the doorstep of Omaha; and similar cases in other parts of the country. In part, this reflects federal licensing policies, but these policies in turn simply codify the fact that the higher-order neighbors of these nonadopting cities adopted earlier and achieved such a degree of market domination that they forestalled any entrepreneurial innovation by nearby smaller centers.

By 1956 the combination of further station openings and increased market penetration by stations in existing cities (most of which added second, third, and more stations and increased their effective radiated power) had led to coverage of all but the least populated parts of the country (see Figure 4). Zones of high penetration stood out in the

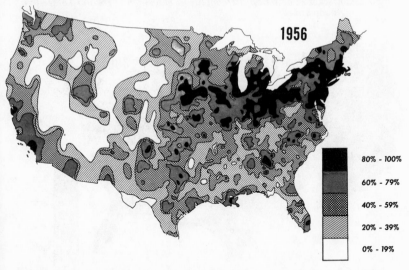

Figure 4. *Market Penetration: Percentage of Households Having Television Receivers.*

national heartland of the manufacturing belt and in California. The areas with the lowest degrees of household innovation were, broadly speaking, the zones of lowest national market access (compare with Figure 2, inset map).

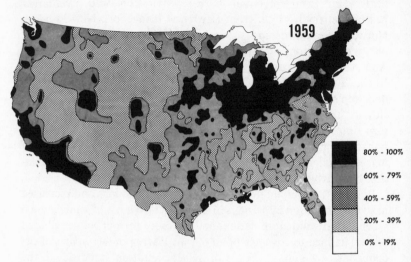

Figure 5. *Market Penetration: Percentage of Households Having Television Receivers.*

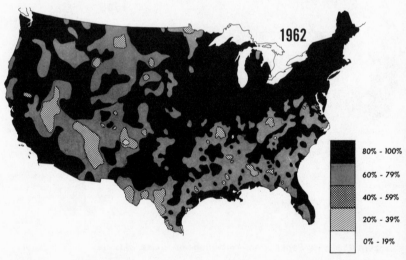

Figure 6. *Market Penetration: Percentage of Households Having Television Receivers.*

Complete national coverage was achieved in 1958–1959 (Figure 5), and the diffusion dynamics were such that the time necessary for geographic spread to make television available for all households in the country was also sufficient for near-complete market penetration to be achieved throughout the north and in California. Three years later (see Figure 6), market penetration had increased apace, and only the relatively poor and more inaccessible parts of the South, the Rio Grande valley and the mountainous West displayed substantially lower degrees of TV ownership, a pattern remaining, although to a lesser degree, in 1965 (see Figure 7).

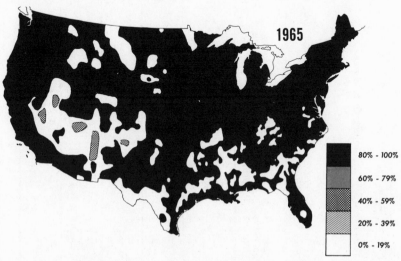

Figure 7. *Market Penetration: Percentage of Households Having Television Receivers.*

MODELS OF THE ENTREPRENEURIAL INNOVATION

That diffusion of television stations among American cities was largely hierarchical is clearly borne out by statistical analysis. Taking the cities with TV stations (270 in all) as the observations, and the date at which the first TV station in each city began broadcasting as the dependent variable, a variety of regression equations consistent with the models developed earlier were estimated, some of which are reported in Table 1.

Three alternative measures of city size or status of urban centers in the hierarchy were examined: city population in 1950, essentially at the beginning of the process; city population in 1960, toward the end; and a multivariate index of the functional size of urban centers in the hierarchy developed in a study of the latent structure of the

TABLE 1

Diffusion of Television Stations among U.S. Cities

Independent variable TV OPENING DATE $x = 53.548$ $Sx = 3.471$	Dependent Variables							
	MEASURES OF CITY SIZE			SIZE OF DEPENDENT AREA	CITY CHARACTERISTICS			GENERAL ACCESSIBILITY
	Functional Size in Urban Hierarchy (Factor 1)[d]	Log. Population 1960	Log. Population 1950	Log. FEA Population	Mining Base (Factor 13)[d]	College Towns (Factor 6)[d]	Foreign Born Population (Factor 7)[d]	Log. Population Potential 1950
MODEL								
1. $R^2 = .565$　b[a]	−1.752	—	—	—	0.752	0.323	−0.341	—
S_b[b]	0.113	—	—	—	0.185	0.144	0.186	—
r^*[c]	−0.687	—	—	—	0.242	0.136	−0.112	—
2. $R^2 = .619$　b	−1.028	—	—	−2.652	0.459	0.436	−0.324	—
S_b	0.159	—	—	0.433	0.180	0.136	0.175	—
r^*	−0.369	—	—	−0.352	0.155	0.193	−0.113	—
3. $R^2 = 0.559$　b	—	—	—	−4.731	0.420	0.542	−0.384	—
S_b	—	—	—	0.311	0.193	0.145	0.187	—
r^*	—	—	—	−0.682	0.133	0.223	−0.125	—
4. $R^2 = 0.599$　b	—	−2.927	—	−1.795	0.517	0.471	−0.285	—
S_b	—	0.581	—	0.655	0.186	0.140	0.180	—
r^*	—	−0.296	—	−0.167	0.169	0.203	−0.097	—
5. $R^2 = 0.587$　b	—	−4.347	—	—	0.645	0.424	−0.258	—
S_b	—	0.268	—	—	0.182	0.140	0.182	—
r^*	—	−0.706	—	—	0.213	0.182	−0.087	—

6. $R^2 = 0.604$	b	—	—	−3.231	−1.522	0.301	0.476	−0.287	—
	S_b	—	—	0.598	0.663	0.185	0.139	0.179	—
	$r*$	—	—	−0.316	−0.140	0.100	0.207	−0.098	—
7. $R^2 = 0.596$	b	—	—	−4.458	—	0.322	0.441	−0.267	—
	S_b	—	—	0.269	—	0.186	0.139	0.180	—
	$r*$	—	—	−0.714	—	0.106	0.191	−0.091	—
8. $R^2 = 0.596$	b	—	—	−4.406	—	0.283	0.448	−0.227	−0.334
	S_b	—	—	0.305	—	0.216	0.140	0.182	0.941
	$r*$	—	—	−0.663	—	0.081	0.192	−0.093	−0.022
9. LOG. TV. Opening date $R^2 = 0.618$	b	—	—	−0.036	—	0.002	0.003	−0.002	−0.004
	S_b	—	—	0.002	—	0.001	0.001	0.001	0.007
	$r*$	—	—	−0.675	—	0.086	0.183	−0.104	−0.036

[a] b—metric regression coefficient
[b] S_b—standard error of b
[c] $r*$—partial correlation of independent variable with dependent-stepwise model.
[d] Berry, Brian J. L., "Latent Structure of the American Urban System." See note 23.

American urban system.[23] Additionally, two measures of accessibility were input: population potentials in 1950, as an index of national market access, and the population of the labor market or functional
economic area dominated by the urban center,[24] as an index of local
access. Experimentation also showed that the diffusion proceeded
more rapidly than expected into the oilfield areas of the Southwest
(where, presumably, more risk capital was available) and into those
"outer rim" sections of the nation where the foreign born population
was greatest, but that it was retarded in college towns where the size
of town is greater than the effective television market because of the
student population and because in the earlier years of television there
was greater resistance to the medium by those of higher educational
levels. Therefore, three indices of those factors were retained in the
regression models.[25] A variety of other variables showed no significant relationship to the diffusion sequence, among them the growth
rate of the cities 1950–1960, the socioeconomic status and stage in
life-cycle of the town's residents, the principal features of the town's
economic base, and the like.

As Table 1 shows, there are few differences in the power of the
alternative models resulting from different combinations of these
variables. City population at the beginning of the process in 1950
gives slightly better fits than the data for 1960 on the multivariate
index, which is a satisfying verification of the gravity formulation.
The measure of local access splits the variance attributable to size
alone, and its inclusion improves the regression estimates only
slightly, suggesting that city population provides an approximately
proportional estimate of market size. Population potentials do not
make a significant addition to the power of the model, however,
confirming that the diffusion pattern graphed in Figure 2 is largely
hierarchical in nature. But this is not unexpected since, as seen in the
inset to Figure 2, the highest order centers occupy and in fact create
the zones of highest population potentials and greatest national
market access. Thus, if model 8 of Table 1 is solved for a range of
population sizes and potentials, assuming that the three other
variables take their average values of zero [the indices are ortho-
normal[26], so the equation is Opening date = 76.26 − 4.406 (Log.
1950 Population) − 0.334 (Log. of 1950 Population Potentials)], the
expected innovation dates are as indicated in Table 2. Potentials
force at most a nine-month delay on the entrepreneurial innovation
process, whereas the expectation is that center of the lowest level in

TABLE 2

*Expected Innovation Dates for Cities
of Different Sizes and Varying Population Potentials*

POPULATION POTENTIALS

City size	10,000	100,000	1,000,000	10,000,000
10,000,000	1944.082	1943.748	1943.416	1943.080
1,000,000	1948.488	1948.154	1947.820	1947.486
100,000	1952.894	1952.560	1952.226	1951.892
10,000	1957.300	1956.966	1956.632	1956.298
1,000	1961.706	1961.372	1961.038	1960.704

the hierarchy above the adoption threshold will lag more than thirteen years behind the nation's largest metropoli. This span coincides with the post-World War II years in which all but nine of the nation's TV cities installed their stations.

MODELS OF THE HOUSEHOLD INNOVATION

We suggested earlier that, given an available entrepreneurial innovation, the individual innovation sequence should be wavelike, increasing in time outward from cities according to effective distance from these cities. Therefore, in our first attempt to model household innovations we took as independent variables the percentages of households with TV in 1953, 1956, 1959, 1962, and 1965, computed for each of the 3,100+ counties in the United States, and regressed them in turn on the broadcasting start date of the TV cities serving as the centers of the Designated Television Market Areas to which the counties belonged (Nielsen, 1967–8)[27] and two measures of local access. The first of these local access measures was the percentage of workers resident in the county who commuted to the TV city to work each day, selected as a nationally meaningful standard for comparing locally-variable accessibility conditions, because the intensity of commuting tends to drop off negative exponentially with effective distance [refer to equation (39)]. The second measure used was population potentials because it was noted that in zones of high potentials local communications access is high even where local commuting may be limited. Thus, the commuting area of Newark, New Jersey, for example, remains tied closely by means of the mass media to New York City.

TABLE 3

Diffusion of Television Sets among U.S. Households

Independent variable	TV start date	Population potential	Log. % workers commuting to city	Population change 1950–1960	Median income	% with more than $9999	% with less than $3000	Median age	Log. % nonwhite	Satellite TV city
A. Market Penetration 1953 MODEL										
1. $R^2 = 0.586$ b[a]	−3.66	0.00008	6.423							
S_b[b]	0.094	0.000003	0.556							
$r*$[c]	−0.564	0.448	0.203							
2. $R^2 = 0.601$ b	−3.489	0.0008	4.825	11.092						
S_b	0.095	0.000003	0.565	1.026						
$r*$	−0.547	0.465	0.151	0.191						
3. $R^2 = 0.633$ b	−3.15	0.000085	3.265	2.704	Deleted by regression	0.546	−0.156	0.342	1,352	Deleted by regression
S_b	0.094	0.000003	0.560	1.153		0.071	0.023	0.080	0.525	
$r*$	−0.513	0.482	0.104	0.042		0.138	−0.121	0.077	0.046	
B. Market Penetration 1956 MODEL										
1. $R^2 = 0.430$ b	−2.033	0.000064	9.800							
S_b	0.096	0.000003	0.557							
$r*$	−0.354	0.367	0.301							
2. $R^2 = 0.446$ b	−1.881	0.000067	8.383	9.833						
S_b	0.096	0.000003	0.569	1.033						
$r*$	−0.330	0.382	0.256	0.169						
3. $R^2 = 0.549$ b	−1.381	0.000065	7.358	3.706	Deleted by regression	Deleted by regression	−0.229	0.834	−1.696	−18.039
S_b	0.090	0.000003	0.525	1.051			0.019	0.075	0.497	1.285
$r*$	−0.265	0.406	0.244	0.063			−0.202	0.194	−0.061	−0.245

C. Market Penetration 1959
MODEL

1. R² = 0.311

	1	2	3	4	5	6	7	8
b	-1.292	0.000034	7.215	Deleted by regression	Deleted by regression	0.659	-1.897	-23.059
S_b	0.079	0.000002	0.463			0.059	0.393	1.015
$r*$	-0.280	0.274	0.270			0.194	-0.086	-0.378

2. R² = 0.327

	1	2	3	4
b	-1.186	0.000035	6.173	7.413
S_b	0.079	0.000002	0.473	0.856
$r*$	-0.258	0.284	0.228	0.154

3. R² = 0.505

	1	2	3	4	5	6	7	8
b	-0.653	0.000036	5.282	2.127	-0.215	0.659	-1.897	-23.059
S_b	0.071	0.000002	0.414	0.830	0.015	0.059	0.393	1.015
$r*$	-0.162	0.302	0.223	0.046	-0.239	0.194	-0.086	-0.378

D. Market Penetration 1962
MODEL

1. R² = 0.040

	1	2	3
b	-0.445	0.00001	5.495
S_b	0.121	0.000003	0.705
$r*$	-0.066	0.056	0.138

2. R² = 0.058

	1	2	3	4
b	-0.298	0.000012	4.058	10.233
S_b	0.121	0.000003	0.722	1.308
$r*$	-0.044	0.064	0.100	0.139

3. R² = 0.167

	1	2	3	4	5	6	7	8	9
b	-0.249	0.00001	3.023	Deleted by regression	0.399	-0.215	0.463	-2.484	-20.428
S_b	0.121	0.000003	0.697		0.085	0.027	0.100	0.646	1.700
$r*$	0.037	0.054	0.078		0.084	-0.138	0.083	-0.069	-0.211

E. Market Penetration 1965
MODEL

1. R² = 0.066

	1	2	3
b	-0.174	0.000012	3.532
S_b	0.067	0.000002	0.392
$r*$	-0.046	0.160	0.122

2. ?

3. R² = 0.332

	1	2	3	4	5	6	7	8
b	-0.338	0.000013	2.236	Deleted by regression	-0.193	0.324	-2.493	-21.302
S_b	0.060	0.000002	0.345		0.011	0.050	0.325	0.857
$r*$	-0.101	0.133	0.115		-0.282	0.115	-0.136	-0.408

[a] b—metric regression coefficient.
[b] S_b—standard error of b.
[c] $r*$—partial correlation of independent variable with dependent-stepwise model.
[d] 1950 census data for 1953 and 1956 analyses, 1960 data for 1959, 1962 and 1965.

The five resulting three-variable regressions are called Model 1 in Table 3. They are augmented by the rate of population change from 1950 to 1960 to form the five Model 2 equations since it was thought that household diffusion might proceed more rapidly in areas of growth than in relatively stagnant or declining areas. Of course, a variety of other considerations might be introduced, and therefore Table 3 also contains more elaborate equations designated Model 3 (actually selected from a large set of more extensive regression estimates). These Model 3 equations are extended to include income and family size data because, looking at the United States Census data on TV ownership in 1950, Dernberg, Rosetti and Watts, in an earlier statistical study of market penetration, concluded that the ownership of TV sets was directly related in 1950 to the length of time TV had been available and the extent of TV station coverage of the country.[28] They found ownership to be directly related to income up to a 1950 figure of $7,000 and inversely thereafter; holding average income constant, it was inversely related to the dispersion of income except in very low income areas. Finally, they found ownership to be highest where educational levels were, on the average, ten to twelve years, and to be lower for higher and lower levels of education. To extend the Dernberg findings, we decided to add variables measuring the median and tails of the income distribution to our model, as well as median age (the tails of the age distribution were not statistically significant), race, and whether or not the TV city was identified by Nielsen as a smaller satellite in a Designated Market Area that had a larger TV city located within it. Other variables initially included but later dropped for lack of statistical significance were educational levels (the effect is already included in the TV start date), occupational characteristics, and a variety of other summary dimensions of county characteristics.[29]

As is seen in Table 3, Model 3 is more powerful than Model 2, and this is in turn more powerful than Model 1, in every year studied; but the power of each model declines year by year from 1953 to 1965, as market penetration proceeds and the county-to-county variance expressed in the dependent variable is progressively reduced, the range being 100 per cent in 1953 but only 25 per cent in 1965.

In 1953, TV start date is clearly of the greatest importance, along with potentials (confirming the value of the gravity formulation in looking at household innovations also). Household adoption declines with distance from the TV city, is greater in growing high-income

TABLE 4

Matrix of Transition Numbers from TV Diffusion Data 1953–1956

PERCENTAGE OF FAMILIES WITH TV IN 1953	PERCENTAGE OF FAMILIES WITH TV IN 1956									
	0–10	11–20	21–30	31–40	41–50	51–60	61–70	71–80	81–90	91–100
0–10	63	152	255	405	292	239	121	60	32	0
11–20	0	0	22	68	103	74	38	32	10	0
21–30	0	0	4	25	63	66	70	29	15	0
31–40	0	0	2	6	16	55	80	47	17	0
41–50	0	0	0	3	8	29	52	63	47	0
51–60	0	0	0	1	0	10	16	35	73	0
61–70	0	0	0	0	0	3	2	23	82	0
71–80	0	0	0	0	0	1	2	12	73	0
81–90	0	0	0	0	0	0	0	5	68	10
91–100	0	0	0	0	0	0	0	0	21	2

TABLE 5

Matrix of Transition Numbers from TV Diffusion Data 1956–1959

PERCENTAGE OF FAMILIES WITH TV IN 1956	PERCENTAGE OF FAMILIES WITH TV IN 1959									
	0–10	11–20	21–30	31–40	41–50	51–60	61–70	71–80	81–90	91–100
0–10	34	0	0	0	29	0	0	0	0	0
11–20	0	0	0	7	117	26	1	1	0	0
21–30	0	0	0	0	77	191	15	0	0	0
31–40	0	0	0	0	2	299	190	17	2	0
41–50	0	0	0	0	0	20	369	91	67	1
51–60	0	0	0	0	0	1	44	364	214	2
61–70	0	0	0	0	0	0	0	165	275	24
71–80	0	0	0	0	0	0	0	7	0	345
81–90	0	0	0	0	0	0	0	0	93	0
91–100	0	0	0	0	0	0	0	0	0	12

TABLE 6

Matrix of Transition Numbers from TV Diffusion Data 1959–1962

PERCENTAGE OF FAMILIES WITH TV IN 1962

PERCENTAGE OF FAMILIES WITH TV IN 1959	0–10	11–20	21–30	31–40	41–50	51–60	61–70	71–80	81–90	91–100
0–10	34	0	0	0	0	0	0	0	0	0
11–20	0	0	0	0	0	0	0	0	0	0
21–30	0	0	0	0	0	0	0	0	0	0
31–40	0	0	0	1	13	1	1	3	2	0
41–50	0	0	0	1	7	23	48	67	65	8
51–60	0	0	0	0	1	30	118	225	142	14
61–70	0	0	0	0	0	7	44	217	307	43
71–80	0	0	0	0	0	0	11	99	440	95
81–90	0	0	0	0	0	0	1	9	314	327
91–100	0	0	0	0	0	0	0	1	18	365

TABLE 7

Matrix of Transition Numbers from TV Diffusion Data 1962–1965

PERCENTAGE OF FAMILIES WITH TV IN 1965

PERCENTAGE OF FAMILIES WITH TV IN 1962	0–10	11–20	21–30	31–40	41–50	51–60	61–70	71–80	81–90	91–100
0–10	34	0	0	0	0	0	0	0	0	0
11–20	0	0	0	0	0	0	0	0	0	0
21–30	0	0	0	0	0	0	0	0	0	0
31–40	0	0	0	0	0	0	0	0	0	0
41–50	0	0	0	0	1	2	15	0	0	0
51–60	0	0	0	0	0	5	49	11	0	0
61–70	0	0	0	0	0	1	12	198	13	0
71–80	0	0	0	0	0	0	0	115	504	2
81–90	0	0	0	0	0	0	1	0	585	702
91–100	0	0	0	0	0	0	0	0	4	848

areas, and is retarded in low-income communities and where age
levels are lower.

The findings are similar in 1956, although start date and potentials
have declined in importance, local access has increased, the high-
income variable is no longer statistically significant (presumably,
because penetration in such areas is relatively complete), but lower
penetration in low-income areas and in counties with substantial
nonwhite populations is more marked. In addition, a significantly
lower degree of market penetration by the outlying satellite TV cities
is revealed.

The same findings apply in all succeeding years, and by the
mid-1960s the effects of the variables originally most significant in
molding the household diffusion process (TV start date, potentials,
local access) though still statistically significant, have been surpassed
in importance because of the universally high levels of market penetration in the nation by those variables which identify the "hold-out"
zones of lowest market penetration. These are areas in which the
proportion of the population with incomes less than $3,000 is greatest,
where a greater part of the population is nonwhite, where more of
the population is youthful, and where satellite TV cities are least
effective in penetrating the market. In effect, Figures 6 and 7 pick
out the regions of greatest rural poverty in the United States.

The changing nature of the pattern can be shown in other ways.
Tables 4 to 7 record the transitions made by counties from one penetration category to another in each of the four-year time-spans.
Clearly, the transition probabilities are not stable. Table 8 records
the regression relationships among each successive pair of maps.

TABLE 8

Relationships among Successive Diffusion Patterns:
TV Market Penetration 1953–1965

Dependent[a] Variable	Independent Variable	Multiple R	Intercept	Regression Coefficient Metric	Standard- ized
% with TV 1956	% with TV 1953	0.713	40.29	0.609	0.713
% with TV 1959	% with TV 1956	0.945	34.14	0.712	0.945
% with TV 1962	% with TV 1959	0.498	37.27	0.643	0.498
% with TV 1965	% with TV 1962	0.615	58.87	0.346	0.615

[a] Data for 3101 counties.

Basically, one set of relationships holds until complete geographic coverage of the national market had been achieved, and a distinct shift in pattern develops thereafter. *This is consistent with the notion that an orderly wavelike process of household innovation follows from a hierarchical pattern of entrepreneurial innovation. Hierarchical diffusion extends down to some threshold, and then entrepreneurial innovation ceases. Household innovations continue until some saturation level is reached within all areas accessible to the hierarchy of places that have experienced entrepreneurial innovation. Remaining unserved are these areas peripheral to the adopting hierarchy.*

Income Changes Accruing from the Diffusion Sequence

It is not unreasonable to expect that adoption of an innovation will provide a given employment and therefore a population growth impetus to the adopting region,[30] and that if a succession of innovations diffuses down the urban hierarchy all regions benefiting will experience the same population growth rate (thus satisfying Gibrat's law that all regions below the smallest threshold will stagnate and those regions lying in the range of sizes between the smallest and the greatest innovation thresholds will have growth rates directly related to size). If, on the other hand, the income effect of an innovation declines in time so that later adopters receive a lesser income increment than earlier adopters, a sequence of cases will arise:

1. Large cities that adopt early and have rapidly rising incomes.
2. Medium and smaller-sized cities above all thresholds, experiencing the same population growth rates as those of class 1 but rates of real income growth more nearly those of the nation. In general, the larger and/or more central cities will gain more than the smaller and more peripheral.
3. Small places satisfying some thresholds but not others. The population growth rate and the rate of change of incomes will be positively related to size, because the larger and/or more accessible of these places will satisfy more thresholds than the smaller and more peripheral.
4. Declining small towns in inaccessible intermetropolitan peripheries, with lagging relative income levels, and declining populations because the more energetic and able residents emigrate, largely to places in class (1), creating in turn the central city ghettoes of these large metropolitan areas.

In each case, of course, the degree to which surrounding populations benefit is indexed by the extent of their participation in the opportunities provided by the central city—in general, measurable by relative location in the city's commuting field.[31]

Again, some statistics bear this out. Between 1950 and 1960, the cities with TV stations grew as follows:

$$\text{Log } P_{1960} = 0.32 + 0.98 \text{ Log } P_{1950}$$
$$R^2 = 0.95$$
$$S_e = 0.13$$

whereas the comparable expression for all 3101 counties in the country was

$$\text{Log } P_{1960} = -0.20 + 1.05 \text{ Log } P_{1950}$$
$$R^2 = 0.95$$
$$S_e = 0.12.$$

Clearly, small counties were declining. In those counties of intermediate size, growth rates were a positive function of size, whereas for TV cities the growth rate was approximately independent of size. On the other hand, median family income of the 3,101 counties in 1960 could be expressed as follows:

$$
\begin{aligned}
\text{Med. family income}_{1960} = {} & -3112 + 736 \text{ Log. population}_{1960} \\
& + 164 \text{ Log. percentage commuting} \\
& - 0.00168 \text{ Pop. potential}_{1960} \\
& - 21 \text{ Percentage nonwhite}_{1960} \\
& + 1716 \left[\text{Income}_{1960}/\text{Income}_{1950} \right] \\
& + 1525 \left[\text{Population}_{1960}/ \right. \\
& \qquad \left. \text{Population}_{1950} \right] \\
R^2 = {} & 0.612.
\end{aligned}
$$

Since the regression model used was stepwise, the only surprising term, that for population potentials, can be easily interpreted as expressing the relative wealth of the southern and western rims of the nation. Otherwise, all the postulates hold: incomes are higher the higher the level in the urban hierarchy and the greater the degree of participation in the employment opportunities of the central city; and in a circular fashion, these same areas are the zones of most rapid growth of incomes. *This suggests that hierarchical diffusion and attendant geographic spread effects characterize the entire range of innovations that bring growth and incomes to cities and regions.*

Hierarchical Diffusion
and Growth Center Theory

In consequence, diffusion theory provides a sound conceptual base for the growth center idea. Growth occurs as a consequence of the filtering of innovations downward through the urban hierarchy and the spread of use of the innovations among consumers residing within the urban fields of the adopting centers. The operation of the growth center mechanism in a country like the United States is spontaneous, and it is subject to minimum threshold conditions that leave abandoned broad peripheral zones of low and declining incomes, substantial emigration and, where natural rates of increase are not exceptionally high, of population decline.

Can growth centers be used to induce development in these lagging poverty regions?[32] If by "development" is meant bringing population growth to approximately that of the nation with steadily rising real incomes, the models presented earlier suggest several variables to be influenced in achieving such goals:

1. *Threshold limitations.* Any policy that reduces thresholds will induce development to penetrate further down the hierarchy and out into the intermetropolitan periphery.

2. *Diffusion times.* Since the income effect is a declining function of time, any hastening of the diffusion process will bring a greater income effect to smaller and more distant areas.

3. *Accessibility.* Particularly in the case of household innovations, the extent to which families make use of new innovations in urban centers that have adopted them is a function of their access to these centers. Any decrease in effective distance will have a multiplicative effect in use of innovations because the distance-decay effect is negative exponential.

Notes

1. Elihu Katz, Martin L. Levin, and Herbert Hamilton, "Traditions of Research in the Diffusion of Innovations," *American Sociological Review* 28 (1963): 237–52.

2. Vida Nichols, *Growth Poles: An Investigation of Their Potential As a Tool for Regional Economic Development* (Philadelphia: Regional Science Research Institute Discussion Paper No. 30, 1969).

3. Francoise Boon, *A Simple Model for the Diffusion of an Innovation in an Urban System* (Chicago: Center for Urban Studies, University of Chicago, 1967); Raymond V. Bowers, "The Direction of Intra-Societal Diffusion," *American Sociological Review* 2 (1937): 826–36; Robert L. Crain, "Fluoridation: The Diffusion of an Innovation among Cities," *Social Forces* 44 (1966): 467–76; John Friedmann, *Regional Develop-*

ment Policy: A Case Study of Venezuela (Cambridge, Mass.: M.I.T. Press, 1966); Torsten Hägerstrand, *Innovation Diffusion As a Spatial Process* (Chicago: University of Chicago Press, 1953, 1967); John C. Hudson, "Diffusion in a Central Place System," *Geographical Analysis* 1 (1969): 45-48; Edgar C. McVoy, "Patterns of Diffusion in the United States," *American Sociological Review* 5 (1940): 219-27; Poul Ove Pedersen, "Innovation Diffusion Within and Between National Urban Systems," forthcoming in *Geographical Analysis*; Wilbur Thompson, "Internal and External Factors in the Development of Urban Economics," in H. S. Perloff and L. Wingo, eds., *Issues in Urban Economics* (Baltimore, Md.: Johns Hopkins University Press for Resources for the Future, Inc., 1968).

4. Pedersen, "Innovation Diffusion."

5. Brian J. L. Berry, *Geography of Market Centers and Retail Distribution* (Englewood Cliffs, N.J.: Prentice-Hall, Inc., 1967).

6. Brian J. L. Berry, "City Size and Economic Development: Conceptual Synthesis and Policy Problems, with Special Reference to South and Southeast Asia," in L. Jacobson and V. Prakash, eds., *Urbanization and National Development* (Beverly Hills, Cal.: Sage Publications, 1970); M. J. H. Mogridge, "Some Factors Influencing the Income Distribution of Households within a City Region," in A. J. Scott, ed., *Studies in Regional Science* (London: Pion Limited, 1969), pp. 117-42.

7. Edwin Mansfield, *The Economics of Technological Change* (New York: W. W. Norton & Company, Inc., 1968).

8. Chauncy D. Harris, "The Market as a Factor in the Localization of Industry in the United States," *Annals of the Association of American Geographers* 44 (1954): 315-48.

9. Thompson, "Internal and External Factors in the Development of Urban Economics."

10. Pedersen, "Innovation Diffusion."

11. Hudson, "Diffusion in a Central Place System."

12. Boon, *A Simple Model for the Diffusion of an Innovation.*

13. E. Casetti and R. K. Semple, "Concerning the Testing of Spatial Diffusion Hypotheses" *Geographical Analysis* 1 (1969): 254-59.

14. Pedersen, "Innovation Diffusion."

15. A. G. Wilson, "Towards Comprehensive Planning Models" (Paper presented at the London Conference of the Regional Science Association, August 26, 1967, and identified as MAU Note 72, Economic Planning Group, Ministry of Transport, London).

16. Ibid.

17. Hudson, "Diffusion in a Central Place System."

18. Casetti and Semple, "Concerning the Testing of Spatial Diffusion Hypotheses."

19. Ibid.

20. Brian J. L. Berry, *Growth Centers and Their Potential in the Upper Great Lakes Region* (Washington, D.C.: Upper Great Lakes Regional Commission, 1969); Lawrence A. Brown, *Diffusion Processes and Location* (Philadelphia: Regional Science Research Institute, Bibliography Series No. 4, 1968); Hägerstrand, *Innovation Diffusion.*

21. Mogridge, "Some Factors Influencing the Income Distribution of Households."

22. A. C. Nielsen Co., T.V. Households by Regions, States and Counties, 1953, 1956, 1959; U.S. Television Ownership Estimates by State, County and Designated Market Area, 1962, 1965; Designated Market Areas 1967-68, 1967, 1968.

23. Brian J. L. Berry, "Latent Structure of the American Urban System, in Brian J. L. Berry, ed., *City Classification Handbook* (New York: Wiley Interscience, 1971).

24. Berry, *Growth Centers and Their Potentials in the Upper Great Lakes Region.*

25. Berry, "Latent Structure of the American Urban System."

26. Ibid.

27. Nielsen, Designated Market Areas 1967-68.

28. R. Dernberg, R. Rosetti and H. Watts, *Studies in Household Consumer Behavior* (New Haven, Conn.: Yale University Press, 1958).

29. Berry, "Latent Structure of the American Urban System."

30. Mansfield, Economics of Technological Change.

31. Berry, *Growth Centers and Their Potentials in the Upper Great Lakes Region.*

32. A. O. Hirschman, *The Strategy of Economic Development* (New Haven, Con.:

Yale University Press, 1958); J. B. Parr, *The Nature and Function of Growth Poles in Economic Development* (Seattle: University of Washington, 1965).

References

BROWN, Lawrence A. (1968), *Diffusion Dynamics* (Lund Studies in Geography, Series B, Human Geography, No. 29).

MADDALA, G. S. and P. T. Knight (1967), "International Diffusion of Technical Change—A Case Study of the Oxygen Steel Making Process," *The Economic Journal* 77: 531–558.

MANSFIELD, Edwin (1968), *Industrial Research and Technological Innovation* (New York: W. W. Norton and Co.).

MISRA, R. P. (1968), *Diffusion of Agricultural Innovations* (Mysore: Prasaranga).

MORRILL, Richard L. (1968), "Waves of Spatial Diffusion," *Journal of Regional Science* 8: 1–18.

MYRDAL, Gunnar (1957), *Economic Theory and Underdeveloped Regions* (London: Duckworth).

PERROUX, François (1955), "Note sur la Notion de Pôle de Croissance," *Economie Appliquée* 8: 307–320.

PRED, Allan (1966), *The Spatial Dynamics of U.S. Urban-Industrial Growth, 1800–1914* (Cambridge: The M.I.T. Press).

PYLE, Gerald F. (1969), "The Diffusion of Cholera in the United States in the Nineteenth Century," *Geographical Analysis* 1: 59–75.

REDLICH, Fritz (1953), "Ideas—Their Migration in Space over Time," *Kyklos* 6: 301–22.

ROGERS, Everett M. (1962), *Diffusion of Innovations* (New York: The Free Press).

SIEBERT, Horst (1969), *Regional Economic Growth: Theory and Policy* (Scranton, Pa.: International Textbook Co.).

TIDEMAN, T. Nicolaus (1968), *The Theoretical Efficacy of "Potential" and Transport Cost Models* (Chicago: Center for Urban Studies, University of Chicago).

UNIVERSITY OF GLASGOW SOCIAL AND ECONOMIC STUDIES (1968), *Regional Policy in EFTA. An Examination of the Growth Center Idea* (Edinburgh: Oliver and Boyd).

PROGRAMMING A VIABLE MINIMAL INVESTMENT INDUSTRIAL COMPLEX FOR A GROWTH CENTER

J. PAELINCK
Netherlands Economic Institute (Rotterdam)

Introduction

In recent years, growth center policy has been intensively discussed, especially in French regional literature.[1] On the other hand, from the French, Dutch, Spanish, Portuguese, and Italian policy experiences, the need has emerged for some guidelines about how to conceive and stimulate some sort of optimum bunch of industries to start with, and some progress has been made in this regard. We are able to collect information on a group of industries that, taken together, would constitute a desirable and probably viable complex for a given region. The industrial program resulting from a study sponsored by the EEC. and designed for the Bari-Taranto region of the Mezzogiorno (southern Italy) is a good example of this. We know that complete implementation of such a program, given its total amount of investment, will take a certain number of years (five to ten years at a minimum), but can some sort of strategy be developed that gives some idea about where to start the program?

The present study is a first attack on the problem; it tries to select some criteria and constraints that would direct public authorities in their search for possible candidate-investors. Further work has to be undertaken, especially in the fields of sequential programs and the dynamic (spontaneous association) effects of a first partial investment program. It is hoped that from our attempt a new line of thought will emerge that might lead to the discovery of efficient (and in some sense, optimal) growth sequences for underdeveloped or stagnating regions.

We will first investigate what happened empirically to a certain number of spontaneous and planned industrial complexes. Then we will reconsider the setting of the problem and try to introduce suitable economic viability conditions. These conditions will be worked out mathematically, a solution procedure will be proposed, and the empirical properties of the solutions will be discussed. Finally, we will show, after a summary of the findings, how they can be an aid in devising a suitable policy for a developing area, and, in a later stage, some elementary theory of regional growth.

The Problem Raised by Industrial Complexes

For more than ten years industrial complexes have been a tool in regional analysis and policy. How efficient has this tool been?[2] We would like to investigate what happened in a number of industrial complexes over time and try to put forward a diagnosis of why, on the average, they have not behaved as well as one might have expected. A remedy to this situation will then be proposed and taken up in detail.

Examples of Industrial Complexes[3]

THE INDUSTRIAL COMPLEX OF LACQ (FRANCE)

Potential technical interdependences might be considered as important in Lacq, a gas-chemical complex in the French Basses-Pyrénées, and some of them have been worked out. The complex has been started without full economic-technical study. Most of the industries concerned have their main offices in Paris. Part of the gas is used locally, but much of it is sent off to existing industrial centers.

Two studies have been made to measure *ex post* the effects of the Lacq complex. Vertical integration of the complex has been observed, especially in the chemical sector, but leakages have been important; this is evident in differential growth rates in local incomes and value added, the former being lower than the latter. Some town-and-country planning has been carried out in the vicinity of Lacq.

TORINO (ITALY)

The Torino complex originated in the nineteenth century; it is essentially built on technically complex metalworking and mechanical industries. There are three dominant firms: Fiat, Lancia, and Olivetti. Subcontracting is a typical feature of their operations.

In this case, the problem was how to transmit polarizing effects to neighboring zones. Once more, it is not clear that this will occur spontaneously, and experts think that some public stimulus will be a prerequisite in order to obtain noticeable results. No criteria for rational grouping of the activities to be decentralized have been formulated.

THE PLANNED DUNKIRK COMPLEX (FRANCE)

The core of the Dunkirk complex is a steelworks (USINOR) planned to produce one million metric tons by 1980. Some forty firms composed an embryonic complex in 1966. However, due to a restricted market and consequent high production costs, the potential complex has hardly started to integrate the region, and subcontracting remains at a low level.

When the steelworks was started, no study of possible polarization effects existed. Only a global market and cost analysis has been undertaken, but no formal complex analyses have been attempted.

The general impression is that forward and backward linkage effects are weak for the time being; nevertheless, an industrial climate is tending to develop, training and reconversion of manpower are underway, and some positive effects may be expected in the future.

KOUILLOU (CONGO-BRAZZAVILLE)

At Kouillou is a hydroelectric project directed at energy-intensive consumers (aluminium, magnesium, chemicals). Links seem to be essentially of the tree type, and there exists little evidence of interlinkings between the industries, all of them producing intermediate products. A noteworthy element is that profitability has been considered in measuring the degree of potential successfulness of the proposed pseudo-complex; we will come back to this important factor later. In this case in particular, it is a necessity to coordinate the investments of different types of industries with the degree of overall development. Sequential analysis seems called for.

COMPLEX ANALYSIS OF PUERTO RICO

In Puerto Rico there is a potential complex of the petrochemical type, and it is one of the rare instances where formal analysis has been conducted *ex ante*. In our opinion, the main point to be stressed is the high variability of the profit margin as a function of joint production.[4]

The case is interesting because it indicates something about how efficiency at the analysis stage can guide later policy measures. In fact, oil refining and fertilizers have more or less developed according to the guidelines of the study, though synthetic fibers have lagged behind. On the other hand, there are indications that officials are favorably biased toward these types of studies, which allow them to base their decisions on something more than roughly quantified projections or single development projects whose desirable complements are not described.

It should be noted, however, that no systematic overall selection procedure—either static or sequential—has been developed. Something more on this subject will be said later.

THE GULF OF FOS (FRANCE)

In the Gulf of Fos case, the anticipated size of the complex is much greater than in any of the cases previously discussed.[5] Both a "mixed" complex (petrochemicals, metalworking) and different "layers" (sequential planning) have been considered.

In conformity with this approach, the central authorities will try to attract the chosen industries selectively. These have been designated on the basis of market analyses and technical considerations. An integrated regional policy, based on previously studied complementary industries, together with local planning of the concrete location sites, is thus characteristic for this case.[6]

It is too early to judge the overall effects of the scheme. Potential linkages have been studied, and policy has been conducted along these lines. Outward leakages are still possible, but our guess is that horizontal links will progressively build up to fill these gaps.

THE BARI-TARANTO INDUSTRIAL COMPLEX (ITALY)

As in the Torino case, the Bari-Taranto complex is based on industries of the mechanical "complex cycle" type; as in the Fos case, a thoroughgoing study—stimulated by the Common Market authorities—on potential markets and linkages has been a starting point. Basic industries and linked activities have been distinguished, and subcontracting has been systematically considered. Competitiveness and productivity considerations have prevailed, and external economies have been integrated through a careful study of intermediate flows of goods and services. In fact, a systematic elimination procedure has been applied, based on various criteria (regional specialization, optimal dimensions, availability of qualified manpower, dimension of the national and international markets). It should be noted also that the existence of multiple linkages allows a sequential implementation procedure.

Once more, as in the case of Fos, potential success is high despite the smaller dimensions of the project (8,200 workers in the complex itself). Site planning and state intervention (directly, or through fiscal stimulants) will follow or complement the plan.

Rationalizing the Selection Procedure

The cases discussed have been presented in more or less increasing order of analytic comprehensiveness. The trend is definitely toward the study of completely integrated complexes, utilizing competitive and profitable industries adapted to some strategic local characteristics. How efficient such a policy may be as a tool for regional development is far from clear; experiences are either partial or too recent.

The object of our study is to *rationalize* and *formalize* a certain number of elements that appear to be *a priori* economically important: the complex of industries as such, their interrelations, the externalities that can be locally derived, and finally, the necessary profitability condition in a mixed-economy environment.

To do this, we will set up a simple objective function that, together with certain profitability and level constraints, will allow us to select a reasonable starting point for politically implementing studies of the Fos and Bari-Taranto type. What we have to say is of a highly technical and mathematical nature, but our main conclusions and policy applications will be summed up in the last section of the paper.

The Mathematical Program

DATA

For a certain number, n, of interrelated industries selected as members of a regional industrial complex, we suppose the availability of the following three types of data.

Investment and labour functions. Investment and labor functions are supposed to be of the following form:

$$\frac{I_i}{I_{i0}} = \left(\frac{P_i}{P_{i0}}\right)^{\alpha_i}, \quad \left(\frac{L_i}{L_{i0}}\right) = \left(\frac{P_i}{P_{i0}}\right)^{\beta_i}$$

where I_i = investment for production in industry i, P_i; L_i = corresponding labor required for production; I_{i0}, L_{i0}, P_{i0} = minimal technical levels for the variables concerned;[7] α_i, β_i = characteristic parameters, $0 < \alpha_i$, $\beta_i < 1$. These engineering functions have sometimes been used in the literature;[8] they can be related to neoclassical production functions.[9]

Prices and related data. We are given the following information:

p_i^* = unit price of investment in product i;

p_i = unit price of product i, [net of intermediate inputs not considered in the industrial complex];

w_i = unit wage in producing product i;

ρ_i = unit period depreciation in product i;

π_i = desired relative profitability of investment i, per unit period.

External economies. Input = output links—coefficients a_{ij}—exist among the n productive activities; their matrix is assumed to be nondecomposable. Moreover, proximity of enterprises is assumed to affect unit delivered prices of a given input as a function of the production level of the seller.[10]

Both hypotheses can be formalized as

$$c_{ij} = p_{ij}a_{ij}e^{-\alpha_{ij}P^i}P_j$$

where c_{ij} is the total cost of intermediate product i in production process j, and α_{ij} the typical coefficient for external economies between processes i and j.

THE MODEL

Our model can finally be formulated as

$$\min I = \sum_i p_i^* I_i$$

$$= \sum_i p_i^* \left(\frac{I_{i0}}{P_{i0}^{\alpha_i}} \right) P_i^{\alpha_i} \qquad [1]$$

s.t.

$$p_i P_i - \sum_{j \neq i} p_j a_{ji} e^{-\alpha_{ji} P_j} P_i - w_i \left(\frac{L_{i0}}{P_{i0}^{\beta_i}} \right) P_i^{\beta_i} - \rho_i p_i^* \left(\frac{I_{i0}}{P_{i0}^{\alpha_i}} \right) P_i^{\alpha_i}$$

$$\geq \pi_i p_i^* \left(\frac{I_{i0}}{P_{i0}^{\alpha_i}} \right) P_i^{\alpha_i}, \forall i \qquad [2]$$

$$P_i \geq P_{i0}, \forall i \qquad [3]$$

This formulation is still primitive, in the sense that it does not allow for the presence or absence of production, as constraint [3] imposes a too restrictive condition, meaning that all n activities should be utilized.

We could reformulate [3] as

$$\text{either } P_i \geq P_{i0} \text{ or } P_i = O \qquad [3']$$

but then the obvious solution to program [1], [2], [3'] is $P_i = O$, $\forall i$.

We can, however, write the formal program as follows:

$$\min \sum_i p_i^* \left(\frac{I_{i0}}{P_{i0}^{\alpha i}} \right) P_i^{\alpha_i} x_i \qquad [1']$$

s.t.

$$p_i P_i x_i - \sum_{j \neq i} p_j a_{ji} e^{-\alpha_{ji} P_j x_j} P_i x_i - w_i \left(\frac{L_{i0}}{P_{i0}^{\beta_i}} \right) P_i^{\beta_i} x_i$$

$$- \rho_i p_i^* \left(\frac{I_{i0}}{P_{i0}^{\alpha i}} \right) P_i^{\alpha i} x_i \geq \pi_i p_i^* \left(\frac{I_{i0}}{P_{i0}^{\alpha i}} \right) P_i^{\alpha i} x_i, \forall i \qquad [2']$$

$$P_i \geq P_{i0}, \forall i \qquad [3]$$

$$x_i \geqslant 0, \text{ either 0 or 1, } \forall i \qquad [4]$$

$$\sum_i x_i \geqslant 1 \qquad [5]$$

As the model now stands, it represents a mixed integer, continuous, nonlinear program. No solution algorithm is known to us: we will discuss a possibly efficient way of solving the program, based on its specific characteristics.

Solution of the Program

REWRITING THE PROGRAM

Let us start again with formulation [1], [2], [3]. It can be written

$$\min I = \sum_i c_i P_i^{\alpha_i} \qquad [1']$$

s.t.

$$a_{ii}{}^* P_i - \sum_{j \neq i} a_{ji}^* e^{-\alpha_{ji} P_j} P_i - a_i P_i^{\alpha_i} - b_i P_i^{\beta_i} \geqslant 0, \forall i \qquad [2'']$$

$$P_i \geqslant P_{i0} \qquad [3]$$

where

$$c_i \overset{\Delta}{=} p_i{}^* \left(\frac{I_{io}}{P_{i0}{}^{\alpha_i}} \right)$$

$$a_{ii}{}^* \overset{\Delta}{=} p_i$$

$$a_{ji}{}^* \overset{\Delta}{=} p_j a_{ji}, j \neq i$$

$$a_i \overset{\Delta}{=} (\rho_i + \pi_i) p_i \left(\frac{I_{i0}}{P_{i0}{}^{\alpha_i}} \right)$$

$$b_i \overset{\Delta}{=} w_i \left(\frac{L_{i0}}{P_{i0}{}^{\beta_i}} \right)$$

Now [2'] can be rewritten as

$$\sum_{j \neq i} a_{ji}^{**} e^{-\alpha_{ji} P_j} + a_i^* P_i^{\alpha_i - 1} + b_i^* P_i^{\beta_i - 1} \leqslant 1, \forall i \qquad [2''']$$

where the new coefficients are the corresponding coefficients of [2'] divided by a_{ii}^*.

Constraint [3] can be rewritten as

$$P_{i0} P_i^{-1} \leqslant 1 \qquad [3'']$$

$$P_i \geqslant 0 \qquad [3''']$$

Program [1'], [2''], [3'] calls once more for an interior solution, as is immediately obvious.

It can be transformed into

$$\min I = \sum c_i P_i^{-\alpha_i} x_i \qquad [1'']$$

$$x_i \sum_{j \neq i} a_{ji}^{**} e^{-\alpha_{ji} P_j x_j} + a_i^* P_i^{\alpha_i - 1} x_i + b_i^* P_i^{\beta_i - 1} x_i \leqslant 1, \forall i \qquad [2'''']$$

$$P_{io} P_i^{-1} x_i \leqslant 1 \qquad [3'''']$$

$$P_i \geqslant 0 \qquad [3''']$$

$$x_i \geqslant 0, \text{ either } 0 \text{ or } 1, \forall i \qquad [4]$$

$$\sum_i x_i \geqslant 1 \qquad [5]$$

Condition [2''''] and [5] can be easily transformed so as to get a mixed integer-continuous geometric program.[11]

On the one hand, for E sufficiently large, we can replace in [2''''] the term

$$a_{ji}^{**} e^{-\alpha_{ji} P_j x_j}$$

by

$$a_{ji}^{**} t_j^{-E} \qquad \text{giving a condition} \qquad [2''''']$$

and the additional conditions

$$t_j^{-1} + \frac{\alpha_{ji}}{E} P_j x_j t_j^{-1} \leqslant 1, \forall_j \qquad [6]$$

$$t_j \geqslant 0, \forall_j \qquad [6']^{12}$$

On the other hand condition [5] can be replaced by

$$\frac{n}{\varepsilon} - \frac{1}{\varepsilon(1+\varepsilon)}^{-1} \sum_i (n_i + \varepsilon)^{-1} \leqslant 1 \qquad [5']$$

AN EFFICIENT SOLUTION PROCEDURE.

Despite the fact that (1''), (2'''''), (3'''), (3''''), (5'), (6), and (6') have now been expanded in the standard form for geometric programming, a solution would be intractable for two reasons: (1) no algorithm is known to us for solving mixed integer-continuous geometric programs, and (2) even an ordinary geometric program for our problem would have a large number of degrees of freedom.[13] A two-dimensional program (two production sectors) would already have degree of difficulty 9. This leads us to look for a step-by-step solution procedure.

We will start from the noninteger version, reproduced for the sake of clarity.

$$\text{Minimize I} = \sum_i c_i P_i^{\alpha_i} \qquad [1']$$

s.t.

$$\sum_{j \neq 1} a_{ji}^* e^{-\alpha_{ji} P_j} + a_i^* P_i^{\alpha_i - 1} + b_i^* P_i^{\beta_i - 1} \leqslant 1, \forall i \qquad [2''']^{14}$$

$$P_{i0} P_i^{-1} \leqslant 1 \qquad [3'']$$

$$P_i \geqslant 0 \qquad [3''']$$

The steps of the proposed search procedure can be described as follows:

A. Investigate a one-firm (first order) program.

1. At least one π_i-constraint is satisfied; the minimal $[P_{i0}]$ is optimal if

$$I_{i0} \leqslant \min_{j, k \neq i} (I_{j0} + I_{k0}).$$

The reason for this *sufficient* condition is that no minimal (optimal) l-program, $l \geqslant 2$, could be less expensive than

$$\min_{j, k \neq i} (I_{j0} + I_{k0}).$$

2. No π_i-constraint is satisfied; compute $P_i^{**} \triangleq \min P_i$ s.t. the corresponding π_i-constraint is satisfied. The solution is unique, the π_i-constraints being convex functions bounded from below.[15] If

$$P_i^* \leqslant \min_{j, k \neq i} (I_{jo} + I_{ko})$$

then P_i^* is optimal for the same reason as mentioned under A.1 above.

B. If neither P_{i0} nor P_i^* is optimal, investigate 2-programs.

1. At least one $[\pi_i, \pi_j]$ constraint is satisfied; the minimal $[P_{i0}, P_{j0}]$ program will be optimal if

$$I_{io} + I_{jo} \leqslant \min_{k, m, n, \neq i, j,} (I_{ko} + I_{mo} + I_{no})$$

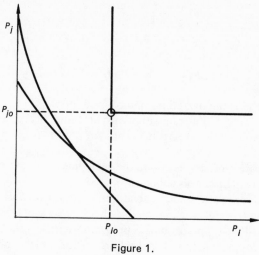

Figure 1.

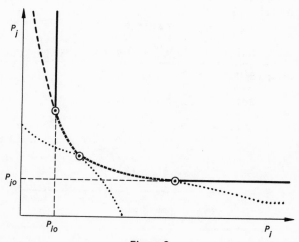

Figure 2.

2. No $[\pi_i, \pi_j]$ constraint is satisfied: compute

$$[P_i^*, P_j^*] \stackrel{\Delta}{=} \min [P_i^g, P_j^g]$$

where $[P_i^g, P_j^g]$ is the optimal $2(ij)$-solution obtained by geometric programming;[16] again if

$$[P_i^*, P_j^*] \leqslant \min_{k, m, n \neq i, j} (I_{ko} + I_{mo} + I_{no}),$$

then $[P_i^*, P_j^*]$ is the overall optimum solution.

Figures 1 and 2 illustrate situations B(1) and B(2);[17] the circled points or curves are the possible candidates for 2- or n-optima.

C. Investigate 3-programs, along the same lines.

The following remarks should be added.

1. Unless special economic conditions prevail (for instance, high required profit ratios), it is probable that on the average an overall optimum will be found for an n/h program where n is the number of industries investigated, and h the horizon for which—on intuitive grounds—the program is drafted; we expect, for instance, that for a 30-industry, 10-year plan a 3-program will generally be optimal.

2. One can give an idea about the importance of the calculations involved (Table 1).

TABLE 1

Stage	π_i-checks	G-programs[a]	Checks for optima[b]
A(1)	n	—	2
A(2)	—	n	2
B(1)	$\binom{n}{2}$	—	2
B(2)	—	$\binom{n}{2}$	2
G(1)	$\binom{n}{g}$	—	2
G(2)	—	$\binom{n}{g}$	2

[a] G-programs = geometric programs; for A(1) it simply means the solution of a posynomial.
[b] Computation of the minimal program and of $\min \sum_{j \in J} I_{jo}$ is straightforward.
(3) $g \leqslant n$.

3. The rationale for proposing the procedure just outlined rests on the presence of the P_{io}-constraints. No feasible program can ignore them; no optimal 1-program can be less costly than the corresponding $1(P_{io})$-program.

A complete enumeration of all feasible solutions $(2^n - 1)$ can be avoided, and is practically reduced to a manageable subset.

INTRODUCING SUPPLEMENTARY CONSTRAINTS

Production could be submitted to upper bounds. If these rest only on previously studied demand conditions, a simple constraint

$$P_i \bar{P}_i^{-1} \leqslant 1 \qquad [7]$$

can be introduced, where $\bar{P}_i$ is the upper level of P_i.

If both demand $(\bar{P}_i)$ and technical conditions $(\bar{\bar{P}}_i)$ fix upper limits to P_i, and if $\bar{\bar{P}} < \bar{P}$, a new variable, P_{2i}, can be defined, and functions of type

$$I_{i2} = c_{i2}(P_{i2} - \bar{\bar{P}}_i)^{\alpha_i}$$

can be introduced with suitable constraints to be written in a standardized geometric program form.

Properties of the Solutions

SOLUTION OF THE GEOMETRIC PROGRAM

Under suitable conditions[18] a dual problem has a common solution for its objective function with the primal; it can be formulated as follows:
Maximize

$$v(\delta) = \left[\prod_{i=1}^{n} \left(\frac{e_i}{\delta_i} \right)^{\delta_i} \right] \prod_{k=1}^{p} \lambda_k(\delta)^{\lambda_k(\delta)}$$

where

$$\lambda_k(\delta) = \sum_{i \varepsilon J[k]} \delta_i, \, k = 1, \ldots, p;$$

$$J[k] = \{m_k, m_{k+1}, \ldots, n_k\}, \, k = 1, \ldots, p;$$

$$m_o = 1, m = n_o + 1, \ldots, m_p = n_{p-1} + 1, n_p = n$$

e_i = coefficients of the primal posynomials

s.t.

$$\sum_{i \varepsilon J[0]}^{\delta \geqslant 0} \delta_i = 1 \text{ (normality condition)}$$

$$\sum_{i=1}^{n} \varepsilon_{ij}\delta_i = 0, j = 1, \ldots m \text{ (orthogonality condition),}$$

the ε_{ij} being the exponents of the primal posynomials.

No general solution algorithm is known to us, but we propose the following transformation to a quadratic problem (with linear constraints) for which solution algorithms are available.[19]

The monotonic increasing transform $\log_h v(\delta)$ attains its maximum for the same values of δ. Two sorts of terms appear in $v(\delta)$. A term

$$\left(\frac{e_i}{\delta_i}\right)^{\delta_i}$$

will be transformed into

$$\delta_i(\log_h e_i - \log_h \delta_i) = e_i^* \delta_i - \delta_i \log_h \delta_i.$$

The concave function $\log_h \delta_i$ can be approximated by

$$F(\delta_i) = a + b\delta_i - c\delta_i^{-1}, a, b, c > 0;$$

approximation can be ensured over a proper range of δ_i for any choice of h. For instance, if we want to cover the range $[0, 100]$, and if we choose $h = 10$, we obtain the system[20]

$$\begin{bmatrix} 1 & 1 & -1 \\ 1 & 1 & -1 \\ 1 & 100 & -.01 \end{bmatrix} \begin{bmatrix} a \\ b \\ c \end{bmatrix} \cdot = \begin{bmatrix} 0 \\ 1 \\ 2 \end{bmatrix}$$

giving the solutions

$$a = 1$$
$$b = .81(80.19)^1$$
$$c = 81(80.19)^1$$

satisfying the positivity constraints; empirical work should give hints as to a proper range for δ_i. Hence

$$\log\left(\frac{e_i}{\delta_i}\right)^{\delta_i} \approx (e_i^* + a)\,\delta_i + b\delta_i^2 - c$$

A similar operation can be performed on the terms λ_k, the proper bounds depending on the number of terms in the function $\lambda_K(\underline{\delta})$.

PROPERTIES OF INTERIOR SOLUTIONS

To investigate some properties of the solutions obtained from the geometric programs that have been outlined, a simple 2×2 example has been worked out.

In standard form the program presents itself as

$$\text{Min } 1 = c_1 P_1^{\alpha 1} + c_2 P_2^{\alpha 2}$$

s.t.

$$c_{11} t_2^{-E_{21}} + c_{12} P_1^{\beta_1 - 1} + c_{13} P_1^{\alpha_1 - 1} \leqslant 1$$

$$c_{22} t_1^{-E_{12}} + c_{21} P_2^{\beta_2 - 1} + c_{23} P_2^{\alpha_2 - 1} \leqslant 1$$

$$t_2^{-1} + c_{21}^* P_2 t_2^{-1} \leqslant 1$$

$$t_1^{-1} + c_{12}^* P_1 t_1^{-1} \leqslant 1$$

$$c_{10} P_1^{-1} \leqslant 1$$

$$c_{20} P_2^{-1} \leqslant 1$$

and

$$P_1, P_2, t_1, t_2 \geqslant 0.$$

Table 2 relates the coefficients to the original data.

TABLE 2

Coefficient	Value
c_1	$p_1^* l_{10} P_{10}^{-\alpha_1}$
c_2	$p_2^* l_{20} P_{20}^{-\alpha_2}$
c_{11}	$p_2 p_1^{-1} a_{21}$
c_{12}	$w_1 p_1^{-1} L_{10} P_{10}^{-\beta_1}$
c_{13}	$(\rho_1 + \pi_1) p_1^* p_1^{-1} l_{10} P_{10}^{-\alpha_1}$
c_{22}	$p_1 p_2^{-1} a_{12}$
c_{21}	$w_2 p_2^{-1} L_{20} P_{20}^{-\beta_2}$
c_{23}	$(\rho_2 + \pi_2) p_2^* p_2^{-1} l_{20} P_{20}^{-\alpha_2}$
c_{21}^*	$\alpha_{21} E_{21}^{-1}$
c_{12}^*	$\alpha_{12} E_{12}^{-1}$
c_{10}	P_{10}
c_{20}	P_{20}

The dual presents itself with 9 degrees of freedom. Suppose that wages are zero, no external economies occur, and that no minimal production is to be attained. Then the dual reduces to

$$\max v = \left(\frac{c_1}{\delta_1}\right)^{\delta_1} \left(\frac{c_2}{\delta_2}\right)^{\delta_2} \left(\frac{c_{13}}{\delta_5}\right)^{\delta_5} \left(\frac{c_{23}}{\delta_8}\right)^{\delta_8} (\delta_5)^{\delta_5} (\delta_8)^{\delta_8}$$

s.t.

$$\begin{cases} \delta_1 + \delta_2 && = 1 \\ \alpha_1\delta_1 + (\alpha_1 - 1)\delta_5 = 0 \\ \alpha_2\delta_2 + (\alpha_2 - 1)\delta_8 = 0 \end{cases}$$
$$\delta_1, \delta_2, \delta_5, \delta_8 \geqslant 0$$

This system can be expressed as

$$\underline{\delta} = \underline{b}^0 + r_1 \underline{b}^1$$

where r_1 is arbitrary. Solution gives

$$b^0 = \begin{bmatrix} 1 - (\alpha_1 - 1)(\alpha_2 - 1) \\ (\alpha_1 - 1)(\alpha_2 - 1) \\ \alpha_1(1 - \alpha_1)^{-1} - \alpha_1(\alpha_1 - 1) \\ \alpha_2(1 - \alpha_1) \end{bmatrix}, \; b^1 = \begin{bmatrix} -(\alpha_1 - 1)(\alpha_1 - 1) \\ -(1 - \alpha_1)(\alpha_2 - 1) \\ \alpha_1(\alpha_2 - 1) \\ \alpha_2(1 - \alpha_1) \end{bmatrix}$$

and $-1 \leqslant r_1 \leqslant B^{-1} - 1$, $B = (\alpha_1 - 1)(\alpha_2 - 1)$

due to the positivity constraints.

In case $\delta_i > 0$, $\forall_i$, the solution can be derived from

$$\frac{\partial \log v(r_1)}{\partial r_1} = 0$$

which gives the optimal value

$$r_1^0 = \left[(C^{-B^{-1}} + 1)B\right]^{-1} - 1,$$

where

$$C = c_1^{-B} c_2^{B} c_{13}^{\alpha_1(\alpha_2 - 1)} c_{23}^{\alpha_2(1 - \alpha_2)}.$$

We know that

$$\frac{\delta_1}{\delta_2} = \frac{c_1 P_1^{\alpha_1}}{c_2 P_2^{\alpha_2}} = \frac{I_1}{I_2} = \frac{1 - (1 + r_1)(\alpha_1 - 1)(\alpha_2 - 1)}{(1 + r)(\alpha_1 - 1)(\alpha_2 - 1)} = C^{-\frac{1}{B}} = \frac{c_1}{c_2} \cdot \frac{c_{13}^{\frac{\alpha_1}{1 - \alpha_1}}}{c_{23}^{\frac{\alpha_2}{1 - \alpha_2}}}$$

This expression allows us to easily study the relative contributions of each investment at the optimum. This relation will, of course, be distorted by external economies, as we shall see now.

By treating the system[21]

$$\text{Min } c_1 P_1^{\alpha_1} + c_2 P_2^{\alpha_2}$$

s.t.

$$c_{11} P_2^{-E_{21}} + c_{13} P_1^{\alpha_1 - 1} \leqslant 1$$

$$c_{22} P_1^{-E_{12}} + c_{23} P_2^{\alpha_2 - 1} \leqslant 1$$

or equivalently maximizing

$$v(r) = \left(\frac{c_1}{\delta_1}\right)^{\delta_1}\left(\frac{c_2}{\delta_2}\right)^{\delta_2}\left(\frac{c_{11}}{\delta_3}\right)^{\delta_3}\left(\frac{c_{13}}{\delta_5}\right)^{\delta_5}\left(\frac{c_{22}}{\delta_6}\right)^{\delta_6}\left(\frac{c_{23}}{\delta_8}\right)^{\delta_8}(\delta_3+\delta_5)^{\delta_3+\delta_5}(\delta_6+\delta_8)^{\delta_6+\delta_8}$$

s.t.

$$\delta_1+\delta_2 = 1$$
$$\alpha_1\delta_1+(\alpha_1-1)\delta_5-E_{12}\delta_6 = 0$$
$$\alpha_2\delta_2-E_{21}\delta_3+(\alpha_2-1)\delta_8 = 0$$

one obtains

$$\delta(r) = \begin{bmatrix} -E_{21}(\alpha_1-1-E_{12}) \\ 1+E_{21}(\alpha_1-1-E_{12}) \\ -\alpha_2(\alpha_1-1-E_{12})-\alpha_1(\alpha_2-1) \\ \alpha_1 E_{21} \\ \alpha_1 E_{21} \\ \alpha_1 E_{21} \end{bmatrix} + \begin{bmatrix} -E_{21}(\alpha_1-1) \\ E_{21}(\alpha_1-1) \\ -\alpha_2(\alpha_1-1) \\ \alpha_1 E_{21} \\ 0 \\ 0 \end{bmatrix} r_1 +$$

$$+ \begin{bmatrix} E_{12}E_{21} \\ -E_{12}E_{21} \\ -\alpha_2 E_{12} \\ 0 \\ \alpha_1 E_{21} \\ 0 \end{bmatrix} r_2 + \begin{bmatrix} 0 \\ 0 \\ \alpha_1(\alpha_2-1) \\ 0 \\ 0 \\ \alpha_1 E_{21} \end{bmatrix} r_3$$

Three remarks can be made. First we have

$$\frac{I_1}{I_2} = \frac{\delta_1}{\delta_2} = \frac{-E_{21}(\alpha_1-1-E_{12})-E_{21}(\alpha_1-1)r_1+E_{12}E_{21}r_2}{1+E_{21}(\alpha_1-1-E_{12})+E_{21}(\alpha_1-1)r_1-E_{12}E_{21}r_2}$$

where

$$-1 < r_1 < -[E_{21}(\alpha_1-1)]^{-1}-1$$
$$-1 < r_2 < (E_{12}E_{21})^{-1}-1$$

due to the positivity condition on δ, as can be easily verified. Taking extreme cases, one verifies that

$$\frac{\partial}{\partial E_{21}}\left(\frac{I_1}{I_2}\right) > 0$$

so that with increasing positive externalities in P_2, the relative burden of I_1 increases.

Furthermore, we know that the lagrangian multiplier corresponding to the first π_i-constraint is[22]

$$\mu_1 = (\delta_3 + \delta_5)v^0 = \frac{\partial I}{\partial \pi_i} > 0$$

As our system minimizes under upper constraints and as an increase in E_{21} corresponds to a relaxation of the constraint, it means that externalities decrease the burden of overall investment. Similar conclusions can be reached, of course, for every E_{ij}.

Finally, we have

$$\frac{\mu_1}{\mu_2} = \frac{\delta_3 + \delta_5}{\delta_6 + \delta_8} = \frac{x^* + \dfrac{B(r_1 r_2 r_3)}{\alpha_1 E_{21}}}{y^*}$$

where

$$x^* = 1 + r_1 > 0, \ y^* = 2 + r_2 + r_3 > 0,$$

and B is a complex expression in various parameters of the problem excluding E_{21}. In the absence of analytical expressions for r_1, r_2 and r_3, it is difficult to say how E_{21} would affect the ratio μ_1/μ_2, as the r-vector would also be changed.

Summary of Findings and Policy Conclusions

The findings of this study can be summarized as follows:

1. Given a bunch of feasible industries for a development region, the selection of a minimal investment complex can be set up as an integer geometric program.

2. This program can be sequentially solved through an approximation of its dual; the result is a subcomplex of minimally profitable industries, of which the levels of production can be computed.

3. Externalities play an important part in calibrating the relative levels of investment in the selected industries; it is probable, too, that the specific bunch selected will depend on these externalities. Moreover, they decrease the minimum amount of investment necessary to sustain an economically viable complex.

4. The objective function and the constraints can be modified. It is evident that the model, as it stands now, is in a sense too simplistic to be implemented as such. Other objective functions can be introduced and might eventually lead to better hypotheses on regional economic growth; in other words, the improved model might be the core for a new line of thinking in the theory of regional economic development. In any case, our findings do have some policy implications.

First, the dual prices of the problem can give an idea of the importance of certain constraints. For instance, given all the technical coefficients, it can be worked out how the solution in I (total investment) depends on the profitability constraints. More specifically, the minimum profitability required by investors or poor labor conditions that result in high nominal wage/labor productivity ratios can be investigated, and this can give indications as to what policy would most be efficient in reducing investment requirements (for example, schooling of unqualified labor, temporary subsidies to investors).

Second, the method allows one to study the impact of externalities. It will automatically select an optimal k-bunch of industries, taking this feature into account. If the total bunch initially selected has poor externality prospects, study of the solutions will possibly allow us to reconsider this selection in favor of a different starting point for setting up an industrial complex.

An efficient way of handling the problem would be to investigate successive truncated minimal investment programs $P^1, P^2, \ldots, P^m$, $m < n$, where the previous minimal programs are considered as given. The sum of these investments will be greater than once-and-for-all overall investment, as the constraints of this overall problem are relaxed compared to those of the partial problems. An indication of the relative cost of this timing would be the quantity

$$C^* = \frac{\sum_{i=1}^{m} I_i}{I^{\text{overall}}} - 1$$

On the other hand, interest cost can be saved over the time-horizon (H) of the program, as Figure 3 shows.

Maximizing this interest saved would lead to postponement of the $P^2, \ldots, P^m$ fractions of the program. An optimal time profile could be computed from

$$\max_{0-H} G = G(-R,P)$$

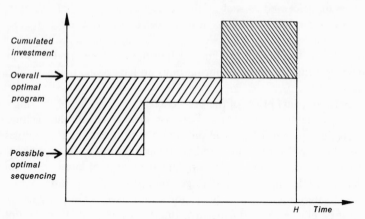

Figure 3.

where R stands for interest sums to be saved, and P for the opportunity value of having programs $P^2, \ldots, P^m$ executed.

Which relations exist between this sort of optimality and other criteria for efficient economic growth (modified golden rules, for example) is still another problem to be tackled.

Notes

1. For an appraisal, see D. F. Darwent, *Growth Poles and Growth Center Concepts: A Review, Evaluation and Bibliography*, Working Paper No. 89, Center for Planning and Development Research, Institute of Urban and Regional Development, University of California, Berkeley, October, 1968.

2. On this efficiency problem of measures of regional economic policy, see J. Paelinck, ed., "L'efficacité des mesures de politique économique régionale," Namur, Faculté des Sciences Economiques, Centre de Recherches, 1967.

3. A student of ours at the University of Paris Development Institute prepared, under our direction, an essay from which much of the material of this section is taken. For further details see J. C. Neffa, "Complexes industriels et programmation régionale," Université de Paris, I.E.D.E.S., 1967.

4. W. Isard, E. W. Schooler and T. Vietorisz, *Industrial Complex Analysis and Regional Development* (New York: John Wiley & Sons, Inc., 1959).

5. One hundred thousand persons would be employed in 1985 (by direct, indirect and induced effects).

6. Even a new town is considered in this respect.

7. Maximal levels can also be considered.

8. Isard, *et al.*, *Industrial Complex Analysis*; J. Kornai (with T. Liptak and P. Wellish), *Mathematical Planning of Structural Decisions* (Amsterdam: North-Holland Publishing Company, 1967).

9. J. C. de Meester and J. Paelinck, "Fonctions de production néo-classiques dérivées de données technologiques: la fonction CES non-homogène," in *Recherches récentes en matière de fonctions de production*, Namur, Faculté des Sciences Economiques, Centre de Recherches, 1968.

10. See also S. Reiter and G. R. Sherman, "Allocating Indivisible Resources Affording External Economies or Diseconomies," *International Economic Review* (1962): 108–35.

11. R. J. Duffin, E. L. Peterson, and C. Zener, *Geometric Programming, Theory and Applications* (New York: John Wiley & Sons, Inc., 1967).

12. Ibid., p. 101.

13. "Degrees of difficulty," in the terminology of Duffin, Peterson, and Zener in *Geometric Planning*.

14. Hereafter condition [2‴] will be referred to as the π_i-constraint, condition [3″] as the P_{i0}-constraints.

15. Duffin, *et al.*, *Geometric, Programming* p. 83.

16. The exponential terms should be approximated by power-functions.

17. Forms of the graphs are derived from convexity and lower boundedness properties. Duffin, *et al.*, *Geometric Programming*, p. 80 ff.

18. Duffin, *et al.*, *Geometric Programming*, p. 80 ff.

19. G. Hadley, *Nonlinear and Dynamic Programming* (Reading, Mass.: Addison-Wesley, 1964), chap. 7.

20. Derived from the condition $f(1) = 0, f(10) = 1, f(100) = 2$.

21. The t_i have been replaced by P_i, as only interior solutions are considered.

22. This can be stated under the strict positivity condition of δ.

DEVELOPMENT POLES
AND RELATED THEORIES:
A SYNOPTIC REVIEW*

TORMOD HERMANSEN
Institute of Sociology, University of Bergen

Introductory Remarks

The concept of development poles (*pôles de croissance*) is a recent one in theories of economic growth and regional development, and it is still far from being well established. It has, nevertheless, together with similar concepts such as growth centres, growth areas, growing points, development nuclei, core areas, and the like attracted increasing attention in the search for tools to resolve problems of imbalance in interregional development in industrialized as well as in nonindustrialized countries. The popularity of these concepts and the basic idea beneath—*i.e.*, the alleged superiority of decentralized concentration of development efforts as a strategy for speeding up the process of economic growth and interregional integration and equalization—is well illustrated by the fact that their validity is assumed to be independent of the economic and social systems of the countries within which they are to be applied.[1]

The concept of *pôles de croissance* and the related body of theory were originally developed as a tool to describe and explain the anatomy of economic development in abstract economic space.[2] However, during the course of time the scope of the theory and the concept have been broadened and reoriented to include also the

* This paper is an abbreviated and adapted version of an earlier one which, under the title "Development Poles and Development Centres in National and Regional Development-Elements of a Theoretical Framework for Synthetical Approach", was written while I was associated with the Program of Research in Regional Development of the United Nations Research Institute for Social Development in Geneva. The author wishes to express his indebtedness to Dr. A. R. Kuklinski for valuable advice during the work on this project.

normative issues of policy intervention and planning. Thus, the theory is now viewed as a general theory of development in a simultaneous sectoral-temporal-spatial setting.[3] A consequence, however, of the generalization of the theory on one side and the increased popularity and abuse of the concepts as catchwords in the political discussion of regional problems has been that they have lost much of their original content and meaning and thereby have become more elusive and ill-suited for empirical testing and practical application on a scientific basis.

As opposed to what is usual in economics, the theory of development poles as founded by Perroux is derived inductively from observations of the actual process of economic development.[4] Based on the observation and subsequent recognition that "development does not appear everywhere and all at once: it appears in points or development poles with variable intensities; it spreads along diverse channels and has varying terminal effects for the whole of the economy,"[5] Perroux was led to the conception of development as essentially polarized in the sense that forces inherent in the development process worked toward clustering of economic activities and growth and toward imbalance between industries and geographical areas. His theory is essentially a theory of development. It purports to explain the entire process of structural change in the economic as well as in the social and even institutional systems, as opposed to a theory of economic growth that concentrates on the conditions for expansion of aggregate production and total income only. Although, as it will be seen, Perroux originally was not particularly concerned with the spatial aspects of development in its purely geographical sense, application of the development pole theory has been concentrated mainly on problems of inter- and intraregional development. Typically, all the closely related concepts mentioned above refer to geographical or territorial aspects of development emphasizing the tendency for clustering of economic development in certain areas or centers as inherent in the economic forces and concomitant to economic development. There are reasons, however, to believe that the confusion of the concepts and theories referring to territorial clusterings with the much more general theory of development poles is one of the causes for the weakening of the analytical strength of the theory.[6]

On the other hand, it is no coincidence that development pole theory has attracted the attention of regional planners and economists.[7] First, it is obvious that the creation of poles or clusters of development is nowhere so clearly demonstrated as in geographical space. Second, the global character of the development pole theory—*i.e.*, its alleged capacity to integrate all relevant aspects of development—is particularly important at the regional level because the success or failure of a region to develop usually is attributed not to single factors but to complexes of entangled cause and effect relations. Or, as it is put by Balassa in suggesting that the interdependence among individual incomes in the process of development should be used as a criterion for identifying regions: "The use of this criterion is not justified by the hypothesis that regions grow and decay as entities rather than having their income changed as outcomes of sums of independent variations in particular activities located in the regions."[8] Therefore, what is searched for in order to provide a scientific basis for regional planning[9] is precisely a global theory of development which integrates all interrelated aspects of development in their geographical setting. The question, therefore, is whether the growth pole theory is capable of providing this theoretical foundation and framework for comprehensive regional planning.

It is my purpose to inquire into this problem and to explore the relations of this relatively loose body of theory to other theories dealing with different aspects of the same subject matter, namely, the spatial dimension of national development and the interrelations between the various aspects and factors of development in their spatial setting. Ultimately, my aim is to provide the essential elements to be included in a synthetic concept of development poles.

It will be clear from my review and discussions throughout that even if development pole theory still is far from being a full-fledged theory of regional development upon which policy making and planning can be safely based, it does provide a core that together with other elements of theory is of considerable interest, at least for practical purposes of planning. It should be stressed, however, that although the ultimate aim should be to arrive at an integrated synthetic theory of development poles in a regional context, the task set here is more limited. It is confined to giving a survey of the various theoretical elements of which such a synthetic theory would be composed, with a particular view to their source of origin and their relations to the basic theme as indicated above. This survey is therefore not intended to include all contributions to the field nor is it meant to undertake a thorough appraisal of the various approaches, conceptual frameworks, and theories touched upon either with respect to their validity under changing conditions or from the point of view of their usefulness in policy making and planning.

Towards a Comprehensive Concept of Development Poles in a Spatial Setting

The conception of the process of development as polarized, *i.e.*, involving a formation of clusters and/or peaks of development, is an essential point of departure in the development pole theory. This process of polarization is alleged to characterize the development process in its entirety as well as its composite aspects. However, this recognition is in itself not a theory. What is needed is, from a *descriptive* point of view, a specification of variables and yardsticks that will enable us to survey and identify the processes of polarization as they actually manifest themselves. From a *positive* point of view, a number of hypotheses must be suggested by which these variables are tied together and thus provide explanations of why the development process tends to exhibit the particular feature of polarization with respect to each subprocess as well as with respect to its totality. From a *normative* point of view, it is necessary to provide a set of criteria in accordance with which the contended superiority of polarized as compared to other patterns of development can be proved. And finally, from a *control* point of view, the theory must identify the degrees of freedom for intervention and the instruments and tools to employ in a deliberate direction of the process of development, aiming at achieving development goals derived from a normative analysis.

The formulation and testing of such a general theory of polarized development is such a tremendous task that one suspects any solution to be either tautological or so general that it can yield very little practical guidance.[10] It is nevertheless precisely such a general theory, albeit at a high level of aggregation, one would need in order to undertake comprehensive development planning in a consistent and meaningful way. In addition to this global theory of development, one would need a set of related theories of the subprocess of development that could provide identification, explanation, and guidelines of a more specific nature.

A critical aspect of the development pole theory is the explanation of how the poles are generated and how the development impulses are spread among such poles. This becomes evident when the theory is extended to include also the time and geographical dimensions of development, *i.e.*, when it is extended to become a tool to understand the interactions between the development process as described by its composite aspects and the distribution of development in time and space. It is precisely to this interaction that the development pole theory in its geographical setting addresses itself.[11] It is important to recognize the interaction character of this problem, namely, that the distribution of development over territorial space that can be found at a certain point in time is a result of the historical process of development that by its very existence will influence the future path of development, which in turn will influence the change in distribution of development in space and time during the future course of the process.[12] A development pole theory applicable to geographical space must in its *descriptive* version be able to identify the nature of the process of polarization as it manifests itself in geographical space. In its *positive* version, it must be able to explain this process by reference to the polarized nature of development in general and to the particular influence of geographical space as a frame of development. The key questions to be answered are those related to the formation and spread of poles in geographical space, the structural characteristics of the spatial pattern of poles, the interaction between this pattern and the development process, and the diffusion of development impulses among the poles.

As a *normative* theory it should suggest criteria for optimum distribution of socioeconomic, cultural, and political administrative activities among geographical poles and criteria to determine how the network of poles should be adjusted during time. Finally, as a *control* theory, it should identify the degrees of freedom for intervention and for steering the changes in the network of poles, and it should identify the instruments and tools to employ in steering and the tools for assessing the efficiency of various baskets of instruments.

It will be clear from the review that follows that no general theory exists that is capable of answering all the questions raised above. However, what can be found is the theory of polarized economic development formulated originally by Perroux[13] with a view to the economic aspects of development in general, which has been extended

by Boudeville to include the geographical dimension as well.[14] Both
these theories are *dynamic* in the sense that the time dimension and
intertemporal relations play an important role. Whereas these two
theories focus upon the mechanisms beneath the formation and
growth of economic development poles largely in an *inductive*
manner, there exists another body of theories (namely, the so-called
central place theories originally developed by Christaller[15] and
extended by Losch[16]) that focuses upon the location and the geographical size distribution of clusters of economic activities. This
body of theories is, however, conceptually and substantially very
different from those of Perroux and Boudeville in that they are
derived in a *deductive* manner within the context of a static framework. A key problem in the formulation of a general theory of
polarized development is, therefore, to establish the relations between
these two bodies of theories. Although this may seem difficult when
seen from a descriptive and/or positive point of view, a reformulation
to a control approach may facilitate such a reconciliation. The
relation between geographical clusters appears to be quite well
established within the *static* models of Christaller and Losch; but
when it comes to the diffusion of development impulses between poles
that occur in a dynamic setting, a new theoretical approach is
required. At this point, attention is drawn to the hypotheses of
Hirschman[17] and Myrdal[18] about the geographical incidence and
spread of economic growth. These hypotheses offer a useful point of
departure for incorporating the spread effects so far as economic
aspects are concerned. However, this theory treats the geographical
dimension only indirectly, and there is still a gap to be filled with
respect to the territorial manifestation of the spread of development.
It is intended that this gap can, to a large extent, be filled by Hägerstrand's[19] theory of geographical diffusion of information and innovation, which is equally applicable to social and cultural elements of
development, and by Pottier's theory of axes of development.[20]
Particular attention is drawn to recent efforts to integrate theories of
geographical diffusion of innovations with the central place theory.
The theories referred to above have all been concerned with *economic*
growth and development. However, to establish a real synthetic
concept of development poles, cultural, social, and administrative
aspects of development should be included as well. However, at this
point, the lack of theory seems even more profound. Attention is
called only to the loose assembly of hypotheses and theoretical

elements that deals with the role of the city in economic and socio-cultural development and with the optimum size of cities.

To sum up, I shall review a number of theoretical elements dealing with the process of development in general and with its geographical dimension in particular. Some of these are descriptive and some positive, some based on deduction and some on induction, and they differ considerably with respect to scope as well. Very few include elements of normative and control approaches. It seems, however, that it is when they are put in a control context that they can be most easily reconciled. The obvious reason for this is that when dealing with problems of a descriptive or positive character, solutions can be found by isolating the variables concerned from the disturbances of other variables simultaneously at work. The methods of descriptive and positive analysis, therefore, by their very nature lead to frag-mentation of theories. However, when one comes to the problem of planning and *development control*, what is needed above all are theories of a comprehensive character that integrate all the frag-ments of theoretical elements and explanations arrived at in descrip-tive and positive analysis. Naturally, what can be gained in compre-hensiveness has to be paid for by less profundity. But insofar as the aims of development control are defined with reference to the process of development in its entirety, there seems to be no way but to pay this price. Therefore, it is my contention here that in attempting to elaborate a comprehensive theory of development poles applicable to geographical space, the control approach should be employed as a device for reformulation and integration.

The elusiveness of the concept of development poles and the diversity of its interpretations in the context of specific problems of interregional balance have already been noted above. As it will be clear from the following review, the difficulties stem not only from the broadening and consequential loss of content of one concept but also from its being put together with a number of similar concepts from related fields and modified under their impact. Therefore, before commencing the following review, it may be advisable to note the desirability of improved conceptual apparatus and precision in the formulation of ideas and hypotheses expressed by two well-known students in the field, Paelinck and Hansen.

In the words of Paelinck:

The development pole concept has often been misunderstood. It has been confused with the notions of key industry, basic industry, and industrial ensemble; from this follows the erroneous conception according to which the development pole would be an industrial monument raised to the glory of future regional industrialization, a guarantee of certain economic growth. Or again ... some would have as a development pole any important establishment of firms, preferably industrial, which would exercise beneficial effects on the geographical area where it is located.[21]

Hansen has this to say:

The theory is badly in need of a thorough semantic re-working, the concepts and the language which characterize it need more precise definitions and more consistent usage. ... In general, then, greater emphasis in conceptual clarity is needed if the development pole theory is to provide tools for more operationally feasible regional developmental models.[22]

However, although recognizing the general validity of the above statements, we shall in this paper be more concerned with the identification of concepts and theories and their mutual relations than with their much-needed semantic reworking.

Economic Space and Development Poles

The concept of growth poles was originally introduced and put into systematic use by Perroux in his classic article of 1955.[23] The concept suggested is closely related to his particular notion of abstract economic space as a field of forces consisting of centers, poles or foci "from which centrifugal forces emanate and to which centripetal forces are attracted. Each center being a center of attraction and repulsion has its proper field which is set in the field of other centers."[24] From the outset, it is important to note that Perroux originally was concerned with *economic growth* and primarily with firms and industries and their interrelations, not with the geographical pattern of economic activity or the geographical applications of economic growth and intra- and interindustrial shifts. To Perroux, geographical space appears to be only one, and a rather "banal," type of space. He maintains that it is possible to distinguish "as many economic spaces as there are constituent structures of abstract relations that define each object of economic science." It is among the centers of this field of forces—working in the various economic spaces that could be defined—that Perroux identifies his growth poles in which economic growth occurs and is spread throughout the rest of the economy. Thus, Perroux's concept of a growth pole is highly abstract.[25] It was introduced as a tool to explore the process by which economic activities, *i.e.*, firms and industries, appear, grow, stagnate, and sometimes disappear. Hence, the process of economic growth is conceived of as essentially unbalanced involving a succession of dynamic poles through time.

Perroux developed his theory in search of a coherent explanation of how the modern process of economic development deviates from Cassel's stationary conception of equilibrium growth.[26] He based his argument heavily on Schumpeter's theories of the role of innovations and large scale firms.[27] Also, to Perroux, entrepreneurial innovations are the prime causal factors behind economic progress. He argues, as does Schumpeter, that most innovating activities take place in the large economic units that are able to dominate their environment in the sense of exercising irreversible and partially reversible influence on other economic units by reason of their dimension, negotiating strength, and by the nature of their operations and so on.[28] The close relationship between scale of operations, dominance, and impulses to innovate appears to be a most significant feature of Perroux's theory, which leads him to the concepts of dynamic firms and leading industries. Although Perroux is far from clear in his conceptualization and in the application of his theory,[29] it seems that the most remarkable characteristics of a *dynamic propulsive firm* are that it is a relatively large one, it generates significant growth impulses to its environment, it has a high ability to innovate, and, finally, that it belongs to a fast-growing sector. The features of a *leading propulsive industry* are similar. Leading propulsive industries are relatively new ones, operating at a technically advanced level in markets with high income elasticities of the products. Moreover, such industries exert a considerable influence on their industrial environment through interindustry linkages.[30]

Interindustry linkages and the theory of industrial interdependence play a major role in the development pole theory. As a matter of fact, this theory together with the Schumpeter theory of development as propelled by waves of innovations can be said to constitute the two cornerstones upon which Perroux bases his theory. The theory of industrial interdependence is basically a tool to conceptualize and give clearer meanings to the rather vague notions of dominance, forward and backward linkages, leading and key industries, industrial complexes, and development poles.[31] The notion of industrial dominance is derived from, among other things, triangularization of the table of interindustry deliveries, *i.e.*, the input-output table, on the basis of the criterion of the best customer. Patterns of dominance are found by arranging the interindustry table into a hierarchical ordering where any industry tends to dominate downward and to be dominated from those above. The meaning of domination is made more precise by the concepts of backward and forward linkage effects.[32] An industry is said to exert a strong *backward linkage* effect if it has a high ratio of intermediary inputs delivered from the other industries to its total production. Such an industry tends to dominate its input-delivery industries in the sense that it induces expansionary or stagnatory forces into them, depending upon its own trend of development. According to Perroux, such a backward linkage industry will depend on other industries for determination of its rate dominating industry can be said to be a *key industry* insofar as it determines the amount of expansion induced in dependent industries relative to its own expansion.[33] *Forward linkage* industries, on the other hand, tend to be dominated and to have a higher ratio of intermediary deliveries to final demand. Thus, a forward linkage industry will depend on other industries for determination of its rate of expansion. However, by producing important intermediaries to other industries, it will be able to induce expansion in these by transmitting innovations or effects of innovations forward.

In any interindustry table, it will usually be relatively easy to establish hierarchical orderings and patterns of domination for some groups of industries, notably those characterized by one-way sequences of production. An example occurs in the case of raw materials that are transformed into intermediaries and further into final products without important feedback effects. This structure of industrial interdependence will create real poles of development only if the key industry is a dynamic or propulsive one (*i.e.*, with an extremely strong capacity to innovate) that faces a highly income-elastic demand curve. Other groups of industries, however, tend to form clusters around a core of industries of a highly propulsive strength (*i.e.*, industries with a high capacity to transmit growth impulses through both backward and forward linkages). Such clusters are said to constitute *industrial complexes*.[34] The prominent feature of such a complex is that the expansion of any of the industries would set in motion a process of development sustained by a very high supermultiplier, *i.e.*, the combined effect of the ordinary final demand multiplier and induced interindustry deliveries, which are further supported by the investment accelerator. Such a process of development would be termed *polarized* insofar as it contributes to the formation and strength of development poles. However, an industrial complex would constitute a *development pole* in industrial space only if the propulsive industries constituting its core also belong to the category of *leading industries*, *i.e.*, those propulsive industries that are relatively new, working at an advanced technological level, facing rapidly increasing demand, and having a strong capacity to generate, adopt, and transmit innovations throughout their sphere of influence. Furthermore the pole as a whole should be large enough to exert a dominant influence over its industrial environment. The development of the national economy can then be visualized as a process of differentiation of growth among industrial complexes and poles of development. The succession of dynamic poles through time then implies that as old poles mature and gradually stagnate, they are replaced by new poles that emerge as the propulsive force of national economic development.[35]

At the level of theoretical reasoning employed so far, there appear to be few substantial difficulties involved in joining the Schumpeter theory of development and the theory of interindustry interdependence. In practice, however, this synthesis has turned out to be very problematic and in fact a major source of confusion, probably because of the choice of Leontief-type interindustry input-output tables as the main tool for empirical testing and application in planning.[36] Basically, the difficulty stems from the fact that whereas Perroux originally aimed at a truly dynamic theory of development and therefore adopted the Schumpeterian theory and framework as one of his cornerstones, the Leontief-type formalization of industrial interdependence is of an essentially static character. And because the latter theory is operational and the former not, or at least not to the same degree, there has been a strong tendency, particularly in planning-oriented literature, to attribute to the development pole theory a much stronger input-output bias than it had originally.[37]

As it is expressed by Lasuén, this has:

... drained the growth pole concept of its original temporal and dynamic meaning and recharged it with a static and/or comparative static content. The heavy use of the input-output technique has shifted the (French) school away from Perroux's original translation of Schumpeterian development. They failed to develop the point that the activity creating a growth pole was essentially a sectoral and a geographical disturbance not because of its larger than average size, nor because of its higher multiplier, but because it was an *innovation*.[38]

Thus, it is clear that by restricting the concept of a leading propulsive industry to only those of its aspects that can be formalized in an input-output framework of the traditional type, *i.e.*, its high supermultiplier, the concept has lost much of its meaning in a developmental context. Input-output data are incapable of explaining the process of economic development, though they may aid in giving insights into its manifestations. Therefore it is necessary to examine more carefully the process of *change* in industrial interdependencies. Systematic study of these linkages and their evolutions is required if regional policy is to have the means for initiating and reinforcing optimal growth patterns.[39] Recognizing that gradual change to inter-industry relations is the rule rather than the exception when development proceeds according to the development pole theory, it appears obvious that lasting development in lagging regions cannot be expected to evolve from the installation of an industrial complex planned on the basis of traditional input-output models so as to achieve as high supermultiplier (internal blocking) and as low net outflow of generated income (external blocking) as possible. Although such a complex may work, it will function as a real development pole only if it contains a dynamic core capable of generating and transmitting innovations that will stimulate the emergence of new industries and new interdependencies. Or, as it is put by Paelinck:

It is not enough ... to limit analysis to the classical interdependencies (of either the Walras or Leontief type) of economic flux, whether in quantity or in value terms. [The analyst] must be able, in addition, to recognize the technical origin of this interdependency, which explains its ever increasing complexity.[40]

This, then, is what is aimed at in the much more disaggregated industrial complex analysis.

In spite of its strong connection to centrally planned economies, the concept of interrelated industrial complexes[41] appears to have a potentially much wider applicability, especially as a means of implementing regional schemes of industrial development.[42] Furthermore, the techniques of industrial complex analysis may be viewed as a step forward as compared with traditional input-output analysis insofar as the origin of technical interdependencies are explicitly recognized. An industrial complex may be defined—in a very wide sense—

as an ensemble of technologically and economically interconnected industrial units usually located on a given territory. Such a complex is normally a planned one, based on common physical infrastructure and developed around one major industry that forms the core or the focal point of the complex. The core often appears to be a heavy industry. The advantages[43] of the creation of industrial complexes are said to be:

1. Substantial economies of investment expenditure. The investment for the whole complex is less than the sum of investment for each enterprise planned and located in isolation.[44]

2. Efficient production due to advantages of specialization, economies of large-scale operation, and organization of common managerial and infrastructural facilities.

3. Possibility of coordinated exploitation of the natural and raw material resources of the area of location.

4. Opportunities for close contact, rapid diffusion of technological innovations, and rapid overall development of the economy.

To a large extent, the concept of industrial complexes is an engineering one. The core unit may nevertheless be compared to the concept of the dominant firm of the growth pole theory, around which there tends to grow up a set of interrelated units based on backward and forward linkage effects. The essential difference is that in an industrial complex these interconnections are directly planned in order to insure an optimal composition of the entire complex involving also the economic and sociocultural infrastructure, auxiliary and servicing plants, and plants working for the local consumer market. Consequently, setting up the complex (*i.e.*, the time sequence of establishing the various units) is also planned.[45]

It should be emphasized, however, that the concept of an interrelated industrial complex basically is a functional one. In French terminology, it belongs to the sphere of organizational space. It should, therefore, be distinguished from concepts referring to geographical space, such as industrial estates, industrial zones and zones and centers, or economic regions. Although the problems of optimal composition of complexes and of their location are closely related and in principle should be solved simultaneously, they belong to different spaces. For example, an industrial center may contain more than one complex or the complex may be geographically divided among more than one center. Because of the engineering approach and its background in central planning, the concept of industrial complexes may seem somewhat static. The dynamics of technological progress, inventions, innovations, income elasticities, and changing tastes are obviously very complicated to master in the stage of planning. Although the successful complexes by their own strength will develop a social and economic environment conducive to innovations and technological progress, the complex planned as an entity may be so rigid that the introduction of new methods, means, and products may be hampered. Solutions to this problem are obviously difficult, but they seem to involve both setting up new complexes, old ones running down, and, above all, planning for flexibility and adaptability.

Development Poles
in Geographical Space

As already pointed out, Perroux was primarily concerned with economic development as manifested in organizational and industrial spaces—*i.e.*, the appearance, growth, and stagnation of firms and industries, the mutual interrelations between poles prevailing in these spaces, and the propulsive forces and mechanisms behind the changes taking place. The development pole theory has nevertheless come to be applied mainly in a regional context, *i.e.*, in geographical space. There are several reasons for this. To start with, inasmuch as all economic activity necessarily takes place in geographical space, organizational and industrial changes in functional space occurring during economic growth can be projected into and manifest themselves in geographical space. Therefore, for the same reasons that the concept of growth poles may shed light on transformations in functional spaces, it may also shed light on the transformations taking place in geographical space during the same process of economic growth.

All economic activities, including the dominant and leading firms and industries, have given locations at a given point in time. Because the growth of these firms and of industries linked to them creates cumulative differentiation and clusterings in functional spaces, a similar cumulative differentiation and clustering may take place in geographical space in accordance with the locational interrelations between firms and industries. Therefore, growth poles may also be

identified as being localized in geographical space. As Lasuén has
put it:

> In brief, the net contribution of Perroux to the basic Schumpeterian
> argument was that he took Schumpeter's tool-box of concepts and hypo-
> thesis from its original sectoral-temporal setting and applied it to a
> sectoral-temporal-geographical universe. He was able to do it, thanks to
> his concept of topological space. He viewed the changes in the system of
> industries as transformations in "sectoral" space, and asked which form
> they would take in "geographical" space. The geographical pole is the
> geographical image of the newly innovated industry and its linked activi-
> ties.[46]

Therefore, far from being a theory of location in geographical space
for firms, industries, or cities, the growth pole concept, when applied
to geographical space, has to rest on the traditional theories of
location, theories of intertemporal locational interrelations, theories
of spatial organization,[47] and theories of external economies of
agglomeration.[48] Although there may be some confusion at this
point, the matter should now be relatively clear. According to
Paelinck, the growth pole theory, when applied to geographical
space, should be regarded as a *conditional* theory of regional growth
that establishes conditions under which accelerated regional economic growth *may* occur.[49] The more intricate problem of establishing necessary and sufficient conditions for regional economic growth
is left unsolved by the development pole theory.

The application of the growth pole concept and theory in a specific
geographical and regional context is primarily due to Boudeville,
who, as opposed to Perroux's abstract conception of space, emphasized the regional characteristics of economic space. To Boudeville,
economic space is tied to geographical space through a functional
transformation that describes the relevant proportions of economic
processes. These transformations can be considered from three
different points of view, in accordance with which economic space
can be defined as homogeneous, polarized, and planning space.[50]
Furthermore, Boudeville distinguishes between space and region. A
region is characterized by being a continuous area localized in
geographical space, whereas economic space is not. *Homogeneous
space* is defined in terms of uniformity of relevant properties of
elements localized in geographical space. *Polarized space* is studied
in terms of interdependence between elements. The concept of
polarized space is closely related to the notion of hierarchy and is
particularly well suited to the study of urban centers and their inter-

relations. Thus, this concept provides a link to one of the other foundations of a synthetic concept of development centers, *viz.*, the central place theory of Christaller.[51]

A *polarized region* is defined as a heterogeneous continuous area localized in geographical space, whose different parts are inter-dependent through mutual complementary and interplay relations centered around a regional center of gravity. The geographical interpretation of growth poles as localized functional growth poles appears, however, to be somewhat more difficult than the original functional concept in that it *involves polarization in geographical as well as in functional spaces.* Not all centers of nodal regions qualify to be called a geographical development pole. A geographical pole of growth should be interpreted as such *only* if it contains propulsive firms (large scale, technically advanced, innovating, and dominating firms) working within propulsive industries (industries with a strong capability to induce growth in linked industries) that exert a strong influence on their environment and are capable of generating sus-tained growth over a prolonged period of time. In short, the notion of regional centers as poles of growth localized in geographical space in the sense of Perroux and Boudeville is based on the assumption that economic growth is polarized in all spaces, *i.e.*, in organizational and industrial as well as in geographical space.[52]

In modifying the original theory of development poles in functional space to be applicable also to geographical space, Boudeville pro-vided a bridge to another and older set of theories dealing with the problem of organization of human activity in geographical space. These theories were originally developed by Christaller[53] and Lösch[54] under the name of *central place theory.* Central place theory purports to explain the structure of spatial organizations: (1) the pattern of clusters of human activity as characterized by relative locational positions and distribution in geographical space, size distribution and functional differentiation; (2) the network of movement facilities for people, commodities, and information that connects the clusters; and (3) the distribution and density pattern of agricultural and other space-exploiting activities. Although central place theory has been further advanced by others,[55] its basic content has not been altered. As opposed to the inductive method of Perroux, both Christaller and Lösch employed a deductive method. Basing their ideas on the underlying assumption that man tries to organize his activities over geographical space in an efficient manner, they contended that the structure of spatial organizations could be deductively derived and explained with reference to a number of ordering principles governing the formation of this structure.

Christaller and Lösch started their analysis with very similar and extremely simplified assumptions. They assumed a homogeneous plain with even distribution and even quality of agricultural conditions and natural resources. At each point of this plain, the population density is equal, and so are consumer preferences and production techniques for each product. They based their models on three basic factors, namely, the existence of space exploiting activities, transporting costs, and economies of scale, of which the two latter generally differ from product to product. Furthermore, they assumed that to each product there corresponds a demand function that is also different from product to product. Finally, all producers and consumers were assumed to behave rationally, minimizing costs and taking production and utility functions as given data. For each product, a hexagonal market area surrounding the production site is assumed. A circle would have been optimal from the viewpoint of the individual firm but a group of touching circular areas would leave "empty" spaces whereas contiguous hexagons exhaust the entire surface being considered.[56] So far, Christaller and Lösch base their models on the same assumptions, disregarding the existence of external economies in the traditional sense as well as disregarding intermediary commodities and interplant linkages. The difference between their two models arises out of their different way of treating the key problem, namely, the combination of the market areas of individual plants into a systematic spatial organizational structure. As it is clearly pointed out by von Böventer, Christaller and Lösch start at opposite ends.[57] Christaller starts with the goods that have the widest spatial range and develops his organization from above, whereas Lösch starts at the bottom with the goods having the smaller spatial range and subsequently derives the organization from below. As it will be shown, the two types of organization that emerge are quite different. Although the one can be seen as a special case of the other, it appears that the two models apply to a different type of goods—Lösch's model to transportable commodities and Christaller's to immobile services.

Following his deductive procedure, Christaller arrived at a model of spatial organization in which human activities are organized in geographical space so that *horizontally*:

1. The activities are located to regularly spaced clusters forming triangular lattices.
2. The activities are centrally located within hexagonally shaped trading areas.
3. Higher order central places are more widely spaced than lower order ones.
4. Lower order central places are located at gravity centers of triangles formed at the next higher order.

Vertical characteristics of the spatial organization are that:

5. Higher order centers supply all goods that are supplied by lower order centers but, in addition, have a number of goods of a wider range that differentiate them from and set them above the lower order.
6. Higher order centers are larger with respect to number of activities, range of goods produced, volume of business and trading areas than lower order centers.

By making an additional assumption, namely, that the number of places served by a central place at the next higher order in the system is fixed,[58] another well known characteristic of the vertical organization of the central place system can be derived, namely, that:

7. A definite hierarchy can be established in the system in which a number of levels corresponding to the number of classes of goods can be identified.[59]

One basic weakness of the model should be immediately noted. It does not allow specialization among central places and division of labor in any other way than what is included in the higher order centers' provision of goods to lower order ones. Thus, all centers are *service* centers in the true sense of the word, their *raison d'être* ultimately determined by the service requirements of the agricultural population. It is natural, therefore, that the area of application of this model is limited primarily to the service sector.[60]

Accepting the basic assumptions of Christaller, but starting from below, Lösch developed a model of spatial organization that has a more elaborate economic base and contains Christaller's model as a special case. The resulting system of spatial clustering can be summarized as follows:

1. There is one superior center where all goods are produced.
2. There is real specialization and division of labor and trade between centers, *i.e.*, smaller centers supply larger centers with their specialized products.
3. There is a concentration of centers in "city-rich" sectors separated by interstitial sectors less densely packed with centers.

4. Without further assumptions, nothing can be said about the relative sizes of centers, except that the superior one is larger than all others. Centers with the same number of functions do not necessarily provide the same kinds of function.

5. Assuming that size of centers is proportional to the number of plants, it can be shown that within city-rich sectors, size of centers increases with distance from the central place and that smaller centers tend to locate about half-way between larger ones.[61]

6. Although Lösch asserts that the vertical organization would be hierarchical, this is doubtful and cannot be proved without further assumptions. On the contrary, it seems to follow from the model that the size distribution is continuous.[62]

On the whole, the Lösch model is far less rigid both in its vertical and its horizontal organization than Christaller's. It appears that Lösch's spatial organization applies particularly to secondary industries in which such complex patterns of specialization are the normal case. If this is so, the models of Lösch and Christaller can be viewed as supplementing each other, the first explaining the spatial organization of secondary activities and the second that of service activities.[63] There is, however, one basic difference between the two models that to a certain extent complicates such mutual complementarity. Although Christaller's model can be looked upon from both a micro point of view (*i.e.*, from the point of view of the distribution of production of individual goods) and from an aggregate macro point of view (*i.e.*, the spatial and size distribution of agglomerations), Lösch's model does not have any aggregative feature. It is, strictly speaking, more a model of spatial specialization, location, and trade of individual goods than a model of overall spatial organization. Criticism has been raised against the Lösch model for two reasons. First, because it is a model of spatial specialization, it appears to be an unnecessary restriction that all goods are produced at the superior center. This criticism does not apply to the Christaller model when it is regarded as a model of the service sector only. The second objection applies to both the Christaller and Lösch models and is more severe since it, in fact, points to an inconsistency in the way of deriving the spatial organizations. Both models take as their point of departure an assumption of even distribution of demand throughout a homogeneous plain. However, when the final pattern of centers is derived on the basis of this assumption, the assumption is no longer fulfilled unless very peculiar additional assumptions are made.[64]

In spite of the lack of evidence supporting the geographical regularities suggested by the theories of Christaller and Lösch, the theories are nevertheless of considerable interest in relation to the problems of localized and development poles. As pointed out by Bos,[65] these theories were the first global theories of location, attempting a simultaneous coherent explanation of the spatial pattern of human settlement including the location of production and consumption to spatial clusters of different locations, size, and functional structure. Although both theories are partly positive—attempting to explain actual patterns on the basis of behavioral assumptions—and partly normative—attempting to determine optimal patterns—they have contributed considerably to the understanding of spatial interrelations and to the evolving view of "cities as systems within systems of cities."[66]

It is contended here that central place theories can be regarded as complementary to Boudeville's theory of localized poles of development. Although Boudeville's theory explains the developmental impact of the existence of localized poles of development in geographical space, it is not by itself a theory of location explaining where the functional growth poles are or where they in the future will be localized in geographical space. To explain this, the growth pole theory must rely on theories of location, of which the central place theory is the only global one that takes stock of the interdependencies among service activities resulting from their spatial division of labor. Therefore, disregarding the lack of spatial regularities, the theory of central places, and in particular the functional interrelations suggested by the theory, may well serve as a point of departure for analyzing the impact of development in a given center on the other centers, problems of how to direct changes in the system of centers, and problems of urban growth control.[67]

On the other hand, a central place theory does not explain growth phenomena. It is a static theory that aims only at explaining the existence of certain patterns of centers, not how this pattern has gradually come into being, and it says nothing about how the pattern may undergo future changes. However, this is a critical question because, as has been stressed recently by Hilhorst, "the spatial structure of a region does not come into being at once, but is a result of a process of time, in which certain things come first and depending upon their configuration determine the other things."[68] To explain these dynamic phenomena it is necessary to look at growth theories,

among which Boudeville's modifications of the growth pole theory
to make it applicable to geographical space seems a most promising
one. In this way, the growth theory of the French and the German
theory of location appear to supplement each other in a fruitful way.

However, to accept the contended relation of complementarity
between the central place theory and the theory of localized development poles is not without difficulty because the first is a deductively
derived, static equilibrium theory pertaining in principle to the level
of the firm and interfirm relations, whereas the other is an inductively
based dynamic theory of development pertaining to the level of
industries and macro-aggregates. Their mutual relations are, therefore, not of the simple type suggested by the principle of correspondence between static and dynamic theories. To clarify, it should be
stressed first of all that central place theory deals with clustering in
geographical space only, whereas the theory of localized development
poles deals simultaneously with both functional (*i.e.*, organizational
and industrial) space and geographical space, aiming at projecting
changes in functional space into geographical space. Following
Boudeville, this can be visualized as being done through a functional
transformation described by the appropriate system of locational
criteria and locational interrelations in which the central place
theory may form the core.[69] In this way, the central place theory
may be viewed, not as some sort of a static version of the dynamic
development pole theory in which all movement has come to an end,
but as the *mechanisms through which development occurring in
functional space can be projected into geographical space*. It appears,
however, that this point of view requires a dynamization of the
central place theory, at least in the sense that intertemporal relations
in the evolution of the spatial organization are recognized, so that
the central place model is continuously up-dated.[70]

So far, we have kept a clear distance between the concept of a
functional pole of growth that may or may not be localized in
geographical space and the clusters or agglomerations of human
activity that, according to the central place theory, are spread
throughout geographical space with definite order in both size and
geographical distributions. However, the development pole theory
may also be thought of as having a direct validity even for geographical space, in the sense that the formation and change of the
distribution of geographical clusters should be explainable with
reference to this theory. If this were the case, one should then expect

a succession of growth, maturation, and stagnation of geographical poles during the course of development leading to alterations in the rank-size relations of centers over time. Such alterations take place, however, on a surprisingly small scale. Spatial organizations, in fact, seem to exhibit a remarkable stability and empirical evidence points to increasing stability during the course of development.[71] Therefore, although the development pole theory may be a powerful tool in explaining industrial development and change in industrial and organizational space, it is certainly not equally powerful when applied to clusterings in simple geographical space, which after all constitute part of the frame rather than a vital aspect of development. However, insofar as clustering in geographical space is related to development in the functional sense, and diffusion of development in geographical space can be related to development in functional space through the locational transformations referred to above, the theory of localized poles of development may constitute a powerful tool to explain not geographical clusterings *per se*, but the geographical incidence and transmission of *development* among such clusterings.

The most important implications of the relation between the theory of localized development poles and the central place theory are brought out, however, when the two theories are put together in the context of development planning and control. Two relevant problems facing many countries are: (1) how to initiate a self-perpetuating process of development in a lagging region, and (2) how to direct the process of urbanization to achieve a spatial organization with a size and geographical distribution of urban centers conducive to further development.

The first problem is one of projecting the development effects of the installation of the core units of a development pole into the specific context of a certain area exhibiting a characteristic structure of linkages in functional and geographical space, and of selecting a type of functional pole that will insure the maximum effect in terms of new functional (*i.e.*, forward and backward) linkages and developmental change *within* the given area and at the same time facilitate the inflow of innovations from outside and their rapid internal diffusion.[72] It seems that such analysis cannot be undertaken without the use of a model of geographical interrelations of which the central place model would form the core.

The second problem is principally one of selecting appropriate locations for industrial and service establishments that may or may not be parts of development poles so that their effects are distributed over the system of centers in geographical space in a way that contributes to an efficient sequence of geographical reorganization. This requires that development in functional space be projected into geographical space, a problem that is particularly difficult since it is necessary to take into account also the feedback effects of change taking place in geographical space on functional development.[73] Obviously, much more research is needed to provide efficient tools for projecting development in functional space into geographical space, and vice-versa. The role to be played by central place theories is far from clear. Even more difficult problems, however, have to be solved in order to establish rational decision criteria for simultaneous control of development in the two types of space. One reason for this is the static character of central place theories that renders them useful mostly for comparative static analysis of intercenter relations. Therefore, central place theory must be supplemented by theories dealing specifically with the geographic incidence and transmission of development that can be used for explaining and directing the dynamic process of development diffusion and change in relations between centers.

The Impact of Development Poles on the Geographical Pattern of Development

A first attempt to integrate a theory of geographical incidence of growth with hypotheses of the mechanisms of geographical transmissions of development impulses was made in Hirschman's now classic study of economic development strategies.[74] Taking it for granted that economic progress did not appear everywhere at the same time, and that once development had appeared, powerful forces would make for a spatial concentration of economic activity and growth at the initial starting points, Hirschman argued that "there can be little doubt that an economy to lift itself to higher income levels must and will first develop within itself one or several centers of economic strength."[75] Hirschman's argument was based on his theory of economic development as an essentially unbalanced process that is propagated through chains of disequilibria. The similarities between Hirschman's theory—developed mainly with reference to the less developed Latin American countries—and the French theories of development poles are many, in spite of the different conditions and levels of development of the basis of which they were developed. This can, however, be explained by the fact that they both were developed as reactions to the balanced growth theories originally developed by Cassel[76] and furthered by Nurkse,[77] Lewis,[78] and Rosenstein-Rodan.[79]

Both Hirschman and the French school view economic growth as unbalanced and occurring in certain leading firms and industries that induce growth in related industries through forward and backward linkages by means of investment incentives resulting from disequilibria. There is one essential difference, however, that reflects their different background. Whereas the French theory is primarily a theory of economic growth, the Hirschman theory deals with economic development. Hirschman's theory includes not only economic variables but also the interrelations between these and certain social and cultural variables, particularly those that determine the emergence of entrepreneurial talents and the ability of entrepreneurs to take investment decisions. It should be stressed, however, that Hirschman, just as Perroux, addressed himself primarily to the economics of development and not to the spatial aspects of the process.

As a matter of fact, Hirschman arrived at a conceptual framework and a theory of development that are much the same as the French development pole theory, particularly with respect to the importance attached to interindustry interdependence. It has already been noted[80] that Perroux must have been influenced by the work of Chenery and Watanabe[81] on comparisons of input-output tables. Since the same is the case with Hirschman, it is not much of a surprise that both employ the concepts of forward and backward linkages and of propulsive respective strategic industries. Attempting to refine the analytical technique, Hirschman speaks of the *strength* and the *importance* of the links extending from a given productive unit. Importance refers here to the potential net output of industries that may be induced, whereas strength refers to the probability that plants producing the said output shall be established as a response to the inducements. Taking the product of strength and importance, one gets a measure for the *total linkage effect*. But since strength and importance tend to vary inversely, the total linkage effect of most primary investments tends to be limited.

So far, Hirschman's theory has no spatial elements, the interaction between strategic industries and the rest of the economy being viewed as taking place in a spaceless matrix of an open national economy. When Hirschman takes up the question of *where* in addition to those of what and how, it is primarily to illustrate further aspects of the inducement mechanisms of unbalanced development, *i.e.*, those conditioned by the need to overcome the "friction of space." He takes as his point of departure the gains of agglomeration that are agreed upon in the traditional theories of location and the psychological advantages of the "industrial atmosphere" in growth centers with its special receptivity to innovations and diffusion (*i.e.*, in the language of economics, the external economies of agglomeration). Development thus always tends to be geographically unbalanced; therefore, for a country to develop, according to Hirschman, there is a need for the emergence of some *growing points*. The existence of these geographical growth centers would then by themselves insure their further growth, primarily because of external economies of agglomeration mechanisms but also because economic operators are inclined systematically to overestimate the importance of these economies and neglect equally good or even better investment opportunities elsewhere in the country.

Despite exaggerated space preferences of economic operators, development occurring in geographical growth points will nevertheless set in motion forces that will induce development in the backward hinterlands. These trickling-down forces work particularly through interregional trade and transfer of capital to the backward regions. Their effect depends largely on the existence of complementarities between the industries in the growth center and the hinterland. In addition, migration from the hinterland to the growth center may absorb some disguised unemployment and raise the marginal productivity of labor and the income per capita of the hinterland. However, the progress of the growth center may also—and particularly in the case of weak complementarities—have unfavorable polarization effects on the hinterland.[82] The industries of the hinterland can be depressed as a result of the competition from the growth center, particularly as the transportation facilities are improved. Owing to better opportunities in the growth center, the hinterland can be drained not only of the most able parts of its labor force but also of a significant share of what savings there can be. The polarization effects generated in the growth centers may well turn out to be stronger than the trickling-down effect, in spite of Hirschman's optimistic view that in the long run external diseconomies of the growth centers together with complementarities will assure a spontaneous spread of development. A lasting dual society may then be created in which industrial and geographical backwardness coincide.

The tendency for the polarization forces to be stronger than the trickling-down forces was exactly the main conclusion of Myrdal when he studied the problem of geographical coincidence and spread of economic development at the same time as Hirschman.[83] Myrdal's spread and backwash effects coincide with Hirschman's trickling-down and polarization effects. Myrdal bases his more pessimistic view of the possibilities for spontaneous spread of development in space on his theory of *circular and cumulative causation*. He maintains that movements of labor, capital, and goods, contrary to what is believed in equilibrium theory, are precisely the "media through which the cumulative process evolves—upwards in the lucky regions and downwards in the unlucky ones." The spread effects, which operate mainly through trade via interregional complementarities, set up opposite counteracting forces to the backwash effects and will in some regions balance them. But, according to Myrdal, this balance is of a temporary character and should not be confused with stable equilibrium because any change induced will generate a cumulative movement up or down. Regions in which the spread and backwash effects of the main growth regions are in balance will, as a rule, be stagnating. In reality, expanding, stagnating, and regressing regions tend to be arranged in a fairly continuous pattern. Myrdal finds, however, that the higher the level of development and the higher the rate of growth of the economy, the stronger the spread effect as compared to the backwash effect. And, the other way around, the *gradual neutralization of the backwash effects as a country develops* can by itself be seen as an important factor to speed up development. Therefore, lasting interregional unbalance in less developed countries represents an impediment to development and a part of the "interlocking relations by which in the cumulative process poverty becomes its own cause." Thus, Myrdal and Hirschman seem to agree that development makes for more efficient spread effects. However, whereas Hirschman argues in favor of the need for initial geographical unbalance through the creation of development centres, Myrdal takes the opposite stand and argues that the mechanisms for spread effects should be strengthened from the outset.

Despite their profound disagreement when it comes to choice of development strategy, the two theories are coincidental in identifying the basic reasons why development is apt to occur in a limited set of urbanized regions and be concentrated there, and in exposing the nature of the mechanisms through which development impulses are propagated throughout the rest of the country. However, although these theories deal with questions of location, they remain fundamentally nongeographical, and they have little to say about the geographical location of the development centers and the geographical manifestation of the development impulses propagated from the centers.

Although the students of development discussed so far agree that development tends to occur in geographical concentrations, and when left to itself tends to stimulate further concentration both of developmental phenomena and people, they have not undertaken a thorough analysis of the whole range of reasons why this is so. Concentrating on economic factors, they largely neglected the whole fabric of social, cultural, and political factors and processes that can be subsumed under the *role of the cities* in sociocultural and political development. This role, however, is crucial both for the national development processes and their relations to urbanization, and for the formulation of policies to cope with the rapid reorganization of spatial organization that takes place in transitional societies.[84] Therefore, to develop a synthetic concept of development poles in geographical space one would need to include also elements of theories attempting to explain not only the mutual impact on each other of development and urbanization but also more specifically the reasons why the social climate of cities is particularly conducive to the generation and adoption of innovations, economic as well as social, cultural, and institutional. Such theories, however, are rare and of a rather descriptive character, a fact that may be explained with reference to the historical character of the urban-industrial revolution. In his classic study of 1955, Lampard viewed the urban industrial development as a cultural process through which modes of life values, customs and socioeconomic relations were gradually transformed.[85] Historically, the emergence of cities could be seen as a synthesis of economic, administrative, defensive, and religious requirements, their spatial setting being determined partly by natural conditions and partly by the existing network of communications and transportation facilities. The modern city, however, can be understood only in its relation to the emergence of industrial technology and organization, according to Lampard. Industrialization is essentially a process of technological innovations, which leads to improved organization, specialization, and division of labor, and which has strong inherent impetuses to foster continuous and cumulative progress.

The roles of the city in this process are several. First, the increasing specialization of functions imposes an *increasing degree of interdependence* among all the differentiated parts. Such interdependencies can be efficiently established only when the friction of space is overcome, *i.e.*, when the functions are clustered together within spatial concentrations. In other words, cities provide a spatial organization of interdependent activities conducive to their further development. Second, owing to its complex composite character with a *high internal accessibility*, the cities develop external economies that to a large extent are spatially immobile and therefore can be utilized only within and close to the cities.[86] These external economies are particularly tied to the labor force and the local service sector but include also what can be called social and cultural urbanization. What is implied here are changes in values, habits, beliefs, and the like and changes in social institutions and mobility patterns that, together with the development of higher levels of education and skills, make for urban communities with much *higher degrees of flexibility* and capability to utilize opportunities and adjust to changes than traditional urban and rural ones.[87] Because of the high level of internal and external accessibility, cities are particularly *conducive to the generation of innovations* and to the spread of their adoption of innovation, not only within the city but also throughout their spheres of influence.[88] Furthermore, as is particularly stressed by Friedmann,[89] cities are the main agent for *geographical integration* of the social, economic, and cultural systems of a nation. This integrationability is owing to the cities' functions as centers of trade and of religious, administrative, and political activities, to their innovative strength in economic as well as in social and cultural fields, and to their geographical arrangement in a hierarchical system of central places that provide mutual relations of interdependence and interplay throughout national space.

The distinction between the spatial incidence of new developmental phenomena and their transmission throughout space is very useful. At a general level, Hirschman and Myrdal identified the transmission mechanisms of development throughout geographical space which spill development over to transitional areas in between geographical poles, as trickling-down and spread effects. These effects can be viewed as materialization of diffusion of innovations in geographical space. Hence, theories dealing with geographical diffusion of innovations are closely related to the theory of localized poles of development both at the general level and as a tool to explain the dynamic process of transmission of development among poles and from poles to their surrounding areas.

Regularities in the geographical pattern and time order of spread of innovation, particularly within rural societies, have been noted for quite a long time in many countries. However, it was not before Hägerstrand's pathbreaking work in the first part of the 1950s that a theoretical basis was laid for an understanding of how the mechanisms of the geographical diffusion of innovations work and give rise to empirical regularities of a strikingly stable nature.[90] The theory, as founded by Hägerstrand and furthered by a number of other scholars in the field, is principally a general positive theory purporting to explain and even predict the process of geographical diffusion of any type of innovation, technical as well as cultural and social, in any society having its population spread out in geographical space.[91] Hägerstrand originally developed his theory inductively from a number of empirical case studies. However, in his conceptualization, he drew upon the body of relevant sociological and geographical theories and arrived at an essentially social theory of diffusion. The salient features of the theory are as follows:

1. Diffusion of innovations comprises two processes: the dissemination of information about the innovation and the adoption of the innovation. The first process is largely a function of social communication. The second is a complex process of learning, accepting, and decisionmaking.[92]

2. The spread of information takes place through a number of channels that can be classified into two main groups—mass media and interpersonal—of which the latter is contended to be the more important.[93]

3. The pattern of social (interpersonal) communication can be conceived as a network consisting of nodes (sources and receivers)

and links (channels). The sources and receivers of information are social actors with definite locations who establish contacts with each other for various reasons.[94]

The basic unit of the network of social communication is the private information or communication fields that describes the spatial range of the contact patterns of the various individuals. The private communication fields are assumed to be classified into a smaller number of groups, mean communication fields, which describes the average spatial range of the contact probabilities of the different functional and social groups. Hägerstrand suggests that the private, and therefore also the set of, mean communication fields can be organized in an hierarchical way.[95] This means that one field is operating at the local level, one at the regional level, one at the national level, and so on. Some individuals are bound to the local range field, others belong also to wider fields. Those belonging to wide range fields and at the same time having links in common with people belonging to fields of more limited range form the channels through which information disseminates between levels. In principle, it should be possible to describe, with respect to its geographical pattern, the whole fabric of social communication by means of a hierarchical ordering of a limited number of mean communication fields. Such a description must then also include the linkages between the levels and their locations.

The introduction of the hierarchical system of interconnected communication fields distorts the simple picture of the spatial spread of innovations derived from a model with only one field dominated by neighborhood effects and terrestrial barriers. The innovations tend to "jump" between larger centers and from centers at higher levels to centers at lower levels whereas the spread throughout the local zones of influence is dominated largely by neighborhood and barrier effects. Empirical evidence for this change in diffusion patterns has been provided recently by Pedersen, who investigated the reciprocal impact of development on the geographical pattern and speed of diffusion processes in Chile. One of his conclusions is:

As the country develops, the transportation and communication network improves. This improvement in communication in general will increase the speed of information diffusion, but it will tend to benefit the largest towns most, and the information diffusion process will therefore change from being a spatial process to being a diffusion down the urban hierarchy from the large to the small towns. As all of the delaying factors tend to be of small importance in the large towns, the chance that intermediate non-adopters will delay the diffusion process decreases. This leads to an even further increase in the speed of diffusion.[96]

Hägerstrand's original approach was strictly microsociological. Recent contributions of Hägerstrand as well as of others have shown that this approach may well be applicable also to the analysis of spatial diffusion at a more aggregated level.[97] The key to the aggregated application is the concept of a hierarchical ordering of the mean information fields, which, together with inductive generalizations from empirical examples, suggests that there may be a close connection between the hierarchy of mean information fields and the hierarchy of cities within the system of central places.

As Hägerstrand puts it, "In all probability there exist rather stable hierarchical systems of normative centres which are very difficult to counteract because they reflect not the accidental status of a few single individuals but a status order between clusters of population."[98] And in another paper, ". . . a closer analysis shows that the spread along the initial 'frontier' is led through the urban hierarchy." In the same paper he says:

. . . also the leading cities within a country should give impulses first of all to towns next in rank. The further spread is then heavily regulated by distance friction; strong ties of the major towns with the capital over a rather long distance occur; the local influence is exerted on lower-order centres closer by.[99]

Although Hägerstrand developed his theory as a positive micro-theory applicable to relatively well-developed societies, it seems likely that the theory may be of equal importance as reformulated to an instrumental aggregate macro theory applicable to developing countries.[100] Because diffusion of innovation is a key process of development, much attention has to be devoted to the formulation of propagation strategies.[101] It is to this complex of problems that the instrumental formulation of the theory may provide useful guidelines. Hägerstrand devoted some attention to this problem of engineering induced innovations in one of his papers, giving particular emphasis to the concept of hierarchical ordering of centers related to a similar hierarchical ordering of communication fields, and to that of normative sources which all suggest that induced innovations should be initially concentrated and utilizing the existing system of communication linkages.[102] Instead of working against or trying to enforce other patterns of diffusion, efforts should be made to identify the prevailing system in order to exploit its ability to disseminate and persuade. Furthermore, insofar as lasting underdevelopment of some regions is due to their being outside the prevailing national patterns of diffusion channels, it may be suggested that the communication patterns should be corrected by the creation of a new class of centers in the urban hierarchy.

At this stage of our discussion, it seems safe to conclude that one of the aims of this study has been fulfilled, namely, the clarification of the relationships between the three cornerstones in spatial theory— central place theory, the theory of localized development poles, and the theory of spatial innovation diffusion. We have also established a much better basis on which to explain the remarkable stability of urban systems during economic development, a fact that is contradictory to what one would expect if the development of urban systems were governed by the theory of localized development poles alone. Therefore, we feel safe in subscribing to the following conclusion of Lasuén:

> The profound geographical regularity (hierarchical) of the patterns of the diffusion and adoption subprocess seems to me the most obvious factors to account for the hierarchical and stable order in which the system of regions grow and develop. For this reason, the factors determining the patterns, which steadily through this time, follow the diffusions and adoptions of successive sets from some leading regions hierarchically down to the regions which follow, are to be considered the factors to explain the invariant behaviour of the system of the nations.[103]

Although urban systems tend to be very stable over time, there is one aspect of their gradual change, relating to the geographical diffusion of development and particularly to the patterns of intercity relations, that is particularly striking. That is the emergence of *axes of high development* between the main urban areas.

As opposed to the rich variety of contributions to industrial location theory,[104] the latter subject has been largely neglected by geographers as well as economists. There is, however, one relatively recent contribution by Pottier that stands out and deserves to be mentioned.[105] Pottier's main contention is that economic development normally tends to be propagated along the *main transportation* routes linking the most important industrial centers, and, therefore, development manifests itself in *linear geographical paths*. Pottier's theory, which to some extent was anticipated by Christaller's transportation principle, has been developed mainly on the basis of the French historical experiences. Nevertheless, it would seem to have more general value, particularly inasmuch as it contributes to integrating theories of the effects of the transportation network with the theories of urban hierarchies and geographical development poles. According to Pottier, there are several factors working together in a process of circular cumulative causations that explain the strong tendency for economic development to concentrate along the original national transportation channels during the initial stages of industrial growth. When traffic increases along a transportation route as a result of interregional trade, economies of scale leading to lower unit costs of transportation can be exploited. Because lower transportation costs stimulate trade and generate increased traffic, the transportation infrastructure and the modes of transport can be steadily improved by means of capital investments and the introduction of new techniques. A cumulative process is started which tends to concentrate transportation demand and facilities along the original axes. Then industry, commerce, and population are attracted and, in turn, create easily accessible factors and product markets likely to attract more industries. This cumulative process is particularly strong in the points where two routes cross each other and create *junction effects*. Agriculture in close proximity to such axes and functions benefits, partly by the improved accessibility to larger markets but also because it is more exposed to agents disseminating information of technological and cultural innovations. This, in turn, induces impulses for social change and makes the areas more conducive to development and growth.[106]

Development Poles
and the Optimum Size of Cities

The notion of optimum city size is, strictly speaking, not a part of the development pole theory, but because discussion of growth pole policies in geographical space appears not to be able to avoid this theme, a few remarks on this subject should be made here for the sake of completeness. The origin of the notion is to be found among city planners who traditionally have been concerned.[107] City planners also posed the problem with reference to the individual city, rather than with reference to the system of cities. Characteristic of the early thinking on the problem—beside the limitation to the single city—is that the conclusions drawn rest heavily on the subjective assumptions and evaluation of the planners, to which scarcely any scientific investigations were added.

The first attempt at a scientific clarification of the problems involved in determining optimum size of cities was made by Duncan, who recognized that inasmuch as there were many criteria that could be applied, no general solution could be given to the problem.[108] Duncan distinguished between the *factual element, i.e.*, the principle objective problem of establishing empirical relations between size of cities and variation in selected welfare indicators, and the *normative element*, which places a positive or negative valuation on the magnitudes of the indicators. His method was static and cannot yield much on the problem of urban and development dynamics. However, an important exception should be mentioned, namely, the role of the cities as centers of innovations and agents for cultural diffusion. Duncan refers to data that indicate a positive correlation between city size, the frequency of innovations and the spread of cultural diffusion.

Another attempt was made by Shindman, who explicitly recognized that cities have always formed parts of larger, functionally interrelated systems.[109] Instead of determining the optimum size of single cities, the problem should be formulated as one of finding the optimum size of the various cities according to their functions and situations in the hierarchy of cities. The optimum sizes could not have absolute values but should rather be seen as ranges in population, having a maximum and minimum determined on the basis of variations of efficiency in the functions performed. Shindman was mainly concerned with economic efficiency as a criterion of optimum size. Although his approach was comparatively static, he did recognize that the functional interrelations between cities are not static but are subject to changes as a result of technical progress, particularly progress leading to improved transportation facilities, changes in values and preferences, and so on. Therefore, the max-min range of city sizes would be subject to corresponding changes.

The first economist who gave serious attention to the problem of optimum size of cities was Clark, who took as his point of departure the different trends of development in terms of employment as between primary, secondary, and service trades.[110] Noting that the distinguishing characteristic of service trades is that they must be carried out in the same city where the consuming population lives, and noting the diseconomies of transportation, he posed the problem of determining the minimum size of a city that could provide its inhabitants and those of the surrounding region with all but the most specialized of services. The underlying assumption was that the production of services should fulfill essential efficiency requirements, giving due attention to the exploitation of economies of scale. On the basis of a large amount of statistical material referring to a number of industrialized countries and making allowances for differences in income per capita among regions, Clark concluded that a region can give its inhabitants an adequate range of commercial services when the population of the principal city is in the 100,000 to 200,000 range and that for most other services a smaller population will suffice. According to Clark's material, manufacturing industries appeared to perform best in cities above 200,000 but below 500,000 inhabitants. Economies of scale in the provision of utilities and the like were significant in cities with up to 150,000 inhabitants but turned to diseconomies after the population reached 300,000. Clark drew the conclusion (in 1945) that the optimum size of a city would be in the area of 175,000 to 200,000 inhabitants, with the city serving a region with an additional 50,000 to 75,000.

Among economists who more recently have discussed this problem are Isard[111] and Klaassen.[112] They are both concerned primarily with urbanization economies and diseconomies that manifest themselves in income levels and in operating costs of urban sectors. However, their discussions do not go far beyond formulating the problem and indicating possible solutions.

According to Klaassen, evidence seems to show that nominal income per capita is likely to increase continuously even if agglomerations become very large. However, as operating costs per capita of the agglomeration are likely to rise even faster, the increments in income are likely to decrease as agglomerations grow larger. Then, if the aggregate operating costs per capita of a city are compared to aggregate income per capita, there must be a size where the difference between income and costs per capita reach a maximum. This size would be the optimum size of the city. Klaassen's conclusion is, therefore, that:

In building cities one should aim at maximizing the contribution of all cities together to the national income. The distribution of population over the existing nucleus, therefore, should be such that marginal disposable income in all of them is equal.

However, Klaassen's approach seems to be too restricted, particularly for one reason. He neglects the interdependence between centers within the urban systems that implies that growth of one center usually will affect other centers of the system, some adversely and some positively. Thus, a situation where all centers have been developed to their individually optimum size may either be not feasible or not compatible with an optimum size of the system as a whole.

As opposed to Klaassen, Isard is rather pessimistic, not only with respect to determining optimum size of cities, but even to formulating the problem in a meaningful way. His approach is similar to Klaasen's. He assumes that the net economy curve of each urban sector would presumably rise to a maximum and then fall. However, when it comes to aggregating the curves to an overall index of urban economy as a function of size, Isard objects. First, there is the obvious fact that no cities are similar and, therefore, the various net curves referring to different cities must be expected to have different shapes. Second, there is the problem of weighting. Because the various cities' economies must be expected to be of different significance, there must be some sort of weighting in the aggregate of curves into a uniform index, and no obvious or objective way of selecting such weights can be found. However, the most significant objection is the third, namely, that aggregating the curves even by means of weighting would imply an assumption that the net economy curves referring to the numerous urban functions simply are additive, whereas their functions in reality are tied together in a complex system of dependency and interplay relations.

To sum up, disregarding all the theoretical problems of defining the problem of the optimum size of cities in a scientifically meaningful way, one is inclined to agree with Allen that, when all costs and benefits are taken together—even in a very crude way—there are reasons to believe that some optimum size of individual cities could be found.[113] However, there are also reasons to believe that the aggregate net economy per capita curve is likely to be rather flat over a wide range of city size. If this is the case, and in fact Allen provides some empirical evidence that suggests that it is, then one can safely conclude that "there is freedom to choose any population level in this range as a target population and still be at optimum."[114]

Table of Synopsis

It should now be clear that the growth pole theory in itself is a very compound and complex body of theory and that it has a variety of relations with other theories. Therefore, instead of trying to summarize the whole in a few sentences, it is more appropriate to end this presentation with a table that in a catchword-like but surveyable way gives a picture of the whole and its composite parts. This table distinguishes vertically between the spaces to which the theory applies, *i.e.*, abstract functional or industrial space, simple geographical space, and their combined super space, in which the interplay between the factors pertaining to the two spaces takes place. Horizontally, the table distinguishes first between the static and the dynamic points of view and second, between the three main cate-

Approach / Space	STATIC and/or Comparative Static		
	Descriptive	Positive/ explanatory	Planning/control
Industrial	Interindustry relations. Input-output tables.	Forward and backward linkage effects. Multiplier effects. Pecuniary external economies. Domination effects.	Input-output models. Interrelated industrial complexes.
Geographical	Urban hierarchy versus rank-size relations.	Central place theory. General theories of spatial organization. Traditional theories of industrial location.	Optimum city size and optimum spatial organization. Network theory. Service center policy. New towns.
Interplay between industrial and geographical space.	Urban industrial patterns. Resource frontiers. Center-periphery relations.	Inertia due to intertemporal relation and locational complementarities. Localized development poles based on industrial complexes.	Optimum location of industrial complexes within the urban systems. Urban system planning.

Approach / Space	DYNAMIC		
	Descriptive	Positive/ Explanatory	Planning/control
Industrial	Trends in industrial changes. Emergence of innovation sets in techniques and products.	Sector theory. Leading industries. Propulsive and strategic industries. Functional development poles. Diffusion of innovations among industries.	Dynamic industrial complex planning. Extension and diffusion policies. Establishment of propulsive or strategic industries.
Geographical	Trends of urbanization. Identification of spatial growth centers. Mapping of polarized (nodal) regional systems.	Role of the city. Hypothesis of urban growth patterns. Regional external economies. Localized development poles. Urbanization economics. Spatial diffusion of innovation.	Planning of urban systems based on location of propulsive industries and localized poles of growth. Extension and diffusion service.
Interplay between industrial and geographical space.	The urban realm and the shift to services. Development stages.	Diffusion of innovations in industrial space conditioned by locational interrelations. Accumulation of advantages. The role of the city. Development stage theory.	Comprehensive urban regional development planning based on central place, development poles, and diffusion theory.

gories of approaches, namely, the descriptive, the positive, and the normative planning/control approach. This gives the table altogether eighteen parts corresponding to different facets of the theory.

Notes

1. Reference can be made to most countries in Europe as well as in western and eastern countries like the Soviet Union, United States, India, Japan, Pakistan, Venezuela, and Chile, to mention only a few examples of the widespread use of these concepts.

2. The path-breaking contributions are those of F. Perroux, who during the first part of the 1950s published several papers on this subject leading to the formulation of the concept and the theory of development poles. See, for example: "The Domination Effects and Modern Economic Theory" *Social Research*, 1950, pp. 188–206. "Economic Space: Theory and Application," *Quarterly Journal of Economics*, 1950, pp. 21–36. "Note sur la notion de Pôle de Croissance," *Economic Appliquée*, 1955 Nos. 1–2. The relevant papers are also published together in his: *L'économie du XXième Siècle*, Paris, 1964.

3. Cf. J. Paelinck *La théorie du développement régional polarisé*, Cahiers de l'ISEA., L.15, Mars, 1965.

4. Perroux, "Note sur la notion de Pôle de Croissance."

5. Ibid.

6. This point is made for example in J. R. Lasuén's "On Growth Poles," *Urban Studies* 2 (1969).

7. This tendency manifested itself early in France and Belgium. See for example J. R. Boudeville *Les espaces économiques* Paris, 1961. J. R. Boudeville "*La région plan*," Cahiers de l'ISEA. Serie L.N.9., Oct. 1961. F. Perroux "*La firme motrice dans la région, et la région motrice*" Cahiers de l'ISEA, Serie L. No. 9., Oct. 1961. L. E. Davin, L. Deger and J. Paelinck, *Dynamique économique de la région Liégoise*, Paris, 1959. Paelinck, *La théorie du développement régional polarisé*, 1965 op. cit.

8. B. Balassa, *The Theory of Economic Integration* London, 1962, Ch. 9.

9. When nothing is said to the contrary, the term *regional planning* will throughout this paper be used to mean both inter- and intraregional planning.

10. One such bold attempt should be mentioned, namely J. Friedmann, *A General Theory of Polarized Development* Santiago, 1967 (mimeo). Revised version, School of Architecture and Urban Planning, University of California at Los Angeles, 1969.

11. Cf. Boudeville, *Les espaces économiques*.

12. On this point see T. Hermansen: "Spatial Organization and Economic Development—The Task and Scope of Spatial Planning" (Mysore, India, 1970).

13. Perroux, "Note sur la notion."

14. Boudeville, 1961, *Les espaces économiques*.

15. W. Christaller, *Central Places in Southern Germany*, Englewood Cliffs, 1965. Translated from the original German version published in Jena, 1933.

16. A. Lösch, *The Economics of Location*. New Haven, 1954; first German edition 1940.

17. Hirschman *The Strategy of Economic Development*, New Haven, 1958 Ch. 10.

18. G. Myrdal, *Economic Theory and Underdeveloped Regions*, London, 1957.

19. T. Hägerstrand, *Innovation Diffusion as a Spatial Process*, Chicago, 1968; first Swedish edition, Lund 1954.

20. P. Pottier, "Axes de communication et développement économique", *Revue Economique*, 1963.

21 Paelinck, "La théorie du developpement regional polarisé". Here quoted after N. M. Hansen, "Development Pole Theory in a Regional Context," *Kyklos*, 1967.

22. Hansen, "Development Pole Theory."

23. Perroux, "Note sur la notion."

24. F. Perroux, "Economic Space: Theory and Application," *Quarterly Journal of Economics*, February 1950; also reprinted in J. Friedmann and W. Alonso, *Regional Development and Planning—A Reader*, Cambridge, Mass. 1964.

25. It should be noted that Perroux and the French school of regional economics use the terms *pole* and *polarization* in a way different from that usually used in English. To Perroux a *pole* simply means a clustering or a concentration of elements in abstract —but also in geographical space—so that a pole is sticking up as a peak in a more or less plain density surface. The term *polarization* is used to mean the process by which poles—as defined above—are created and enlarged. However, since the creation and/or enlargement of one pole may imply stagnation and even decline of other existing poles, the term polarization is used as a general term referring to the enlargement as well as the decline of poles, *i.e.*, as the *process by which poles succeed each other during time*. On the other hand, the *English meaning* of the term polarization is that of the process by which two extremes opposing each other attract the elements in between them. Thus, according to this meaning there will normally be two poles, whereas according

to the French meaning there can be more than two poles at the same time. For more on this point see Lasuén, "On Growth Poles."

26. Perroux, "Note sur la notion," refers to G. Cassel, *Theoretische Sozial ekonomie*, Leipzig, 1927.

27. J. A. Schumpeter, *The Theory of Economic Development*, Cambridge, Mass., 1949; first German edition 1912.

28. Perroux "L'économie dominante" in 1964, here quoted from Hansen, "Development Pole Theory." See also "The Domination Effect and Modern Economic Theory," *Social Research*, 1950.

29. For a very strong criticism see M. Blaug, "A Case of the Emperor's Clothes: Perroux's Theories of Economic Domination," *Kyklos*, 1964.

30. Hansen, "Development Pole Theory" and Lasuén, "On Growth Poles." Lasuén gives particular emphasis to the innovation aspects of leading firms and sectors.

31. When summarizing the development pole theory in the formulation of Perroux, one faces the difficulty of interpreting a relatively loose conceptual framework which furthermore underwent significant changes from the first major paper to the second. While the first puts most stress on the processes of innovation diffusion and development, the second has a much more pronounced input-output flavor. The present summary, which should be regarded more as an interpretation, is besides Perroux's own work based on the reviews of Paelinck and of Lasuén.

32. Although Perroux does not employ these terms himself, it appears clear that the same notions play an important role in his theory. See for example his "Les Points de développement et les foyers de progrès," in *L'économie du XXième siècle*. Perroux seems to have been influenced by A. O. Hirschman's use of these concepts which were originally developed by H. B. Chenery and T. Watanabe in their "International Comparisons of the Structure of Production" *Econometrica*, 1957.

33. The concept of key industry was rejected by Perroux.

34. In his definition of an industrial complex Perroux is strongly influenced by the concept of interindustry linkages giving rise to pecuniary external economies as developed by T. Scitovsky in his "Two Concepts of External Economies," *Journal of Political Economy*, 1954.

35. As pointed out by N. M. Hansen and J. R. Lasuén, Perroux does not provide a satisfactory explanation of how leading propulsive industries come into being or the effects of existing complexes upon emerging ones.

36. The arguments in this paragraph derive largely from J. R. Lasuén, "On Growth Poles."

37. For evidence see references No. 27–34 in J. R. Lasuén, "On Growth Poles."

38. Ibid., p. 171.

39. Hansen, "Development Pole Theory," p. 715.

40. Paelinck, *La théorie du développement régional polarisé*, p. 8.

41. The following summary is based on A. E. Probst, *Industrial Territorial Complexes in the USSR*, paper prepared for the UNIDO Interregional Seminar on the Role of Industrial Complexes in Economic Development, Tashkent, 1964.

42. Similar concepts have been employed in a study of regional development and promotion of industrialization in Southern Italy, undertaken by the EEC Secretariat, 1966, and in a study of industrialization of Puerto Rico. See EEC and Italconsult *Study on the Promotion of an Industrial Development Pole in Southern Italy*, Brussels, 1966; and W. Isard, E. G. Schooler, and T. Vietorisz *Industrial Complex Analysis and Regional Development: A Case Study of Refinery-Synthetic Fiber Complexes and Puerto Rico*, New York, 1959.

43. As stated in E. B. Alayev *Location and Regional Planning—A Short Dictionary*, United Nations Economic Commission for Africa, Addis Ababa, 1968.

44. Compare the concept of pecuniary external economies in Scitovsky, "Two Concepts of External Economies."

45. Probst, *Industrial Territorial Complexes*. See also W. F. Lutrell, "Industrial Complexes and Regional Economic Development," paper presented to the Regional Planning Conference, Ireland, 1969.

46. Lasuén, "On Growth Poles."

47. T. Hermansen, "Spatial Organization and Economic Development."

48. This was recognized at least partly by Perroux already in his 1955 paper. See *L'économie du XXième siècle*, pp. 152–53.

49. Paelinck, *La théorie du developpement régional polarisé*.

50. J. R. Boudeville *Les espaces économiques*, Paris, 1961. See also his *Problems of Regional Economic Planning*, Part 1, Edinburgh, 1966.

51. Christaller, *Central Places in Southern Germany*.

52. Boudeville appears, however, to be somewhat loose in his definitions. In *Problems of Regional Economic Planning*, p. 11 he states that "a regional growth pole is a set of expanding industries located in an urban area and inducing further development of economic activity throughout its zone of influence." While this definition stresses the functional pole aspect, his definition on p. 112 seems to give most weight to the geographical aspect when he says, "It would be preferable to describe poles as geographical agglomeration of activities rather than as a complex system of sectors different from the national matrix. In short, growth poles will appear as towns possessing a complex of propulsive industries."

53. Christaller, *Central Places in Southern Germany*.

54. Lösch, *Economics of Location*.

55. Notably by M. Beckmann in his "City Hierarchies and the Distribution of City Size," *Economic Development and Cultural Change*, 1958 pp. 243–248; E. von Böventer in "Towards a United Theory of Spatial Economic Structures," *Regional Science Association Papers and Proceedings*, 1961; and B. J. L. Berry in "Cities as Systems within Systems of Cities," *Regional Science Association Papers and Proceedings*, 1963.

56. This was first proved by Lösch. For a recent discussion of this problem see, for example, P. Haggett, *Locational Analysis in Human Geography*, London, 1965, pp. 48–56.

57. von Böventer, "Towards a United Theory."

58. This is a key assumption in the theory. By varying this parameter, different forms of spatial organization are generated. Christaller considered three possible values—the market principle in accordance with which the nesting follows the rule of 3, the administrative principle following the rule of 7, and the traffic principle following the rule of 4.

59. This is one of the most controversial aspects of the theory. The case for hierarchies is argued theoretically by M. Beckmann, "City Hierarchies." There are also a number of empirical verifications. Reference can be given to the bibliography contained in B. J. L. Berry and A. Pred, 1965, op. cit. The case against hierarchies is argued perhaps best by R. Vining in his "A Description of Certain Spatial Aspects of an Economic System," *Economic Development and Cultural Change*, 1958. When a hierarchy is identified, the number varies from 5 to 7. In general, the following types of centers are identified: farmsteads, hamlets, villages, towns, cities, regional capitals, and national capitals.

60. For further discussion on this point see, for example, von Böventer, "Towards a United Theory"; R. L. Morrill, "Migration and the Spread and Growth of Urban Settlement," Lund, 1965; T. Hermansen, "Service Trades and Growth Centres" in *Regional Policy in EFTA. An Examination of the Growth Centre Idea*. Edinburgh, 1968.

61. B. Gardner, "Models of Urban Geography and Settlement Location" in R. J. Charley and P. Haggett, *Models in Geography* London, 1967.

62. W. Isard, *Location and Space Economy*, New York, 1956.

63. This section is extracted from T. Hermansen, *Spatial Organization and Economic Development*.

64. von Böventer, "Towards a United Theory."

65. H. C. Bos, *Spatial Dispersion of Economic Activity*, Rotterdam, 1965, chap. 1.

66. Berry, "Cities As Systems." See also E. E. Lampard, "The Evolving System of Cities in the United States—Urbanization and Economic Development," in H. S. Perloff and L. Wingo Jr., *Issues in Urban Economics*, Baltimore, 1968.

67. Hermansen, "*Service Trades and Growth Centres*." Part 3 in "*Regional Policy in EFTA. An Examination of the Growth Center Idea*." Edinburgh, 1968.

68. J. G. M. Hilhorst, *Regional Development Theory—An Attempt to Synthesize*, The Hague, 1967.

69. See e.g. J. R. Boudeville, *Problems of Regional Economic Planning*.

70. cf. T. Hermansen 1969 *Spatial Organization and Economic Development* op. cit., particularly Ch. V: "Impact of Economic Development on Spatial Organization." It would also require an extension of the central place theory so that due account is taken of locational interrelations among manufacturing industries.

71. Reference can be given particularly to research undertaken by Lasuén. See for example his "Urbanization Hypothesis and Spain's Cities System Evolution," *Journal of the Institute of Social Studies* (The Hague) 1970. See also "On Growth Poles." And see *Multiregional Economic Development—An Open System Approach*, paper prepared for the Seminar on Information Systems for Regional Development, Lund, 1969; and with A. Lorca and J. Oria, *City Size Distribution and Economic Growth, Ekistics,* 1967.

72. On this point see M. Penouil, "An Appraisal of Regional Development Policy in the Aquitaine Region," in E. A. G. Robinson, *Backward Areas in Advanced Countries*, London, 1969. See also J. Friedmann, "The Strategy of Deliberate Urbanization," *AIP Journal*, Nov. 1968; C. W. Hale, "The Mechanism of the Spread Effect in Regional Development," *Land Economics*, Nov. 1967; and G. C. Cameron: *Urbanization—Industrialization, Strategy and Growth Centres*, paper presented at the Regional Planning Conference, Ireland, 1969.

73. See *e.g.*, J. R. Lasuén, A. Lorca, and J. Oria, "City Size Distribution." See also J. G. M. Hilhorst, *Regional Development Theory*; T. Hermansen, "Spatial Organization and Economic Development"; T. R. Lakshamanan and A. Silvers, "Developmental and Adaptive Planning for Dynamic Regional Systems" in R. P. Misra, ed., *Regional Planning—Concepts, Techniques, Policies and Case Studies*, University of Mysore Press, Mysore, 1969.

74. A. O. Hirschman, *The Strategy of Economic Development*, New Haven, 1958, Ch. 10.

75. Ibid., p. 183. It is interesting to note that Hirschman uses the terms *growing points* and *growing centers* and not the French term *pole*. Furthermore, although Hirschman uses the terms *polarization* and *polarization effects*, he does not use these terms in the same way as the French school, but in the usual English meaning of widening the gap between two extremes—namely, between rich and poor areas.

76. G. Cassel, 1927, *Theoretische Sozial ekonomic*, Leipzig, 1927.

77. R. Nurkse, *Problems of Capital Formation in Developing Countries*, Oxford, 1953.

78. W. A. Lewis, *The Theory of Economic Growth*, Homewood, Ill., 1965.

79. P. N. Rosenstein-Rodan, "Problems of Industrialization of Eastern and Southern Europe," *Economic Journal*, 1953.

80. See above.

81. H. B. Chenery and T. Watanabe, "International Comparisons of the Structure of Production."

82. The use of the term *polarization* by Hirschman must not be confused with that used by Perroux, Boudeville and others, as discussed in note 34. Perroux appears to use the term *effets de stoppage* in the same sense as Hirschman uses *polarization effects*.

83. G. Myrdal, *Economic Theory and Underdeveloped Regions*, London, 1957.

84. See for example L. Rodwin "Metropolitan Policy for Developing Areas," in W. Isard and J. Cumberland, *Regional Economic Planning*, Paris, 1960. J. Friedmann, "The Strategy of Deliberate Urbanization," *Journal of the American Institute of Planners*, November, 1968, and by the same author, *The Role of Cities in National Development*, Santiago, 1968 (mimeo). See also M. D. Rivkin, "Urbanization and National Development: Some Approaches to a Dilemma," *Socio-Economic Planning Sciences*, 1968. For some critical views reference is given to B. F. Hoselitz, "Generative and Parasitic Cities," in *Sociological Aspect of Economic Growth*, Chicago, 1960, and A. L. Mabogunje, "Urbanization in Nigeria—A Constraint on Economic Development," *Economic Development and Cultural Change*, 1965.

85. E. E. Lampard, "The History of Cities in the Economically Advanced Areas," *Economic Development and Cultural Change*, 1955.

86. C. Furtado, "Intra-Country Discontinuities; Towards a Theory of Spatial Structures," *Social Science Information*, 1967. See also E. A. J. Johnson, *Market Towns and Spatial Integration in India*, New Delhi, 1965.

87. G. Sjoberg, "Cities in Developing and Industrial Societies: A Cross-cultural

Analysis," in P. M. Hauser and L. F. Schnore, *The Study of Urbanization*, New York, 1966.

88. R. L. Meier, *A Communications Theory of Urban Growth*, Cambridge, Mass., 1962. See also J. Friedmann, "An Information Model of Urbanization," *Urban Affairs Quarterly*, 1968.

89. J. Friedmann, *Cities in Social Transformation, Comparative Studies in Society and History*, 1961. See also his "Integration of the Social System: An Approach to the Study of Economic growth," *Diogenes*, 1961.

90. T. Hägerstrand, *Innovations-förloppet ur korologisk synspunkt*, Lund, 1953. Also translated into English and published under the title, *Innovation Diffusion as a Spatial Process*, Chicago, 1967; and by the same author, *The Propagation of Innovation Waves*, Lund, 1952.

91. T. Hägerstrand, "Aspects of the Spatial Structure of Social Communication and the Diffusion of Information," *Regional Science Association Papers and Proceedings*, 1966, p. 27.

92. For a full treatment of the adoption process see, for example, F. E. Emery and O. A. Oeser, *Information, Decision and Action: A Study of the Psychological Determinants of Changes in Farming Technique*, Melbourne, 1958.

93. Hägerstrand is here in accord with the findings in rural sociology. See, for example, E. M. Rogers, *Diffusion of Innovations*, New York/London, 1962.

94. T. Hägerstrand, *Aspects of the Spatial Structure of Social Communication*.

95. The concept is introduced in the later papers of Hägerstrand. See for example, "A Monte Carlo Approach to Diffusion," in *S. Archiv. Europe, Social*, 1965, p. 47; "Quantitative Techniques for Analysis of the Spread of Information and Technology," same publication 1965, p. 277; and, "Aspects of the Spatial Structure of Social Communication and the Diffusion of Information," same publication, 1966, p. 30.

96. P. O. Pedersen, "Innovation Diffusion in Urban Systems," paper prepared for the Seminar on Information Systems for Regional Development, Lund, October, 1969.

97. When the various papers of Hägerstrand are compared, this development stands out clearly. See also P. J. Pedersen, "Innovation Diffusion in Urban Systems," and R. L. Crain, "Fluoridation: The Diffusion of an Innovation among Cities," *Social Forces*, 1966.

98. T. Hägerstrand *"Quantitative Techniques for Analysis of the Spread of Information and Technology"*, p. 277.

99. T. Hägerstrand *"Aspects of the Spatial Structure of Social Communication and the Diffusion of Information"*, pp. 40–42.

100. See, for example, J. A. Ponsioen, *National Development—A Sociological Contribution*, The Hague, 1968.

101. The most obvious cases are the various types of extension services in agriculture, small industries, health improvements, and the like.

102. T. Hägerstrand *"Quantitative Techniques for Analysis of the Spread of Information and Technology."*

103. J. R. Lasuén: "Multi-regional Economic Development, An Open Systems Approach." Paper prepared for the seminar on Information Systems for Regional Development, Lund, Sweden, 1969.

104. See, for example, B. H. Stevens, C. A. Brackett, *Industrial Location—A Review and Annotated Bibliography of Theoretical, Empirical and Case Studies*. Philadelphia, 1967.

105. P. Pottier, "Axes de communication et développement économique," *Revue Economique*, 1963.

106. For similar views advanced in an African context see Z. Piero, "Growth Poles and Growth Centres in Regional Policies in Tanzania." Report prepared for UNRISD, August 1969.

107. E. Howard, *Garden Cities of To-morrow*, London, 1946. See also C. E. Jeanneret-Gris, *City of To-Morrow and its Planning*, London, 1947 (C. E. Jeanneret-Gris is the pseudonym used by Le Corbusier).

108. O. D. Duncan, "Optimum Size of Cities," in P. K. Hatt and A. J. Reiss, Jr., *Cities and Society: The Revised Reader in Urban Sociology*, Glencoe, Ill. 1957 (First ed. 1951).

109. B. Shindman, "An Optimum Size for Cities", *Canadian Geographer*, 1955.

Also reprinted in H. M. Mayer and C. F. Kohn, *Readings in Urban Geography*, Chicago, 1959.

110. C. Clark, "The Economic Functions of a City in Relation to its Size," *Econometrica*, 1945. See also by the same author, "The Distribution of Labour Between Industries and Between Locations," *Land Economics*, 1950.

111. W. Isard, *Location and Space Economy*, New York, 1956.

112. L. H. Klaassen, "Regional Policy in the Benelux Countries", *Area Development Policies in Britain and the Countries of the Common Market*, U. S. Department of Commerce, Washington, D.C., 1965.

113. K. Allen, "Growth Centres and Growth Centre Policy" in *Regional Development in EFTA. An examination of the growth idea.* A similar conclusion is reached by K. Fox in his *The Role of Growth Centers in Regional Economic Development*, Ames: Iowa University Press, 1966.

114. The above review relates basically to industrialized countries. For the relevance of the concept and discussion of optimum city size to developing countries reference is given to J. J. Spengler, "Africa and the Theory of Optimum City Size, in H. Miller, ed., *The City in Modern Africa*, London, 1967.

GROWTH
POLE POLICY
IN CANADA

BENJAMIN HIGGINS
University of Montreal

Introduction

Canada has never experienced the marked centripetal tendency that has characterized the growth of regional income in the United States during the last three decades. Income figures by province have been available only since 1926. From that time to the present, dispersion indices, whether for the ten provinces or for the five regions, show no clear tendency to fall. The unweighted index of dispersion for major regions is, moreover, substantially higher than in the United States, and the gap between richest and poorest region is also greater.[1] Figures for occupational structure have been available since 1911; these suggest that the gaps have been there at least since that date (occupational structure is a good proxy variable for income). Historical records and other sources of information indicate that the regional disparities have changed little since Confederation in 1867.

Over the thirty-five-year period following 1926, real per capita personal income in Ontario grew faster than the national average. Ontario moved from second place in 1927 to first place in 1962. The second highest rate of growth, it is true, occurred in the Maritime Provinces, which were the poorest region in 1927. They remained the poorest region in 1962, and the absolute gap in real per capita income between the Maritimes and the richest region widened considerably. The Prairie Provinces shared with British Columbia the dubious honor of having the slowest rate of growth and retained the middle position among major regions in the country. British Columbia slipped from first to second place. Quebec had the same overall growth rate as Ontario; but its position as the second poorest region was unchanged—a striking fact, given Quebec's vast mineral and forest resources and its tremendous supplies of hydroelectric power.

In terms of earned income per member of the labor force, growth in the Maritimes was below the dominion average for 1931–1955, although it was slightly higher than the dominion average for 1941–1955. Quebec and Ontario lagged behind the dominion in both periods, but British Columbia was above the national average in both periods. Finally, the Prairies were well above the country as a whole in both these periods.

Up to World War II, there was some tendency toward convergence of regional incomes. Since the war, unfortunately, this tendency has been reversed; in the words of the Economic Council, "the forces tending to narrow differences between regional income levels have weakened considerably."[2] The Atlantic Provinces failed to share in the acceleration of growth that took place in other regions. Even in percentage terms, the income gap between the Maritimes and the rest of the country widened.

Quebec enjoyed the highest rate of growth of all regions during the early post-war period (1947–1962), improving its relative position significantly over 1947, although not much over 1927. Since then, Quebec's growth rate has been close to the national average. Its rank among Canadian regions remains the same. The Prairie Provinces lost ground during the post war years, despite the oil discoveries in Alberta; their growth rate was barely above that of the Atlantic Provinces. The relative position of British Columbia was unchanged, while Ontario grew faster than the national average and strengthened its position as the "rich" region of Canada. There was some slight tendency toward convergence in the late 1960s.

Both in the Atlantic Provinces and in the Province of Quebec there are people who feel, with some justice, that confederation did not bring the same economic benefits to their regions as to other parts of the country. No other highly regionalized country has anything quite like the Province of Quebec, with nearly 30 per cent of the national population living in a sharply defined geographic and political region with a religion, language, history, and culture different from that of the great majority of people in the rest of the country. It is not surprising that regional differences (not in themselves particularly large in comparison to some other countries) should bring more serious political problems in Canada than in other countries. It is not too much to say that the survival of the federation depends on finding a solution to the problems of regional disparities.

Legislation

Given the serious political problems arising from regional differences, it is not surprising that Canada has a welter of legislation dealing with regional disparities.

AREA DEVELOPMENT AGENCY

The Area Development Agency was established by the Department of Industry Act of July, 1963. Its powers were extended by the Area Development Incentives Act of June, 1965. The original act established the Department of Industry under a minister and set up within this ministry an Area Development Agency under the direction of a Commission for Area Development. The original act empowered the minister to undertake research on means of increasing employment and income in designated areas and to carry out programs and projects to improve the economic development of designated areas that cannot suitably be undertaken by other departments. It also empowered the governor-in-council to authorize and direct departments, branches, and agencies of the government to undertake special measures to facilitate economic development in any designated areas.

The original legislation provided tax incentives for enterprises willing to locate in designated areas. Such firms were exempted from income tax for three years; and after that they were allowed to write off their machinery and equipment for tax purposes in two years and their buildings in five years. The 1967 legislation went further, providing outright capital grants. For new facilities, the grant could amount to one-third of the capital costs up to $250,000. For capital costs between $250,000 and $1,000,000, the grant could be one-third of the first $250,000 and one-quarter of the remainder. If the capital costs exceeded $1,000,000, the grant would be one-third of $250,000 plus one-quarter of $750,000 plus one-fifth of the remainder or $5,000,000, whichever was less. For expanded facilities, the formula was: subtract from capital cost of the extension 10 per cent of the "approved" value of existing plant or $10,000, whichever was larger;

and then apply the formula for new facilities. The capital grants did not reduce the value of capital or depreciation for tax purposes, and enterprises could choose between the grants and the tax holiday.

It will be noted that the formula discriminates in favor of relatively small firms; in so doing it also discriminates in favor of French Canadian firms, since these tend to be on a smaller scale than English-speaking firms. Also, the firms likely to be attracted to growth poles east of Montreal are likely to be mainly "foot-loose" industries which do not need to be close to a major market or to sources of energy and raw materials; and these will tend to be relatively small, scientifically-oriented industries.

The areas for special assistance were first designated solely in terms of chronic unemployment, and assistance was limited to reductions in effective rates of taxation on private enterprises undertaking to establish new ventures within the designated areas. The legislation of June, 1965, went further and provided outright development grants for private enterprises establishing undertakings in designated areas. The grants were exempt from income tax and were not excluded from capital costs for tax purposes up to 1,000,000 or up to one-fifth of amounts above a 1,000,000 up to 5,000,000. The grants were also available for expansion of existing plants provided they contributed appreciably to improving income and employment opportunities in the area.

When this legislation was introduced, the Department of Industry also announced its intention to achieve closer cooperation among the firms receiving these financial incentives, the interested provincial authorities, and the national employment service so as to assure effective planning to meet the long-term manpower needs of the new industries as well as their immediate requirements. As part of this new manpower planning aspect of the Area Development Program, the Department of Labor undertook joint surveys with provincial and local authorities to assess training needs and facilities. Assistance to provinces with training activities is provided under the technical and vocational training assistance act. The definition of "designated areas" was also expanded. There is also federal legislation for assisted migration, including free transportation and reestablishment grants; but this legislation has never been thoroughly integrated with other facets of regional development policy.

The ADA legislation made some contributions to alleviating the problem of differentials in income and employment among ethnic groups as well as among regions. Only three counties and seven national employment service areas were designated in Ontario, the province with the biggest share of the national labor force. In New Brunswick, nine national employment service areas and one county were designated, covering a large proportion of the area in that small province where French Canadians are concentrated. In Quebec twenty-two national employment service areas and three counties were designated, far more than any other province. Thus, the administration of the legislation, by the very fact of being directed toward unemployment and low incomes, did discriminate in favor of French Canadians.

DEFECTS IN THE ADA APPROACH

The importance attached to having a simple, measurable criterion to be applied uniformly throughout the country was in accordance with Canadian traditions and was understandable in terms of administrative problems under existing arrangements; but it was totally inadequate in terms of development policy, either national or regional. Virtually every economist commenting on this policy pointed out that the presence of large-scale or chronic unemployment in a particular area is in itself no recommendation for encouraging investment in that area. More than any other aspect of federal regional and area development policy, the ADA approach was destined to run into conflict with integrated regional development policy at the provincial level.

THE ATLANTIC DEVELOPMENT BOARD

The Atlantic Development Board was established by the Atlantic Development Board Act of December, 1962. The original board had five members appointed by the governor-in-council. The act stated specifically that although the board is financed from federal funds, it is not an agency of the federal government nor are members of the board a part of the public service. The revision of July, 1963, increased the number of members of the board to eleven, the board remaining as a public corporation, and established the Atlantic Development Fund with an initial capital of $100 million. The legislation was quite broad so far as the use of the fund is concerned. It was to be used "for the purpose of financing and assisting in financing the undertaking and the carrying out of programs and projects, that, in the opinion of the Board, will contribute to the growth and development of the economy of the Atlantic Region and for which satisfactory financing arrangements are not otherwise available." So far as the legislation was concerned, the fund could be used to provide capital assistance to private enterprise. In practice, however, the board preferred to use the bulk of its funds to assist private enterprises through financing the infrastructure. The larger grants went to hydroelectric power and transportation. Smaller grants were made for research and to provide facilities associated with food processing industries. The federal grants were matched on a fifty-fifty basis by Nova Scotia, New Brunswick, and Newfoundland, and on a twenty-five-seventy-five basis by Prince Edward Island.

The act provided that the board might "prepare in consultation with the Economic Council of Canada an overall coordinated plan for the promotion of the economic growth of the Atlantic Region." The chairman of the board was a member of the Economic Council of Canada, and research leading toward such a comprehensive plan was launched jointly by the board and the council.

ARDA

The Federal Agricultural Rehabilitation and Development Act was passed in December, 1961, establishing the Agricultural Rehabilitation and Development Agency. Under this legislation ARDA, through bilateral agreements with the provincial governments, might pay two-thirds, one-half, or one-third of the costs of agricultural rehabilitation programs and projects. The ARDA program was under the Ministry of Lands and Forestry, and programs and projects receiving federal assistance were approved by the minister or his designate. A sum of $125 million for allotment to the provinces was provided but with a limitation to total expenditures of $25,000,000 by the federal government in any one fiscal year. In addition, the federal government set up a special fund for rural economic development in the amount of $50,000,000 to finance major development projects in all provinces.

The allotment to each province was made on the basis of a formula, with an initial amount of $375,000, increased in accordance with the ratio of rural population of the province to the total rural population of Canada, the ratio of rural nonfarm families with less than $3,000 income relative to the national total, and the proportion of the total number of farms having a capital value of less than $25,000 and annual sales of farm products of less than $3,750. The provinces might submit either an annual overall program for approval or individual projects.

The legislation had among its objectives the promotion of physical, social, and economic research related to agricultural rehabilitation. Efforts to formulate comprehensive rural development plans were acceptable as "programs" under the act, as were feasibility studies for individual projects. Another objective of the legislation was "the establishment of viable farms through the enlargement, consolidation, regrouping and basic improvement of submarginal farms." A third objective was to reestablish rural people in effective employment and income opportunities. In this connection the federal government assisted in financing allowances for transportation and for living costs for people undertaking retraining. For such agricultural development projects as establishment of pastures, community foliage, forests, and recreation areas, the federal government assumed 100 per cent of the total costs. Federal funds might also be used in comprehensive programs in special rural development areas.

ARDA–QUEBEC

In June, 1963, the province of Quebec passed its own ARDA legislation, *Aménagement Rural et du Développement Agricole* (ARDA). It authorized the Minister of Agriculture and Colonization, who was the minister concerned with negotiating ARDA programs for the Province of Quebec, to elaborate plans for economic, technical, and social progress in rural regions and to undertake research toward this end. In May, 1965, a convention was signed by the governments of Canada and of Quebec. The document stated that the major role of the federal government would consist of review and ultimate approval or rejection of programs submitted by the government of Quebec and transmitting to the province the financial contributions foreseen in the *entente* to meet the costs of approved programs. Planning and implementation of projects and programs were to remain the function of the government of Quebec. The provincial government would forward projects suggested by local and regional organisms and establish an order of priority, taking account of the needs and characteristics of diverse regions within its territory; it would initiate programs and projects designed to achieve the objectives of the ARDA legislation; and it would submit projects and programs for the approval of the federal government and execute approved programs and projects.

From the beginning, ARDA-Quebec undertook to bring into the planning process the people actually to be affected by the execution of particular projects. The Quebec government laid considerable stress on the point that any project proposed should ultimately be part of a plan of "a certain scope" (*certain envergure*); that is, a plan prepared, for example, by a particular group of farmers having identical problems or by a group of citizens interested in the preparation of a site for tourism, interested in bringing into use a particular resource, and so on.

The availability of funds under the ARDA legislation and the fact that the majority of projects that could be undertaken with these funds would be of interest to several ministers led to the formation of the *Comité Permanent d'Aménagement des Ressources* (CPAR). This committee included the Ministries of Agriculture and Colonization, Tourism, Hunting and Fishing, Industry and Commerce, Natural Resources, Lands and Forest, and Roads. The deputy ministers are the actual members of CPAR. The basic research is done by the ARDA administration, but priorities are determined by the CPAR.

The Quebec government stated at the outset that, with respect to projects aimed at increasing income and employment opportunities, the Quebec government intended to consider only those demands that comprise a part of a local or regional program "of a certain scope." In short, the province was feeling its way toward a system of comprehensive regional planning and did not intend to have its progress in this direction hampered by any limitations that might be involved in federal legislation.

THE GENERAL INVESTMENT CORPORATION

The GIC was established in July, 1962, by the government of Quebec, with an authorized capital of $150,000,000. Its stated purpose is:

(a) to stimulate and promote the formation and development of industrial undertakings, and accessorily, of commercial undertakings, in the

province, so as to broaden the basis of its economic structure, accelerate the growth thereof, and contribute to full employment;
(b) to induce the people of Quebec to participate in the development of
such undertakings by investing a part of their savings therein.

The share of private capital in the corporation exceeds the share of
government capital, and the privately nominated directors constitute
a majority of the board. The GIC provides the government of Quebec
with a financial instrument of its own for altering the pattern, including the regional distribution, of investment in the province. Its policy
to date has been flexible; it has bought control of some companies,
created new enterprises of its own, participated with other firms in
establishment of new companies, and has made straightforward
loans to companies in which the GIC has little or no direct participation.

In June, 1968, the Province of Quebec adopted the Regional
Industrial Development Assistance Act, which provides additional
incentives for manufacturing or processing plants willing to establish
themselves in two designated zones outside the Montreal region. In
Zone I the grants can reach 25 per cent of capital costs or $500,000,
whichever is lower; in Zone II, comprising the Abitibi region and the
Gaspésie north and east of Rivière-du-Loup, the grants are higher.
The legislation is designed to encourage middle-sized enterprises;
capital investment must amount to $50,000 to be eligible for
assistance.

In September, 1969, the province introduced a still more interesting
system of incentives, defined not in terms of regions, but in terms of
"leading sectors": electronic, electrical, chemical, industrial equipment, and aerospace industries. The grants can amount to $5,000,000
and are designed to assist large corporations in these fields that are
unable to take advantage of the new program of the Federal Ministry
of Regional Economic Expansion. The sole obligation imposed on
the firms receiving these grants is that they should employ graduates
in engineering, sciences, technology, or business administration of
Quebec universities.

THE MINISTRY OF REGIONAL EXPANSION

In March, 1969, the various pieces of federal legislation relating to
regional development were pulled together in the Government
Organization Act, which established the Ministry of Regional

Economic Expansion. The new ministry takes over the administration of federal assistance granted under the former ADB, ADA, and ARDA legislation, and henceforth all federal assistance for regional development in the provinces is to be administered by the Ministry of Regional Expansion. The new legislation provides for much more flexibility in granting federal funds for programs or projects designed to reduce regional disparities. The former "designated areas" of the ADA are replaced by "special areas," designated by the governor-in-council after consultation with the province, and they may be "any area in that province that is determined to require, by reason of the exceptional inadequacy of opportunities for productive employment of the people of that area or of the region of which that area is a part, special measures to facilitate economic expansion and social adjustment." Although this phraseology does not allow for "economic space" or for the possibility that raising income and employment in a retarded area may best be accomplished by investment in a totally different area, it does permit federal assistance to regional development programs, instead of tying federal aid to particularly ill-favored counties or electoral districts.

The minister is also empowered to formulate plans for regional development in cooperation with other departments or agencies of the government of Canada and to provide for coordination in the implementation of such plans. In exercising these powers, the minister is required to provide for the cooperation of the provinces. The minister may also formulate joint plans in cooperation with a province, and implement the plans under an agreement with the province. He may also make grants or loans toward the capital cost of specific works or facilities in special areas if he is satisfied that they are "essential to the successful implementation of a plan." Finally, he may make grants or loans to any commercial undertaking in a special area, if it is essential to the plan, for "establishment, expansion, or modernization." This wording provides much more administrative discretion than the former ADA formula. For the time being, it has been decided to limit cash grants to a ceiling of $12,000,000 for any one project; and the formula has been established as "up to 25 per cent of capital cost plus an amount not exceeding $5,000 for each manufacturing job created." Up to the end of January, 1970, the ministry had considered 517 applications, rejected forty-one, made offers for ninety-six, and was still considering the rest. The grants varied widely in total amounts and in proportion of capital costs covered and subsidy per job created. In terms of total grants as a proportion of total capital costs, the federal assistance ranged from about 15 per cent to about 40 per cent.

From the standpoint of growth pole theory and practice, the size of zone designated is of special interest. To begin with, the entire Atlantic Provinces region has been designated, including the metropolitan area of Halifax-Dartmouth. In Quebec, virtually the whole province north and east of Montreal has been designated; in effect, seven of the ten administrative regions of the entire province, including the metropolitan areas within them, are eligible for federal grants to private enterprises established or expanding there, and for federal investment in the infrastructure.

In the more prosperous provinces much smaller zones have been designated—only the north of Ontario, for example, and only the southeast corner of British Columbia. It is interesting to note, however, that among the grants already made up to the end of January, 1970, are four in the Prairie Provinces' largest metropolitan center, Winnipeg. Thus, the Canadian legislation permits a policy of strengthening true *pôles de croissance*, in the Perroux sense of large aggregations of propulsive, innovating enterprises.

GROWTH POLE STRATEGY IN QUEBEC

This, then, is the legislative background against which growth pole strategy may be formulated in Canada. The joint powers of federal and provincial governments, including budgets for public investment and incentives for private investment, would seem to be sufficient to alter the regional pattern of development. In point of fact, however, only Quebec is currently talking seriously of creation of *pôles de croissance* as a means of reducing regional disparities and undertaking the studies necessary for the formulation of growth pole policy. No doubt because of the influence of French theory and practice in Quebec, the concept of growth poles is at the core of current planning in that province. The notion also has some currency in the Atlantic Provinces (where half of francophone Canadians outside of Quebec make their homes), but the political commitment to such a strategy of development is less clear cut than in Quebec. In the other provinces, regional planning tends to be more physical than economic, and concern for retarded areas reflects basic norms of social justice, rather than an economic theory which argues that

accelerating growth of the entire province is closely linked to reduction of gaps within it, with growth poles as a major instrument. Thus,
for the economist and particularly for the economist concerned with
growth pole theory and practice, Quebec holds the greatest interest at
the present time.

The Quebec Economy

For as long as records exist, there has been a persistent lag in per
capita incomes in Quebec behind those of the neighboring province
of Ontario and of Canada as a whole. Between 1927 and 1964 (the
period for which comparable data are available), Quebec's personal
income per capita ranged from 67 per cent to 75 per cent of that of
Ontario; it was 74 per cent in 1927 and close to 75 per cent for the
years 1961 to 1964. Hourly wage rates in Quebec manufacturing have
lagged a persistent 15 per cent below the Ontario level for some twenty
years. Value added per man-year in manufacturing in Quebec has
lagged a persistent 15 per cent below Ontario ever since 1870. The
relationship of Quebec personal income per capita to the national
average shows similar stability. It was about 88 per cent in 1927,
averaged 83.4 per cent for 1949–1952, rose slowly to 87.6 per cent
for 1961–1964, and was about 90 per cent in 1968. Historical sources
suggest that the gap in productivity and income prevailed throughout
the nineteenth century and perhaps even earlier than that. No clear
and continuing trend toward a narrowing of the gap is discernible
despite the industrial boom that has taken place in Quebec since
World War II.

QUEBEC AND "FRENCH CANADA"

Partly because three-quarters of the French Canadians live in Quebec,
the regional difference in economic and social status are reflected in
ethnic differences. French Canadians are clearly at an economic disadvantage in comparison with the British Canadian population or
with Canadians in general. It is a striking fact that in every province
in Canada, the incomes of French Canadians are below the average
and well below the average income of Canadians of British origin.
For the country as a whole, only the Italians among major ethnic
groups have lower average incomes.[3]

In 1961 the total income of French male members of the labor force was 87.7 per cent of the Canadian average, as compared to 109.9 per cent for the British. When women are included, the figures are 88.9 per cent for the French and 109 per cent for the British. In Ontario the situation was much the same as for the country as a whole; male French Canadians earned 87 per cent of the provincial average, whereas British Canadians earned 106.9 per cent of the provincial average. In Quebec, because of the great preponderance of French Canadians, the average income of the French members of the labor force must be close to the provincial average; it was 91.7 per cent of that average. However, because of the concentration of the British population in the higher income occupations in Quebec, their average income was 140 per cent of the provincial average.

In the Province of Quebec, the Jews, the Germans, the Ukrainians and "others" all earn higher incomes than French Canadians. Indeed, as we have said, only the Italian population had lower incomes. Except in Newfoundland, where the average income of the British population is about equal to the provincial average, the incomes of the British are above the average in all provinces.

It is worth noting that there is more difference between the incomes of French Canadians in the province where French Canadians are richest and where they are poorest than there is between French Canadians and British anywhere in the dominion. In Prince Edward Island the income of French Canadians is only 66 per cent of the average income of French Canadians in Canada as a whole, whereas in British Columbia the figure is 117.3 per cent. This range is less than the equivalent range for the British, from 61 per cent of the Canadian average in Newfoundland to 121.9 per cent of the Canadian average in Quebec. If, on the other hand, we compare the French incomes where they are lowest with British incomes where they are highest, the range is from $4,957 to $2,251, a difference of 120 per cent.

The difference in per capita income as between Quebec and the national average is almost identical with the difference between incomes of French Canadians and the national average. Moreover, if the extreme cases of the Province of Prince Edward Island and the Jewish group are eliminated (both distort the picture because they are a very small part of the total population), the coefficient of variation from the national average becomes almost the same for provinces and for ethnic groups: 15.1 per cent versus 13.1 per cent.[4]

Quebec is by no means the poorest province or even the poorest region. Newfoundland had a per capita personal income in 1962 only 59 per cent of the national average, and Prince Edward Island, 61 per cent. Ontario, on the other hand, had a per capita personal income 17 per cent above the national average in that year. In 1968 per capita personal incomes in Ontario were about 10 per cent above the national average, Quebec was some 10 per cent below, and the Atlantic Provinces some 20 per cent below. Thus, the regional gaps are considerably greater than the gaps between French and British incomes, whether in Canada as a whole or in individual provinces. Obviously, there is an association between the relatively low figures of French Canadian incomes and the fact that most French Canadians live in the Province of Quebec, whereas about half the remainder live in the Atlantic Provinces.

With incomes measured as total income of members of the labor force, Saskatchewan as well as the Atlantic Provinces drops below the province of Quebec. Once again, it is interesting to note that average incomes of the British population, so measured, range from 67.1 per cent of the national average for all ethnic groups in New-foundland to 134.1 per cent of this national average in Quebec. Similarly, the incomes of French Canadians range from 57.9 per cent of the national average (for all groups) in Prince Edward Island to 102.9 per cent of the national average in British Columbia. Thus, the predominant role of regional differences is once again apparent.

UNEMPLOYMENT

Unemployment is, of course, a factor contributing to lower average incomes, but a relatively high incidence of unemployment in Quebec (and among French Canadians) might also be regarded as an economic disadvantage in its own right. Unemployment in the province of Quebec shows a persistent tendency to run higher than the Canadian average, and it is indeed higher than in any region except the Atlantic Provinces. Moreover, unemployment has shown a sharper increase in Quebec since the war than in any other region. In 1948 unemployment in Quebec was only 2.4 per cent of the labor force, and in five years, 1946–1950, the average was 3.3 per cent. In 1961 unemployment was 9.4 per cent of the labor force, and the average for 1956–1960 was 7.4 per cent. Thus, the five-year average for 1956–1960 was more than double the five-year average for 1946–

1950, and peak unemployment in 1961 was nearly four times as high as the nadir in 1948. For Canada as a whole, the corresponding figures are 2.9 per cent and 5.6 per cent for the quinquennia 1946–1950 and 1956–1960, and 2.2 per cent and 7.2 per cent for the minimum and maximum figures.

Unemployment fell throughout the country between 1964 and 1968 but remained higher in Quebec than in the country as a whole. The figures for Quebec are 6.4 per cent, 5.4 per cent, and 4.7 per cent for the three years; for Canada, they are 4.7 per cent, 3.9 per cent, and 3.6 per cent.

The Atlantic Provinces are the only region where unemployment has been higher than in the province of Quebec. In Quebec unemployment is concentrated in subregions with high proportions of French-speaking people. All areas in the Atlantic Provinces with large French Canadian populations are also areas of high and chronic unemployment. In the city of Montreal, where figures are available by ethnic groups, the higher level of unemployment among French Canadians explains 6.3 per cent of the income difference between French and British.[5]

TABLE 1

Average Unemployment in Administrative
Regions of Quebec, 1955–1964

Region	Rate of Unemployment	Percentage of Quebec Level
Gaspésie	15.2	176.7
Saguenay/Lac St-Jean	13.7	159.3
Quebec	9.0	104.6
Trois-Rivières	11.1	129.0
Cantons de l'Est	9.0	104.6
Montréal and metropolitan Montréal	7.5	87.2
Outaouais	8.5	98.8
Abitibi-Témiscamingue	9.1	105.8
Côte-Nord	12.7	147.7
PROVINCE OF QUEBEC	8.6	100.0

Source: *Tableau* XI, p. III/46 "Pour une politique québécoise de développement régional." *première partie,* Ch. III *(Projet de rapport).*

POVERTY

The proportion of French Canadians among the poor, as usually defined for policy purposes, is higher than their proportion of the total population. In Canada as a whole, 37.4 per cent of French Canadian members of the labor force receive less than $3,000 a year, as compared to the overall figure for Canada as a whole of 30.6 per cent. The proportion of French Canadians earning less than $3,000 a year ranges from 75 per cent in Prince Edward Island to 24 per cent in British Columbia. Another 40.8 per cent of French Canadians are in the $3,000 to $5,000 class, making 78.2 per cent of the French Canadians below $5,000, as compared to 70.1 per cent for the country as a whole and 73.0 per cent for the British.

SUBMARGINAL FARMS

During 1963 ARDA undertook an Eastern Canada Farm Survey. They found that in Quebec and the Atlantic Provinces at least 50 per cent of the farm units are redundant, economically nonviable, and should be done away with as soon as possible. These farms' 20 per cent contribution to the total farm output could easily be picked up by the expanded and improved viable units. In general, farms producing less than $2,500 per year were regarded nonviable, but the survey team also applied other criteria that gave a figure of 42.7 per cent versus 50 per cent of the farm units as being nonviable.

Oversettlement and underemployment characterized the nonviable farms. Most farms with less than 100 acres were found to be non-economic. Quebec and Nova Scotia were found to be the worst offenders. The team found that almost 8 percent more of Quebec farms were in the below-$2,500 bracket, so both in terms of number and size the problem is more acute there.

OCCUPATIONAL STRUCTURE

Like unemployment, differences in occupational structure are a major factor in explaining differences in income. However, apart from their contribution to income gaps, differences in occupational structure may be regarded as a symptom of economic disadvantage in themselves, reflecting inequalities of employment opportunity.

In terms of broad industrial structure, the province of Quebec might be regarded as the second most "advanced" of the major regions of Canada. In 1961 the proportion of the labor force in manufacturing was much higher in Quebec than in any province except Ontario and was therefore well above the national average.

Conversely, the share of the labor force engaged in primary industry (other than agriculture) is lower in Quebec than in any province except Ontario, where the proportion in the agricultural sector is also low, and in Manitoba and Saskatchewan, where the proportion in agriculture is high. In comparison to any region except Ontario, Quebec has a relatively low proportion of its labor force in primary industry, including agriculture. In finance, insurance, and buildings, also, Quebec ranks just below Ontario and thus above the national average.

On the other hand, Quebec had relatively few people in public administration and in general services; in both of these categories the proportion of the labor force in Quebec is below several provinces and below the national average.

URBANIZATION

Quebec is also highly urbanized and has for generations been one of the most urbanized of Canadian regions. In 1961 54 per cent of Quebec's population lived in the Montreal region, 75 per cent lived in cities. Of the urban population, 67 per cent lived in cities of 100,000 or more, and some 85 per cent lived in cities of 10,000 or more.

THE PROBLEM OF "CONTROL"

Perhaps the most disturbing of all the characteristic features of Quebec as an economic region is its "enclave" nature; the "modern sector" is very largely in the hands of "foreigners." In 1961 less than 26 per cent of the number of manufacturing establishments (with 25 or more employees) were under the control of the French Canadians. Some 57 per cent of the establishments were controlled by other Canadians, and 17 per cent were under foreign control. The proportion of establishments under French Canadian control, moreover, tended to be relatively high in such traditional or consumer-oriented sectors as food and drink, leather, wood products, and furniture, involving mainly the application of simple techniques to local raw materials. The proportion was very much lower in more recent and more dynamic industries such as tobacco, textiles, clothing, electric equipment, machinery, and chemicals requiring higher technical skills.

In part, the underrepresentation of French Canadians in the control of the growth industries is a matter of size. The proportion of French Canadian control over value of production is very much lower than their share in number of establishments: 10.2 per cent for manufacturing as a whole, as compared to 44 per cent for other Canadians and 46 per cent for foreigners. Measured in this way, the French Canadian share of control drops to 0.9 per cent in tobacco, 2 per cent for textiles, 7.3 per cent for clothing, 7.6 per cent for paper, 11.1 per cent for machinery, 5.1 per cent for transport equipment, 4.1 per cent for electrical equipment, and 2.5 per cent for chemicals. On the other hand, the share in value of output remains at 39.9 per cent for leather and 66.3 per cent for wood products.

Even in trade, the French Canadian control is surprisingly low: 30.4 per cent of the number of wholesale establishments, 32.2 per cent of the number of retail establishments, and 31.2 per cent for commerce as a whole. Here the differences by size of establishment are less striking; measured by the value of sales, the French Canadian share is 31.7 per cent. When we move to mining, so important in the recent development of Quebec, French Canadians control only 11 per cent of the number of establishments and only 2.2 per cent of the value added.

The lack of proportionate representation of French Canadians in management also shows up in the salary structure. About 45 per cent of the total labor force in Quebec operations is French-speaking. In the $5,000 to $6,500 salary bracket, French-speaking personnel constitute 36 per cent of the total. Only 25 per cent of all salaried personnel is French-speaking. In the over-$15,000 salary range, the French-speaking comprise only 15 per cent. In English Canadian, Quebec-based firms the picture is as shown in Table 2.

TABLE 2

Percentage French-Speaking in
English Canadian Quebec-based firms

Labor force	58 per cent
Lower level management	40 per cent
Middle level management	13 per cent
Presidents and vice presidents	10 per cent
Directors	19 per cent

Source: Oswald Hall, "Equal Partnership and the Control of Industry," Working Paper No. 2 July 26, 1966, p, p. 7.

It will be noted that the representation of French Canadians among directors is higher than among top management; this fact may reflect a growing tendency for English Canadian Quebec firms to have one or two "showpiece" French Canadian directors, who are always in the minority and may exercise very little effective control. Thus, French Canadians play a minor role in the management of large English Canadian or foreign corporations operating in the province of Quebec. Even if one takes manufacturing enterprises as a whole, including the smaller firms, at the highest levels of management French Canadians appear at only one-quarter of the statistically expected frequency whereas other Canadians appear at four times the expected rate.

These are the conditions that give rise to the French Canadian demand to be *maîtres chez nous*. This demand is more vociferous than the demand for equal economic status in terms of income and employment. In terms of reducing tensions, increasing the degree of control of French Canadians over industrial, commercial, and mining enterprises in their own province is probably a more pressing policy objective than reducing income gaps between French Canadians and others.

CONTROL, INCOME, AND EMPLOYMENT

There is a direct relationship between the problem of control and the differences in income levels between French Canadians and others. English-speaking top management, trained in English-speaking universities, likes to have around it in the higher echelons of managerial, scientific, and technical personnel, men with the same background as their own. That means "speaking the same language" in professional terms, as well as in purely linguistic terms. Thus, the limited scope of French Canadian ownership and management in the Province of Quebec leads directly to limitations of employment opportunities for French Canadians. Genuine equality of employment opportunity in the province requires the presence in the region of a far greater number of enterprises with French-speaking top management, willing to entrust the higher positions in the firm to graduates of French language educational institutions.

REGIONAL DISPARITIES WITHIN QUEBEC

The Quebec economy is dominated in large measure by Montreal, which has within its metropolitan region some 50 per cent of the population and more than half the gross regional product. The Montreal region is the richest of the ten official regions of the province, with a per capita income 21 per cent above the provincial average. The frontier area of Côte Nord-Nouveau Québec, a prosperous mining and forestry region with some 2 per cent of the provincial population, has a per capita income close to the average and an income per worker above the average. As mentioned above, Gaspésie-Bas St. Laurent is the poorest region, with an average income about 40 per cent that of Montreal. The regions north and west of Hull (across the river from Ottawa) are decaying mining areas that are losing population through net emigration. The Cantons de l'Est, south and east of Montreal, consist of poor farms and (except for Sherbrooke) stagnant or decaying old industrial towns, specialising in such problem industries as textiles, furniture, leather goods, and the like. Some of the counties on the south shore of the St. Lawrence, between Quebec and the steel town of Sorel, are also very poor, although outside of the East of Quebec.

THE BAEQ

The major program undertaken under ARDA legislation in Quebec thus far has been the reconstruction and development of the East of Quebec. The planning for this undertaking was done by a special agency set up for the purpose, the *Bureau d'Aménagement de l'Est du Québec*. The BAEQ was formed in 1963 out of two existing regional councils, le Conseil d'Orientation Economique de Bas-St-Laurent and le Conseil Régional d'Expansion Economique de la Gaspésie et des Iles-de-la-Madaleine. The East of Quebec was legally defined as a pilot region for development planning in the province. It was selected as the *territoire-pilote* essentially because it is the poorest of the ten administrative regions of Quebec. A large proportion of the region's 325,000 people were earning their livelihood in traditional fishing, farming, and woodlot activities, and per capita income was less than half that of the region of Montreal. Half the families in the region were judged to be below the legally defined poverty line and were receiving government subventions of one kind or another; government transfer payments constituted one-quarter of personal income of the region.

Over three years the BAEQ managed to spend close to 4,000,000 dollars in the preparation of a plan; half of this amount was provided by the federal government, half by Quebec. One reason for the high cost of the plan was the stress laid upon *animation sociale*. It was considered highly important for the population to feel a sense of participation in the planning process; it was also thought that in a region that had been so long stagnant it was essential for the people to have a vision of a different and better way of life, if the implementation of the plan was to be effective.

One of the difficulties confronting the team of young and enthusiastic planners who formed the core of the BAEQ staff was the fact that when they began their work there was little or no indication of the way in which planning for the rest of the province might proceed. Thus, in effect, they were precluded from considering a solution to the problems of the region that would involve moving the population to growth poles or centers of attraction outside the region. The major objective was the elimination of poverty and raising the average income of the region to the average of the province. It was estimated that to achieve these objectives within a plan framework based on exploitation of natural resources, it would be necessary to reduce the population to 200,000. This solution was rejected; instead, it was assumed that the population would remain stable. In effect, the existing tendency for net emigration to offset natural population growth was projected to the future. The team thus accepted the challenge of devising a regional plan that would permit 325,000 people to live in the region at a level equal to the provincial average.

The major objective was then translated into six operational goals:

1. Modernization of traditional sectors (farming, fishing and forestry).
2. Creation of dynamic new enterprises in tourism, industry, and mining.
3. Manpower training designed to increase geographic and occupational mobility.
4. Installation of an institutional framework suited for continuing planning and implementation.
5. Implantation of a "regional conscience" that would identify the population with the objectives and instruments of development.
6. A rational structuring of geographic space.

Although the solution of emptying the region was rejected, the plan did envisage the emptying of some of the more hopeless of the farming, fishing, and forestry areas and the attraction of population to new enterprises to be established in the larger cities of the region (none of which is large). It is interesting to note, too, that the team accepted a 10 per cent unemployment rate as the best one could hope for in the region. However, they did establish goals for reduction of total and seasonal unemployment that involved the creation of the equivalent of 9,000 additional full-time jobs with an initial labor force of 83,000. These requirements were broken down into sectors in considerable detail and translated into specific investment projects, public and private. The labor force in agriculture was to be reduced from 30,000 to 13,000 while output per farmer was to be raised from $2,000 in 1965 to $4,000 in 1971. Modest increases in secondary employment were envisaged, while the share of the labor force in services was to rise from 45 per cent in 1961 to 59 per cent in 1982.

It should perhaps be pointed out that the BAEQ did not start with a clean cut "decision function" and design a plan to fit; the definition of objectives itself came out of the first round of detailed research and represented a gradual adjustment of the desirable to the possible. The plan itself is essentially a sector-plan and a project-plan; there is no macroeconomic model underlying it, and little in the way of analysis of regional interaction, either with respect to relations among subregions of the *region pilote* itself, or with respect to the relation of the East of Quebec to other regions in the province or elsewhere in Canada and the United States.

The provincial government changed just as the BAEQ was finishing its work. The new government took some time to make up its mind to implement a plan prepared under the auspices of its predecessor. However, implementation is now under way, with a budget of $250,000,000 (some $800 per capita) provided by federal and provincial governments for five years. Ordinary multiplier effects alone of spending on this scale can hardly help but bring significant increases in income in the region.

LAC SAINT-JEAN–CHICOUTIMI

As this paper was being written, work was being completed on a plan for the second *region pilote* in Quebec: Lac Saint-Jean–Chicoutimi. This region is a good deal more prosperous than the East of Quebec, although incomes are below the provincial average. Although *animation sociale* continues to be given considerable attention, the lessons learned by the BAEQ have permitted the second regional plan to be completed much more quickly (about one year) and at less than one-quarter the cost of the plan for the East of Quebec. In addition, a good deal of work was being done on other parts of the province while the plan for the second pilot region was being prepared; much more attention was paid this time around to the interrelationship between development of the region and economic development in other parts of the province.

THE STRATEGY OF REGIONAL DEVELOPMENT IN QUEBEC

The Province of Quebec (and particularly the *Bureau des études en aménagement régional*) first approached growth pole policy in terms of creating two or three *pôles de croissance* east of Montreal, designed to pull industrialization and urbanization eastward from Montreal toward the retarded areas of the province. I have recently served, together with my colleagues, Professors André Raynauld and Fernand Martin, as a member of a three-man Task Force, established by the Ministry of Regional Economic Expansion and the Office of Planning of Quebec, to design an overall strategy for development of the province. The team was asked to consider three cities as potential *pôles de croissance*: (1) Sept-Iles to the northeast, on the Gulf of St. Lawrence, a small but rapidly growing port and the major outlet for the mining frontier of Côte Nord/Nouveau Québec; (2) Quebec City, the capital, a thriving metropolis of some half million people; and (3) Trois Rivières, a relatively stagnant pulp, paper, and textile city of about 125,000 population.

It did not take long for the team to decide that none of these three cities was, ever had been, or was likely soon to become a *pôle de croissance* in Perroux's sense of major aggregations of propulsive, technologically advanced, innovating enterprises. Sept-Iles and Quebec City, it is true, are strong reactors to basic development generated by investment elsewhere in the province—in the case of Sept-Iles, largely in the frontier region; in the case of Quebec City, largely in Montreal. But neither of these cities is a generator of growth for the rest of the province; indeed, only Montreal is that. This recognition led to a distinction between *pôles de croissance*, fast-growing urban centers that are strong reactors to development generated elsewhere, and *pôles de développement*, which are strong generators of spread effects to the whole provincial economy—in effect, Montreal.

Further study revealed that far from throttling the growth of other urban centers in the province, as some observers have contended, the growth of Montreal has generated supermultiplier effects such that the urban hierarchy has remained largely unchanged over several decades. Industrial production in Quebec City, for example, has grown somewhat faster than industrial production of metropolitan Montreal since 1939, and Montreal's share of total industrial production in the province remains essentially unchanged.

However, a much more serious trend appeared on closer examination: a tendency for Montreal (and the entire urban structure of Quebec) to lose out to Toronto (and the entire urban structure of Ontario). Moreover, the industries that are losing relatively to Toronto are the more scientifically advanced and sophisticated ones. Although Montreal is the bigger city, the total population within a sixty mile radius is higher in the Toronto area. Toronto is surrounded by a group of dynamic and prosperous small satellite cities. The cities in the crown of Montreal are relatively stagnant and relatively poor, with high levels of unemployment. One favorable sign, on the other hand, is the beginning of a process of decentralization of Montreal industrial activity and the establishment of branch activities of high-productivity and high-growth enterprises in Montreal in the satellite cities.

The team concluded, therefore, that any regional development policy that might weaken the Montreal economy would be seriously misguided. Rather than trying to attract sophisticated enterprises *away* from Montreal to establish new development poles further east, policy should be designed to strengthen the Montreal enterprises and to accelerate the new trend toward an improved industrial structure in the satellite cities. The powerful incentives available, in other words, should be used mainly to attract high-productivity, high-growth enterprises to the satellite cities. Most of these enterprises are likely to have head offices in Montreal. Once the economic strength of the Montreal administrative region is assured, the spread effects can be lured further east to Trois Rivières and Quebec City. Meanwhile, some investments will be needed in other regions of the province to assure that the spread effects are maximized; there must be investment in the transmission lines and in the reactors at the end of the line, as well as in the generator. But with the strategy recommended there would be clear recognition that the Montreal area is the generator. Eventually, with such a process of regional expansion, other cities could pass the threshold dividing "growth poles" from "development poles." Quebec City is the strongest candidate for the first city to make this transition, given its size, its charm, the beauty of its site, its excellent university and research institutions, its port. Probably Sherbrooke, with a vital new university and its role as a subregional central city, would be second.

In terms of growth pole policy in the United States, however, the significance of these recommendations is that in the opinion of the team, even Montreal with its 2.5 million people is not too big; it is still too small to be safe, in competition with other large North American cities for its position as a development pole. And without a dynamic Montreal the prospects for Quebec are dim. It would be easy enough to convert Montreal into another Quebec City by a policy of neglect; turning Quebec City into a second Montreal will be a long and difficult process. At the time of writing, the team's report was being studied in Ottawa and Quebec; it remains to be seen whether the recommended strategy will be adopted by the governments concerned.

Notes

1. When incomes of regions are weighted by population of the region, the dispersion index is much the same in the United States and in Canada.

2. The year 1961 or 1962 seems to have been the peak year for relative growth of Quebec; per capita income of Quebec in percentage of Ontario reached its peak in 1962; and in percentage of Canada, Quebec incomes fell after 1961.

3. For a more thorough analysis of income differences in Canada, see Raynauld, Marion, and Beland, *La répartition des revenus selon les Groupes ethniques au Canada.* Rapport de recherche préparé pour la Commission royale sur le bilinguisme et le biculturalisme, 1966.

4. Raynauld, *et al., op. cit.,* p. 2–16.

5. Ibid., introduction, par. 7.6.

SPONTANEOUS GROWTH CENTERS IN TWENTIETH-CENTURY AMERICAN URBANIZATION

WILLIAM ALONSO and ELLIOTT MEDRICH
University of California, Berkeley

Most discussion of growth centers concentrates on the where, the how, and the why of inducing growth in areas where by some criterion, development is lagging. In this the discussion reflects a concern with the equity or distributional objective of equalizing levels of welfare in different regions of the national territory. In developing nations, the concern is usually with countering the phenomenon of primacy as a manifestation of the duality of the economy. It most developed countries, as in the United States, the concern is rather that depressed or underdeveloped areas do not participate in the levels of social and economic welfare of most of the nation. Even those developed countries that want to diminish the concentration in their largest cities appear to consider their growth center efforts primarily as distributive ones.

It would seem that this view is too narrow for the formulation of national urbanization policies, that is to say, for policies to guide the growth of the national system of cities. Even a developed country is a developing country, and its development implies a structural evolution over time that will be reflected in the differential growth among territorial units as well as among economic sectors. In brief, development is not mere growth but also change. A national urbanization policy, as an element of a national urban policy, should address itself to the issues of efficiency or development, as manifested in growth centers that may be termed spontaneous, as well as to the questions of equity through inducing growth in centers where the overall functioning of the system is not producing it. A national urbanization policy should include developmental objectives for guiding the phenomenon of growth as well as equity considerations for dealing with retardation.

There are, then, two varieties of growth centers. Induced growth centers are those in which public policy is trying to promote growth. In this sense, the designation of a locality as a growth center is a normative one. Spontaneous growth centers are those that are growing without benefit of special assistance, or at least without benefit of conscious or explicit policy. In a lively socioeconomic system, there will always be a number of these centers, whose growth derives from the dynamics of the system. It would seem worthwhile to study the characteristics of such centers and the importance of their role in national urbanization, both for the lessons they may hold for inducing growth where it does not occur spontaneously and for their own sake as a valid subject of national developmental policy, since growth also has its problems.

Our aims are modest. We shall not try to analyze the reason for the development of spontaneous growth centers, nor shall we enter into the economic history of particular ones. Neither shall we try to suggest policy, except in the broadest outlines. We shall try to describe the magnitude of the role of spontaneous growth centers in the urbanization of the American population since the turn of the century and shall try to describe some of the shifts that have occurred. We shall limit ourselves to a consideration of time series of the numbers of people who lived between 1900 and 1965 in each of the 212 Standard Metropolitan Statistical Areas as defined territorially in 1960.[1] Estimates of net migration into all metropolitan areas (SMSAs) and into or out of each of them were constructed by assuming that they all followed the decade's rate of natural increase in the nation and that the difference in the observed population at the end of each decade from that which would have resulted from natural increase alone was attributable to migration.[2] Spontaneous growth centers were operationally defined as those which showed substantial in-migration.[3] Most of the presentation will use as a criterion for designating a metropolitan area as a growth center a rate of net in-migration twice that into the total set of SMSAs, but we have also looked at more stringent criteria. For convenience we will use 2M, 3M, and so on for twice, three times, and so on, the rate of migration into all metropolitan areas. We shall also use SGC at times as shorthand for Spontaneous Growth Centers. Thus, a 2M SGC is a metropolitan area that had a net rate of in-migration at least twice that into all metropolitan areas.

Several disclaimers are necessary as to the precision of our data.

Estimates of natural increase in the early part of the century are not
very reliable and neither are population estimates for 1965, our last
date.[4] Other problems arise. For instance, we assume nationwide
rates of natural increase, but poorer and smaller areas tend to have
higher rates of natural increase, as do fast growing areas whose
population is heavily weighted toward the young. Our practice of
using the 1960 SMSA territory implies, of course, that the early
figures for many areas include farmers and villagers; but this effect
may not be too serious, because, although it makes it harder for an
area to qualify for the growth criterion by expanding the base on
which growth is computed, the areas where the areal definition is
most excessive in the early years must be those that experienced the
most growth. In more recent years, two other problems arise. The
first is that suburban and exurban diffusion are proceeding very
rapidly, and many urban scholars think that the SMSA boundaries
cut off substantial population that is functionally associated with the
metropolis.[5] This effect is probably strongest for the larger metropolitan areas, and thus SMSA figures will tend to understate their
most recent populations and their growth. The other problem is a
more profound conceptual one. It is that, just as the single-centered
nineteenth century city gave way to the multicentered metropolis,
there are now recognizable congeries of metropolitan areas, sometimes called megalopolises, with strong interdependent functional
relations. These are higher order systems that are inadequately
recognized in our analysis, which is based on SMSA's; some glimmer
of this effect is visible in the last of our maps in what we call "suburban metropolises." But for all these difficulties, we believe that the
general outlines of our findings, if not the details, are reliable.

Figure 1 shows the share of all metropolitan growth accounted for
by Spontaneous Growth Centers. In general, the share increases from
the beginning of the century to the present, regardless of the criterion
used, with a sharp temporary rise during the depression decade of
1930–1940. At the 2M level, SGC's account for nearly half of all
metropolitan growth since 1940, while 3M centers, with a net in-
migration at least triple that into all metropolitan areas, account for
nearly one-third in the most recent period. Although the secular rise
since 1900 is unmistakable, the 2M share shows no clear trend since
1940 and the 3M share has clearly declined slightly. But there has
been a clear rise at the 5M level from 12.6 to 23.7 per cent and at the
10M level from 1.2 to 6.1 per cent. Thus, contrary to what might be

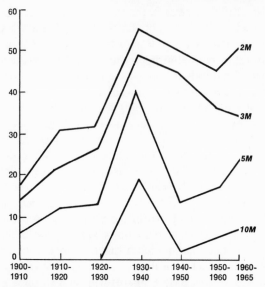

Figure 1. *Percentage Share of Metropolitan Growth Accounted for by SGCs at 2M, 3M, 5M, and 10M, 1900-1965.*

imagined in a nation that has achieved our degree of economic maturity, rapidly growing cities account for an increasing rather than a decreasing share of total metropolitan growth, and this increase is most marked for the higher growth criteria.[6]

More detailed information is presented in Table 1. The rate of growth of the metropolitan areas is remarkably stable from decade to decade (line 2), except for the high first decade (which resulted from a high rate of in-migration into metropolitan areas), the 1930–1940 decade (when both natural increase and in-migration were very low), and the most recent period (when again low natural increase and low in-migration combined to slow metropolitan growth). Migration's share of metropolitan growth (line 4) shows a marked decline over the period. Because of the increasing preponderance of vegetative growth for the metropolitan area set, it might be expected that growth rates would become more nearly equal among metropolitan areas, but we have seen that, in fact, the fast growers account for an increasing share of the total growth (line 7). Part of the explanation may be found in line 8, which shows that the SGCs account for a dramatically increasing share of all migration into the metropolitan set and currently receive as in-migrants a greater absolute number

TABLE 1

Population, Growth, and Migration
of Standard Metropolitan Statistical Areas
(SMSAs) and of 2M Spontaneous Growth Centers (SGC),
1900–1965

	1900–1910	1910–1920	1920–1930	1930–1940	1940–1950	1950–1960	1960–1965
1) SMSA population at the beginning of the period (000)	31,955	41,955	52,524	66,804	72,834	89,317	112,885
2) Decennial rate of SMSA population growth (%)	31.4	25.2	27.2	9.0	22.6	26.4	17.8[a]
3) Decennial rate of migration into SMSAs (%)	21.0	16.4	15.0	2.2	9.0	9.6	5.0[a]
4) Migration as % of growth	70	65	55	25	40	37	29
5) 2M criterion [(2)+(3)] (%)	52.4	41.6	42.2	11.2	31.6	36.0	22.8[a]
6) Share of SMSA population in 2M SGCs (%)	5.5	10.3	11.1	20.4	21.4	19.7	25.1
7) Share of all SMSA growth accounted for by 2M SGCs (%)	18.7	30.5	31.8	54.2	49.7	43.5	48.6
8) Share of net immigration into all SMSAs accounted for by 2M SGCs (%)	24.5	41.3	48.8	157.3	92.2	85.0	109.1
9) Number of 2M SGCs	40	40	48	87	69	52	60
10) Number of SMSAs with net out-migration	18	31	52	77	50	60	82

[a] The 1960–1965 rates have been doubled to convert to the common decimal base.

than all the SMSAs (including themselves) put together. This means that in the earlier decades migration from nonmetropolitan areas and from abroad was more evenly distributed among SMSAs, whereas

TABLE 2

Percent Share of All SMSA Growth Accounted for by 2M SGCs, by Size Class and Cumulatively, 1900–1965

SGC size (000)	1900–1910 (Cum.)	1910–1920 (Cum.)	1920–1930 (Cum.)	1930–1940 (Cum.)	1940–1950 (Cum.)	1950–1960 (Cum.)	1960–1965 (Cum.)
Under 50	5.6 (5.6)	3.3 (3.3)	3.6 (3.6)	2.2 (2.2)	1.2 (1.2)	0.9 (0.9)	0 (0)
50–100	4.4 (10.0)	5.8 (9.1)	3.6 (7.2)	8.8 (11.0)	5.9 (7.1)	3.2 (4.1)	1.1 (1.1)
100–150	3.8 (13.8)	5.0 (14.1)	4.2 (11.4)	8.1 (19.1)	3.9 (11.0)	3.1 (7.2)	3.3 (4.4)
150–200	5.0 (18.7)	2.5 (16.6)	2.8 (14.2)	4.6 (23.7)	4.2 (15.2)	2.0 (9.2)	2.6 (7.0)
200–250	0 (18.7)	0 (16.6)	2.3 (16.5)	6.2 (29.9)	1.1 (16.3)	0.5 (9.7)	3.7 (10.7)
250–300	0 (18.7)	0 (16.6)	0 (16.5)	1.4 (31.3)	7.5 (23.8)	3.8 (13.5)	1.2 (11.9)
300–500	0 (18.7)	0 (16.6)	0 (16.5)	8.2 (39.5)	3.6 (27.4)	9.1 (22.6)	3.8 (15.7)
500–750	0 (18.7)	13.9 (30.5)	0 (16.5)	4.9 (44.4)	5.8 (33.2)	6.8 (29.3)	7.1 (22.8)
750–1000	0 (18.7)	0 (30.5)	9.3 (25.7)	0 (44.4)	3.0 (36.2)	1.9 (31.2)	7.0 (29.8)
1000–2000	0 (18.7)	0 (30.5)	6.1 (31.8)	0 (44.4)	4.7 (40.9)	2.3 (33.5)	6.6 (36.4)
2000+	0 (18.7)	0 (30.5)	0 (31.8)	9.8 (54.2)	8.8 (49.7)	10.1 (43.5)	12.3 (48.6)

in recent decades marked differences in growth rates have resulted from intermetropolitan migration. Illustrating this point, the number of SMSAs estimated to have been net exporters of population rose from eighteen in 1900–1910 to eighty-two in 1960–1965 (line 10).

Table 2 shows the shares of total SMSA growth contributed by SGCs of each size class and cumulatively. Disregarding the decade of the 1930s, which was anomalous in many ways and which will be discussed later, the main trends are apparent. SGCs below 200,000 population have contributed a declining share of all metropolitan growth since the beginning of the period. The fast-growers' increasing share of all metropolitan growth is the result of the emergence of larger SGCs. Since the 1940s, the population categories above the 300,000–500,000 bracket have each increased their shares while most of the lower categories have had declining shares. In that period, the share of growth of all SGCs under 300,000 has declined from just under one-fourth to just over one-tenth, while that of SGCs over 500,000 has increased from 22.3 per cent to 32.9 per cent. The relatively narrow categories in the table are somewhat unstable in their rates of change, but reading across the cumulative figures makes evident the overall shift toward larger urban sizes.

Because much present United States and foreign legislation and common practice in regard to induced growth centers focus on centers below 250,000 population, it is interesting to examine further the experience of areas between 50,000 and 250,000. Since the turn of the century, SGCs of this size have contributed a declining share of all metropolitan growth (from 18.7 per cent to 10.7 per cent); this, of course, reflects the declining share of all SMSA growth by all SMSAs in this size class (from 36.5 per cent to 16.1 per cent) and the decline of the share of all metropolitan population of metropolises in this class (from 33.8 to 11.7). Contrary to what might be thought, the decline does not stem from there being fewer such areas or fewer successful ones. The number of SMSAs of that size actually increased from 106 to 111. More surprisingly, their chances of success have increased markedly. Table 3 shows the percentage of SMSAs in each size category that qualified as 2M SGCs for each period. This percentage may be taken as a naive *a priori* expectation that a metropolis of that size will qualify as a 2M SGC.[7] This expectation was 12.3 per cent in 1900 for all SMSAs between 50,000 and 250,000 but rose by 1960 to 31.6 per cent, substantially above the 24.7 per cent expectation of larger areas. Further, the centers between 50,000 and 250,000

TABLE 3

Percentage of SMSAs in Each Size Class
That Were 2M SGCs

SGC size (000)	1900–1910	1910–1920	1920–1930	1930–1940	1940–1950	1950–1960	1960–1965
Under 50	32.9	30.0	55.6	72.2	75.0	80.0	0
50–100	13.1	17.1	18.8	44.6	36.7	34.2	36.4
100–150	13.0	21.4	22.2	47.4	29.7	14.9	23.8
150–200	13.3	21.4	15.0	47.4	29.2	25.0	30.8
200–250	0	0	25.0	44.4	13.3	5.6	42.9
250–300	0	0	0	25.0	43.8	27.8	15.0
300–500	0	0	0	27.3	20.0	30.8	21.4
500–750	0	33.3	0	12.5	36.4	35.7	27.3
750–1000	0	0	20.0	0	20.0	14.3	71.4
1000–2000	0	0	20.0	0	20.0	14.3	21.4
2000+	0	0	0	14.3	14.3	12.5	20.0
All SMSAs (212)	18.9	18.9	22.6	41.1	32.6	24.5	28.3

TABLE 4

Number of SMSAs by Size and Growth Rates
of Size Classes (1960–1965)

Population Class (.000)	Less than −5%	−5 to 0%	0–5%	5–15%	15–25%	25–40%	40+%	Avr. Gr.[a]
50–100	0	2	4	11	2	0	0	6.8
100–150	1	3	11	18	1	1	0	6.0
150–200	0	2	10	8	7	0	1	9.4
200–250	0	3	3	10	1	0	2	11.4
250–300	0	3	8	9	6	0	0	7.6
300–500	0	1	8	17	3	1	0	8.8
500–750	0	0	5	12	1	0	0	8.4
750–1000	0	0	1	7	1	1	0	13.6
1000–2000	0	0	3	9	4	1	0	11.2
2000+	0	1	1	7	1	0	0	7.2

[a] Average of the growth rates of SMSAs in each size class.

accounted for 52 per cent of all 2M SGCs in 1950–1960 and 58 per cent in 1960–1965.

The sources of the declining national importance of these smaller metropolitan areas lie elsewhere. First, of course, there is the declining share of all metropolitan population in metropolitan centers of this size and the increasing share in larger centers. Second, there is the increasing probability of larger areas' being fast growers, which increased from nil (none of the twenty-one SMSAs greater than 250,000 qualified as a 2M SGC in 1900) to 24.7 per cent of 101 in 1960. Third and most important, there is the greater variability of growth rates for the smaller centers. Table 4 illustrates this point. The distribution of growth rates for larger centers is skewed to the right: with rare exceptions these centers grow either fast or at least steadily. Although some of the smaller centers grow faster than the larger ones, nearly one in ten is in fact losing population in absolute terms. This greater spread and symmetry in the distribution of smaller center growth rates means that the average rates of the smaller metropolitan size classes will be lower. Thus, information such as that in Table 5, although correct and frequently cited, must be accepted with some caution. It must not be thought that all smaller areas are

TABLE 5

Population Change and Migration Rates
for Metropolitan Areas 1960 to 1966,
By Size in 1966

Size Category	Number of Areas	Population 1966 (000)	Percentage of Change 1960–1966	Net Migration 1960–1966 as Percentage of 1960 Population
All metropolitan areas	221	132,160	10.8	2.4
2,000,000 and over	11	49,223	8.7	1.2
1,000,000–2,000,000	19	25,192	14.3	5.2
500,000–1,000,000	36	24,572	11.5	2.9
200,000–500,000	76	22,757	11.9	2.7
100,000–200,000	61	8,858	9.4	0.3
under 100,000	18	1,557	7.6	−2.1

Source: Adapted from Table D, p. 5, U.S. Bureau of the Census, Series P-25 No. 427, "Estimates of the Population of Counties and Metropolitan Areas, July 1, 1966: A Summary Report" (Washington, D.C.: Government Printing Office, 1969).

growing slowly. Rather, smaller metropolitan sizes are unstable, tending either to grow very fast into larger sizes or to lose ground.[8] But just what is meant by losing ground is not clear. There are as yet no instances of massive decline, such as has occurred in some towns and small cities, although many of the currently declining centers have been alternating absolute decline with insignificant growth for decades. It may be that policies and programs are needed in some cases not to induce growth but to facilitate and make decline less painful.

In brief, our discussion suggests that (1) smallish growth centers are possible and frequent, (2) smallish growth centers will not significantly affect national urbanization, although they may have great local regional importance, and (3) many successful smallish growth centers will grow to be far bigger because, as will be discussed below, spontaneous growth centers have considerable staying power.

Map 6 (1950–1960) and Map 7 (1960–1965) best illustrate the longevity of the SGCs. The numbers within the figures, which represent the number of decades each of the active SGCs has grown since 1900, make clear that most of the SGCs have had a long history of growth. It is harder to document this longevity statistically. For the 148 SMSAs that have met the 2M criterion at some point since 1900, the median number of years in the 2M category or higher is twenty-nine. But this would represent an underestimate of the typical growth period if one thinks of an S-curve of growth, since the sixty-five-year period would cut off portions of such curves before 1900 and, presumably, after 1965. The median number of growth years for the 1950–1960 2M centers was thirty-four years. Although this dropped to twenty-six years in 1960–1965, this drop was attributable to the rather large number (nine) of first-time centers. Looking at it another way, if a center had been growing in 1950–1960, its chances of growing at 2M in 1960–1965 were 61 per cent; if it had grown at 2M at any time since 1900, its chances of growing at this rate in 1960–1965 were 36.6 per cent. On the other hand, a metropolitan area that had never been an SGC had only a 12.3 per cent chance of being a 2M SGC in 1960–1965.

The decade of the 1930s presents discontinuities in some of the trends and continuities in others. It was, of course, the decade of the Great Depression. It saw a proliferation of 2M SGCs and a great increase in the number of metropolitan areas that had net out-migration. In this it anticipated the most recent periods, in which

SGCs accounted for increasing shares of all SMSA growth by inter-metropolitan migration. Similarly, it anticipated the increasing share of the fastest growers (see Figure 1). However, it was an untypical regression to smaller places. Except for Washington, D.C. and one other, all SGCs were under 500,000 population, and nearly one-half of the SMSAs under 250,000 population qualified as 2M SGCs. Most of this growth was only a spurt, and the South and the Midwest in particular are crowded with centers that grew only in this decade because the trend toward bigger places resumed in the 1940s. On the one hand, this exhibits the weakness of demographic criteria for socioeconomic purposes, for one may imagine the dismalness of these smaller metropolitan areas, crowded with impoverished farmers and with those who had given up on bigger cities. Such demographic growth under conditions of economic hardship can hardly be inter-preted as development. The snuffing out of the growth of these centers with the return of economic vitality testifies to the pathology of this growth. On the other hand, for reasons that are unclear, the 1930s may have provided a boost to the viability of smaller centers, according to Table 3. In this table, the frequency or probability of high growth for the smaller centers may be viewed either as a long-run trend, or it may be viewed as an enduring effect of the 1930s, which pegged their growth levels to higher levels that are maintained even today. But there is no theoretical base for either interpretation, and although there appears to be pattern rather than randomness in these numbers (Table 3), a choice between these interpretations depends on squinting, preference, and numerology.

Maps 1 through 7 indicate several interesting features of the geographic distribution of SGCs. Perhaps the most striking is the antiquity of the growth in what may be called the "new regions": the older regions base their current growth on newer centers. The mid-west's current SGCs are all new, and in fact there was a complete turnover of SGCs between the 1950s and the 1960s. The South, excepting Florida, experienced a flurry of growth in the 1930s, but the majority of these centers were quickly extinguished. There has been, however, sustained growth since then in centers in Virginia, the Carolinas, and Georgia. The Northeast presents most recently a flurry of quite recent centers, and these may be called "suburban metropolises." They include Brockton and Manchester in relation to Boston and a number of Connecticut areas in relation to New York. Such growth centers have a greater degree of functional

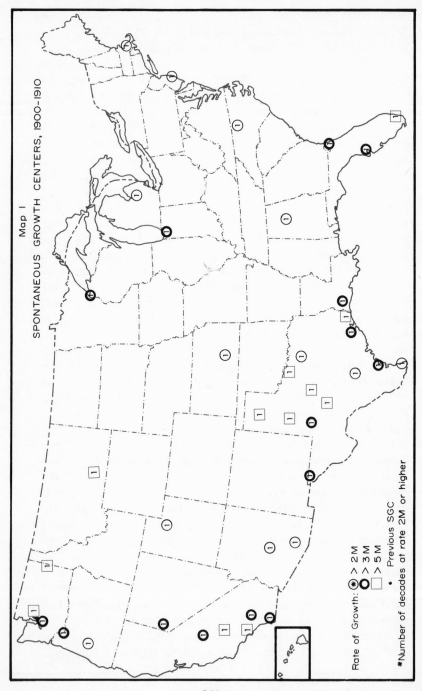

Map I

SPONTANEOUS GROWTH CENTERS, 1900-1910

Rate of Growth: ⊛ > 2M
         ⬤ > 3M
         ☐ > 5M
         • Previous SGC

*Number of decades at rate 2M or higher

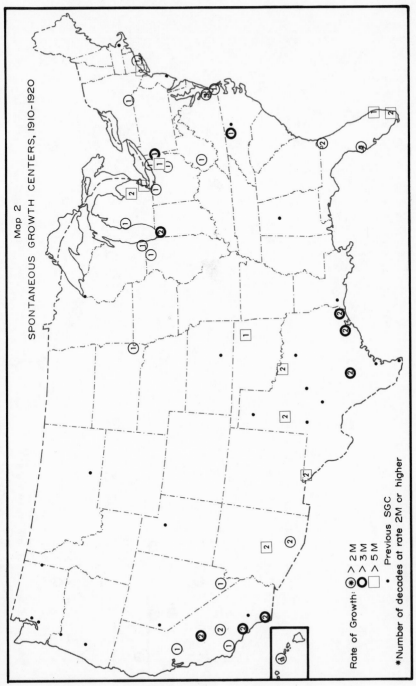

Map 2

SPONTANEOUS GROWTH CENTERS, 1910-1920

Rate of Growth: ⊛ > 2 M
           ◯ > 3 M
           ☐ > 5 M
           • Previous SGC

*Number of decades at rate 2M or higher

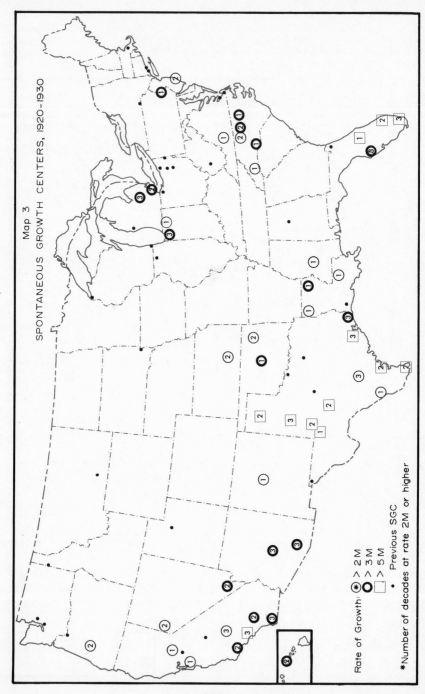

Map 3

SPONTANEOUS GROWTH CENTERS, 1920-1930

Rate of Growth:
⊛ > 2M
◯ > 3M
▢ > 5M
• Previous SGC

*Number of decades at rate 2M or higher

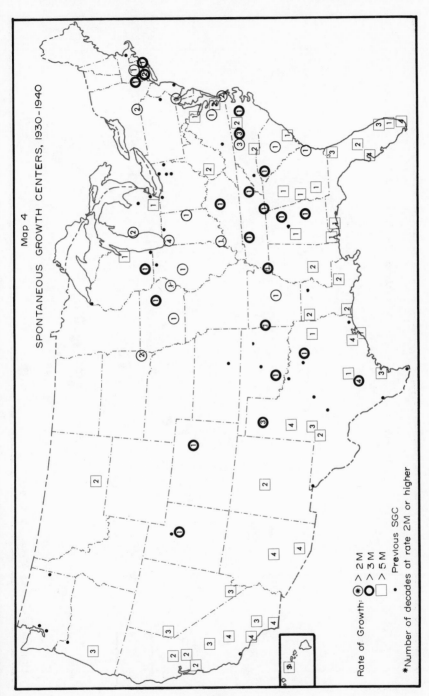

Map 4

SPONTANEOUS GROWTH CENTERS, 1930-1940

Rate of Growth:
⊛ > 2 M
◉ > 3 M
□ > 5 M
• Previous SGC

*Number of decades at rate 2M or higher

243

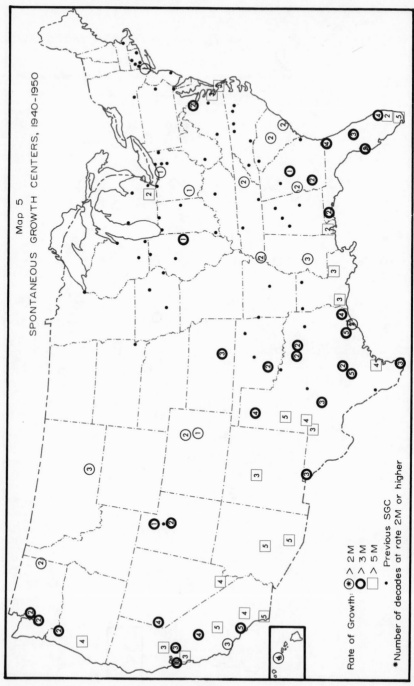

Map 5

SPONTANEOUS GROWTH CENTERS, 1940-1950

Rate of Growth:
⊛ > 2M
● > 3M
□ > 5M
• Previous SGC

*Number of decades at rate 2M or higher

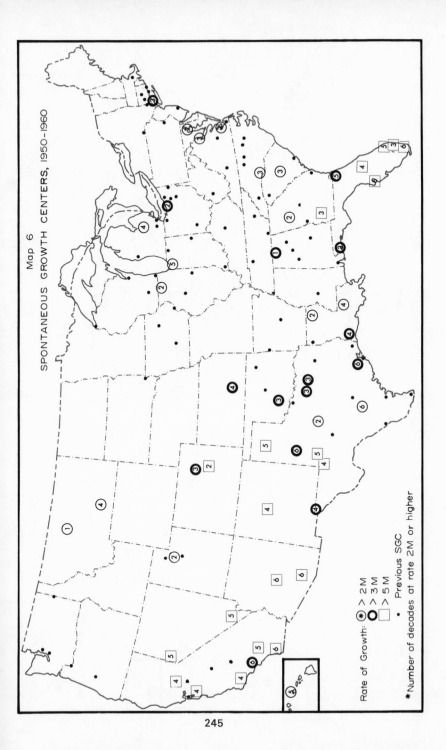

Map 6

SPONTANEOUS GROWTH CENTERS, 1950-1960

Rate of Growth: ✳ > 2M   ⭕ > 3M   ☐ > 5M   • Previous SGC

*Number of decades at rate 2M or higher

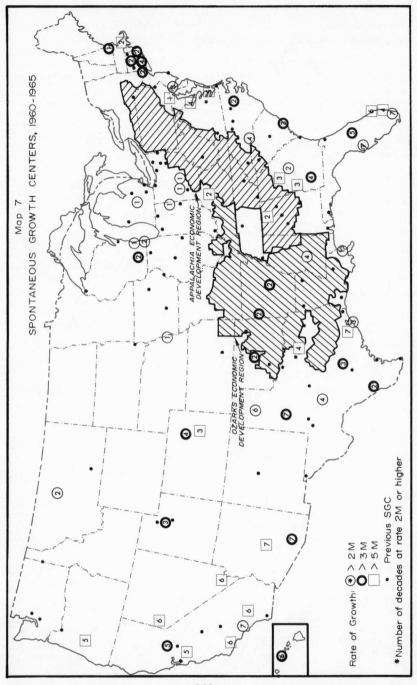

Map 7

SPONTANEOUS GROWTH CENTERS, 1960-1965

APPALACHIA ECONOMIC
DEVELOPMENT REGION

OZARKS ECONOMIC
DEVELOPMENT REGION

Rate of Growth:
⊛ > 2 M
◯ > 3 M
▢ > 5 M
• Previous SGC

*Number of decades at rate 2M or higher

closure than an ordinary suburb, but they clearly owe their development to their adjacency to the larger centers. The phenomenon is not limited to the Northeast, as instanced by the continued growth of the San Jose area in relation to the San Francisco-Oakland metropolis. It is clear that in many cases and for many purposes the relevant unit for analysis is the complex of linked metropolitan areas, and that to deal with individual SMSAs in such cases may be as misleading as to work with data for a single municipality within a metropolitan area.[9]

The Appalachia Economic Development Region, shaded on Map 7, has had only one SGC since 1950. This is Huntsville, Alabama, and Huntsville owes its growth to the National Aeronautics and Space Administration activities. Other than this, Appalachia has had ten SGCs since 1900, but none has managed to grow for more than two decades; the majority of those in the southern half grew only in the 1930s, whereas most of those in the northern half grew only in the 1910s. It is not surprising that a region defined by its economic difficulties should be rather light in spontaneous growth, but the barrenness of this record is striking. In contrast, just to the east of southern Appalachia, a file of metropolitan areas in Virginia, North and South Carolina, and Georgia are exhibiting sustained growth with a median of twenty-seven years at 2M.

A Southwest depressed region, shown on Map 7, consisting of the Ozarks Economic Development Region plus all the contiguous authorized districts, presents a slightly better aspect. It has had seven SGCs since 1900 and has three current ones, as it had three in the 1950s. Curiously, the three in the 1960s are not the same as those of the earlier decade, so that there have been six SGCs in the area since 1950.

Conclusion

Since the beginning of the century (and presumably earlier), a very large share of American metropolitan growth and a far larger share of the net in-migration into metropolitan areas have been absorbed by those metropolises that grew substantially faster than the metropolitan set. This share has been increasing recently, in spite of the declining importance of metropolitan in-migration, as a result of a more active and selective intermetropolitan migration. As the number of areas with substantial net in-migration has increased, so has the number of metropolises that are net exporters of people.

Although at any one time there are many metropolises putting on a spurt of growth that is not sustained, fast growth is more typically a long-run, sustained phenomenon, adding novae to the constellation of metropolitan areas. The metropolitan population of America continues to increase by means of these novae as well as by means of vegetative growth. At the same time, some of the new fast-growers are suburban metropolises in close relation to lower-growth, large metropolitan areas, suggesting that, as the metropolis transcended the city, new clusters of metropolitan areas are emerging as functional systems. But spontaneous growth centers are few and thus far eposodic in areas of economic retardation such as Appalachia and the Ozarks.

Explicit American urbanization or urban growth policy has tended to limit itself to the question of induced growth centers in areas of retarded development. But growth has its problems, too, and national policy should concern itself with guiding the social, physical, institutional, and economic development of the emerging novae and of the evolving clusters of interdependent metropolises. On the other hand, growth might not be possible in some backward areas or not desirable in terms of the alternatives, and there national policy should concern itself with welfare rather than developmental considerations. More generally, such a national policy should be framed in terms of guiding the development of the system of urban areas in accordance with national objectives. Within this more general system perspective, particular programs and policies, whether focused on the problems of growth or the lack of it, would be more intelligent and effective.

Appendix

The territorial definition of Standard Metropolitan Statistical Areas is revised periodically. We have calculated the population of the 212 SMSAs from 1900 to 1965 according to their territorial definitions by the Bureau of the Budget for 1960.[10] These population figures are shown in the Appendix Table. In some cases it was not possible to convert the available data to conform to the B.O.B. definition; these instances are noted and explained. Population growth rates are also shown in the table, which may be read as follows:

	1920
Abilene, Tex.	46404: population
	08.3: growth rate for the decade 1910–1920

APPENDIX TABLE

Population and Growth Rates of Standard Metropolitan Statistical Areas, 1900–1965

SMSA		1900	1910	1920	1930	1940	1950	1960	1965(e)[a]
ABILENE, TEX	pop	17552	50592	46404	65256	67525	85517	120337	126000
	%		188.2	−8.3	40.6	3.5	26.6	40.7	4.7
AKRON, OHIO	pop	71715	108253	286065	344131	339405	410032	513569	551600
	%		50.9	164.3	20.3	−1.4	20.8	25.3	7.4
ALBANY, GA	pop	13679	16035	20063	22306	28565	43617	75680	89000
	%		17.2	25.1	11.2	28.1	52.7	73.5	17.6
ALBANY-SHTDY-TRY, NY	pop	395209	446094	468627	520069	531249	589359	657503	697000
	%		12.9	5.1	11.0	2.1	10.9	11.6	6.0
ALBUQUERQUE, NM	pop	28630	23606	29855	45430	69391	145673	262199	288000
	%		−17.5	26.5	52.2	52.7	109.9	80.0	9.8
ALNTN-BTH-ETN, PA-NJ	pop	231361	289686	246664	391516	396673	437824	492168	515000
	%		25.2	−14.9	58.7	1.3	10.4	12.4	4.6
ALTOONA, PA	pop	85099	108858	128334	139840	140358	139514	137270	137000
	%		27.9	17.9	9.0	.4	−.6	−1.6	−.2
AMARILLO, TEX	pop	2783	15736	20385	53151	61450	87140	149493	168000
	%		465.4	29.5	160.7	15.6	41.8	71.6	12.4
ANN ARBOR, MICH	pop	47761	44714	49520	65530	80810	134606	172440	187000
	%		−6.4	10.7	32.3	23.3	66.6	28.1	8.4
ASHEVILLE, NC	pop	44288	49798	64148	97937	108755	124403	130074	143000
	%		12.4	28.8	52.7	11.0	14.4	4.6	9.9
ATLANTA, GA	pop	198322	273288	348580	452386	558842	726989	1017188	1216000
	%		37.8	27.6	29.8	23.5	30.1	39.9	19.5
ATLANTIC CITY, NJ	pop	46402	71894	83914	124823	124066	132399	160880	179000

Sources for Appendix Table
U.S. Bureau of the Budget, *Standard Metropolitan Statistical Areas* (1961).
U.S. Department of Commerce, Bureau of the Census, *Eighteenth Decennial Census of the United States* (1960), Vol. 1-A, Table 31.
Sixteenth Census of the United States (1940), Vol. 1, Table 4.

Metropolitan Area															
AUGUSTA, GA-SC	92767	54.9	100735	16.7	109266	48.8	120393	-.6	131779	6.7	162013	21.5	216639	11.3	237000
AUSTIN, TEX	47386	8.6	55620	8.5	57616	10.2	77777	9.5	111053	22.9	160980	33.7	212136	9.4	247000
BAKERSFIELD, CALIF	16480	17.4	37715	3.6	54843	35.0	82570	42.8	135124	45.0	228309	31.8	291984	16.4	319000
BALTIMORE, MD	689907	128.9	770427	45.4	902122	50.6	1036753	63.6	1139529	69.0	1405399	27.9	1727023	9.3	1854000
BATON ROUGE, LA	31153	11.7	34580	17.1	44513	14.9	68208	9.9	88415	23.3	158236	22.9	230058	7.4	255000
BAY CITY, MICH	62378	11.0	68238	28.7	69548	53.2	69474	29.6	74981	79.0	88461	45.4	107042	10.8	109000
BEAUMONT-PT ART, TEX	20144	9.4	47710	1.9	88499	-.1	148540	7.9	162711	18.0	235650	21.0	306016	1.8	313000
BILLINGS, MONT	6212	136.8	22944	85.5	29600	67.8	30785	9.5	41182	44.8	55875	29.9	79016	2.3	84000
BINGHAMTON, NY	69149	269.3	78809	29.0	113610	4.0	147022	33.8	165749	35.7	184698	41.4	212661	6.3	222800
BIRMINGHAM, ALA	140420	14.0	226476	44.2	310054	29.4	431493	12.7	459930	11.4	558928	15.1	634864	4.8	644000
BOSTON, MASS	1320593	61.3	1602023	36.9	1868859	39.2	2168566	6.6	2209608	21.5	2410572	13.6	2589301	1.4	2669600e
BRIDGEPORT, CONN	84609	21.3	125717	16.7	190803	16.0	210764	1.9	225268	9.1	273723	7.4	334576	3.1	382100e
BROCKTON, MASS	62704	48.6	98229	56.7	51.8	110012	12.0	10.5	111259	1.1	6.9	110463	-.7	21.5	119728	8.4	22.2	149458	24.8	14.2	178000e	19.1

Fourteenth Census of the United States (1920), Vol. 1, Table 50.

U.S. Department of Commerce, Bureau of the Census, *Statistical Abstract of the United States* (1967), Table 15, Table 126.

Historical Statistics of the United States: Colonial Times to 1957, Series C 88–114.

U.S. Housing and Home Finance Administration, *Population Growth in Standard Metropolitan Areas: 1900–1950* (December, 1953), Appendix, Table 1.

	1900	1910	1920	1930	1940	1950	1960	1965
BRNSVL-HLGN-SBO, TEX	16095	27158	36662	77540	83202	125170	151098	151000
		68.7	35.0	111.5	7.3	50.4	20.7	− .1
BUFFALO, NY	508647	621021	753393	911737	958487	1089230	1306957	1320000
		22.1	21.3	21.0	5.1	13.6	20.0	1.0
CANTON, OHIO	94767	122987	177218	221784	234887	283194	340345	356000
		29.8	44.1	25.1	5.9	20.6	20.2	4.6
CEDAR RAPIDS, I	55392	60720	74004	82336	89142	104274	136899	148000
		9.6	21.9	11.3	8.3	17.0	31.3	8.1
CHAMPAIGN-URBAN, ILL	47622	51829	56959	64273	70578	106100	132436	133000
		8.8	9.9	12.8	9.8	50.3	24.8	.4
CHARLESTON, SC	88006	88594	108450	101050	121105	164856	216382	251200
		.7	22.4	− 6.8	19.8	36.1	31.3	16.1
CHARLESTON, WVA	54696	81457	119650	157667	195619	239629	252925	245000
		48.9	46.9	31.8	24.1	22.5	5.5	− 3.1
CHARLOTTE, NC	55268	67031	80695	127971	151826	197052	272111	309400
		21.3	20.4	58.6	18.6	29.8	38.1	13.7
CHATTANOOGA, TENN-GA	82763	113160	139324	185703	211502	246453	283169	292000
		36.7	23.1	33.3	13.9	16.5	14.9	3.1
CHICAGO, ILL	2056554	2669033	3394996	4395646	4569643	5177868	6220913	6689000
		29.8	27.2	29.5	4.0	13.3	20.1	7.5
CINCINNATI, OHIO-KEN	527293	590456	628999	756281	787044	904402	1071624	1138100
		12.0	6.5	20.2	4.1	14.9	18.5	6.2
CLEVELAND, OHIO	460800	660352	972162	1243129	1267270	1465511	1796595	1881000
		43.3	47.2	27.9	1.9	15.6	22.6	4.7
COLORADO SPRINGS, COL	31602	43321	44027	49570	54025	74523	143742	176000
		37.1	1.6	12.6	9.0	37.9	92.9	22.4
COLUMBIA, SC	72853	87183	113798	124161	140837	186844	260828	289000
		19.7	30.5	9.1	13.4	32.7	39.6	10.8
COLUMBUS, GA-ALA	62709	67750	76909	93829	126407	170514	217985	260000

Area	Pop	%	Pop	%	Pop	%	Pop	%	Pop	%	Pop	%	Pop	%	Pop
COLUMBUS, OHIO	164460	34.7	221567	28.2	283951	27.2	361055	7.7	388712	29.5	503410	35.7	682962	12.1	765600
CORPUS CHRISTI, TEX	10439	110.3	21955	3.9	22807	127.0	51779	79.0	92661	78.6	165471	33.9	221573	7.2	237500
DALLAS, TEX	211190	27.7	269656	30.2	351215	30.6	458689	14.9	527145	41.0	743501	45.7	1083601	19.0	1289000
DVNPT-RI-MLNE, I-ILL	106807	22.1	130404	27.5	166249	5.6	175523	12.8	198071	18.3	234256	15.3	270058	19.0	286800
DAYTON, OHIO	204864	16.5	238570	21.2	289181	23.8	358041	7.2	383975	35.1	518642	33.9	694623	6.2	755700
DECATUR, ILL	44003	23.1	54186	20.3	65175	25.4	81731	3.6	84693	16.7	98853	19.6	118257	8.8	122000
DENVER, COL	183867[c]	34.2	246787	34.1	330948	16.3	385019	15.6	445206	37.5	612128	51.8	929383	3.2	1073000
DES MOINES, I	82624	33.7	110438	39.5	154029	12.2	172837	13.3	195835	15.4	226010	17.8	266315	15.5	271000
DETROIT, MICH	426829	43.8	613773	112.7	1305798	66.7	2177343	9.2	2377329	26.9	3016197	24.7	3762360	1.8	3987000
DUBUQUE, I	56403	1.9	57450	1.4	58262	5.1	61214	4.2	63768	11.9	71337	12.2	80048	6.0	87000
DULUTH-SUPR, MIN-WIS	119267	76.7	210696	21.6	256162	-1.9	251179	1.1	254036	-.5	252777	9.4	276596	8.7	267000
DURHAM, NC	26233	34.5	35276	19.7	42219	59.2	67196	19.4	80244	26.7	101639	10.2	111995	9.4	123000
EL PASO, TEX	24886	34.5	52599	19.7	101877	59.2	131597	19.4	131067	26.7	194968	61.1	314070	-3.5	344000

a The territorial definitions of forty-four metropolitan areas were changed between 1960 and July 1, 1965. To keep the data consistent with the 1960 SMSA definitions, estimates for the following metropolitan areas were calculated by multiplying the population as defined in the 1960 SMSA by the estimated population change for the newly defined SMSA, 1960–1965. These areas are:

Akron, Ohio   Charleston, South Carolina
Binghamton, New York   Charlotte, North Carolina

City		1900	1910	1920	1930	1940	1950	1960	1965
ERIE, PA	%		111.4	93.7	29.2	−.4	48.8	61.1	9.5
	pop	98473	115517	153536	175277	180889	219388	250682	255000
EUGENE, ORE	%		17.3	32.9	14.2	3.2	21.3	14.3	1.7
	pop	19604	33783	36166	54493	69096	125776	162890	194000
EVANSVILLE, IND-KEN	%		72.3	7.1	50.7	26.8	82.0	29.5	19.1
	pop	104676	106790	119902	139615	157803	191137	199313	200000
FALL RIVER, MASS-RI	%		2.0	12.3	16.4	13.0	21.1	4.3	.3
	pop	114616	131031	133348	133599	135137	137298	138156	142400^e
FARGO-MRHEAD, ND-MIN	%		14.3	1.8	.2	1.2	1.6	.6	3.1
	pop	46567	53575	61117	71855	78186	89240	106027	110000
FITCHBRG-LMSTR, MASS	%		15.0	14.1	17.6	8.8	14.1	18.8	3.7
	pop	46935	58938	64667	66852	68853	74943	82486	86000^e
FLINT, MICH	%		25.6	9.7	3.4	3.0	8.8	10.1	4.3
	pop	41804	64555	125668	211641	227944	270963	374313	412500
FT LDALE-HOLYWD, FLA	%		54.4	94.7	68.4	7.7	18.9	38.1	10.2
	pop	N.A.	N.A.	N.A.	20094	39794	83933	333946	441000
FT SMITH, ARK	%					98.0	110.9	297.9	32.1
	pop	36935	52278	56739	54426	62809	64202	66685	76000
FT WAYNE, IND	%		41.5	8.5	−4.1	15.4	2.2	3.9	14.0
	pop	77270	93386	114303	146743	155084	183722	232196	259000
FT WORTH, TEX	%		20.9	22.4	28.4	5.7	18.5	26.4	11.5
	pop	86195	143032	190086	230870	255905	392643	573215	627000
FRESNO, CALIF	%		65.9	32.9	21.5	10.8	53.4	46.0	9.4
	pop	37862	75657	128779	144379	178565	276515	365945	403000
GADSDEN, ALA	%		99.8	70.2	12.1	23.7	54.9	32.3	10.1
	pop	27361	39109	47275	63399	72580	93892	96980	94000
GALVESTON-T CTY, TEX	%		42.9	20.9	34.1	14.5	29.4	3.3	−3.1
	pop	44116	44479	53150	64401	81173	113066	140364	157000
GARY-HMND-ECHGO, IND	%		.8	19.5	21.2	26.0	39.3	24.1	11.9
	pop	57067	103404	180213	284131	321031	408228	573548	596000

City	Printed values (in order)
GRAND RAPIDS, MICH	129714 · 81.2 · 159145 · 22.7 · 74.3 · 183041 · 15.0 · 57.7 · 240511 · 31.4 · 13.0 · 246338 · 2.4 · 27.2 · 288292 · 17.0 · 40.5 · 363187 · 26.0 · 3.9 · 394000 · 8.5
GREAT FALLS, MONT	25777 · 28833 · 11.9 · 38836 · 34.7 · 41146 · 5.9 · 41999 · 2.1 · 53027 · 26.3 · 73418 · 38.5 · 82000 · 11.7
GREEN BAY, WIS	46359 · 54098 · 16.7 · 61889 · 14.4 · 70249 · 13.5 · 83109 · 18.3 · 98314 · 18.3 · 125082 · 27.2 · 137000 · 9.5
GREENSBORO-HP, NC	39074 · 60497 · 54.8 · 79272 · 31.0 · 133010 · 67.8 · 153916 · 15.7 · 191057 · 24.1 · 246520 · 29.0 · 267000 · 8.3
GREENVILLE, SC	53490 · 68377 · 27.8 · 88498 · 29.4 · 117009 · 32.2 · 136580 · 16.7 · 168152 · 23.1 · 209776 · 24.8 · 218800 · 4.3
HAMLTON-MOLTWN, OHIO	56870 · 70271 · 23.6 · 87025 · 23.8 · 114084 · 31.1 · 120249 · 5.4 · 147203 · 22.4 · 199076 · 35.2 · 208000 · 4.5
HARRISBURG, PA	164787 · 190631 · 15.7 · 211694 · 11.0 · 233467 · 10.3 · 252216 · 8.0 · 292241 · 15.9 · 345071 · 18.1 · 363000 · 5.2
HARTFORD, CONN	141993 · 175293 · 23.5 · 234981 · 34.1 · 300017 · 27.7 · 336991 · 12.3 · 406534 · 20.6 · 525207 · 29.2 · 583000[e] · 11.0
HONOLULU, HAWAII	58504 · 82028 · 40.2 · 123527 · 50.6 · 202923 · 64.3 · 258256 · 27.3 · 353020 · 36.7 · 500409 · 41.8 · 571000 · 14.1
HOUSTON, TEX	63786 · 115693 · 81.4 · 186667 · 61.3 · 359328 · 92.5 · 528961 · 47.2 · 806701 · 52.5 · 1243158 · 54.1 · 1495800 · 20.3
HNGTN-ALND, WV-KEN-O	111239 · 133698 · 20.2 · 160579 · 20.1 · 210382 · 31.0 · 225668 · 7.3 · 245795 · 8.9 · 254780 · 3.7 · 260000 · 2.0
HUNTSVILLE, ALA	43702 · 47041 · 7.6 · 51268 · 9.0 · 64623 · 26.0 · 66317 · 2.6 · 72903 · 9.9 · 117348 · 61.0 · 170600 · 45.4
INDIANAPOLIS, IND	197227 · 263661 · 33.7 · 348061 · 32.0 · 422666 · 21.4 · 460926 · 9.1 · 551777 · 19.7 · 697567 · 26.4 · 748500 · 7.3
JACKSON, MICH	48222 · 53426 · 10.8 · 72539 · 35.8 · 92304 · 27.2 · 93103 · .9 · 107925 · 15.9 · 131994 · 22.3 · 137000 · 3.8
JACKSON, MISS	52577 · 63726 · 21.2 · 57110 · −10.4 · 85118 · 49.0 · 107273 · 26.0 · 142164 · 32.5 · 187045 · 31.6 · 211200 · 12.9
JACKSONVILLE, FLA	39733 · 75163 · 32.0 · 113540 · 37.0 · 155503 · 35.1 · 210143 · 44.7 · 304029 · 49.8 · 455411 · 31.6 · 497000 · 9.1

	1900	1910	1920	1930	1940	1950	1960	1965
JERSEY CITY, NJ		89.2	51.1	37.0	35.1	44.7	49.8	9.1
	386048	537231	629154	690730	652040	647437	610734	619000
JOHNSTOWN, PA		39.2	17.1	9.8	-5.6	-.7	-5.7	1.4
	154298	233848	279951	283910	298416	291354	280733	270000
KALAMAZOO, MICH		51.6	19.7	1.4	5.1	-2.4	-3.6	-3.8
	44310	60427	71225	91368	100085	126707	169712	181000
KANSAS CITY, MO-KAN		36.4	17.9	28.3	9.5	26.6	33.9	6.7
	305427	422180	528833	665655	686643	814357	1039493	1125800
KENOSHA, WIS		38.2	25.3	25.9	3.2	18.6	27.6	8.3
	21707	32929	51284	63277	63505	75238	100615	114000
KNOXVILLE, TENN		51.7	55.7	23.4	.4	18.5	33.7	13.3
	111142	132713	160024	209613	246088	337105	366080	390000
LAKE CHARLES, LA		19.4	20.6	31.0	17.4	37.0	9.2	6.0
	30428	62767	32807	41963	56506	89635	145475	135000
LANCASTER, PA		106.3	-47.7	27.9	34.7	58.6	62.3	-7.2
	159241	167029	173797	196882	212504	234717	278359	289000
LANSING, MICH		4.9	4.1	13.3	7.9	10.5	18.6	3.8
	96622	106938	134041	172489	191411	244159	298949	336000
LAREDO, TEX		10.7	25.3	28.7	11.0	27.6	22.4	12.4
	21851	22503	29152	42128	45916	56141	64791	76000
LAS VEGAS, NEV		3.0	29.5	44.5	9.0	22.3	15.4	17.3
	N.A.	3321	4859	8532	16414	48289	127016	232000
LWRNCE-HVRHL, MAS-NH			46.3	75.6	92.4	194.2	163.0	82.7
	123746	159828	184212	178230	178404	182442	187601	193400[e]
LAWTON, OKLA		29.2	15.3	-3.2	.1	2.3	2.8	3.1
	31738	41489	26629	34317	38988	55165	90803	99000
LEWISTON-AUBURN, ME		30.7	-35.8	28.9	13.6	41.5	64.6	9.0
	40315	45427	52867	57221	62538	68426	70295	74000[e]
LEXINGTON, KEN		12.7	16.4	8.2	9.3	9.4	2.7	5.3
	42071	47715	54664	68543	78899	100746	131906	159000

City	(1)	(2)	(3)	(4)	(5)	(6)	(7)	(8)
LIMA, OHIO	47976	13.4 / 56580 / 17.9	14.6 / 68223 / 20.6	25.4 / 69419 / 1.8	15.1 / 73303 / 5.6	27.7 / 88183 / 20.3	30.9 / 103691 / 17.6	20.5 / 112000 / 8.0
LINCOLN, NEB	64835	73793 / 13.8	85902 / 16.4	100324 / 16.9	100585 / .3	119742 / 19.0	155272 / 29.7	161000 / 3.7
LITTLE ROCK, ARK	63179	86751 / 37.3	109464 / 26.2	137727 / 25.8	156085 / 13.3	196685 / 26.0	242980 / 23.5	279000 / 14.8
LORAIN-ELYRIA, OHIO	54857	76037 / 38.6	90612 / 19.2	109206 / 20.5	112390 / 2.9	148162 / 31.8	217500 / 46.8	240000 / 10.3
LA-LONG BEACH, CALIF	189994	538567 / 183.5	997830 / 85.3	2327166 / 133.2	2916403 / 25.3	4367911 / 49.8	6742696 / 54.4	7551800 / 12.0
LOUISVILLE, KEN-IND	294502	323473 / 9.8	346411 / 7.1	420769 / 21.5	451473 / 7.3	576900 / 27.8	725139 / 25.7	771000 / 6.3
LOWELL, MASS	109437	122133 / 11.6	132861 / 8.8	126991 / -4.4	132633 / 4.4	135987 / 2.5	157982 / 16.2	162900[e] / 3.1
LUBBOCK, TEX	293	3624 / 1136.9	11096 / 206.2	39104 / 252.4	51782 / 32.4	101048 / 95.1	156271 / 54.7	185000 / 18.4
LYNCHBURG, VA	60011	71469 / 19.1	76557 / 7.1	82566 / 7.8	90862 / 10.0	96936 / 6.7	110701 / 14.2	119000 / 7.5
MACON, GA	73114	80255 / 9.8	93268 / 16.2	88322 / -5.3	95086 / 7.7	135043 / 42.0	180403 / 33.6	201000 / 11.4
MADISON, WIS	69435	77435 / 11.5	89432 / 15.5	112737 / 26.1	130660 / 15.9	169357 / 29.6	222095 / 31.1	260000 / 17.1
MANCHESTER, NH	59515	72642 / 22.1	80775 / 11.2	80673 / -.1	81932 / 1.6	88370 / 7.9	95512 / 8.1	110100[e] / 15.3
MEMPHIS, TENN	153557	191439 / 24.7	223216 / 16.6	306482 / 37.3	358250 / 16.9	482393 / 34.7	627019 / 30.0	687800 / 9.7
MERIDAN, CONN	24296	27265 / 12.2	29876 / 9.6	38481 / 28.8	39494 / 2.6	44088 / 11.6	51850 / 17.6	55300[e] / 6.7
MIAMI, FLA	4955	11933 / 140.8	42753 / 258.3	142955 / 234.4	267739 / 87.3	495084 / 84.9	935047 / 88.9	1061000 / 13.5
MIDLAND, TEX	1741	3464	2449	8005	11721	25785	67717	67000

258 WILLIAM ALONSO AND ELLIOTT MEDRICH

	1900	1910	1920	1930	1940	1950	1960	1965
MILWAUKEE, WIS		99.0	−29.3	226.9	46.4	120.0	162.6	−1.1
	365246	470287	582061	777621	829629	956948	1194290	1234900
MINNEAPOLIS-SP, MINN		28.8	23.8	33.6	6.7	15.3	24.8	3.4
	459748	620832	728327	882266	967367	1151053	1482030	1612000
MOBILE, ALA		35.0	17.3	21.1	9.6	19.0	28.8	8.8
	62740	80854	100117	118363	141974	231105	314301	337900
MONROE, LA		28.9	23.8	18.2	19.9	62.8	36.0	7.5
	20947	25830	30319	54337	59168	74713	101663	112000
MONTGOMERY, ALA		23.3	17.4	79.2	8.9	26.3	36.1	10.2
	72047	82178	80853	98671	114420	138965	169210	175500
MUNCIE, IND		14.1	−1.6	22.0	16.0	21.5	21.8	3.7
	49624	51414	56377	67270	74963	90252	110938	117000
MUSKEGN-MN HTS, MICH		3.6	9.7	19.3	11.4	20.4	22.9	5.5
	37036	40577	62362	84630	94501	121545	149943	153000
NASHVILLE, TENN		9.6	53.7	35.7	11.7	28.6	23.4	2.0
	122815	149478	167815	222854	257267	321758	399743	441300
NEW BEDFORD, MASS		21.7	12.3	32.8	15.4	25.1	24.2	10.4
	72862	110537	140641	139557	138073	141984	143176	147600[e]
NEW BRITAIN, CONN		51.7	27.2	−.8	−1.1	2.8	.8	3.1
	37525	57042	76168	88541	90499	104251	129397	143600[e]
NEW HAVEN, CONN		52.0	33.5	16.2	2.2	15.2	24.1	11.0
	132322	164702	203850	232227	244294	269714	311681	332300[e]
NLONDN-GTN-NWH, CONN		24.5	23.8	13.9	5.2	10.4	15.6	6.6
	60497	66488	80996	90815	106207	123141	156913	182200[e]
NEW ORLEANS, LA		9.9	21.8	12.1	16.9	15.9	27.4	16.1
	307456	362599	413750	505306	552244	685405	868480	983100

Cincinnati, Ohio-Kentucky
Cleveland, Ohio

Columbus, Ohio

The following table is printed sideways on the page. Each city row gives the population at successive censuses together with the intercensal percentage change. (The column-heading row does not appear on this page.)

City	1900	1910	%	1920	%	1930	%	1940	%	1950	%	1960	%	1970	%
NEW YORK, NY	3792787	5276879	39.1	6246398	18.4	7975100	27.7	8706917	9.2	9555943	9.8	10694633	11.9	11366000	6.3
NEWARK, NJ	523562	727787	39.0	934940	28.5	1249167	33.6	1291416	3.4	1468458	13.7	1689420	15.0	1851000	9.6
NEWPRT NEWS-HPTN, VA	51465[d]	55228[d]	7.3	80308[d]	45.4	77078[d]	-4.0	93353	21.1	154977	66.0	224503	44.9	272000	21.2
NORFOLK-PRTSMOTH, VA	126023	164912	30.9	241148	46.2	229635	-4.8	258927	12.8	446200	72.3	578507	29.7	637000	10.1
NORWALK, CONN	11740	12919	10.0	34141	164.3	44245	29.6	50936	15.1	65685	29.0	96756	47.3	110500[e]	14.2
ODESSA, TEX	3108	3768	21.2	760	-79.8	3958	420.8	15051	280.3	42102	179.7	90995	116.1	93000	2.2
OGDEN, UTAH	25239	35179	39.4	43463	23.5	52172	20.0	56714	8.7	83319	46.9	110744	32.9	120000	8.4
OKLAHOMA CITY, OKLA	104550[b]	127576	22.0	157984	23.8	274801	73.9	299216	8.9	392439	31.2	511833	30.4	585000	14.3
OMAHA, NEB-I	204006	233652	14.5	275444	17.9	313272	13.7	325153	3.8	366395	12.7	457873	25.0	516000	12.7
ORLANDO, FLA	N.A.	N.A.	—	30876	—	68472	121.8	92378	34.9	141833	53.5	318487	124.6	372000	16.8
PATERSN-CFTN-PSC, NJ	233643	353904	51.5	469877	32.8	667106	42.0	718999	7.8	876232	21.9	1186873	35.5	1307000	10.1
PENSACOLA, FLA	38606	52926	37.1	63056	19.1	67677	7.3	90752	34.1	131260	44.6	203376	54.9	224000	10.1
PEORIA, ILL	121829	134282	10.2	150250	11.9	187426	24.7	211736	13.0	250512	18.3	288833	15.3	295500	2.3
PHILADELPHIA, PA	1892128	2268209	19.9	2714271	19.7	3137040	15.6	3199637	2.0	3671048	14.7	4342897	18.3	4664000	7.4
PHOENIX, ARIZ	20457	34483	68.6	89576	159.8	150970	68.5	186193	23.3	331770	78.2	663510	100.0	818000	23.3

	1900	1910	1920	1930	1940	1950	1960	1965
PITTSBURGH, PA		68.6	159.7	68.5	23.3	78.2	100.0	23.3
	1083846	1471800	1759989	2023269	2082556	2213236	2405435	2372000
PITTSFIELD, MASS		35.8	19.6	15.0	2.9	6.3	8.7	-1.4
	31318	42855	52291	60700	60996	66567	73839	75000e
PORTLAND, ME		36.8	22.0	16.1	.5	9.1	10.9	1.6
	66113	77668	91055	99874	106566	119942	120655	130000e
PORTLAND, ORE-WASH		17.5	17.2	9.7	6.7	12.6	.6	7.7
	150711	303829	372777	455037	501275	704829	821897	897000
PROVIDENCE-PWKET, RI		101.6	22.7	22.1	10.2	40.6	16.6	9.1
	407432	522591	588090	677195	695253	760202	816148	839000e
PROVO-OPEM, UTAH		28.3	12.5	15.2	2.7	9.3	7.4	2.8
	32456	37942	40792	49021	57382	81912	106991	118000
PUEBLO, COL		16.9	7.5	20.2	17.1	42.7	30.6	10.3
	34448	52223	57638	66038	68870	90188	118707	119000
RACINE, WIS		51.6	10.4	14.6	4.3	31.0	31.6	.2
	45644	57424	78961	90217	94047	109585	141781	160000
RALEIGH, NC		25.8	37.5	14.3	4.2	16.5	29.4	12.9
	54626	63229	75155	94757	109544	136450	169082	195000
READING, PA		15.7	18.9	26.1	15.6	24.6	23.9	15.3
	159615	183222	200854	231717	241884	255740	275414	283000
RENO, NEV		14.8	9.6	15.4	4.4	5.7	7.7	2.8
	9141	17434	18627	27158	32476	50205	84743	113000
RICHMOND, VA		90.7	6.8	45.8	19.6	54.6	68.8	33.3
	143631	172364	211135	236957	266185	328050	408494	453800
ROANOKE, VA		20.0	22.5	12.2	12.3	23.2	24.5	11.1
	37332	54497	73237	104495	112184	133407	158803	173000
ROCHESTER, NY		46.0	34.4	42.7	7.4	18.9	19.0	8.9
	217854	283212	352034	423881	438230	487632	586387	643300
ROCKFORD, ILL		30.0	24.3	20.4	3.4	11.3	20.3	9.7
	47845	63153	90929	117373	121178	152385	209765	225500
SACRAMENTO, CALIF		32.0	44.0	29.1	3.2	25.8	37.7	7.5
	45915	67806	91029	141999	170333	277140	502778	592300

City														
SAGINAW, MICH	81222	47.7	89290	34.2	100286	56.0	120717	20.0	130468	62.7	153515	81.4	190752	17.8	208000
ST JOSEPH, MO	121838	9.9	93020	12.3	93684	20.4	98633	8.1	94067	17.7	96826	24.3	90581	9.0	95000
ST LOUIS, MO-ILL	820276	-23.7	1023453	.7	1166432	5.3	1387075	-4.6	1464111	2.9	1719288	-6.4	2060103	4.9	2200200
SALT LAKE CITY, UTAH	77725	24.8	131426	14.0	159282	18.9	194102	5.6	211623	17.4	274895	19.8	383035	6.8	447000
SAN ANGELO, TEX	6804	69.1	17882	21.2	15210	21.9	36033	9.0	39302	29.9	58929	39.3	64630	16.7	73000
SAN ANTONIO, TEX	69422	162.8	119676	-14.9	202096	136.9	292533	9.1	338176	49.9	500460	9.7	687151	13.0	755100
SAN BERNARDINO, CAL	45826	72.4	91402	68.9	123698	44.7	214924	15.6	266632	48.0	451688	37.3	809782	9·9	1026000
SAN DIEGO, CALIF	35090	99.5	61665	35.3	112248	73.7	209659	24.1	289348	69.4	556808	79.3	1033011	26.7	1136000
SFRISCO-OAKLAND, CAL	542964	75.7	773975	82.0	1009467	86.8	1347772	38.0	1461804	92.4	2240767	85.5	2783359	10.0	3067300
SAN JOSE, CALIF	60216	42.5	83539	30.4	100676	33.5	145118	8.5	174949	53.3	290547	24.2	642315	10.2	885000
SANTA BARBARA, CALIF	18934	38.7	27738	20.5	41097	44.1	65167	20.6	70555	66.1	98220	121.1	168962	37.8	243000
SAVANNAH, GA	71239	46.5	79690	48.2	100032	58.6	105431	8.3	117970	39.2	151481	72.0	188299	43.8	192000
SCRANTON, PA	193831	11.9	259570	25.5	286311	5.4	310397	11.9	301243	28.4	257396	24.3	234531	2.0	226000
SEATTLE, WASH	134003	33.9	343847	10.3	456963	8.4	542378	-2.9	593734	-14.6	844572	-8.9	1107213	-3.6	1179000
SHREVEPORT, LA	68652	156.6	79938	32.9	105531	18.7	153058	9.5	183365	42.2	216686	31.1	281481	2.0	289000

	1900	1910	1920	1930	1940	1950	1960	1965
SIOUX CITY, I	54610	16.4 67616 23.8	32.0 92171 36.3	45.0 101669 10.3	19.8 103627 1.9	18.2 103917 .3	29.9 107849 3.8	2.7 102700 —4.8
SIOUX FALLS, SD	23926	29631 23.8	42490 43.4	50872 19.7	57697 13.4	70910 22.9	86575 22.1	94000 8.6
SOUTH BEND, IND	58881	84312 43.2	103304 22.5	160033 54.9	161823 1.1	205058 26.7	238614 16.4	237400 —.5
SPOKANE, WASH	57542	139404 142.3	141289 1.4	150477 6.5	164652 9.4	221561 34.6	278333 25.6	267000 —4.1
SPRINGFIELD, ILL	71593	91024 27.1	100262 10.1	111733 11.4	117912 5.5	131484 11.5	146539 11.5	153000 4.4
SPRINGFIELD, MO	52713	63831 21.1	68698 7.6	82929 20.7	90541 9.2	104823 15.8	126276 20.5	140000 10.9
SPRINGFIELD, OHIO	58939	66435 12.7	80728 21.5	90936 12.6	95647 5.2	111661 16.7	131440 17.7	147000 11.8
SPRINGFIELD, MASS	202199	258959 28.1	338033 30.5	376699 11.4	371972 -1.3	413494 11.2	478592 15.7	494400[e] 3.3
STAMFORD, CONN	34253	49164 43.5	65298 32.8	91865 40.7	98890 7.6	134896 36.4	178409 32.3	203700[e] 14.2
STNVILLE-WRTN, O-WVA	58269	86986 49.3	114082 31.1	141481 24.0	155214 9.7	157787 1.7	167756 32.3	170000 14.2
STOCKTON, CALIF	35452	50731 43.1	79905 57.5	102940 28.8	134207 30.4	200750 49.6	249989 6.3	273000 1.3
SYRACUSE, NY	280161	311251 43.1	352045 57.5	400621 28.8	405981 30.4	465114 49.6	563781 24.5	606000 9.2
TACOMA, WASH	55515	120812 11.1	144127 13.1	163842 13.8	182081 1.3	275876 14.6	321590 21.2	343000 7.5

Corpus Christi, Texas
Davenport–Rock Island–Moline, Iowa–Illinois
Dayton, Ohio
Evansville, Indiana–Kentucky

Flint, Michigan
Fort Smith, Arkansas
Grand Rapids, Michigan
Greenville, South Carolina

City	Code	(1)	(2)	(3)	(4)	(5)	(6)	(7)
TAMPA-ST PBURG, FLA	36013	117.6 / 78374	19.3 / 116522	13.7 / 215668	11.1 / 272000	51.5 / 409143	16.6 / 772453	6.7 / 873000
TERRE HAUTE, IND	62035	117.6 / 87930	48.7 / 100212	85.1 / 98861	26.1 / 99709	50.4 / 105160	88.8 / 108458	13.0 / 105500
TEXARKANA, TEX-ARK	44234	41.7 / 54382	14.0 / 63493	−1.3 / 79149	.9 / 82082	5.5 / 94580	3.1 / 91657	−2.7 / 100000
TOLEDO, OHIO	153559	22.9 / 192728	16.8 / 275721	24.7 / 347709	3.7 / 344333	15.2 / 395551	−3.1 / 456931	9.1 / 476100
TOPEKA, KAN	53727	25.5 / 61874	43.1 / 69159	26.1 / 85200	−1.0 / 91247	14.9 / 105418	15.5 / 141286	4.2 / 149000
TRENTON, NJ	95365	15.2 / 125657	11.8 / 159881	23.2 / 187143	7.1 / 197318	15.5 / 229781	34.0 / 266392	5.5 / 296000
TUCSON, ARIZ	14689	31.8 / 22818	27.2 / 34680	17.1 / 55676	5.4 / 72838	16.5 / 141216	15.9 / 265660	11.1 / 307000
TULSA, OKLA	55390[b]	55.3 / 81319	52.0 / 208039	60.5 / 299023	30.8 / 290368	93.9 / 327900	88.1 / 418974	15.6 / 433000
TUSCALOOSA, ALA	36147	46.8 / 47559	155.8 / 53680	43.7 / 64153	−2.9 / 76036	12.9 / 94092	27.8 / 109047	3.3 / 118000
TYLER, TEX	37370	31.6 / 41746	12.9 / 46769	19.5 / 53123	18.5 / 69090	23.7 / 74701	15.9 / 86350	8.2 / 93000
UTICA-ROME, NY	183849	11.7 / 210513	12.0 / 247795	13.6 / 262769	30.1 / 263163	8.1 / 284262	15.6 / 330771	7.7 / 346000
WACO, TEX	59772	14.5 / 73250	17.7 / 82921	6.0 / 98682	.1 / 101898	8.0 / 130194	16.4 / 150091	4.6 / 156000
WASHINGTON, DC-MD-VA	378605	22.5 / 445401 / 17.6	13.2 / 571882 / 28.4	19.0 / 672198 / 17.5	3.3 / 967985 / 44.0	27.8 / 1464089 / 51.3	15.3 / 2001897 / 36.7	3.9 / 2424300 / 21.1

Harrisburg, Pennsylvania
Houston, Texas
Huntsville, Alabama
Indianapolis, Indiana
Jackson, Mississippi
Kansas City, Missouri-Kansas
Los Angeles, Long Beach, California
Memphis, Tennessee
Milwaukee, Wisconsin
Mobile, Alabama
Montgomery, Alabama
Nashville, Tennesse
New Orleans, Louisiana
Peoria, Illinois
Richmond, Virginia
Rochester, New York
Rockford, Illinois
Sacramento, California
St. Louis, Missouri-Illinois
Salt Lake City, Utah
San Antonio, Texas
San Francisco-Oakland, California
Sioux City, Iowa
South Bend, Indiana
Terre Haute, Indiana
Toledo, Ohio
Washington, D.C., Virginia-Maryland
Wichita, Kansas
Wilmington, Delaware-New Jersey

	1900	1910	1920	1930	1940	1950	1960	1965
WATERBURY, CONN	60891	90949 / 49.4	113266 / 24.5	122125 / 7.8	138779 / 13.6	154656 / 11.4	181638 / 17.4	193600e / 6.6
WATERLOO, I	32399	44865 / 38.5	56570 / 26.1	69146 / 22.2	79946 / 15.6	100448 / 25.6	122482 / 21.9	124000 / 1.2
WEST PALM BEACH, FLA	N.A.	5577 / 11.5	18654 / 234.5	51781 / 177.6	79989 / 54.5	114688 / 43.4	228106 / 98.9	281000 / 23.2
WHEELING, WVA-O	135343	166816 / 23.3	189766 / 13.8	206627 / 8.9	208918 / 1.1	196305 / -6.0	190342 / -3.0	188000 / -1.2
WICHITA, KAN	44037	73095 / 66.0	92234 / 26.2	136330 / 47.8	143311 / 5.1	222290 / 55.1	343231 / 54.4	349400 / 1.8
WICHITA FALLS, TEX	8314	22619 / 172.1	78165 / 245.6	84100 / 7.6	81203 / 5.1	105309 / 29.7	129638 / 54.4	130000 / 1.8
WILKES BARRE-HTN, PA	257121	343186 / 33.5	390991 / 13.9	445109 / 13.8	441518 / -3.4	392241 / 29.7	346972 / 23.1	346000 / .3
WILMINGTON, DEL-NJ	135227	150187 / 11.1	184811 / 23.1	197866 / 7.1	221836 / -.8	268387 / -11.2	366167 / -11.5	413400 / -.3
WINSTON SALEM, NC	35261	47311 / 34.2	77269 / 63.3	111681 / 44.5	126475 / 12.1	146135 / 21.0	189428 / 36.4	207000 / 12.9
WORCHESTER, MASS	177800	205546 / 15.6	246347 / 19.9	272704 / 10.7	276453 / 13.2	303037 / 15.5	323306 / 29.6	336900e / 9.3
YORK, PA	116413	136405 / 17.2	144521 / 5.9	167135 / 15.6	178022 / 1.4	202737 / 9.6	238836 / 6.7	290000 / 4.2
YOUNGSTOWN-WARREN, O	116725	168917 / 44.7	270230 / 60.0	359205 / 32.9	372566 / 6.5	416544 / 13.9	509006 / 17.6	523000 / 21.7

b Based on special census, July 1, 1907.
c No data for Adams and Denver Counties.
d Includes Warwick and Elizabeth City Counties.
e Population estimates for 1965; for the twenty-three New England SMSAs were not available. Estimates were calculated by multiplying the percentage of change in the population of the State Economic Area in which the SMSA was located by the census population of the SMSA in 1960.

Notes

1. Definitions of SMSAs from U.S. Bureau of the Budget, *Standard Metropolitan Statistical Areas* (1961). Population of individual SMSAs from *Eighteenth Decennial Census of the United States* (1960), Vol. I-A, Table 31; *Sixteenth Census of the United States* (1940), Vol. I, Table 4, *Fourteenth Census of the United States* (1920), Vol. I, Table 50; and U.S. Housing and Home Finance Administration, *Population Growth of Standard Metropolital Areas: 1900–1950* (December, 1953), Appendix, Table 2.

2. Based on Series C 88–114, *Historical Statistics of the United States: Colonial Times to 1957*; and Table 126, *Statistical Abstract of the United States* (1967).

3. Since the analysis is based solely on demographic data, we do not consider possible alternative modes of being a growth center, such as by increases in employment without increases in residentiary population (by drawing on a commuter shed), or economic growth without population growth, as may occur through capital-intensive industrialization.

4. 1965 estimates from *Statistical Abstract of the United States* (1967), Table 15.

5. See the map of commuting territories in B. J. L. Berry and E. Neils, "Location, Size, and Shape of Cities as Influenced by Environmental Factors: The Urban Environment Writ Large", in H. Perloff, *The Quality of the Urban Environment* (Baltimore: Johns Hopkius Press, 1969), pp. 276–77.

6. It is interesting to contrast the 1960–1965 shares of growth (which range from 48.6 per cent for 2M to 6.1 per cent for 10M) with the recent proposals of the National Committee on Urban Growth Policy, which suggested settling 20 per cent of the forthcoming urban growth in 100 new towns and in ten new cities. See D. Canty, *The New City* (New York: Frederick A. Praeger, Inc., 1969).

7. The percentage of fast-growers among centers below 50,000 is high throughout and rises steadily, but this derives from the self-selectivity of this group, which had to grow in order to qualify as an SMSA in 1960.

8. Similar observations have been made recently by several authors. See E. Lampard, "The Evolving System of Cities in the U.S.," in H. S. Perloff and L. Wingo, eds., *Issues in Urban Economics* (Baltimore: Johns Hopkins Press, 1968), and W. R. Thompson, "The Future of the Detroit Metropolitan Area," in W. Haber *et al.*, eds., *Michigan in the 1970's: An Economic Forecast* (Ann Arbor: University of Michigan Graduate School of Business Administration, 1965). See also Berry and Neils, "Location, Size, and Shape of Cities," who base their argument on a break of the Pareto distribution.

9. The term *megalopolis* has sometimes been used for similar concepts, but it has some value connotations and is predicated on physical adjacency and geographic continuity of conurbation rather than on functional interdependence. *Megalopolis* means a very big city, and from medical usage, *megalo* implies abnormally big. Our meaning of a functional cluster of metropolitan areas would be better rendered by *genopolis*, meaning a tribe of cities.

10. U.S. Bureau of the Budget, *Standard Metropolitan Statistical Areas*, 1961.

GROWTH CENTER POLICY IN THE UNITED STATES

NILES M. HANSEN
University of Texas

At this writing regional policy in the United States is based on two legislative acts, both passed in 1965: the Appalachian Regional Development Act and the Public Works and Economic Development Act. Both acts are intended to provide financial aid as well as planning and technical assistance to areas experiencing high unemployment and/or low income. Although no definitive growth center strategy has been worked out within the context of these acts, the agencies that have been created to implement the programs that they outline have utilized the growth center concept in their operations. This chapter briefly describes and evaluates the nature of the growth center policies that were developed during the 1960s.

The Appalachian Region

The Appalachian region, as defined by the Appalachian Regional Development Act, extends from northeastern Mississippi to southern New York. It represents a rather unusual case among lagging regions of industrialized countries in that whereas these regions tend to be peripheral to their countries' economic heartlands, Appalachia is located between two of the most highly industrialized and urbanized regions of the world—the Atlantic megalopolis and the industrial Midwest.

In 1966 the estimated population of the Appalachian region was 18.3 million. Between 1960 and 1966 the population of the United States grew by 9.8 per cent, whereas that in Appalachia increased by only 3 percent. Net out-migration of 606,100 persons was largely

responsible for the region's lower growth rate. The proportion of
the Appalachian population living in metropolitan areas or in
counties with a total urban population over 50,000 was 49.7 per cent
in 1966, compared to a corresponding national value of 72.4 per
cent.[1] In 1960 over 30 per cent of the families living in Appalachia
had an annual income of less than $3,000, the frequently used
approximate borderline between poverty and a minimally comfort-
able standard of living. Between 1959 and 1966 per capita personal
income in Appalachia increased from $1,661 to $2,297; in the
United States as a whole the increase was from $2,161 to $2,963.
Thus, the absolute income gap between the region and the nation
increased from $500 to $666.[2]

In discussions of Appalachian development problems much has
been made, and rightly so, of the lack of urban centers in the region
capable of providing the services, concentrated labor force, and other
external economies needed to support growth. This lack is especially
evident in the Southern Appalachians. Many people feel that difficult
adjustment problems related to migration would be less severe if the
region's own cities could absorb more of the migrant population.
Unfortunately, the performance of Southern Appalachia's SMSAs
(standard metropolitan statistical areas) has not been bright.

From 1940 to 1950 the SMSAs of Southern Appalachia, as
defined by Brown and Hillery, increased in population by 20 per cent,
but from 1950 to 1960 the gain was only 7 per cent, while all SMSAs
in the country were increasing in population by 26 per cent. During
the 1950–1960 decade, only thirty of the 212 SMSAs in the United
States had population declines or increases of less than 10 per cent.
Four of the six Southern Appalachian SMSAs—Huntington-
Ashland, Charleston, Asheville, and Knoxville—were among these.
The growth rates of the other two—Chattanooga (13.3 per cent) and
Roanoke (18.1 per cent)—were below the national median for
SMSAs. Moreover, during the 1950–1960 decade the combined
SMSAs of the region actually lost population related to migration,
the net migration rate being −10.1 per cent. Only Roanoke did not
lose population due to migration and most of the other SMSAs had
relatively high net out-migration rates. Thus, it is apparent that the
region's SMSAs have been less attractive to migrants than other
SMSAs in the country.[3] Moreover, according to Bureau of the
Census projections, this pattern is going to continue. The Bureau
estimates that between 1965 and 1975 the six SMSAs in question

will, taken together, grow by only 3.5 per cent. If Roanoke is excluded, the ten-year growth rate will be only 1.9 per cent.[4] Brown and Hillery have correctly pointed out that:

> As metropolitan centers have become more important in national life, the incapacity of the Appalachian Region to develop and sustain many large metropolitan areas has resulted in a decline of its national significance. Furthermore, various parts of the area have tended to fall into the spheres of influence of the cities that have developed outside the Region. Consequently, it is less meaningful today to consider the Appalachians as a region in itself, since it is becoming increasingly segmented so far as its economic ties are concerned.[5]

Thus, a regional policy that is primarily concerned with people would give high priority to integrating the growth of urban areas outside of Appalachia with their Appalachian hinterlands and to providing comprehensive relocation assistance. In general, it is to be expected that migrants will be less and less influenced in choosing their destinations by the previous choices of their families and that they increasingly will become more sensitive to opportunities in the job market.[6] The Appalachian Regional Commission, the agency charged with implementing the provisions of the Appalachian Regional Development Act, has taken account of the commuting possibilities that are and can be made available to residents of the region who live relatively close to growing urban areas on the fringe of the region. Many of the commission's human resource investments within the region also imply that the beneficiaries may have to relocate to find gainful employment for their skills and training. But as yet there has been no systematic effort to guide migration, particularly if it involves movement outside the region.

For the near future, at least, the principal response to Appalachia's lack of urban centers capable of providing the services, trained labor, and other external economies needed to support sustained growth apparently will be to encourage the development of such centers within the region.

In contrast to the wide scattering of public investments that characterized earlier efforts to aid depressed areas, the Appalachian Regional Development Act specified that "the public investments made in the region under this Act shall be concentrated in areas where there is the greatest potential for future growth, and where the expected return on public dollars will be the greatest." At the outset of the Appalachian program, there was strong support in some quarters of the Appalachian Regional Commission to work with a relatively few major urban centers in response to this stipulation. However, states such as Kentucky—which represented to many the plight that the Act was to ameliorate—objected that they would be left out of a growth center approach that was built on only a few Standard Metropolitan Statistical Areas. In consequence, the determination of growth centers was given to the various states.

Within each of the sixty development districts (the number has since grown slightly) into which the region was divided, the states attempted to identify areas where future economic growth would probably occur. In this process a distinction was made between a growth center, a growth area, and the surrounding hinterland:

By a '*growth center*' or 'centers' is meant a complex consisting of one or more communities or places which, taken together, provide or are likely to provide, a range of cultural, social, employment, trade and service functions for itself and its associated rural hinterland. Though a center may not be fully developed to provide all these functions, it should provide, or potentially provide, some elements of each, and presently provide a sufficient range and magnitude of these functions to be readily identifiable as the logical location for many specialized services to people in the surrounding hinterland. A '*growth area*' is an extension of the growth center itself. It is the adjoining area likely to experience residential and employment growth because of proximity to a center or location between centers. The hinterlands are surrounding rural areas which rely upon the growth center and growth area for services and employment. The hinterlands contribute resources and manpower to the overall district economy.[7]

Among the key factors to be considered in analyzing the relationship between centers and hinterlands were: commuting patterns, wholesale trade services, education and cultural services, professional services, interfirm and interindustry trade, government services, natural resources and topography, and transportation networks.

It will be noted that the definitions of growth centers and growth areas are based on the performance of certain functions—there is no reference made to growth or to how the performance of the functions mentioned gives a center or area growth potential. This is a matter to which we shall return shortly.

The Appalachian Regional Commission attempts to concentrate appropriate investments in designated growth areas, though human resource investment may be made in the hinterlands to enable the rural population to take advantage of the opportunities expected to develop in the growth areas. Although the states have followed diverse procedures in designating growth centers, the ARC has classified them into three types: regional centers, primary centers, and secondary centers.

Regional Centers are important metropolitan centers providing specialized services and employment opportunities that extend well beyond the boundaries of the district in which they are located. Investments made in these centers are mainly 'region-serving,' i.e., they help improve services and employment prospects for a large area of the Appalachian Region embracing several state planning districts.

Primary Centers are communities or a complex of communities where preliminary analyses indicate a major portion of the future employment base of a district is likely to be located. Investments in these centers will develop their competitive advantages by providing the public facilities and services needed to make the area attractive to increased private investment and growth.

Secondary Centers are communities from which it is necessary to provide services to a large surrounding rural hinterland if isolated populations are to be given the skills and training they need to compete for opportunities wherever they choose to live and work.[8]

The growth center policy of the Appalachian program is constrained in principle by its district program. Instead of beginning by delimiting a select number of growth centers, it has been necessary to define the centers so that each of the districts has at least one. Thus, the states have designated some 125 areas that are deemed to have "significant potential for future growth." If each district really has a genuine growth center, it would seem that there would be no need for out-migration from Appalachia nor for commuting to outside metropolitan areas. There would need to be only commuting—and perhaps some limited relocation within each district—from the hinterlands to the growth center.

Given the relatively low level of urbanization in Appalachia, given the great comparative advantages of larger urban centers in terms of external economies (proximity to suppliers, buyers, and services; a relatively skilled labor force; amenities; infrastructure, and so on) attractive to most firms, and given the enormous financial effort needed to bridge the gap between a "potentially promising" location and actually providing it with enough external economies to be competitive, it seems that greater selectivity should have been used in designating growth centers. When one considers that public capital investment in established metropolitan areas in the United States may range from a quarter to a third of the total capital outlay,[9] it becomes apparent that Appalachian program funds available for growth centers are not sufficient to make all of the designated centers attractive relative to urban centers in more advanced regions, at least not by a process of balanced growth of public facilities within each center. The Appalachian Regional Commission is aware of this, but it believes that the problem is less one of strategy than of inadequate funding. However, even if "ample" funds were available, it still would seem inadvisable to spread them over so many centers, especially when many of them do not really have promising growth potential.

In practice, Appalachian growth center investments have been relatively concentrated. During fiscal years 1965–1969, the Appalachian Regional Commission placed about 40 per cent of its nonhighway investment in rural hinterlands. These expenditures were primarily for health and education. The other 60 per cent was placed in growth areas. However, about 75 per cent of the growth center investments were concentrated in thirty of the seventy-eight regional and primary centers.[10] In Northern Appalachia, relatively great emphasis has been put on growth areas as service centers and on their potential for developing employment on principal transportation routes. In Central Appalachia, trade and service functions, proximity to the Appalachian Development Highway System, and plant site availability have been given particular attention. Recent population and employment growth have been emphasized in Southern Appalachia, whereas the Highlands have emphasized service functions, especially in relation to tourism and recreation. The following areas have been principal recipients of growth center investments:[11]

Northern Appalachia

Greater Pittsburgh (Pa.)	$9,883,216
Cumberland (Md.)	4,993,114
Wilkes-Barre-Scranton (Pa.)	4,441,903
Altoona-Johnstown (Pa.)	3,898,746
Binghamton (N.Y.)	3,537,020
Sharon-New Castle (Pa.)	3,498,638
New Philadelphia-Cambridge (O.)	3,368,493
Hornell (N.Y.)	2,717,173
Parkersburg-Marietta (O.)	2,483,329
Williamsport (Pa.)	2,432,975
Huntington-Ashland-Ironton (O./W.Va./Ky.)	N.A.
Hagerstown-Martinsburg (W.Va./Md.)	1,731,948
Elmira (N.Y.)	1,773,357
Erie (Pa./N.Y.)	1,650,000
Charleston (W.Va.)	1,392,211

Southern Appalachia

Florence-Decatur-Huntsville (Ala.)	$10,454,584
Gadsden-Anniston (Ala.)	7,168,953
Greenville-Spartanburg (S.C.)	4,914,596
Birmingham (Ala.)	3,491,231
Tri-Cities (Tenn./Va.)	2,997,983
Knoxville (Tenn.)	2,344,287
Asheville (N.C.)	2,133,906
Chattanooga (Tenn./Ala./Ga.)	1,860,901
Carrollton (Ga.)	1,869,889
Tuscaloosa (Ala.)	1,771,742
Pontotoc-Tupelo (Miss.)	1,479,529

Central Appalachia

Cookeville-Crosville (Tenn.)	$3,083,841
Paintsville-Prestonburg-Pikeville (Ky.)	2,859,256
London-Corbin-Middlesboro (Ky.)	2,403,480

Appalachian Highlands

State College (Pa.)	$1,465,523

Although large absolute expenditures have been made in some of the region's bigger cities, the highest proportion of commission obligations has gone to growth areas in the 10,000 to 250,000 range. These areas account for 75.3 per cent of all growth area obligations, compared to 15.6 per cent for areas with populations over 250,000 and 9.0 per cent to areas with fewer than 10,000 inhabitants. It is the policy of the commission to invest more in per capita terms in communities of 250,000 or less than in larger cities because the impact of program funds is likely to be greater in these communities. Moreover, the most rapid growth in Appalachia is occurring in communities in the 10,000–50,000 population range, rather than in the larger cities or rural areas. Between 1960 and 1966, communities in the 10,000–50,000 range accounted for 40 per cent of Appalachia's population growth even though they had only 24 per cent of the region's population.[12]

In summary, then, the distribution of growth center investments has been more concentrated than might have been expected from a policy that would give each of sixty districts at least one growth center, and some districts more. On the other hand, even though the designation of growth center has little economic basis in many cases, it may well have political and morale value. In any event, the decision to concentrate investment in human resources in the hinterlands and other investments in growth centers and growth areas was well taken.

It should be noted, however, that the people in some of the nominal growth areas, which are in fact hinterlands to more viable growth centers, might benefit more from improvements in health and education facilities than from growth-type investments that are likely to be ineffective. Finally, the Appalachian Development Highway Program provides links to growing metropolitan areas outside the region (for example, Atlanta, Cincinnati, Lexington, Nashville, Harrisburg, and Piedmont Crescent cities in the Carolinas), but these links have primarily been viewed in terms of commuting opportunities for Appalachian people living near the fringe of the region or in terms of markets for Appalachian firms. In the future a more systematic effort might be made to encourage and aid migration to growth centers outside of but still near to Appalachia.

The Economic Development Administration

The Public Works and Economic Development Act of 1965 authorized the Secretary of Commerce to designate, with the concurrence of the states involved, multistate regions that contain common problems of economic distress or lag that extend beyond the capability of any one state to solve. Once a region has been designated, the relevant states are invited to participate in a Regional Commission, which is patterned in structure after that created for the Appalachian region. In 1966 five Regional Commissions were established. The regions concerned are the Ozarks, New England, the Four Corners, (the only point where four states touch—New Mexico, Arizona, Colorado, Utah) the Coastal Plains, and the Upper Great Lakes. Because of funding delays, the new commissions are only now getting off the ground, so it is not yet possible to evaluate their programs. However, some are developing growth center strategies.[13]

Implementation of the more general aims of the Public Works and Economic Development Act of 1965 is the responsibility of the Economic Development Administration. In addition to assisting the Regional Commissions, EDA provides development aid to "redevelopment areas," that is, counties, labor areas, Indian reservations, or certain larger municipalities. Redevelopment areas are designated on the basis of criteria that reflect chronic economic distress. These criteria include substantial and persistent unemploy-

ment, population loss, and low median family income. "Substantial
and persistent unemployment" is defined by two criteria. First, 6 per
cent or more of the work force must have been unemployed during
the latest calendar year. Second, the annual average rate of unemployment must have been at least 6 per cent and (1) 50 per cent above
the national average during three of the last four years, or (2) 75 per
cent above the national average during two of the last three years, or
(3) 100 per cent above the national average during one of the last
two years.

Areas that lost 25 per cent or more of their population between
1950 and 1960 owing to a lack of employment opportunities are
eligible for designation as redevelopment areas, provided they did
not have an annual median family income over $2,830 in 1960. An
area where this figure was less than $2,264 in 1960 may be designated
as a redevelopment area without regard to the rate of out-migration.

When loss of a major source of employment causes the unemployment rate of an area to exceed the national average by 50 per cent or
more, or when such a loss is expected, a redevelopment area designation is authorized. In addition, Indian reservations with a high degree
of economic distress are eligible for designation as redevelopment
areas. Finally, when a state does not have any area that qualifies on
the basis of high unemployment, low family income, or population
loss, the area in the state that most nearly meets these criteria may
be designated as a redevelopment area.

Another kind of geographic entity eligible for EDA assistance is
the multicounty economic development district. Individual redevelopment areas often lack efficient resources to provide a solid base
for their development. However, because of economic interdependencies among adjacent areas, successful development on a larger
scale may be promoted by grouping together economically distressed
areas and economically healthy areas. EDA has therefore encouraged
groups of counties—usually five to fifteen in number—to pool their
resources for effective economic planning and development. The
district program offers incentives to promote the economic growth
of the entire district, but it is aimed particularly at redevelopment
areas. Thus, a district must contain at least two redevelopment areas.
In addition to the benefits authorized for all redevelopment areas,
those located within districts may receive up to 10 per cent more of
the total cost in grant assistance for projects that are consistent with
the district program. With the exception of an EDA-designated

economic development center, counties in the district that are not redevelopment areas are not eligible for project funding from EDA. However, all participating counties are expected to benefit from coordinated, district-wide development planning.

Counties that wish to form a district must submit a formal proposal for qualification to EDA through the governor of the state involved. In considering whether and to what extent a proposed district will effectively foster economic development, EDA considers a number of factors, including the percentage of district population living in redevelopment areas, district per capita income, the percentage of families with annual income of less than $3,000, trading area patterns, the character of the proposed development center and its ties to the redevelopment areas, and unemployment and labor force participation rates. Once a district becomes qualified, its major organizational task is to formulate a district Overall Economic Development Program, or OEDP, which must be approved by EDA before a district can be formally designated. EDA requires that the district organization be broadly representative of the major economic groups of the area, including business, labor, agriculture, minority groups, and representatives of the unemployed and underemployed.

Each economic development district must contain an economic development center (growth center). The center must be a city or an area with sufficient population, resources, public facilities, industry and commercial services to insure that its development can become relatively self-sustaining.

The growth of the development center is then expected to carry over into the redevelopment areas within the district. Cities or contiguous groups of incorporated places outside the redevelopment area may be designated as economic development centers if they have a population of 250,000 or less. Once designated, development centers are eligible for EDA assistance on the same basis as redevelopment areas. It may also be noted that EDA distinguishes between economic development centers and redevelopment centers; the latter lie within redevelopment areas, whereas the former do not.

The development center is expected to provide an economically efficient marketing and service center for surrounding counties, both by providing job opportunities for depressed area residents who could commute to jobs and by encouraging those rural area residents who do migrate to move to the center. EDA's program would relieve migration pressure on the big cities while at the same time lifting

rural areas by the boot straps. This approach implies that job opportunities can be easily induced because growth factors are already
present even though the community may be located in a low-income
area. It is hoped that migration flows can be channeled to the growth
centers through a combination of forces including jobs, schools,
transportation systems, social amenities, and improved equal
opportunity programs. The program can also be linked with parallel
programs for resettlement assistance and manpower training and
development to assist the rural migrant to adjust to an urban
employment environment.

How do the realities of EDA's development policy compare with
the strategy just outlined? First, although a development center
strategy implies concentrating projects in a relatively few locations,
EDA simply does not have the funds to create the many external
economies that will be needed if rapid, self-sustained growth is to be
induced or reinforced in development centers. Second, even if EDA
had considerably more funds to devote to growth centers, the nature
of the centers that are actually being chosen leaves great doubt as to
their ability to provide a significant number of increased job opportunities for migrants from rural areas. The results of a study conducted by Brian Berry are instructive on this point.

Berry's analysis of the commuting behavior of the population of
the United States in 1960 shows that all but 5 per cent of the country's population resides within the daily commuting fields of metropolitan centers.[14] These fields spread over the entire land area of the
United States except where population density is less than two persons per square mile or where there are national parks and forests
and Indian reservations. Berry finds that the degree of metropolitan
labor market participation is the key variable in what he terms the
"regional welfare syndrome," a pattern of urban influence on the
surrounding hinterland's level of economic well-being as measured
by such factors as income and unemployment. In general, the degree
of labor market participation declines with increasing distance from
the city, as do the average value of farm land and buildings, median
family income, median school years completed, rate of population
increase, and population gain through migration. The proportion
of families with annual incomes less than $3,000 and the unemploy-
ment rate are both directly related to distance from the city. The
lowest levels of welfare are thus at the edges of metropolitan labor
markets and especially in the nonurban interstices between them.

When employment centers are closely spaced and their labor markets overlap, so that residents of one center can take advantage of employment opportunities in another, the decline in welfare levels that accompanies distance from centers is reduced or eliminated. Conversely, the wider the spacing of employment centers, the lower the level to which the measures of regional welfare fall. Berry attributes these results to the lack of opportunities for economies of production in rural areas. His findings also support efforts to stimulate development in growth centers that can give immigrants higher incomes and better job opportunities. He also concurs with the maximum size limit of 250,000 set by the Public Works and Economic Development Act of 1965 for development centers.

> Above that size, the necessary conditions for self-sustaining growth seem satisfied. Perhaps the greatest payoff in terms of both employment and unemployment is in concentrating on cities close to 250,000 population rather than on those very much smaller. Generally labour markets appear to need a population of more than 250,000 to be viable parts of the urban system.[15]

On the other hand, Berry finds that:

> The regional influence of smaller centers is too limited to justify putting public resources into them. Few cities of less than 50,000 population appear to influence the welfare of surrounding regions; those that do are located in the more peripheral areas.[16]

In conclusion, Berry advocates policies designed to encourage migration from rural areas to viable growth centers, but not "to the cores of the largest cities, where isolation in ghettos produces a parallel and perhaps more debilitating isolation than in rural areas."[17]

The growth centers that have been designated by EDA are generally smaller than the 50,000-population level that Berry finds to be a minimum for a city to have a positive influence on its surrounding hinterland. As of April 15, 1970, there were eighty-seven EDA-designated Economic Development Districts with one hundred seventy-one Development Centers (one hundred twenty-six Economic Development Centers and forty-five Redevelopment Centers). Only thirty of the Development Centers had a population of more than 50,000 and only thirteen had a population greater than 100,000. Forty-two of the Centers had fewer than 10,000 persons.[18] Moreover, between 1960 and 1970, sixty-one per cent of the Economic Development Centers that had been designated as of April 1970, had population growth below the national average; thirty-eight per cent of the

Economic Development Centers (and more than fifty per cent of the Redevelopment Centers) experienced population *declines*.[19]

The approach taken by EDA presents two major problems. First, it leaves out of consideration areas that are neither congested urban agglomerations nor towns and small cities that are part of or in close proximity to lagging areas. This no man's land—in terms of policy considerations—has growth centers that probably can absorb more migrants more efficiently than the EDA growth centers, especially if they too benefited from federal aid aimed at helping migrants from lagging areas to find employment. Of course, it might be argued that rapidly growing centers obviously have no need for federal subsidies. This would be true if one were concerned only with the rapidly growing center and its own population. However, the concern here is the relationship of centers of rapid growth to the people of lagging areas. If a federal subsidy can accelerate growth in a center that is already rapidly growing, and if this subsidy is made conditional on providing employment opportunities for residents of lagging areas, then it might well be more efficient for EDA to tie into the growing environment than to attempt to create growth in a relatively stagnant area by putting in water or sewer lines.

Second, it is not clear that the public works projects in which EDA is primarily involved, chiefly infrastructure in the narrow sense, will really lead to a rational migration policy. If the unemployment and welfare difficulties of rural migrants in large metropolitan areas are largely a function of lack of job skills and education, as EDA correctly maintains, why should the migration of these people to smaller growth centers not pose similar problems? Here we come to the very heart of the problem of helping residents of depressed areas.

Conclusions

The Regional Commissions and EDA were created on the assumption that the people in the poorest areas primarily need improved public works facilities. Yet in most cases the greatest relative need of these people is for more investment in human resources and for expanded manpower programs. This point has been stressed in a great deal of recent research. Edward Denison, for example, has shown that increased education is "one of the largest sources of past and prospective economic growth," in addition to being "among the elements most subject to conscious social decision."[20] And Theodore Schultz has pointed out that "investment in human capital accounts for most of the impressive rise in real earnings per worker" in western countries.[21]

The most efficient use of public funds for regional development programs might be to encourage the growth of medium-sized cities, especially those that have already given some real evidence of possessing growth characteristics. In these centers public funds may be integrated with actual or potential external economies to produce rapid growth with a minimum of external diseconomies of congestion. Although such centers do not "need" any government subsidy, it is easier to accelerate their growth than it would be to accelerate growth in a lagging region. However, the accelerated growth of intermediate growth centers must be made conditional on the granting of newly created employment opportunities to a significant number of workers from lagging regions who could either commute or migrate. In cases where local unemployment rates are relatively high despite high growth rates, a policy of growth acceleration could also be made conditional on the employment of the local jobless.

The type of growth center policy proposed here contradicts both those who claim that large metropolitan areas are not too big and those who claim that the only alternative to force-feeding the growth of rural areas is for rural people to migrate to metropolitan ghettos. Such evidence as we have concerning both public locational preferences and efficient city sizes suggests that a growth center policy should build on growing cities in the 250,000 to 750,000 range, though somewhat wider limits should be considered for the sake of flexibility.[22] It should be emphasized that not every rapidly growing city within this range would be eligible for designation as a federally assisted growth center. Only those cities that could be expected to benefit a significant number of persons from lagging regions (and the unemployed within the center) would be eligible for designation. Thus, growth centers would have to be selected on the basis of study of commuting and migration data, as well as data on unemployment and employment growth. Such a growth center policy would not reinforce existing migration patterns that represent movement from rural areas to metropolitan ghettos. However, migration and commuting studies would give valuable insights into the migration streams linking lagging rural areas to rapidly growing, intermediate-sized cities, streams that could be reinforced by a growth center policy. This in turn implies that education and training programs in lagging areas be geared to employment opportunities in growth centers. Those who benefit from such programs will be under no compulsion to move, but at least they will have a choice. A national regional policy should attempt to help areas with problems arising from out-migration to attain new equilibria with a minimum of friction. People in these areas, such as older workers whose prospects for either local employment or retraining and migration are dim, might be aided by the nation as a whole, though here we are talking about welfare rather than economic development policy. In any event, public policy for lagging regions should still emphasize active manpower and human resource programs.

Notes

1. Eli P. March, "Indicators of Appalachian Progress: Population and Income," *Appalachia* 2 (1969): 24.
2. Data supplied by the Appalachian Regional Commission.
3. James S. Brown and George A. Hillery, Jr., "The Great Migration, 1940–1960," in Thomas R. Ford, ed., *The Southern Appalachian Region* (Lexington, Ky.: University of Kentucky Press, 1962), pp. 59–61.
4. U.S. Bureau of the Census, *Current Population Reports*, Series P-25, No. 415, "Projections of the Population of Metropolitan Areas, 1975,' (Washington, D.C.: Government Printing Office, 1969), pp. 16–18.
5. Brown and Hillery, "Great Migration," p. 71.
6. Ibid., p. 76; and Niles M. Hansen and Richard YuKhin, "Locational Preferences and Opportunity Costs in a Lagging Region: A Study of High School Seniors in Eastern Kentucky," *Journal of Human Resources*, Vol. 5, No. 3 (Summer, 1970), pp. 341–53.
7. *State and Regional Development Plans in Appalachia, 1968* (Washington, D.C.: Appalachian Regional Commission, 1968), p. 12.
8. Ibid., pp. 19–20.
9. John W. Dyckman, "The Public and Private Rationale for a National Urban Policy," in S. B. Warner, Jr., ed., *Planning for a Nation of Cities* (Cambridge, Mass.: M.I.T. Press, 1966), p. 28.
10. *Testimony of John B. Waters, Jr., Federal Cochairman, Appalachian Regional Commission, Before the Special Subcommittee on Economic Development Programs, Committee on Public Works, House of Representatives, October 2, 1969*, p. 14.
11. *The Role of Growth Centers and Growth Areas in Appalachian Development*, Appalachian Regional Commission staff paper, n.d.
12. Ibid.
13. See, in particular, B. J. L. Berry *et al.*, "Potential Growth Centers and Growth Center Potentials in the Upper Great Lakes Region," a report to the Upper Great Lakes Regional Commission, October 15, 1968.
14. B. J. L. Berry, "A Summary—Spatial Organization and Levels of Welfare: Degree of Metropolitan Labor Market Participation as a Variable in Economic Development," *EDA Research Review*, June 1968, pp. 1–6.

15. Ibid., p. 6.
16. Ibid. It should be pointed out that many EDA growth centers are in peripheral areas.
17. Ibid.
18. Mary A. Toborg, "Assistance to Development Districts and Growth Centers," EDA Staff Paper, October, 1969, pp. 16–18.
19. Computed from data supplied by EDA.
20. Edward Denison, *The Sources of Economic Growth in the United States and the Alternatives Before Us* (New York: Committee for Economic Development, 1962), p. 74.
21. Theodore Schultz, "Investment in Human Capital," *American Economic Review* (1961): 1.
22. For a detailed discussion of this point see Niles M. Hansen, *Rural Poverty and the Urban Crisis: A Strategy for Regional Development* (Bloomington, Ind.: Indiana University Press, 1970).

EMPLOYMENT GROWTH AND CHANGES IN UNEMPLOYMENT AT THE COUNTY LEVEL*

GENE LABER
University of Vermont

Between 1950 and 1960 the Census-week unemployment rate for the United States rose from 4.8 to 5.1 per cent. An interesting concomitant development at a less aggregated level was an increase of one or more percentage points in unemployment for 58 per cent of the 3,100 counties in the United States.[1] Thus, despite the rather minor rise in overall unemployment, a majority of counties experienced rather sharp increases in local unemployment.[2]

Because Federal policies[3] aimed at reducing regionally disparate unemployment focus principally on county units, the behavior of unemployment in such areas is of considerable policy importance. Notwithstanding the policy implications, there has been little investigation of unemployment at the county level. Typically, high unemployment in regions is viewed as a "lagging areas" phenomenon caused by slow growth or decline of employment. But during the 1950–1960 decade, about 36 per cent of all United States counties that grew in employment at the national average or above (656 of the 3,100 counties) experienced increases in unemployment of one or more percentage points.[4] Some of these counties were designated for Federal aid during the 1960s.

My purpose here is to examine the changes in county unemployment between 1950 and 1960, with particular emphasis on the relationship between employment growth and changes in unemployment. The first section summarizes unemployment developments

* Financial support for this study was provided by the Economic Development Administration.

TABLE 1

County Unemployment in 1950 and 1960[a]

Unemployment Rate 1950	Unemployment Rate 1960											Total
	0–1.49	1.50–2.99	3.00–4.49	4.50–5.99	6.00–7.49	7.50–8.99	9.00–10.49	10.50–11.99	12.00–13.49	13.50–14.99	15.00–16.49	
0– 1.49	45	169	126	55	15	11	–	–	1	–	–	422
1.50– 2.99	21	189	378	258	86	26	11	6	2	1	–	978
3.00– 4.49	7	51	261	278	122	60	16	22	4	3	1	825
4.50– 5.99	3	11	74	149	122	55	25	17	6	3	–	465
6.00– 7.49	–	3	16	59	57	38	29	11	2	1	1	217
7.50– 8.99	–	–	12	11	30	14	9	11	6	3	1	97
9.00–10.49	–	2	1	3	9	7	2	2	2	1	2	31
10.50–11.99	–	–	–	4	5	3	2	2	3	2	2	23
12.00–13.49	–	–	1	–	1	2	4	1	1	1	1	12
13.50–14.99	–	–	–	1	–	2	–	1	1	4	1	9
15.00–16.49	–	–	–	1	1	3	–	–	–	–	1	5
Total	76	425	869	818	448	221	98	73	28	19	9	3084

[a] Source: Calculated from County and City Data Book, 1952 and 1962.

that occurred at the county level between 1950 and 1960. The second section outlines a conceptual approach to an analysis of these changes, and the data are discussed in the third section. The last section reports results of regression equations that test the conceptual approach.

A Summary of Unemployment Change
Over the 1950–1960 Decade

As noted above, many United States counties experienced sharp increases in unemployment over the 1950–1960 decade, notwithstanding the rather small increase in the aggregate unemployment rate. To bring this pattern into sharper focus, Table 1 shows Census-week unemployment rates in 1950 and 1960 for the 3,084 counties that had rates of 16.5 per cent or less in both years.[5] Any county with unemployment at least .3 percentage points below the upper class boundary in 1950 would have stayed in that class in 1960 if that county experienced the national increase in unemployment. It is likely, therefore, that entries to the upper right of the principal diagonal in Table 1 show an upward shift of unemployment in excess of the national change.

The median unemployment rate in Table 1 rose from 3.2 in 1950 to 4.8 in 1960. It is evident from the table that a majority of United States counties experienced an upward drift in unemployment between 1950 and 1960, as indicated by the entries to the upper right of the principal diagonal. The impression conveyed by the table and supplemented by the data given at the outset of this chapter is one of substantially sharper change in unemployment for the typical county than is seen in the movement of the aggregate unemployment rate.

A Conceptual Approach
to Employment Growth
and Unemployment Change

The ratio of employment to labor force (the employment ratio) is defined as

$$e \equiv E/L, \tag{1}$$

where E is employment and L is labor force. Taking logs and differentiating, the percentage change in e is

$$e^* = E^* - L^*, \tag{2}$$

where the asterisks indicate percentage change.

We shall examine e^* at the county level for the period 1950–1960. Assume E^* is given by long-run trends in industry location and by whatever cyclical forces were applicable at the county level in early 1950 and 1960.[6] The question then is, "What variables explain L^*, such that some counties, given E^*, experience a fall in the ratio of employment to labor force, while others experience a rise in that ratio?" The answer to this question thus focuses attention on L^*.

Changes in L can be viewed in three parts:

$$\Delta L = r \cdot \Delta P_L + P_L \cdot \Delta r + L_m, \tag{3}$$

where r is the labor force participation rate, P_L is local (nonmigrant) population, and L_m is net migrant labor. Now let us consider the variables that will explain changes in these three components of labor force variation.

It seems clear, *a priori*, that employment growth will play a key role in explaining the changes in participation rates and migration. With respect to participation rates, evidence at the national level shows that participation rates respond positively to employment opportunities.[7] We can expect a similar relationship at the county level, where we shall measure employment opportunities by the growth in employment.

Net migration accounts for some of the most dramatic changes in county labor forces, and these movements also respond to employment growth. On one hand, rapid employment growth attracts migrants as an area becomes known as a place where jobs are available, whereas slow growth or decline of employment opportunities stimulates emigration as workers are either released from jobs or are unable to find employment. In addition, however, migration will be enhanced by employers who geographically broaden their search for labor. Recruiting in areas of slow employment growth is an alternative to raising wages for employers attempting to expand their work forces.

From what has been said above about employment growth and its effect on migration and participation rates, it is conceivable that employment growth could increase unemployment, if migration and participation rates respond enough to increase the labor force by a greater percentage than the initial employment increase. This is a possibility we want to test with the regressions.

Income levels in counties will affect the labor force changes through migration. Classical theory of labor mobility would suggest migration from areas of low income to areas of high income, and empirical studies support this theory.[8]

Unemployment rates will also affect migration. High rates of unemployment lower the probability that a potential migrant will be employed, an effect that will tend to offset some of the pull of employment growth and high income.

In addition to the relationships among the variables outlined above, several plausible relationships appeared in the course of running the regressions. These variables will be discussed in connection with the appropriate equations.

The Data

Comprehensive data at the county level on employment, labor force, population, net migration, median family income, and other important economic variables are limited to Census figures. Consequently, our approach to analyzing unemployment changes at the county level is profoundly affected by the fact that time series data on important variables do not exist.

Census data include observations on employment, labor force, and population for 1950 and 1960; from these data we can calculate changes in employment and labor force over the decade and unemployment rates for 1950 and 1960. The Census figures also provide net migration for 1950–1960. Using survey estimates of labor force participation rates[9] of migrants for the United States as a whole, we can separate the change in county labor force into the three components of equation (3). The participation rate estimate for migrants was applied to the net migration data to estimate L_m. Then participation rates were calculated for 1950 and 1960, after the 1960 data had been adjusted for the migrants' influence on both labor force and population.[10] (This adjustment was necessary because the participation rate of migrants tends to be higher than participation rates for the population in general.) Changes in participation rates were calculated as the difference between the 1960 and 1950 figures.

Natural increase in county labor force was calculated as a residual after migrant labor and participation rate changes were subtracted from the total labor force change between 1950 and 1960. Although it is undesirable to make the natural increase component dependent on the other components of labor force change, this method has the advantage of forcing the three components to equal the actual labor force change.

The data described above, including other variables that will be discussed later, form the base for a series of regression equations reported in the next section. Observations on 3,095 counties[11] were used in those regressions, and we now turn to definitions of the variables before proceeding to the statistical results. In the regressions below,

e^* = percentage change in the ratio of employment to labour force (all changes are for the 1950–1960 period);

e = employment ratio in 1950 (E/L);

E^* = percentage change in employment;

E_a = ratio of employment in agriculture to total employment in 1950;

L_m^* = percentage change in labor force caused by migration;

L_n^* = percentage change in labor force caused by natural increase;

N = ratio of births minus deaths to labor force (1950);

r = labor force participation rates in 1950, measured as a percentage of total population;

Y = median family income in 1949.

The Regression Results

Regression equations (4) to (6) below attempt to explain the various components of labor force change shown in equation (3). Equation (7) attempts to explain e^*, which, from equation (2), is equal to $E^* - L^*$. Thus, equation (7) combines the variable used in equations (4) to (6) with the employment growth variable to estimate the net impact on e^* of variables significant in explaining L^*.

$$L_m^* = -.882 + .012\ Y + 1.012\ E^* - .085\ (E^*)^2 + .760\ e - .057\ E_a \quad (4)$$
$$\qquad\quad (.002)\quad (.009)\qquad (.002)\qquad\quad (.096)\quad (.002)$$
$$R^2 = .859$$

$$L_n^* = .057 + 2.36\ N \tag{5}$$
$$(.149)$$
$$R^2 = .075$$

$$\Delta r = .047 - .029\ E^* + .001\ (E^*)^2 - .309\ r + .069\ e \tag{6}$$
$$(.002) \quad (.0003) \quad (.011) \quad (.020)$$
$$R^2 = .299$$

$$e^* = .324 + .023\ E^* - .002\ (E^*)^2 + .202\ r - .437\ e + .025\ E_a \tag{7}$$
$$(.001) \quad (.0003) \quad (.009) \quad (.018) \quad (.002)$$
$$R^2 = .297$$

Standard errors of the regression coefficients are listed in parenthesis; all variables in these equations are significant at the 1 per cent level.

Equation (4) is a regression of net migration (divided by 1950 labor force) on income, employment growth, the 1950 employment ratio, and the percentage of employment in agriculture. Income and employment growth as determinants of migration were discussed above, and the signs of these variables in equation (4) are as expected: the percentage change in labor force caused by migration increases with income and employment growth. The coefficient on employment growth squared says that employment growth causes L_m^* to increase at a decreasing rate, which is an intuitively plausible result.[12]

The employment ratio in equation (4) is, of course, the complement of the unemployment rate, whose influence on migration was discussed above. The coefficient of the employment ratio says that L_m^* increases with low rates of unemployment (*i.e.*, high employment ratios). We should remember that our unemployment variable is for the beginning of the migration period (1950) because complete county unemployment rates are available only for the Census years. It would be interesting to experiment in this equation with observations on unemployment for other periods during the decade, for migration near the end of the period is no doubt reacting to unemployment more current than the 1950 figures.

The relative importance of agricultural employment in 1950 is highly significant in equation (4), with a negative sign. This suggests that conditions in agriculture not explained by median income figures were giving rise to emigration from that sector.[13]

Equation (5) relates the natural increase in labor force (as a percentage) to the crude rate of population growth, which is expressed as a ratio of the 1950 labor force. The explanatory power of this equation is very weak, and a large part of this weakness probably stems from errors in measurement of the dependent variable. Since L_m is highly correlated (positively) with E^*, and since participation rates of migrants may respond to E^*, L_n may be subject to systematic errors because it is a residual estimate. If participation rates of migrants increase with employment opportunities, estimated values of L_n will be overstated in areas of fast employment growth and understated in areas of slow growth, because we used a constant labor force participation rate for migrants to estimate L_m.

In equation (6), which describes changes in r, we find a negative sign on employment growth. This result is in contradiction to the work cited earlier in which participation rates were found to expand with employment opportunities. The negative sign on E^* in equation (6) appears to be showing a tendency for marginal workers to withdraw from the labor force to a greater extent than they enter during expansion of employment opportunities. A possible explanation for the unexpected sign may lie with the method of calculating participation rates. Participation rates were calculated by dividing civilian labor force by *total* population, after the 1960 labor force and population figures were adjusted to exclude migration. Rates calculated in this fashion differ from the usual measures of labor force participation rates, which use noninstitutional population over fourteen or sixteen years of age. More specifically, the measure used in this study can be expressed

$$L/P \equiv L/P_N \cdot P_N/P$$

where P is population, P_N is noninstitutional population over the age fourteen or sixteen, and L/P_N is the usual measure of participation rates.

Now we can see a possible reason for L/P to decline (over the decade) in areas where employment opportunities are expanding: even though L/P_N may rise in response to employment opportunities —as empirical studies have shown—migration probably tends to reduce the ratio P_N/P because migrants tend to be relatively young persons with families. Consequently, L/P could fall despite the positive response of L/P_N to employment opportunities, because P_N/P probably will decrease as employment growth attracts migrants. My adjustment of 1960 population (namely, the subtraction of net migration) would not remove the effects of migration on the age distribution of county populations.

Participation rates in 1950 are negatively related to Δr (changes in
participation rates) in equation (6). It is reasonable to expect areas
with depressed participation rates in 1950 to experience relatively
large increases in r over the decade, for any improvement in economic
conditions likely would bring persons into the labor force to a greater
extent than would occur in areas with high participation rates at the
start of the period.

The positive coefficient of e in equation (6) is unexpected. We
would expect areas with high rates of unemployment at the start of
the decade (low employment ratios) to show larger changes in participation rates than areas with low unemployment, because high rates
of unemployment should reduce participation rates in 1950. However, examination of the simple correlation between 1950 unemployment rates and 1950 labor force participation rates reveals a correlation coefficient of virtually zero.

Equation (7), of course, is our primary interest, and the problems
of measurement of the dependent variables in equations (5) and (6)
do not affect our ability to explain e^*. Coefficients in equation (7)
result from substituting into $e^* = E^* - L^*$ the variables significant in
equations (4) to (6). This means that many coefficients in equation (7)
show the net impact on e^* of variables that affect several components
of labor force change. Employment growth, for example, would have
a coefficient of one in equation (7) if employment expansion did not
affect changes in the labor force. The estimated coefficient of E^*,
however, is only .023, which shows a net positive effect on e^*
markedly smaller than 1. It is important to note that, *ceteris paribus*,
employment growth does have a stabilizing influence on e^*, in the
sense that employment growth does contribute to reduced rates of
unemployment (increases in the employment ratio). It is also interesting to note that, other things being equal, unemployment has a
stabilizing effect on e^*; a fall in the employment ratio (*i.e.*, an increase
in the unemployment rate) tends to increase e^*. This follows from
the strong impact of e on migration in equation (4).

The variable designed to measure natural rate of population increase (N) was not significant in equation (7). This suggests that
either N is not an adequate measure of natural increase or that differences in natural rates of increase among counties are not significant in explaining e^*.

Income (Y) would enter equation (7) significantly. But income and
1950 participation rates (r) were correlated at a .49 level, and, as

noted above, Y and E_a show rather high correlation. Because both r and E_a were more significant than Y in equation (7), it was decided to omit Y.

Equation (7) also shows that high participation rates (r) in 1950 contributed positively to e^*, as did agricultural employment (E_a). These effects, according to equations (6) and (4), stem from the impact of r on Δr and of E_a on L_m^*.

The explanatory power of equation (7) is not high. There are evidently other variables contributing to e^* that have not been included in the regression.[14] Approximately 100 of the larger residuals from equation (7) were examined and compared with residuals for the same counties from equation (4). In roughly 30 per cent of the cases counties had large residuals for *both* equations. This suggests that errors in predicting L_m^* were causing large errors in predicting e^* in only a minority of cases.

Summary

I have examined the relationship between employment growth and unemployment change at the county level. I was motivated in this inquiry by the observation that fast employment growth was often accompanied by increased unemployment over the 1950–1960 decade.

The percentage change in the ratio of employment to labor force was regressed on employment growth and other explanatory variables for 3,095 counties. Although I recognize that the cross-section data used in these regressions may conceal some important lag structures, the following conclusions are offered tentatively.

1. The effect of employment growth at the county level is to reduce unemployment, other things being equal. This occurs despite a sharp response of net migration to employment growth. Increased unemployment for many fast-growth areas is not the result of an unstable relationship between employment growth and changes in unemployment rates. The phenomenon of fast employment growth and increased unemployment can be traced to low participation rates in 1950 or to low unemployment in 1950 for some counties, although the results of this study have failed to explain that develop-

ment for many areas. It is worth noting, however, that the impact of employment growth on reducing unemployment is markedly less than would be the case if county labor forces did not respond to employment growth.

2. The impact of unemployment on changes in unemployment is stabilizing, because increased unemployment reduces additions to the labor force caused by migration. This suggests that the problem of fast employment growth accompanied by increased unemployment should be assuaged over time, as migrant labor reacts to increased unemployment.

These findings can be related to policy decisions affecting areas where employment grows relatively fast. We have seen that fast growth of employment does not mean necessarily a reduction in unemployment. Suppose, for example, government policy indeed succeeds in accelerating employment growth in a growth center where unemployment is initially high. If the area starts growing from a condition of depressed participation rates, it is not inconceivable that, given the results of our regression equations, unemployment in the growth center will rise. If policymakers look at changes in the unemployment rate in the growth center to evaluate the success of their efforts, they likely will conclude that the policies have worsened the problem. My point is that changes in unemployment rates *in the growth center* are a poor indicator of the effectiveness of the policy in improving economic well-being. The increased unemployment may be telling us that potential output of the growth center is now greater than before the employment growth because of increased participation rates. Or it may be telling us that labor has been attracted to the growth center—thus expanding potential output—because of the economic opportunities in the center, although the migrants are absorbed into the ranks of the employed only after some period of time. But the increased unemployment does not tell us what has happened to per capita real output in the growth center, and increases in per capita output should be the objective of regional development efforts.

Notes

1. The 3,100 figure excludes Alaska and Hawaii and a few counties that did not exist in both Censuses.

2. It is apparent from the movement in overall unemployment that counties with large increases in unemployment tended to have small labor forces.

3. I refer to the policies of the Economic Development Administration (EDA).

4. See my "Unemployment in Major Labor Areas: 1950–1965—A Comment," *Journal of Human Resources*, Fall 1968, pp. 515–19.

5. The 3,084 figure is from a possible 3,095 counties. (See note 11 for an explanation of why the sample size is 3,095 instead of 3,100.) Thus, eleven counties had rates in excess of 16.5 per cent in either 1950 or 1960.

6. There are grounds for arguing that employment growth is a function of migration. This poses a potential bias problem for some of the equations reported later.

7. See, for example, Thomas Dernburg and Kenneth Strand, "Hidden Unemployment 1953–1962: A Quantitative Analysis by Age and Sex," *American Economic Review* 56 (1966): 71–95.

8. See, for example, Robert Raimon, "Interstate Migration and Wage Theory," *Review of Economics and Statistics*, November 1962, pp. 428–38.

9. I used an average of participation rates calculated from two surveys—one for the period 1950–1951 and one for 1965–1966. The difference between surveys was negligible; both rates were about .42. See Bureau of the Census, *Current Population Reports*, "Mobility of the Population of the United States," Series p-20, Nos. 39 and 156.

10. Specifically, the (estimated) labor force portion of the migration was subtracted from 1960 labor force, and net migration was subtracted from 1960 population before 1960 participation rates were calculated.

11. Five of the 3,100 counties referred to earlier in the paper were omitted in the regressions because of a change in the EDA data file that was used for this study. That change eliminated five counties that did not exist in 1965 as well as in 1960 and 1950.

12. Equation (4) was run with both L_m^* and E^* expressed as ratios rather than percentages. The point at which $\frac{\partial L_*^m}{\partial E^*} = 0$ is 5.94, which is 594 per cent when expressed in percentage form.

13. The correlation between Y and E_a is $-.58$; thus, the separate effects of these two variables cannot be estimated precisely. It is worth noting, however, that the change in the coefficient of Y was very small when E_a was added to the equation.

14. Variables tested in equation (7) and found nonsignificant include the percentage of 1950 population that was nonwhite and the population size of counties. Growth of non-agricultural employment was highly correlated with total employment growth but did not provide better explanatory power in equations (4) or (7).

INDEX

Allen, K., 195
Alonso, William, viii, xiii, 229
Appalachia, 39, 247-48, 266-73
Appalachian Regional
    Commission, 268-73
Arrow, K. J., 70
Authority-dependency relations,
    84-85, 91-101
Axes of development, 192-93

Bain, J. S., 63
Bauchet, P., 24
Bell, Daniel, 19
Berry, Brian J. L., xii, 108,
    276-77
Boon, F., 109
Bos, H. C., 52, 179
Boudeville, J. R., 24, 57, 68,
    165, 174, 179-80
Bowers, Raymond V., 109
Brazil, 34-35
Brown, James, 267
Brown, M., 67
Brownlee, O., 67
Bruni, L., 63
Burns, A. F., 75

Canada
    Agricultural Rehabilitation and
        Development Act, 209-11
    Area Development Agency,
        206-208
    Atlantic Development Board,
        208-209

Growth pole policy, 204-228
    Ministry of Regional
        Expansion, 212-14
    Provincial growth rates,
        204-205, 215
    Quebec development policies,
        210-12, 214-28
Cassel, G., 22, 168, 183
Central place theory, 165,
    175-82, 196, 197
Chenery, H., 51, 55-56, 60-62,
    183
Chile, 189
Christaller, 165, 175-79, 191
Clark, Colin, 21, 193-94
Comanor, W. S., 65-66
Communication network, 188-89
Core regions, 57, 85, 93-101;
    see also Peripheral region;
    Spatial system
Crain, Robert L., 109

Dahrendorf, Ralph, 84
Davin, L. E., 24
Denison, Edward, 278
Dependency, 91-96
Dernberg, R., 130
Derwa, L., 24
Development control, 166
Development vs. growth, 86-87
Diffusion processes, 68-70,
    112-36, 188-93, 197; see
    also Innovations